MORAL VALUES
AND
THE MORAL LIFE

The Ethical Theory of St. Thomas Aquinas

BY
ETIENNE Henry GILSON

*Professor at the Sorbonne, and Director of the Institute of
Mediaeval Studies, St. Michael's College,
University of Toronto*

TRANSLATED BY

LEO RICHARD WARD, C.S.C.
University of Notre Dame

THE SHOE STRING PRESS, INC.
1961

NIHIL OBSTAT

> *Sti. Ludovici, die 25. Maii, 1931,*
>
> > *Joannes Rothensteiner,*
> >
> > > *Censor Librorum*

IMPRIMATUR

> *Sti. Ludovici, die 26. Maii, 1931,*
>
> > ✠ *Joannes J. Glennon,*
> >
> > > *Archiepiscopus*

Copyright 1931
By B. Herder Book Co.

Reprinted 1961
with Permission

All rights reserved
Printed in the United States of America

TRANSLATOR'S NOTE

In search of the scheme of moral values in Thomas Aquinas, I have found nothing more convincing than this study by M. Gilson. A theory of moral values almost evidently must, as a contemporary has urged, work out into a system, an integral and harmonious way of human life; and it seems that such a view is at least implied by nearly all writers on the subject. If this is so, students may hardly neglect the present statement of the ethics of Thomism, which aims to give, and I think does give, a good deal in the way of both completeness and effectiveness to the moral life.

The translation is from the fourth edition (Paris, J. Gabalda, 1925). Of course, the thought and the words of Saint Thomas are in all instances translated from the original Latin.

CONTENTS

INTRODUCTION BY THE AUTHOR 1

PART FIRST

THE THOMISTIC THEORY OF MORALS

CHAPTER
I. THE MASTER VALUE 15
II. STRUCTURE OF THE HUMAN ACT 52
III. MORAL VALUE AND DISVALUE 79
IV. LOVE AND OTHER EMOTIONS 91
V. THE INNER PRINCIPLES OF MAN'S ACTION . 134
VI. LAW ON THE HUMAN LEVEL 193

PART SECOND

THE MORAL LIFE IN PRACTICE

VII. LOVE OF OUR NEIGHBOR 215
VIII. THE PRUDENT MAN 233
IX. EVERY MAN HIS DUE 246
X. THE MAN OF VALOR 276
XI. THE PRACTICE OF SELF-CONTROL . . . 288
XII. THE AIM OF GROUP-LIVING 309
BIBLIOGRAPHICAL NOTES 329
INDEX 333

INTRODUCTION BY THE AUTHOR

Thomas was born in 1225 at the Castle of Roccasecca of the noble family of the counts of Aquino, and given at the age of five by his parents to the neighboring abbey of Montecassino, with the hope of seeing him become abbot so as greatly to further their own influence. After ten years with the Benedictines he was sent to the University of Naples, where he met the followers of Saint Dominic and made up his mind to join them. But his people objected, because his plan interfered with theirs. He won against their stand, however, and studied at the University of Paris from 1245 to 1248 under the direction of Albert the Great; then at Cologne under the same master from 1248 to 1252. In that year he returned to Paris, where he took his degree and taught until 1259; then till 1268 he taught in Italy, most of the time at the papal court, and came a second time to teach at Paris from 1268 to 1272, when he left for Italy to teach theology at Naples. Called by Pope Gregory X to the Council of Lyons, he fell sick on the way and died on March 7, 1274, at the Cistercian monastery of Fossanuova near Terracina.

After a life comparatively short but fully given to

intellectual labor, Saint Thomas left a notable product: a whole series of commentaries on the main works of Aristotle, compiled and edited steadily from 1265 till the time of his death, and such as to give us a key to the philosophical elements of all his teachings; a commentary on the *Sentences* of Peter Lombard, the *Summa Contra Gentes,* a *Manual of Theology* and the *Summa Theologica,* which form an ordered statement of everything he taught; then a group of *Questiones Quodlibetales* and *Disputatae,* in which we find the profoundest treatment Saint Thomas has bequeathed us on the many problems which he studied; and a collection of *Opuscula,* one of which at least we find indispensable for explaining his views on government.

The great richness of this intellectual fruit can be understood only as the work of a choice disposition and of habits of a life of labor exceptionally well controlled. In fact, tradition represents him as a man of vast size, extremely fat, habitually quiet in manner, and we shall see, on his own word, that he thought the ideal human life to be one that is contemplative all the time, except for the intermissions needed to rest without interrupting it. We should get a most incorrect idea of his life if we did not remember that the secret spring which never ceased to be its soul, was a deeply religious inspiration. It is true that the whole bent of his thought was given to forming an integral synthesis of Christian thought and chiefly to bringing to light the unity of a system of ideas through which we can express in the same language and interpret with the aid of the same concepts the truths of reason and those of faith. Yet Saint Thomas knew how to keep for his own mystic life the place which it has in his theory, and the way he speaks of it is one with the record of his biographers on the spirit in which he practiced it. We know that a little while before his death, and after he had had an ecstacy, Saint Thomas had to give up the composition of the *Summa Theologica,* and when he was asked to go on with it, he answered simply: "I can do no more; all that I have written seems to me only chaff." And indeed we could guess what was the preferred topic of his mystical meditations, when we see the central place the mystery of transubstantiation has in the poems he left us. Unmistakably he is the poet of the Eucharist; this is the deep devotional source from which his mind never ceased to draw.

Of his extensive works, we undertake to interpret only the ethics. But any attempt to define the spirit of the ethics independently of the spirit that breathes in all his studies would be useless. The first condition for grasping the ethics of Saint Thomas is to know that in this system there is no detached ethics; no one can define the spirit that rules over the elaboration of this ethics without defining the spirit of the whole of Thomism.

For the historian who puts the work of Saint Thomas into the history of Christian thought, the two traits that appear most striking are the extraordinary newness of Thomism, and the extraordinary quickness of the success which, in spite of opposition that lasts till this day, his teaching won.

When we try to say precisely what is the newness of his thought, we see at once the exceptional place that the philosophy of Aristotle has in the system. In the strictly ethical field, it is clear that the *Summa* is the first work of its kind in which the Ethics of Aristotle took such a part. Reflection on this procedure cannot fail to impress us with the decisive importance it has for the history of human as well as Christian thought. That a work which stands as a full synthesis of the religious truths a man must believe to be sure of his salvation by faith in Christ, should think it needs to work into that synthesis the Grecian ideal of human life, as Aristotle had worked it out by reason alone, indicates that Thomistic thought, at the height of the thirteenth century, had integrated with Christianity all the capital acquired by civilization. The genius of Thomas took this step and settled a question from which the thought of man had suffered for a long time, and also opened up a future of promise.

This question was the conflict which had many times since the coming of Christianity brought the followers of the older culture and the confessors of the new life almost to blows; a conflict which not only set one group of men against another, but very often set two men against each other in the breast of the same individual: the man who saw the road of salvation only as the radical supernaturalism of the Christian religion, and the man who could not resign himself to a denial of nature in the presence of the intelligibility and the beauty which the Greeks had found. This future of promise was what we now call the Renaissance and the whole of modern civilization. If it is true that, with the Ethics of Aristotle, it was the man of the Greek city who reclaimed his place in Christendom and installed himself there without giving up any of his rightful demands, we may say that the problem of the unity of human history, broken in the past, was solved, and that the unity of human history was assured for the future. More than that—and the answer to the question in a Christian philosophy was possible only at this price—Saint Thomas did not intend to show simply that the Greek man could, by going to an extreme limit, accommodate himself to Christianity, but that Christianity was necessary for him and that only it could fully guarantee his ideal and let him fully realize it.

Christianity, with all its supernaturalism of faith and grace, coming to fulfil the dreams of Hellenism, which did not know how to or hardly dared to hope —this is how the philosophy of history understands the ethics of Thomas Aquinas. This is also why his coordination of Aristotelianism with Christianity is not like the reconciliation of two heterogeneous realities, but like the fulfilment of the promise of

Aristotelianism + Christianity

nature by the gift of grace and like the unhoped realization of Hellenism, which is quite satisfied only in Christianity. This is why the Renaissance dates, in its source, from the thirteenth century,—the Renaissance of esthetics and of form, which in the sixteenth and seventeenth centuries was to result from the former, being simply its last but not its most important consequence. When William Budé, in 1535, raised the problem *De Transitu Hellenismi ad Christianismum,* it was a long time since Saint Thomas had settled the problem by finding in Christianity a complete Hellenism. To summarize this first distinctive trait of the ethics of Thomism, we would say that it is a *Christian humanism,* meaning not that it is the result of a combining of humanism and Christianity in any proportions, but that it witnesses to the fundamental identity of a Christianity in which the whole of humanism is included, an integral humanism that finds in Christianity its rounded satisfaction.

It is true that this newness and fruitfulness of Thomism may appear, and often has appeared, to endanger its agreement with the spirit of Christian tradition. And in fact, the accepting of all that Christianity can assimilate of the elements of Aristotelianism supposes the accepting of the philosophical basis on which such a doctrine rests. We must admit that there may be, within Christianity, a moment when the humanism of the Greeks is legitimate, and that human nature may therefore be seen and defined as

INTRODUCTION BY THE AUTHOR 7

unrelated, with its rights and duties derived from its essence, and also with a value in itself—even before the supernatural has entered to sanction its rights and duties and value. But in that case does not Thomism merit the lasting reproach of Augustinianism? <u>One can give to nature only what one takes away from grace</u>; to introduce Aristotle into Christian thought is to give to philosophy a place that one necessarily takes from religion. Besides, Greek thought is above all interested in man, and teaches that this concrete being, whose essence is body as well as soul, is actually, before it quits this life, to enjoy a life that has no tomorrow. The Christian view, on the contrary, promises man an immortality because his soul is spiritual, and even promises during this life a communing between God and the soul because of the very independence the soul has with regard to the body.

This is the quintessence of the protest made by Augustinianism. As to how far it is justified, we shall grant that it is just in the measure that Augustinianism expresses one of the most imperious demands of Christian thought: to let man rejoin God and, even in the order of nature, wholly to reclaim God. In writing a history of Augustinian thought, it would not be impossible to show the dangers which gave rise to it and against which it was a needed reaction. The enduring aim of Augustinianism is to afford a basic philosophy of conversion and of the soul's union with God, against all false notions of independence or sufficiency that the soul or nature might raise counter to the rights of God.

There is another tradition also, and this, contrary to popular belief, is not less ancient than Augustinianism; but Saint Thomas was able to use this second tradition. If anyone will run through the Greek and Latin Fathers from the second to the fourth century, he will see that all of them are interested primarily in man, and that it is the whole man of body and soul, not of soul alone, that they endeavor to save. Whoever despises the body or contemns nature on the pretext of better securing the rights of the soul or of God, by that fact is outside the Christian Church. Depth of thought, keenness of philosophical genius, even ardor of belief can do nothing for such persons; and if anyone doubts it, the history of the Christian Gnostics—for instance of Tertullian or of Origen—is proof of it. And just as Augustinianism shows new vigor every time that in the history of Christian thought the danger is an encroachment on the nature or rights of God, as in Pelagianism and in the naturalism of the Renaissance, so Thomism deploys all its powers and tells why it exists every time that the peril lies in a breakdown of human individuality, by confusing it with the race or nature or God; as happened in the crisis of Averroism in the thirteenth century and again in the modernistic crisis originated at the beginning of the nineteenth century by German Romanticism. That is why the Thomistic reform, though it seemed new, was not novel in intention or in fact, but ran its roots deep into the heart of tradition, and this is precisely the reason of its brilliant success. If we were to designate this aspect of Thomism in a single phrase, we would call it a *Christian naturalism*—meaning by this, not a balancing or running together of naturalism and Christianity, but that mere nature needs the Christian confession for its own perfect development, and that in its turn Christianity needs a distinct nature that it is to perfect and to save.

When we grasp this leading place that Thomism has in the history of Christian thought and understand the tradition that inspires it, we have still, if we would get a just general idea of it, to see how it has also tried to meet the demands of the other tradition. For the endurance of Thomism and Augustinianism within Christian philosophy would be an inexplicable fact if these two systems of thought were contradictory, and they would be if each did not make an effort to meet the rightful demands that the other makes it its business to maintain. Augustinianism wishes to keep to one reason, one nature, one human individuality which is to be saved, body and soul, and if we had space we could show how it succeeds. But Saint Thomas not less expressly wishes to be sure of putting man and all things in their places, and of giving to nature that which is nature's and to God that which is God's. If Augustinianism should object that its standards are different and that it would that all were God's, one speaks simply the truth in answering that Thomism also wishes this. It wishes this most manifestly in ethics, and we shall see that without God nature would be nothing, could do nothing, and would come to nothing. Indeed, the proper gift of nature consists in willing what God wills, and as it finds that its goal is beyond its reach, nature has to seek in God its full attainment.

The ethics of Thomas is quite intellectualistic, because God, to whom man is subject, is pure intelligence; it is an ethics of law and order, because the problem of the autonomy of man is solved by his freely entering into the universal divine scheme. It is an ethics without obligation or sanction, at least if we think of obligation and sanction as imposed on a human act from the outside to guarantee its moral character; for the only obligation that the ethics of Thomism knows for man is that he be wholly a man, for by that fact he is sure that he is what God wishes him to be. As for sanction, we should badly deceive ourselves in imagining it as a complementary disposition limiting the very life of morality from the outside, whereas it results from the morality of the act as soon as the act is performed, and it indicates a natural balance between the act and its consequences in a universe ruled by justice and reason.

In the following study we shall see how these views are worked out in the thought of Saint Thomas. We try to show the connections between the parts of Thomistic morals and the spirit that breathes through it. His teaching on the Supreme Value, with which we begin, is the key to his entire ethics and makes clear how this hinges on metaphysics. We have attempted to outline his metaphysics elsewhere (*Le Thomisme: Introduction au system de Saint Thomas d'Aquin,* 2nd ed., Paris, J. Vrin, 1924).[1] But at that time we ran into the impossibility of stating, in a work that aimed to make plain the metaphysical framework of the system, the almost endless detail of the ethics; and Saint Thomas himself will tell us that it is only when morals comes to control the detail of our action that it has its full significance. It will therefore be understood that we have gladly undertaken to explain the ethics of Saint Thomas in the group of studies called *The Christian Ethicists,* and that we were ready to welcome the plan suggested by our colleague and friend, the Abbé Baudin, professor at the University of Strasbourg. Even the form of the modest and really easy task given to us is in line with one of our constant preoccupations. We have often deplored how very hard the teacher of the history of philosophy finds it to get students away from textbooks and secondary sources and to go directly to the originals themselves. Yet what he wishes as historian is to turn his readers over, just as often and as surely

---

[1] Translated by E. Bullough, under the title *The Philosophy of St. Thomas Aquinas,* 2nd revised ed., Cambridge, W. Heffer; St. Louis, B. Herder, 1929.—Tr.

as it can be done, to the great philosophers themselves.

The language of Thomas is difficult and might discourage beginners from tying themselves to the work of reading him. We have therefore hoped that some rather simple passages, as those from the *Summa,* might be a good way to bring readers to study him at first hand. This aim of ours is also the reason for the kind of translation we have attempted to keep to. We have not feared, for instance, to transpose, if this seemed indispensable for a clear statement; yet we have meant to retain in the translation the technical color and tone of the original, so that thought upon our study might serve to lead the inquirer to Saint Thomas himself and, when he had got so far, might be good enough guide to help him to be at home there.

NOTE: The student is respectfully referred to pages 330 and 331 *infra* for suggestions as to how best to use the present volume.

Part First

THE THOMISTIC THEORY OF MORALS

Chapter I

THE MASTER VALUE

I. MORALS AND METAPHYSICS

In the system of Thomas Aquinas the study of morals cannot be isolated from that of metaphysics. We see this as soon as we realize that an ethics apart from the scheme of sciences would imply that man and his moral activity are detached from the general run of things. This is not so. Man's moral and social action carry forward a movement which in origin, power and direction are independent of it. At the outset of his study of God, which is the subject of inquiry in the *Summa Theologica,* St. Thomas shows in a summary way the rounded oneness of the big field that is to be parcelled out for study, into parts, questions and articles.

The main purpose of this sacred science is to make us acquainted with God, as he is in Himself and as the source and goal of things, and in a special way the goal of man. We mean to give an analysis of this problem, and shall treat first of God, secondly of the movement of man towards God, and thirdly of Christ, who, as man, is our way to God (*cf.,* I, q. 2).[1]

---

[1] The passages set in smaller type are directly from St. Thomas. —Tr.

The moral life is a kind of continuance of the creative act. We cannot study God in every light available to man until we study him as Creator, and if not, and if the act by which God creates things outside Himself is vitally one with the act by which He draws them back to Himself, the study of morals lies in the following metaphysical problem: Where do the power and direction of movement branded by God into things go when that movement reaches the human creature? The text will show how this question is posed for all creation and what special aspect it wears in the instance of the rational creature or man. The notion of morality enters precisely when beings gifted with reason receive power to guide themselves to their goals and to select this or that end, though they are among great numbers of beings that are directed from without and that are subject to them.

One first being called God exists and has the full perfection of being. We showed this in an earlier book (*Contra Gentes*, 1, c. 13). From the richness of His perfection He gives being to all things that are and so is witnessed to as the first being and as the source of whatever is. No necessity is written in His nature that He give being to others, but He does it of His own purpose and choice. And so God is master of His works, as we are masters of things subject to our will. But this dominion of God over things made by Him is complete. He is the one maker of their total being; He does not need any outside agent as prop or any original stuff.

When an agent gifted with will does anything, he means it for some purpose. In fact, good or end is the objective of will,

MORALS AND METAPHYSICS

and it must be that whatever comes from the will is arranged for some end. Each thing reaches its farthest goal by its own action, and this action is inescapably shaped by the giver of the nature in line with which that thing acts. It is for this reason that God, perfect in Himself and of His power the giver of being to all things, is the guide of all, and guided by none, and as there is nothing that has not being from Him, so there is nothing that is exempted from His governance. He is perfect as being and as cause, and He is perfect also as ruler.

If we take a look now at the effect of the aim integrated by God with things, we shall see that it differs with the natures of the things in question.

Some beings are so made by God that they have minds, and in that sense are like Him and are His image. These are directed, and also by means of their actions they direct themselves to their goal. If, in guiding themselves, such beings accept the divine guidance, they come by the help of it all the way to their goal; but if they choose to go by any other road, they do not arrive.

Other beings have not got minds, and so cannot direct themselves to their journey's end, but are guided wholly by another. Some of them are existents that cannot disintegrate, and as they are not subject to any defect in their natural being, so in their actions they never leave the orb or path toward the goal prearranged for them, but yield without fail to the ultimate governance. The celestial bodies, whose motion is ever uniform, are of this kind. Others, however, can suffer decay, though this is compensated for by the gain of some other being, for when one goes to pieces, another is built up. So, too, in their actions they do not keep to the order of nature, but some good comes of their defection. It is thus plain that not even those things that seem to break from the primal scheme and rule get around the power of the main guide, because, as these bodies were made by God, so they are fully subject to His might (*C. G.*, 3, c.1; cf. *De Veritate*, q.13, a.1 and 2).

We see at once that the moral life, precisely because it is but a specific instance of divine control, comes to the following problem: How can and how should a rational and free creature use the movement toward God which he has received from God? In other words, the pivotal notion of morals will be that of finality or, more exactly, of free finality: not of a forced finality like that of beings that have not reason; of these St. Thomas says that they are only instruments in the hands of God (1, q.22, a.2; q.105, a.8; and 1-2, q.1, a.2).

Of the acts that a man does, only some are "human" in an exact sense. These are proper to man precisely as man. The difference between man and the irrational animal is that man is master of his acts. So only those actions are properly called "human" of which he is master. Now he has this mastery through reason and will, and free will is known as the "faculty of will and of reason." Human, then, is the correct term for acts that arise from a deliberative will. There are other acts that a man does, but because they are not man's simply as man, they may be called "acts of man," but not strictly human acts. And, of course, any action that issues from a faculty is effected by it in line with the kind of object that faculty has, and the object of will is end or good; so every human action is necessarily for an end (1-2, q.1).[1]

[1] References specified by numbers only, are from the *Summa Theologica*.—Tr.

Hence, the dignity of man. Uniquely in our world, this creature is not an inert medium in the hands of the Creator. Yet it is also his responsibility, which is heavy and fearful when we remember that his own destiny is thus put into his keeping. The point is this, man is either to maintain order in his life and be saved or to destroy order and perish. In the drama of his fate he is at once actor and, by a commission of liberty like the divine trust of causality to beings, he is author. Morals is the science of how man is to conduct himself so that the story of his life may have a happy ending, and we shall see that this coincidence unavoidably comes from the principle with which we have begun: care to shape his life towards a prosperous end is one with care to bring his own humanity to the very peak of achievement.

If this is so, no task is more urgent on the student of the moral life than to give close study to the goals which human action strives for and to sort them with the discernment of a judge.

II. MORALS AND THE END OF ENDS

Any strictly human act is for an end. This end may be exterior to the act, as, for instance, a house built by a contractor or health brought about by a doctor. Or the act itself may be its own end, like an act of knowing, sufficient for itself and not willed for anything further (*C.G.*, 3, c.2). But all these acts, both those that are their own end and those that have an exterior end, should have an ordered relation to one another and to a single end. This is not simply a matter of fitness. The existence of the acts is at stake. We shall not grasp the meaning of St. Thomas on the moral life, unless we bear in mind the close analogy between the argument by which we are going to show that all human actions are for one final end, and the metaphysical arguments for the existence of God. There would be neither movement nor causality in the world of secondary causes if there were not a First Cause to which the changes and effects that we see are tied by a limited number of links in a graduated series. So, too, there would actually be no human actions for specific ends if there were not an end of ends that gives place and meaning to the things people want, and again by a finite group of intermediaries ranked and ordered.

Nothing is more natural than this position for one who remembers that the two arguments answer to two aspects of one and the same problem. The problem is this: How does the divine causality work, first in the field of the efficient cause, secondly in that of the final cause? The text that follows is a good explanation of their metaphysical correspondence.

> From the point of view of essences (*i. e., per se loquendo*, in contrast to *per accidens*) it is not possible to regress *ad infinitum* to end after end, no matter what the kind of change one begins with, for in any series of interrelated essences it must be that to take away the first is to knock down the whole series. This is the basis of Aristotle's proof, in the *Physics*

(8, c.5), that it is impossible to go on forever from cause or mover to cause or mover, because, if there were not a first mover, or if that were supposed out of it, the others could not do anything: they would not stir unless they were started by a first mover.

There are two kinds of order in the realm of ends—the order of purpose and the order of doing. In each of these there must be a first term. That which is primal in purpose is a kind of source that sets desire afoot, and without that source or starter no desire would ever arise. And what is original in doing gives us the story of action getting under way; if that original were lopped off, no one would begin to do anything. Now, this source of purpose or objective is the end of ends, and the first doer is whatever is first in view of the end. So in neither case can we have an infinite regression; without an end of ends nothing would be wanted, no action would have a terminus, and the bent of the agent would never come to rest; and if there were no first of the series toward an end, a person would not get started to do anything, but would go on making up his mind forever.

We may, however, have an infinity of things that are not related in an essential way, but conjoined by accident. Causes of an accidental kind are not determinate, and it is only in this way that there can be an accidental infinity of ends and of steps to an end (1-2, q.1, a.4; *cf. C.G.,* 3, c.2).

We have now to define the relations which are sure to arise between the end of ends and our moral activity. In the first place, this end will be unique for the individual man. Any action of ours is moral if it is willed, and we know an act is willed if it tends toward an end clearly seen by the intellect. Thus it is the nature of the object or goal which a movement makes for, that allows us to class it as willed (1-2, q.1, a.3). And if this is so, what is true of each of our acts taken alone, should be equally true of all taken together; because as in each genus there is a first principle which defines it, so we have seen that in the genus of willed acts there is one end of ends which forms the true urge of all acts of will. The fact that we can group all willed acts into one class implies that they have just one end (*ibid.*, a.5), for which alone man wills whatever he wills and which is the same for humankind in general as for each man in particular.

A second point is that this farthest and unique end of all a man's actions, precisely because it has a share in the definition of man's nature or essence, holds for all men, but only for men. Here, however, an important distinction must be made. We may study man's ultimate end from either of two points of view: in itself, or in the way it is attained. From the former point of view, the end of ends for man is one with that of all creatures, for there is a kind of morality immanent in senseless nature, and it is in some sense a living thing, but not conscious and reflective like ours. Everything indeed tries to be like God (*C.G.*, 3, c.19), and this is why, even without knowing Him, all things desire Him. This point is brought out in a remarkable chapter of the *Contra Gentes*. After noting that, in Aristotelian cosmology, the stars are moved and guided by pure intelligences

MORALS AND THE END OF ENDS

and the movements of these stars are willed by these intelligences with the aim of bringing lower beings into life, Saint Thomas proceeds:

It is not hard to see how natural bodies that have no knowledge are moved, and in what sense they act for an end. They move toward an end as directed to it by an intelligent substance, just as the arrow goes for the mark because aimed by the archer. And as the arrow gets a start for the target or its definite goal from the impetus of the archer, so natural bodies take a line toward their natural ends because of the natural movers from which they have their natures and powers and motion. So it is clear that every work of nature is the work of an intelligence, since an effect is ascribed more to the one who starts a process and guides it to its end, than to the tools which he uses. For this reason the works of nature, like the actions of a wise man, take an orderly path toward their goals.

The following points begin to stand out. Beings that know nothing, can yet act for an end; they have a native bent and desire for good; they even desire to be like God and to attain their own perfection. It is all the same which of these two last we say. For by the fact that a being tends toward good, it tends toward its perfection: anything is good so far as it is realized. And tending toward the good, it nears and resembles God: indeed, everything is like God so far as it has goodness, and a particular thing is so far good or valuable as it is a likeness of the supreme value. So in achieving the goodness of God, it achieves its own, and not vice versa. All things then desire as the end of ends that they be like God.

And, of course, there are several senses in which the value of a thing may be taken. For instance, there is a good that goes with it as an individual unit, and so an animal looks out for its own good when it seeks food to sustain itself. Besides, it has a specific good that is its own, and it is this that the animal desires in the appetite to beget and nurture, or in taking any turn to protect or screen the individuals of its kind. Again, there is a good of the genus, and it is in this sense that the sun (*caelum*), let us say, acts for its own good when it causes beings different from itself. And in a fourth sense, things are good by reason of analogy or likeness of effects to causes, and in this way we may note that God, though outside any class or genus, gives being to all things for the sake of His self-value.

We plainly see that as anything has more perfection and is higher on the scale of value, the broader its taste for good and the wider its quest to realize good. This is because quite imperfect beings work only for the good of their individual selves, the perfect for the good of their type, the very perfect for the good of their group, and God as sovereign and perfect in goodness for the good of everything. So some have reasonably said that the good as such is diffusive, because a thing is better if it pours out its bounty on things farther away. And as what is more perfect in any class is model and measure of all in that class, it must be that God, perfect and rich in goodness and universal giver of goodness, is model for every giver of goodness. And a thing is higher on the ladder of causes if it is a more liberal dispenser of good.

We see now that everything takes on a divine likeness as it tends to be a cause of others. It works *pari passu* towards its own good. It is not out of the way, then, to remark that the movements of the planets and the intelligent actions which start them, are in view of others inferior to them and put together or broken up by them. They do not aim at this as end of ends, but they do effect their begetting and at the same stroke their own good and a divine likeness, as the end of ends (*C.G.,* 3, c.24).

It is another question, however, when we look into the end of ends from the point of view of how it is attained by each creature, for:

As Aristotle says in his *Metaphysics* (bk.5; also in his *Physics,* 2, c.4) the word "end" has two senses: that which and that by which: it means the thing on account of which one wishes anything, and that by which he seeks it: in other words, the thing itself the nature of which is good, and the use or attaining of that thing. For instance, we may say that the end of the movement of a heavy body is either a lower position, which is a thing, or it is the enjoyment and use of this thing. We say that the aim of a stingy man is money, which is certainly a thing, or it is to have money for use. Now, if we speak of the end of ends for man and mean the thing itself which is the end, it is true to say that all other things have the same end as man has, for God is the end of ends for man and for all other things. But if by the end of ends for man we mean the acquiring of this end, we should say that in this sense irrational creatures have no part in the strictly human goal, for man and other reasoning creatures reach their end by knowing and loving God, but the end for others is only a kind of likeness to God, whether these beings merely exist or live or have sense knowledge (1–2, q.1, a.8).

So man and other things have one common end of ends, but beings which are like that end by being or living or being conscious, attain this end without ever understanding it and hence without enjoying it. This is the reason why, though all have one end of ends, man alone has happiness. We shall now go on to inquire in what happiness consists.

III. IN QUEST OF THE MASTER VALUE

Our introductory study has shown that Thomistic morals is integrated with metaphysics. We now proceed to point out that the metaphysics itself is built on a solid empiric basis. St. Thomas begins with the data of sense experience, explains these with the aid of the first principles of thought, and, abetted by the elementary notion of the analogy of being and by the principle of causality, works out a philosophy of God. So in morals, and especially on the question of discerning the Master Value. We know, to begin with, that this should be the end of ends for a creature that has reason, and also that it will lie in our gaining, by an act of knowledge, the one object that has the ability to fill up and to satisfy wholly our power of knowing. But one does not at a glance see precisely which object will be able to meet these demands. The ethician, like the metaphysician, searches the field. The latter, immediately sure that the sensible world requires an original source, must all the same try to fashion an idea of that source; so the other, at once certain that the moral life would not so much as exist if it had no objective, should nevertheless go over the ground of our moral

IN QUEST OF THE MASTER VALUE

experience to discern the nature of this end of ends.

St. Thomas then begins the quest of the Master Value. He commences with what is most thoroughly outside the meaning of man and inquires whether money is not the great human good.

It cannot be that man's happiness is comprised of riches. In fact, riches, as Aristotle remarks (*Politics,* I, c.3) are of just two kinds, natural and artificial. The natural are those a man uses to support his born weaknesses; they are such riches as food and drink, clothes, conveyances, and houses. The artificial, such as money, do not directly come to man's aid, but human ingenuity has devised them to facilitate trade and to serve as a measure of exchange.

Now it is evident that man's happiness is not one with natural riches. For we want these to sustain nature, and so they cannot be man's final end, but man is rather their end, and they are meant for him, as we read in the Psalms: "Thou hast subjected all things under his feet." Nor do we want artificial riches except in view of natural: we want them only that we may buy what we need to live, and so they answer even less to the definition of the end of ends. It simply cannot be, then, that the end of ends for man be made up of riches (1–2, q.2, a.1; *cf. C.G.,* 3, c.30).

A more interior value than money and bodily goods is honor, which is directed to the soul and satisfies it. Is it not the reward of virtue, and is it not even said that honor is due to God alone? (1 *Tim.* 1).

We must grant that human happiness is quite other than honor. After all, why is honor given to anyone? Because of his excellence. Honor is a mark and a kind of witness to the excellence that is in the honored person, and we know that human excellence lies mainly in happiness, which is the rounded and perfect human value, and that it lies secondarily in those branch values which make happiness accessible to us under some aspect. So it may be that honor is a close associate of happiness, but it is not its chief ingredient (1–2, q.2, a.2; *cf. C.G.,* 3, c.28).

We may say as a corollary of this, that the end of ends for man is not human acclaim or reputation. For one thing, these are so little dependable that they do not class with a stable and abiding goal; and besides they are rather a by-product of happiness (1-2, q.3, a.3, ad 2). Supposing, of course, that it is earned, reputation follows perfection and is the companion of the good wherever this goes, and so it cannot make either of them. Still, a person might ask whether efficiency is not the great goal. No, efficiency or power, which in the Latin is another name for faculty (*potentia, vis*), is the source of action, and for this reason cannot be the end. And anyway, wealth, honor, reputation, and ability—all of these values have a common failing: they are morally neutral, they are good, but not good enough; they are a bother and at times harmful to those who possess them; worst of all, they are external to human nature.

Four general arguments may be cited to make it clear that happiness is not made up of any of the outer values that we have just mentioned. The first is that happiness as the Master Value for man can have no part with evil, and everyone knows that any of the values cited may be met with among good people, but also among the wicked. Besides, it is the way of happiness that it has a self-sufficiency about it, as we read in the *Ethics* (1, c.6) that once happiness is had, no value needful for man is wanting. And we may suppose a man to have got all of the aforesaid values and yet he might be without many good things that are humanly needed, such as education and health. The third reason is that happiness is wholly a value and is never the source of evil to anyone, which may not be said of the values in question; for instance, Ecclesiastes (V, 12) says that riches is sometimes "kept to the hurt of the owner," and so of the others. A last argument is that man is meant for happiness by reasons that are at work within him; he is by nature meant for it. But the four values we have passed in review hinge on the world outside man, and often on luck or fortune: so they are called goods of fortune. All this makes it plain that happiness cannot in any way lie in them (1–2, q.2, a.4).

With so much known, our demonstration takes a forward step. The present conclusion allows us to see that the four discussions which it sums up are a sort of induction that excludes from the essence of the Master Value any and every element external to the essence of man. And in fact the concept of "nature," which in Thomistic thought always has the decisive rôle, enters now to close the debate. If man is by nature made for happiness, and if this is so for anyone who is truly a man, it is within his nature that the source of happiness is to be sought.

The quest, then, is still before us, but on another field. What is it within man that can form the Master Value for him? He is made of body and soul, so it may be that the great good is some good of the body.

My view is that this cannot be. Human happiness cannot consist in values of the body, for two reasons:

It cannot be that the main goal of a thing that is used as a means for something else should be to protect its own existence. For instance, a captain does not take as his chief purpose the safety of the ship that he commands, because a ship is made for some other business or end, namely, to sail. Now as a ship is entrusted to the pilot that he steer her, so man is given in charge to his own reason and will; and so Ecclesiasticus says (c.15): "God made man from the beginning, and left him in the hand of his own counsel." Well, man, since he is not the Master Value, plainly is meant for some other end, and so the eventual goal of human reason and will cannot be simply the survival of the human self.

Besides, even if one were to concede that the aim of human reason and will were the survival of the human self, one could not say that the goal of man was a value of the body. It is true that man is made up of body and soul, yet though the being of the body depends on the soul, the being of the soul does not depend on the body, as we showed in an earlier passage (1, q.65, a.1, and q.90, a.4). The very body is for the sake of the soul, as matter is for form or as tools are for him who uses them to do his work. Values of the body are subordinated to those of the soul as their end, and it becomes

IN QUEST OF THE MASTER VALUE

evident that happiness or the Master Value cannot be any goods of the body (1-2, q.2, a.5; *cf*. *C.G.*, 3, c.32).

Because our search has run aground in the realm of the body, we turn to the domain of the soul. We first study pleasures of sense, as these are known to everyone and in the eyes of many are the Master Value. But we must at once rate them down and out of our quest. They are sense enjoyments, common to animal and man, and hence not specifically "human." Besides, they relate in every instance to the working of our organism and never raise us one inch above the goods of the body (*C.G.*, 3, c.33).

There is a broader and deeper reason. It is this: the enjoyment which we shall call by the technical name of delectation, is a result, an appendage, or at most a detail, of happiness, but not its essence. To cast the link between enjoyment and happiness into form and compare it to the well-known relation between essence and accident, we would say: to have happiness is to possess the value which makes up the highest end. This is the central thing or core, and whatever is not included in this definition is outside the essence of happiness and joined to it only by accident. We would not deny that an accident may always accompany an essence and as a proper accident, but it remains an accident even though it be inseparable from the essence. To laugh is proper to man, but his essence is that he is an animal that reasons. Hence the conclusion (1-2, q.2, a.6): even the delectation which accompanies the having of the perfect value is not the essence of happiness, but only a by-product and a chance result of it (1-2, q.4, a.2).

At this moment, it appears that we are headed toward a conclusion the mere announcement of which looks paradoxical, and that we are in a blind alley: human happiness is not found outside man, nor in his body, nor in his soul; and for these reasons:

As we said a while ago, the word "end" has two meanings. First, it stands for the very thing which we seek to gain, and then for the use that is the gaining or the having of this thing. If we mean by the human goal the thing itself that men want as an end, the full human goal cannot be the soul or anything belonging to it. The reason is that the soul, studied in itself, is a kind of potential thing: it is potentially wise before it is actually wise, and potentially good before it is actually good. Now, the potential exists for the actual, which is its complement, hence the impossibility that anything, the nature of which is to be in potency, should play the rôle of end of ends. This rules out the soul as its own objective, and likewise any activity or habit or power of it. For the value which is the main goal is a value that fufils one's whole desire for good, but human desire or will is a desire for the universal value, whereas any value tied up with the soul is shared and fragmentary. So the end of ends for man is not any of these things.

If, however, we mean the attaining of the end of ends for man or the having or using of it, it is true that the human soul has something to do with the end of ends, for it is

IN QUEST OF THE MASTER VALUE

through the soul that man reaches happiness. The very thing, then, which is sought as an end, is that in which happiness consists, and which makes man happy, and the attaining of this thing is called happiness; hence it must be granted that happiness is a feature of the soul. Still, that in which happiness lies is something outside the soul (1–2, q.2, a.7).

We have but one more step to take to obtain a distinct view of the aim of the moral life. If the end of ends is neither outside nor within us, where is it? Plainly, it must be above us. Still, how can it transcend us, yet be our goal, how can it be external to us, yet be our objective? These are questions that demand an answer; but if they can be cleared up, they offer a full solution to the problem of the meaning of man.

To begin with, we may remark that the contradictory look of the form which the problem takes does not warrant despair of its solution. The form of the question expresses experienced facts, and to try to put it otherwise, would involve disloyalty to the facts which we have come upon inch by inch in the course of our inquiry. It is too late to turn back now, and we should think it too soon to contest the validity of our quest. Where, then, is the mistake, and how can we with the conscience of good philosophers regret that we made it? Is it that there is no end of ends? In that case we should have to give up any satisfactory account of the existence of human action. Or is it rather that we are to let the values of body and soul, which seem fitted to our nature and proper to us, take us by surprise? In that case we should renounce the discovery of the Master Value as man's nature defines it.

But after all why regret having taken facts always as given and having never foresworn the deciphering of them in the light of the original leads of reason? We cannot turn back; we must face the problem isolated in our analysis. If fact seems to stand against fact, this is doubtless because we have not carried our analysis far enough. Whatever is real is possible, and our business is to find the conditions of its possibility.

Let us look into the heart of the difficulty. Even when their own logic urges them, people are loath to give up the values which they think suited to them to acquiesce in a chief goal outside their own nature. Yet it may be that this transcendent, outer objective is the only one that is really suited to us, and the only one that fully answers to the needs of our nature. Here again we shall find it vital to return to the essence of man and to inquire whether the necessity of locating the great goal outside and above himself is so far from being a stumbling-block to him that it is a demand written into the essence of a being gifted with reason. What kind of thing, for instance, is the will of a reasoning creature?

It helps us to know that each kind of form has a corresponding tendency. Take fire for example; because of its form, it tends to rise and to beget a flame like itself. And the

IN QUEST OF THE MASTER VALUE

form of things that have reason is a step ahead of those that have not reason. In fact, among beings that have not reason we find simply a form which fixes them in a unique type of being proper to them and constitutive of the being natural to each of them. An inborn tendency, called a natural appetite, answers to this natural form. It is different with beings that can know. Each of them is limited by its native form in a natural being proper to it, but in such a way that it can take into itself types of other things, as the senses take in types or images of all things that can be sensed and the mind of all that can be known. This is how the soul of man, helped by sense and intellect, can in a measure become all things, and so beings that know are in their way like God in whom all things pre-exist, as Dionysius says (*De Div. Nom.*, 5, 1). Now just as the forms in beings that know are of a kind superior to natural forms, so we ought to find in them something higher than the natural tendency that we have called natural appetite. This higher inclination belongs to that power of the soul by which the living creature can desire the things it perceives, and not only those toward which it is inclined by its natural form (1, q.80, a.1).

It begins to appear that there is a large and clear disproportion between man, in his total experience, and in the object of his desire. God is fulness of being, and His infinite love can find in His infinite substance a source of full contentment. But man is too perfect to represent or be like God without knowing it, and not perfect enough to fill up by his own power the gap between what he is and what he represents. He is not just one thing, as the body is or as a natural being is; and he is not everything, like God.

He can only become all things, and it is because he becomes things in the degree that he knows them, that we have reason to locate in his power of knowing, by which he copies the divine infinity, his proper human likeness to God. Thus it is the very nature of man that imperiously calls for the transcendent and divine. Since he can be like the fulness of being, that is, in his knowledge and in his thus becoming an indefinite series of other beings, his will or desire, like the intellect of which it is the companion, will always remain torn and dissatisfied. At least, says St. Thomas, this is the case, unless man's will and desire at last find the infinite object that will give it peace and happiness.

Man's happiness cannot lie in any created good. For happiness is a consummate value which satisfies all desires: if beyond it there were something still to be desired, it would not be the end of ends. Now, just as intellect has for its object all truth, so will, which is the human form of desire, has for its object everything that is good. Hence the evident conclusion that nothing short of the sum-total of good things can content the will of man. This is not found in any created thing, but only in God, because no creature is all good, but each has only a share in goodness. This is why God alone can give complete peace to man's will, as it is written in Psalm 102: "Who satisfieth their desire with good things." Man's happiness, we conclude, is in God alone (1–2, q.2, a.8).

We know now what is the Master Value, but we have yet to define the act by which man comes into possession of it.

IV. HAPPINESS AND MORALS

The end of ends, or Master Value, is beyond our nature, because the object or cause of our happiness is an uncreated good, and this cannot be included in the finite or participated order which is ours. But the taking of it by man, the attainment, or possession, or experience—in a word, the enjoyment of this Master Value—is happiness in a truly human sense. And as there is question here of a contact which must be made within the human soul, we remain in the field of the finite, the bit by bit, the created. To inquire what is this happiness or enjoyment of the Master Value, is thus to set out on a quest of a spiritual state which, of course, could lead the soul to the peak of its perfection and to the rounded realization of its essence. But we know beforehand that this state will leave the soul outside God, face to face with an infinite which it will perhaps see, but will never become. A being by participation will never be happy except by participation (1-2, q.3, a.1, ad 1). However, we should outline how this participation can be effected.

We know, first, that it is sure to consist in an activity, or in the use of one of our powers. By definition, happiness can leave nothing to be desired. Hence it must realize to the full every possibility of our nature. But it would not do this if it were to make us able to perform the noblest act imaginable and yet not bring us all the way to the accomplishment of this act (1-2, q.3, a.2). Besides, the activity by which we shall be happy, ought not to be directed to any outside material to work it over, for we would then act for its good, and not for our own (*ibid.*, ad 3). It will be an act within or, as the philosophers say, immanent to the soul. And because we know only three types of acts which have their terminus within the soul, our choice lies among these three only. We may eliminate acts of sense at the start, for we have seen that happiness means a union of the soul with an uncreated and spiritual good, which cannot come within the range of the senses (*ibid.*, a.3). Therefore, any hesitation could only be between an act of the intellect and an act of the will.

As we pointed out earlier, happiness comprises two things: one is the very essence of it and the other is as its natural companion, that is, the enjoyment which goes with it. As for that which is the very essence of happiness, I say that this cannot possibly be an act of the will. From what has preceded, it is clear that happiness is the attainment of the end of ends, and this does not consist in an act of the will, for the will is moved by desire toward the end when this is not had and by rejoicing and being at rest in it when it is had. But the desire of the end, taken in itself, is not the attainment of the end; so much is plain: it is only a movement toward the end. And as for enjoyment, we would say that this comes to the will from the fact that the end is present—and not, on the contrary, that anything becomes present from the fact that the will enjoys it. There must, then, be

HAPPINESS AND MORALS

something other than the act of the will to make the end present to the will. This is evident in the instance of sense objectives. If one could get hold of money by the act of wanting it, the miser would have gold as soon as he began to desire it. The fact is, he has not got it to begin with, and he obtains it only by getting his hands on it, or in some such way, and his joy over possessing it dates from that moment. The same procedure holds in the case of knowable objects: in the beginning we wish to reach some intelligible end, but we cannot do this unless it becomes present to us by an act of the intellect, and it is only then that the will finds joy and comes to rest in the end attained. Thus the very heart and meaning of happiness lies in an act of the intellect, but the joy resulting from happiness belongs to the will. That is why St. Augustine says in his *Confessions* (bk.10, c.23) that happiness is a joy born of truth (*gaudium de veritate*), since in fact this joy is the crowning touch of happiness (1-2, q.3, a.4; *cf. Quodlib.*, q.9, a.19).

Thus the limits within which our quest moves become narrower and narrower. It might seem that we even now reach the goal, since we know that the Master Value can lie only in an activity of the intellect. However, the intellect has two functions. By one of these it grasps objects of knowledge, and in this sense is said to play a speculative rôle; by the other it fixes the rules of action and is said to take a practical part. How are we to choose between the two workings of this one faculty? This is a problem of decisive import, because the question here is one of either maintaining for the future the rights of the highest human ideal ever conceived, that is, the definitive integration of Christian morals with the Hellenic ideal of contemplation, or of yielding to the tendency which would have us set out for the goal, but locate the end of ends in the going. Yet, before solving this problem, we must note a vital distinction. Every query about happiness will be given two answers at the present juncture, according as the view is of a complete happiness beyond actual human experience, or of the relative happiness which takes the other as a model and helps to make us ready for it.

Happiness always means a kind of rounded perfection. But we are to understand this word in different senses, because the types of being which are capable of happiness can reach uneven levels of perfection. Thus happiness is essentially present with God: His being and activity are one, His joy is in Himself and not in another. But among the angels, happiness is the grand perfection of an activity that joins them to the uncreated good, which act of theirs is eternal and unique. As for men in the present life, the peak of perfection is marked by an activity linking them to God, but it is an activity that cannot be kept up, as it has to be broken off and begun all over again and, therefore, is manifold and not unique. This is precisely why in our normal life complete happiness is out of our reach. It is also why Aristotle, when he locates human happiness in this life (*Ethics,* I, c.10), says it is imperfect, and after much thought concludes, "we call them happy as men." But we for our part have from God the promise of a perfect happiness when, as

HAPPINESS AND MORALS

St. Matthew says (c.22), we shall be as the angels in heaven, and when there is question of this full felicity, all objection gives way, for it is by an act that is one, unbroken, eternal that the mind of man is united to God in a state of happiness. In the case of our earthly life, however, we fail of the oneness and continuity of such action, and so far we fall short of realization. All the same we have some bit of this happiness, and the more continuous and unified our activity, the more nearly it expresses the essence of happiness. It is for this reason that the active life, taken up with many things, is farther from the meaning of happiness than the contemplative, which is concerned with just one thing, that is, with attending to truth; and even if man does sometimes interrupt this act, it is always at hand and he can go on with it; and if he breaks it off, for instance, to sleep or to satisfy some human need, this is done only in view of resuming it, and the act seems to enjoy a kind of continuity (1–2, q.5, a.4).

We see now why happiness, as contemplation of the truth, cannot be merely the exercise of scientific thought.

We just remarked that happiness for man is of two kinds, perfect and imperfect. By perfect happiness we understand that which arrives at the true meaning of happiness, and by imperfect that which does not arrive there, but has some share in it, and is like it from some particular point of view. We may compare these two types to the perfect prudence which man has because he knows the reason for what he does, and the imperfect prudence which animals exhibit when they follow their instincts and go through particular acts like those that suppose prudence. This happiness cannot be the study of the speculative sciences. To prove our case, we note that the field of speculative science does not reach farther than the power of its principles, for in the principles of a science is its whole potential content. But the leading principles of the speculative sciences are learned by the aid of the senses, as Aristotle shows in the opening of his *Metaphysics* and in the conclusion of his *Analytics*. This is why the entire field of the speculative sciences does not go beyond the point to which sense knowledge can bring us. And man's happiness, that is, his full realization, is not in sense knowledge. For nothing receives any perfection from what is lower than itself, unless there is in the lower some share of the higher. Now, because it is plain that the form of a stone, or of any thing of sense, is lower than man, the human intellect cannot get its perfection from the form of the stone as such, but it can in so far as there is in that form, by participation, a likeness of something above the human intellect, as, for example, an intelligible light or anything of that kind. But anything that exists by favor of another can be reduced to something that exists in its own right. Hence, the final human perfection must come through knowing something above the human mind. And as we have shown (1, q.88, a.2) that one cannot, by means of sense experience, come to a knowledge of separate substances which are above the human intellect, we are left with the fact that man's full happiness cannot consist in a study of speculative science. For all that, when there exists in sense forms a shared likeness of higher things, the study of speculative science gives us a little corner of true and perfect happiness (1–2, q.3, a.6).

So, when we look deeper into our spiritual activity, we are brought back more decisively to the point at which the analysis of our desires had left us: within man's essence is a need of the transcendent and absolute, and this, like the very definition of man, cannot content us with what we are or give us what we are not. We accept, then, without any arbitrary hobbling, every demand written into the structure of our thought. Unless we maim it in its loftiest flights, human thought will never be satisfied with less than having reached the essence of God.

Things can be in potency in either of two ways. The first is a natural way, that is, it concerns that which can be reduced from potency to act by a natural agent. The second is to be in potency with regard to that which cannot be reduced to act by a natural agent, but by an agent of another kind. We show this from the realm of organisms. Take, for example, a child grown to be a man: this is within his natural power; or again sperm developed into an animal. But take wood made into a chair, or a blind man become clear-sighted; this is not within their natural power.

It is the same way with our intellect. To be sure, the intellect is in natural potency as to some knowable things, that is, those that can be actualized by "the active intellect," which is that inner principle by whose functioning we can actually know. But it is impossible for us to reach the human end of ends by thus bringing our intellect into operation, for the work of the active intellect lies in making actually intelligible the images which are but potentially so. Now, because these images are received by the senses, our intellect can be actualized by the active intellect only with regard to those knowable objects of which we can acquire knowledge by the aid of the world that can be sensed. But the end of ends cannot consist in such knowledge, because once the end of ends is reached, natural desire should abate and die down. And yet let a man use his intellect, and make all the progress he can in the kind of knowledge that is got from the senses, still he always has a desire to know something more. In fact, the things that our senses cannot know, and of which we can get only a modicum of knowledge by beginning with the senses, are beyond number, so much so that we can perhaps come to know *that* such things are, but not *what* they are, because the essences of spiritual things are of another kind than those of physical things, and we may say that, in comparison with these, they are incommensurably transcendent. And even if we did fully grasp that which comes within the range of the senses, there are things whose nature we cannot know with certitude, for we do not know certain things at all, and we know others poorly.

The desire to know, to have a perfect knowledge, always remains with us; it is inborn, and an inborn or native desire cannot be aimless. We shall, therefore, reach our end of ends only if a higher agent than those connatural with us actualizes our intellect and satisfies our characteristic bent for knowledge. Now, this urge to know is such that when we know effects, we want to know the causes, and no matter what the thing in question be, or which of its properties we may know, our desire does not rest until we know the essence of it. And so our born desire to know is restless until we know the first cause, and not in any haphazard way, but in its essence. This first cause is God. The end of ends, then, for an intelligent creature is to see God as he essentially is (*Compendium Theologiae,* c.4).

United with God as the one object in which human happiness consists, the soul will have reached the

HAPPINESS AND MORALS 45

end of ends towards which its whole moral activity tends (1-2, q.3, a.8). Yet it might seem that by putting off to a future experience the union of man with God, we had rather deferred than solved the problem of happiness, because if God is in essence transcendent to us, He will ever remain so.

How this can be is what we have now to study. For one thing, it is clear that, since our mind cannot know anything except through an image of it, we cannot know the essence of one thing through the image of another, and the farther the image through which the mind knows is from the thing known, the less perfect the knowledge our intellect has of the essence of this thing. If, for instance, our mind were to know an ox through the image of an ass, it would know its essence imperfectly, that is, only in its genus; and it would know its essence even more imperfectly if it knew it through the image of a stone, because that is a genus farther removed. And if it should know it through the image of something whose genus had nothing in common with any ox, it would not know the essence of it at all.

At any rate, it is clear that no created thing can have a common genus with God. And if this is so, God cannot be known in His essence through any created species, whether this is known to sense or to intellect. That God Himself be known to us in His essence, therefore, He must take the form of the intellect which knows Him, and unite Himself to it, not making one nature with it, but as the intelligible image becomes one with the intellect which knows it. For as He is in His being, so He is in His truth, and truth is the form of the intellect. Besides, it is needful that, whatever acquires a form, should have some fitness or disposition for that form. But our intellect by its nature is not in complete readiness to receive the form of truth, else it would have had it from the beginning. Therefore, when it does take it on, it must be raised toward it by a new and superadded disposition. We call this disposition the Light of Glory. Just as heat, which disposes to the form of fire, can come only from fire, so our intellect can attain its perfection only as helped by this Light and led by God, whose nature it is to have this same Light. Of this Light of Glory it is written (Psalm 35): "In thy light we shall see light (*in lumine tuo videbimus lumen*)."

Now, if we suppose this end reached, our natural desire should surely be satisfied, because the divine essence, united, as we have said, to the intellect of him who sees God, is at once the sufficient source of all knowledge and the fountain of all goodness, so that nothing remains to be desired. To know God in His essence and as He knows Himself, this is the most perfect manner of becoming like God. And if we do not comprehend Him as He comprehends Himself, this is not because we are ignorant of a part of Him, for He has no parts; but because we do not know Him as perfectly as He can be known, or because the power of our intellect, though it knows Him, is not possibly equal to the truth by which He is knowable. For His splendor or truth is without limit, whereas our intellect is limited; His intellect, like the truth which is its object, has no bounds. This is why God knows Himself exactly as He is knowable, or as a person knows a conclusion who sees it demonstrated, and not as one knows it imperfectly and as a hypothesis.

We have said that the end of ends for man is happiness. Human felicity or happiness consists in seeing God in His essence. But as regards its perfection, man's happiness is far from God's, because it is by His nature that God has this happiness, whereas man, as we have explained, gets hold of it only by sharing the divine light (*Compend. Th.,* c.105–6; cf. *Quodlibet.,* 7, q.1, a.1).

These luminous pages are their own fit commentary; yet for those who have not in mind the organic structure of the system, we underscore three distinctive points of the teaching unfolded here.

The first is the much-censured *transcendence* which Thomistic thought attributes to God—a feature so deeply imbedded in the divine essence that not only no creature, in any state, can ever be or become God, but no creature, in any state, may pretend to a "natural" knowledge of His essence. The direct seeing of God will always be beyond the reach of the human intellect by the whole distance that God is above man, and hence, to see God can never be anything but a supernatural grace (1, q.12, a.2, and a.5; *C.G.,* 3, c.53). This grace does not bring the created mind into the interior of the divine essence, but is poured out on it to enlighten it and enable it to look upon that essence.

The second mark is the *continuity* of Thomistic thought, based on the applicability of the principle of causality to the visible world. At the height of his grandest speculations, St. Thomas never loses hold of the guiding thread of "analogy," which he has taken at the beginning. The expression "Light of Glory" is a comparison, but it is very reasonable.

In fact, just as there are objects of sense, for instance, these stones, a means to perceive them by, namely the sense image, and a medium that makes them visible, the light of the sun; so we have objectives of the intellect, such as the essence of the stones, a means by which we know them, that is the phantasm of visible things, and one that makes them intelligible to us, namely, the active intellect, which is a kind of light in relation to them. In a similar way we have at the last, in our state of realization, a perceived object, the divine essence, but in this case knowledge is direct and intuitive, and we have no medium through which we know that essence, but only a kind of light which makes it known to us (3, d.24, q.1, a.2; *C.G.,* 3, c.53).

A third chief feature is the *oneness* which this analogy implies between man's moral activity, with the relative happiness that goes with it, and the absolute happiness which is the substance of morality come to its full flower. Because the intellectual seeing of God is to bring human nature to the very peak of its expression and wholly to actualize this "humanity," which is otherwise realized but brokenly, we are sure that, by gathering them up and bringing them to a pointed perfection, happiness will warrant all the acts, all the desires, all the joys which, agreeing with the noblest and most "human" needs of our nature, are beforehand like the state of the soul whose boundless hopes will at last be fulfilled. This is why no moral system merits better than that of

HAPPINESS AND MORALS

Thomas the epithet "humanistic," and without the slightest paradox we may describe Thomism as an integral humanism.

From what has been said, it is plain that in the joy which comes of seeing God, all human desire will be realized, as it is said in Psalm 105: "Who satisfieth thy desire with good things." And in fact all human desires do find their completion in that vision, as we may show by taking them one by one.

Because he has an intelligence, one of man's desires is to know the truth. It is this desire that men satisfy by living a life of contemplation. Evidently, such a desire will come to fruition when, at sight of the first truth, all that the mind naturally wishes to know will become known to it (*cf. C.G.,* 3, c.59).

Man, as a rational animal, also has a desire to put affairs into their places. It is this desire he tries to satisfy by devoting himself to a life of action and social service. The main objective of this desire is to organize the whole of human life in a reasonable way, that is, to live a life of virtue; for the end or value proposed to himself by every active good man is his own virtue, as the end or aim of the strong man is a strenuous life. And this desire will be gratified when reason shall come to its full vigor and be enlightened by a divine light, so that it is no longer open to deception.

Social life also is accompanied by certain goods, such as high honors, which men need for life in society (if a man wants these over-much, he is ambitious and proud). But a man comes to the highest honors by seeing God, because, as we showed (c.51), he is in a way united to God. That is why the blessed or happy in union with Him are called "kings," just as we say that He is the king of the ages. "They shall reign with Him" (Apocalypse, c.20). Another thing that people want in social life is name and reputation, and if their desire for it is uncontrolled, we say they seek empty glory. But at the sight of God, men become renowned, not in human opinion, which deceives and is deceived, but in the absolute knowledge of God and of all the saints. It is for this reason that in Scripture happiness is often called "glory," as we read (Psalm 149): "The saints shall rejoice in glory." And there is one last thing that men are after in social life, namely riches, and when our taste for these and our pursuit of them runs out of bounds, we either become tight or unjust. But in happiness with God there is plenty of all values, because the blessed there enjoy Him who sums up the perfection of all good things. So we read in the Book of Wisdom (c.7): "All good things came to me together with her," and in Psalm 111: "Glory and wealth shall be in his house."

A third desire common to man and all animals, is to be satiated with pleasure. Men seek to satisfy this desire mainly by voluptuous living and, when they overwork it, become intemperate and incontinent. Now, in happiness with God joy is perfect, and this as deeply overshadows sensual pleasure, which even the brute animals take delight in, as intellect outdoes sense. And as this good which we shall enjoy is higher than any sense good, and more intimate and persistently delicious, so this delectation is freer from any admixture of what could sadden or disquiet us. Psalm 35 speaks of this: "They shall be inebriated with the plenty of Thy house, and Thou shalt make them drunk of the torrent of Thy pleasure."

Yet one more inborn desire, common to all creatures: they struggle with all their might for self-preservation. When overdone, this urge makes men timid, and afraid, and sparing of hard work. This desire will be fully satisfied when the happy or blessed, shielded from every harm, shall rejoice in a genuine and lasting way, as is told by Isaias (c.49) and in the Apocalypse (c.16): "They shall no more hunger nor thirst, neither shall the sun fall on them, nor any heat."

The patent inference is that it is in seeing God that intelligent beings find real happiness. In this vision all desire comes to rest, and in it is found that true sufficiency of all values which, in Aristotle's view (*Ethics,* bk.10), is required for happiness. So Boëthius also says (*de Consol. Phil.,* 3) that happiness is "a state made perfect by the assembling of all good things." In our present life, however, nothing comes closer to this full and final happiness than the way of those who contemplate truth as well as can be done now. The philosophers, not quite able to know this chief felicity, have said that man's grand happiness is the contemplation which he can reach in this life. For the same reason, Holy Scripture commends the contemplative above other ways of life, as Our Lord says (Luke, 10): Mary has chosen the better part, namely, the contemplation of truth, which shall not be taken from her. In fact, contemplation of truth begins in the present life, but is completed in the future life; whereas the active and social life does not last beyond the present (*C.G.,* 3, c.63).

Such is the end, and the whole moral life leads us safely to it. But as we can reach it only by action, we must inquire what a human act is.

Chapter II

STRUCTURE OF THE HUMAN ACT

Ethics is of the practical order, it is the science of what is to be done to win happiness. It thus relates closely to the description and the prescription of specific actions. And because it is a science, it has to be grounded on the universal. We must begin, therefore, with the very broadest principles of action and come down to the concrete detail of moral doings. And since happiness, the attaining of which is our problem, is man's own peculiar value, we should inquire first into voluntary acts, which are man's own, and leave to a later chapter the acts common to man and beast and known as the emotions. What is a voluntary act?

1. THE WILLED ACT

A willed act is a reasonable act. And as man of course is a rational being, human acts are willed.

For a clear understanding of this we must remember that the source of some acts or movements is within the being which acts or is moved, and that the source of others is without that being. For example, when a stone is raised, as when you give it a throw, the source of its motion is outside

THE WILLED ACT

the stone; but when it falls (*i. e.,* when it naturally falls) the origin of its motion is within the stone itself. Now, of those things that are moved from within, some move themselves and some do not. And as everything that moves or is moved does so for an end (as we saw: 1–2, q.1, a.2), we shall consider as wholly moved by an inner principle those beings in which there is both a principle to move them and a principle to move them for an end.

If anything is to be done for an end, some knowledge of this end is required. So every being that acts or is moved by some inner principle implying a knowledge of the end, has truly within itself the source of its activity, and it not only acts, but acts in view of the end. As for those beings that have no knowledge of ends, even though they have an inner principle of action or movement, the principle which causes them to act or be moved for an end is not in them, but in some other, who impresses on them the principle of their movement towards the end. This is why we say of such beings that they do not move themselves, but are moved, and of those that know their end we say that they move themselves, precisely because they have within them the principle which moves them both to act and to act for an end. And thus, because their acting and their acting for an end are both from an inner source, their movements and acts are called *voluntary*. The word voluntary means that the movement or activity comes from a being's own inclination. For this reason, Aristotle and Gregory and John Damascene did not define the willed act simply as something whose source is within, but they added, "with knowledge." And because man best of all knows the purpose of what he does and initiates his own activity, his actions are out and out willed or voluntary (1–2, q.6, a.1).

Particularly or out and out, we say; and, in this visible world, we might say, uniquely. For if the willed act is a function of knowledge, it comes and goes with knowledge and varies with it. Where, then, there is strictly speaking no knowledge of end, as in the case of animals pursuing ends without seeing them as such, there is, strictly speaking, no will. On the other hand, it is enough that there be inner freedom of action, with consciousness of the end sought, for the willed act to exist, though it may be that no external action is carried out. In a word, we call voluntary anything that proceeds from the will.

We may say that one thing can come from another in either of two senses. First, it can spring directly from it if it arises out of the activity of the other, as, for instance, warmth comes from the action of heating. Secondly, it can come in a roundabout way, from the mere fact that the thing does not act, as the sailing of a vessel is said to be from the pilot, even when he has ceased to govern her. It must be understood, however, that what results from the absence of one's action is not imputed to him as cause, merely for the reason that he does not act, but only when he could and should do something. For example, if a pilot could not man his ship, or if the running of her was not in his hands, we would not charge him with anything that might happen in his absence. In like manner, the will, by willing and acting, can put a stop to not-willing and not-acting, and sometimes ought to do it: and of course the not-willing or not-acting is then imputed to the will as arising from it. And so there can be "a willed act without an act"; first, at such times as there is no external act,

THE WILLED ACT

but an interior one, as when one wills not to act, and again when there is not even an interior act, as when one does not will to act (1–2, q.6, a.3).

This absolute within-ness of will is explained by the fact that will is the most finished work of nature. Of course, we know that, in the Aristotelian sense, "nature" is the inner and direct source of the activity and doings of any being. And we now come to what is most interior in nature—its finality; and in understanding this as within nature itself, we have met the will. Henceforth we shall realize why this will, which does not let even its own finality come in from the outside, would much less let its movement and action be imposed on it from without. By the inner-ness, then, which is its own essence, the will is strictly inviolable. Violence can be brought from without only on acts that are exterior to it and so are different in character from it; and these acts remain subject to its control.

The will has two acts; one belongs immediately to it because it comes from it. This is the act of willing. The other is an act of the will in the sense that the will commands it, but it is done with the help of some other faculty. For example, to walk or to speak is an act commanded by the will, though carried out by some other power. As for acts commanded by the will, plainly the will can suffer violence, to the extent that the exterior members can be kept by force from obeying the order of the will. But violence cannot enter the field of the proper action of the will itself. The reason is that an act of the will is simply the type of inclination that comes from an inner principle with knowledge, as the "natural" appetite is an inclination arising from an inner source, but without knowledge. Now, whatever is forced or violent has some external origin. It is thus against the very meaning of an act of the will that it be forced or violent, precisely as it is against the essential inclination or natural tendency of a stone to rise. A stone can be lifted up by force; but it is not possible that this forced movement be from its native tendency. So, too, a man can be taken by force; but that he should go of his own will is a contradiction to the kind of thing that force is (1–2, q.6, a.4).

Such is the character of the voluntary act. We have a means now to qualify every act, and with no great risk of error to put it among acts which do or do not arise from the will. It is clear, first of all, that that which is forced is still less compatible with the voluntary than it is with the "natural," for the two terms are opposed to each other as that which comes from within and that which is endured from without. We know at the outset, then, that no act resulting from outer force brought to bear upon our body, is chargeable to our will (*ibid.,* a.5). Yet it is just as clear, and the point is central and important, that nothing which might try to act directly on the will, can violate it. We inflict on the body, which is commanded by the will, acts condemned by the will, but no one can impose anything on the will by force; not even God could do it, for whatever He might impose on it, would become voluntary in passing through the will. We do not doubt that it is correct to say with Scripture (Prov. 22): The heart of the king is in the hand of God: whithersoever he will, He shall turn it. All the same, the heart is a human heart, and God does not cause it to will anything but voluntary acts (*ibid.*, a.4, ad 1).

Here, then, we see the profound oneness of the coöperation given by God to the material world with that which he gives to the moral world. This unity is explained by the fact that the will is a nature whose finality is conscious and within. Now, it occurs to no one to deny that the natural movement of a body is and remains natural, even though it has received its nature from God and is started by God as its first mover; nor would anyone wish to deny that the voluntary movement of a being remains voluntary in the very measure that its will is moved by God (*ibid.*, a.1, ad 3). In a word, the coöperation of God does apply to beings, but is not a substitute for them. It moves nature as nature, and will as will (*De Veritate*, q.22, a.8).

Here some one might cite the endless repercussions which such a principle would start on a detailed criticism of human acts, and even now he senses how hard it is for a man to pass off on others the responsibility for his own acts. We have said that nothing from without can force this principle; let us get rid now of the notion that anything can force it from within. The great interior sources of violence are the emotions, and the most general of these are concupiscence and fear. We now inquire whether the first can smother the voluntary character of our acts. Evidently it cannot. Concupiscence does really take us hot after the object of our desire, it inclines the will to choose what we want, and consequently it reënforces the free character of the act and does not tend to efface it (*ibid.*).

The problem raised by fear is more subtle; but, with a shade of difference, the same conclusion is sound. We cannot judge absolutely of the quality of an act unless we hold a complete list of the circumstances that go with it. An act born of fear may seem involuntary if taken in the abstract, but it is always seen to be voluntary when we look into the specific motives that mark it off. No one, for instance, would throw goods into the sea just for the fun of it, but no one would hesitate to do so to escape a wreck. This is a voluntary act, then, though he who does it is driven by the circumstances (*ibid.*, a.6 and *Quodlibet.*, 5, q.10).

There remains a problem which, because of its practical consequences, is even more important; namely, the bearing of ignorance on the free character of human acts.

By the very fact that it excludes knowledge, ignorance makes an act involuntary. For we have seen (a.2) that knowledge must precede an act if that act is to be free. Yet not every kind of ignorance negates this needed knowledge.

THE WILLED ACT

We must understand that ignorance can be related to the free act in different ways: it may accompany the act, or it may go before the act, or it may follow the act.

Ignorance accompanies the act when a person does not know what he is doing, but would do it just the same, even if he knew. In fact, in such case it is not ignorance that leads him to will what he does: it is simply an accident that the action is unknown. An example of such ignorance would be this: a man who is willing to kill an enemy, does unknowingly kill him under the impression that he is killing a deer. Now, this ignorance does not make the act involuntary, as Aristotle notes (*Ethics,* 3) because it does not imply anything averse to the will; it only makes it not-voluntary, because what is not known can not be actually willed.

Secondly, ignorance follows an act of the will when that ignorance itself is willed. This can happen in two ways, according to the two kinds of voluntary acts which we have cited above (a.3, ad 1). An example of the first is this: the act of the will has ignorance for its end, when one wishes not to know in order to have an excuse for wrong-doing, or so as not to give it up, as Job says (c.21): "We desire not the knowledge of Thy ways." We call this ignorance *affected*. In a second way, one is said to be voluntarily ignorant if he does not know what he could and should know, for to do nothing and not to will are acts of the will, as was said before (a.2). We have an example of this sort of ignorance when a person does not actually think of what he might and should think of. This is the ignorance of a bad will and arises from emotion or from habit. The same is true if a man does not take care to acquire the knowledge which he should have; and in this sense we take as voluntary an ignorance of the principles of right, which a man neglects and lets slip, even though he is required to know them. The ignorance is willed, because in each of these instances it cannot give rise to an act that is simply involuntary; yet it makes the act involuntary in a relative degree, namely, in the sense that it precedes the movement of the will to do a particular act, which, if a person knew he were doing, would not be done.

Besides, ignorance can go before the will in such a way that, though it is voluntary, it still causes the willing of what otherwise would not be willed; as when a man is ignorant of some detail about an act, which he is not required to know, and as a result does what he would not do if he knew. For instance, a man may take all precaution and yet not know that anyone is going along the road: he fires and kills a passerby. Such ignorance as this makes an act purely and simply involuntary (1-2, q.6, a.8).

Thus all these inquiries lead us to one conclusion, namely, that the willed act is present with, and only with, an inner principle of action, plus knowledge of the end pursued. Hence, the formula: "*Actus proprie dicuntur humani, prout sunt voluntarii,*" i. e. an act is rightly called human only if it is free. And this is simply to say that the human and the willed act are one and the same. From all of which we may conclude that the voluntariness of an act resides not in the materiality even of the movement which outlines it, since men, animals, plants, and things are all moved; but man is unique in willing for the reason that he is the sole creature that has in itself a principle for the orientation of its own life.

II. WILL IN THE CONCRETE

We know now what are the bounds of the willed act as such, and we go on to examine the will, taken in itself and in its concrete reality. The order we are to follow in this inquiry will necessarily be imposed on us by an analysis of the relations which the will has to its end, that is, to its proper object. It is plain, in the first place, that the will has no other object than the good, and we shall have to understand in a literal way that it is of the very essence of the will never to do anything except for a good. The proposition is evident from the very definition of desire, of which will is one kind, and the definition of the good. The good is that which we desire; we desire only the good: these are equivalent terms. Now, will is a reasoned desire, that is to say, it is the desire of a good known by reason (*C.G.*, 1, c.96; *De Veritate*, q.22, a.1; 1-2, q.8, a.1). But what is not at once seen, though it is brought to light by St. Thomas' analysis, is the complexity into which this fact throws the several elements of the moral act.

Sometimes the word "will" means the power of willing, and again it stands for the exercise of this power. If we want to speak of will in the sense of a power, it extends to both means and end. The truth is, each faculty takes in everything that in any way shares the nature of its object, as sight extends to everything which in any way has color, and the substance of good, which is the proper object of the will, is found in the end, but just as surely in the means. However, if we speak of the will in the limited sense of voluntary action, then, to be exact, it is a question of end only. For any act that gets its name from a faculty, properly means only the act of that faculty, as, for example, to know means solely the act of intellect. Now, the simple act of a faculty is directed towards what is strictly the object of that faculty. And as everything that is good and willed for itself is an end, in a literal sense the will points to the end; and as the means, on the contrary, are not good or willed for themselves, but in relation to the end, the will never moves unless it moves towards the end, so that what it wills in them, is the end. In the same way, an act of intellect strictly deals with what is knowable in itself, that is to say, with principles; and knowledge deduced from these principles is not knowledge, except in the light of the principles. For in the field of the desirable the end is what first principles are in the order of the knowable (1–2, q.8, a.2).

Here, then, we have the way in which the complexity of the willed act just mentioned flows from this analysis.

Because the end is willed for itself and the means only for the end, it is plain that the will can aim at the end as such without aiming at the means, but that it cannot aim at the means without aiming at the end. The will, therefore, can go towards the end in either of two senses—first toward the end seen precisely as the end, and secondly, toward the end regarded as the cause of willing the means.

It is also patent that one and the same act of the will bears on the end, in the sense of the reason of desiring the means, and on the means themselves. But a different act points the will towards the end taken in itself, and sometimes it precedes the other; as when a man first of all wants health, and afterwards, figuring out how to get it, is willing to call in a doctor to cure him. In the domain of intellect also we have the same procedure: first we know the principles in themselves, and afterwards we understand them in the conclusions drawn from them, in the sense that we assent to the conclusions because of the principles (1–2, q.8, a.3).

This basic duality in the act of the will outlines the order we must follow in studying the will. We shall examine successively: (a) the willing of the end; (b) the willing of the means; which will put us in a position to emphasize the interpenetration really and ceaselessly occurring between the two moments of willing which we have just defined.

A. WILLING THE END

In a study of the act by which the will seeks the end, we should first ask ourselves, what sets the will in action? And no doubt such a method seems to avoid the moot question: Is the will not able by its essence to start itself towards the good? Yet the fact is that it is to this very question that our research will answer: seeking whether such or such a faculty, such or such a being exterior to us, can or cannot move our will, we inevitably find the deep source of its activity, what the will receives from this source and what the will gives to it. Let us take the problem first from the point of view of the intellect and its relation to the will.

One thing needs to be started by another only in so far as it is somehow in potency: what is in potency can be brought into act only by something that is in act; and it is this last which is justly called a starter. Now, a power of the soul may be said to be in potency with regard to several things in either of two senses: first, as to the fact of acting or not acting; secondly, as to the fact of doing this act rather than that. Take, as an example, vision: sometimes we actually see, sometimes we do not see; sometimes we see white and sometimes black. There is need, then, that something move the vision in these two senses, namely, to the *exercise* or use of its act and to the *determination* of its act. The first of these depends on the subject, who may be disposed to act or not to act; the other, however, depends on the object which gives a specific turn to the act.

We may first take the movement of the subject. This arises from some agent, and because every agent acts for an end, as we have shown (q.1, a.2), the source of the movement is in the end; and so the art to which the end belongs commands and moves the art to which the means belong: for instance, the art of navigation commands maritime talent, as Aristotle says in the second book of his *Physics*. Now the good in general, which has the nature of an end, is the object of the will; and from this point of view the will brings the other powers of the soul into activity. For we use other powers of the soul when we will: the ends and perfections of all other powers of the soul are comprised, as specific values, under the object of the will. And always an art or power to which a universal end belongs calls into action the art or power to which a particular end, included under that universal end, belongs. Thus the general of an army, whose aim is the common good, that is, the order of the whole army, moves and commands each of his subordinates, and these aim at order on the battle front.

However, the object moves in its turn, for it specifies the act after the fashion of a formal principle by which an action is specified in subhuman things, as heating from fire. And the first formal principle is being and the truly universal, which is the object of the intellect, and it is by this kind of motion that the intellect moves the will by presenting its object to it (1–2, q.9, a.1; *cf. De Veritate,* q.22, a.12).

The purpose of this analysis is to make evident the essentially mixed character of every act of the will. It is a fact that the psychologist always has trouble when he has to describe the will from the point of view of the concrete acts in which it is exhibited. The will is everywhere in our inner life, but nowhere if we try to isolate it. Especially in what concerns our reasoned acts, we may say that there is not one of our faculties whose operation cannot eventually become matter for an act of the will: I will to eat, to take a walk, to feel, to know; I will to will. The will makes use of all the other faculties at its pleasure. It sets them in motion or keeps them from acting, so much so that, in the last analysis, it is because we have a will that we can always will or not will what we do will or do not will. Yet, correlatively, the will of itself can never determine the nature of an act. The will is a tendency which of itself is blind, and it becomes voluntary or reasonable only at the moment when reason puts within its reach the several objects among which it may choose. An act is voluntary because the will wills it, but the will takes this object rather than that only because reason offers it as good; and it is the successive presentations of reason, making known to the will the divers possible objects among which its choice may be made, that successively move the will toward this object rather than toward that other. It is the will that causes me to will, but it is the intellect that causes my will to will what I will; and in this sense my intellect acts upon my will as my will acts on my intellect.

Itself indifferent, the will is always a fertile source of spontaneous determination towards whatever the intellect proposes to it as good. This spontaneity, however real it be, does not suppose that the will is the first origin of its activity; for just as there must be an external object to specify a voluntary act, so there must be an exterior principle to give a reason for the first impulse which our decisions actually make use of. At least, to run back infinitely in the conditions for the exercise of our acts, would be as absurd here as anywhere else. So we must suppose a first mover of our will, as we had to conclude to a first mover of all movement in general (a.4). And this first mover of willed activity ought to be exterior to our will, precisely as the mover of the world is exterior to the world. Yet we must find an exterior mover of the will who respects the inner character that is of the essence of the will. Who, then, could move the will from the outside and yet not keep the will from being an inner principle which determines itself from the inside? God alone. For He who moves nature as nature can also move the will as will, and even, far from there being here one of those forced dialectical conclusions to which reason gives in, but the intellect does not, we may say that the cause of an inner movement being a cause of the internal character of this movement, this cause alone can act upon it, and that this cause cannot not act on it, since without the cause the movement would not be. Hence this decisive formula: *"Deus igitur est causa nobis non solum voluntatis, sed etiam volendi"* (*C.G.*, 3, c.89), *i.e.*, God is the cause of both our will and our willing. And yet the action of God, however deeply it penetrates, respects the spontaneity which it has given to the human will.

The providence of God is not a destroyer of the nature of things, but their preserver. This is why it moves each thing according to its status, so that from necessary causes the effects of the divine action follow necessarily, but from contingent causes the effects are contingent. Thus because the will is an active principle not set on just one effect, but can indifferently work out any of several, God so moves it as not to force it to one effect, and its action is not inevitable but free, except of course in relation to that to which it is naturally moved (1–2, q.10, a.4).

Now, will is naturally in act toward the good in general, and hence necessarily wills all that is good: love, science, joy, and so on, and it would unavoidably will any concrete object in particular if this object were an absolute good. But there is no such object in our human experience. Morals, then, is the process of the will seeking the absolute value by way of particular values, just as science is the exercise of intellect intent upon being which it seeks by way of particular beings. This procedure of the will should be described under its two chief aspects: it enjoys the good when it has it, and it tends towards good when it has it not. What is this, "to enjoy"? In the Latin, enjoyment is called *fruitio*, which word is plainly from *fructus* or fruit. Now fruit is what we get last from the tree and eat with pleasure, and by analogy we give the name fruition or enjoyment to the possession of the ultimate good which we hope for and which we love. It lies, then, in an act of the will, and it never exists perfectly unless there is the actual seizing of the end that is the last end, for it is only there that the movement of will is completed and comes fully to rest. And this means that there cannot be perfect joy in an experience and a morals which are solely of earth, for as yet we have not this consummatory end: we only tend towards it; so we have but imperfect joys (q.1, a.4) which go along with and crown every striving or conation on their way to being realized. And what is conation?

WILLING THE END

Conation, as the Latin word (*intentio*) suggests, means *to tend toward some thing*. Now that which tends toward some thing can either be the activity of a being that does move, or the movement of a being that is moved. But the movement of a being that is moved tends toward some thing because of the activity of that which moves it; and for this reason purpose and conation belong in the first place and mainly to that which moves things towards an end: as let us say the architect, or any leader moves others by his authority to the purpose which he himself has in view. And the will moves all the other faculties of the soul toward its end, as we proved. Thus it is plain that conation is an act of the will (1-2, q.12, a.1).

Now that we see their intimate unity, how can we keep apart these several aspects of the willed act: willing, enjoyment, conation? They are only three distinct relations which link one and the same act of the will to the end which it pursues. Taken absolutely and in itself, the act of willing is will: I will knowledge, I will health, and so on. Seen as come to its goal and content with victory, this act is enjoyment. As the will to reach an end by using the required means, this same act is conation (*ibid.,* ad 4). We have reached the precise point where analysis of the willed act may bear, according to cases, either on the willing of the end or on the willing of the means (*De Veritate,* q.22, a.14, 1-2, q.12, a.4). For conation consists essentially in the movement of the will which goes by way of the means to the end: to want medicine for the sake of health is yet to will health, for whoever wills the end, wills the means. But there may and there necessarily will come a moment when I shall have to take the medicine; and, in order that the remedy give as little pain as possible, I shall make an empiric distinction of the wanting of an end and the willing of the means. The dissociation which is made in such instance between the two acts should serve as a guide in our analysis. Beginning, then, with the three relations of will to end, we shall study its three relations to the means. These relations are *choice, consent, use.*

B. CHOICE OF MEANS

An end is always willed, and the means to it should always be taken. Before choosing among them, one should think them over, and after they are chosen, the only thing to do is to use them. We shall examine first the nature of the pivotal act which ties will to means, that is their choice or selection. St. Thomas analyses this act with great care to bring out its essential complexity. Nevertheless, choice, as he sees it, is properly the will's.

The term selection means something that belongs both to reason (or intellect) and to will. Aristotle says in the *Ethics* (vi, 2) that choice is a conative knowing or an intelligent desire. However, when two things work together to make a whole, one of them serves as form for the other; and it is for this reason that Gregory of Nyssa says that choice is not desire taken in itself, nor deliberation taken in

CHOICE OF MEANS

itself, but a composite of the two. As we say that an animal consists of body and soul, and is not body alone or soul alone, so we may say of choice. And we should note that in acts of the soul the act which is of the essence of a power or a habit gets its form and species from a higher faculty or habit, because the lower functions under the higher. If, for instance, a man performs an act of courage for the love of God, this act materially is an act of courage, but formally, it is an act of charity. Still it is evident that reason precedes will in a sense and orders its act, that is, in so far as the will tends towards its object, as reason outlines it, because it is the faculty of knowing which presents the object to the faculty of desire; so the act by which will tends toward anything offered it as good, is, from the fact that it is reason which orders it towards its end, materially an act of the will, but formally an act of reason. In such case, the substance of the act enjoys the rôle of matter with regard to the order which a superior faculty imposes upon it, and that is why, substantially, choice is not an act of the intellect but of the will, for choice is a movement of the soul toward the good which the soul selects. This makes choice manifestly an act of the power of desire (1–2, q.13, a.1; *De Veritate,* q.22, a.15).

Arising from the will, selection or choice is as free as the will. Besides, as choice has to do only with the means, it is always free; for the only instance in which the will would cease to be free will never presents itself for selection or choice. This is the instance: in presence of the Supreme Value, the will, defined as desire of good, would of necessity will it. But the Supreme Value can only be an end, and never a means. It can thus be willed, but not chosen; and, as a consequence, selection, as we define it, moves in the realm of relative values, and this domain is the one place of our freedom.

Man does not choose of necessity. This is because that which can not-exist need not exist. In the dual nature which is man's, we can give a reasonable account of the fact that it is possible for him to choose or not to choose. Man can will or not will, act or not act, and he can will either this or that. The basis of this power of willing is found in our very power of knowing: will can tend toward anything that reason can see as good. Now reason sees as good not only willing and acting, but also not-willing and not-acting. Besides, if we consider any particular good, the intellect can view it under the aspect of its good or its lack of good, which is what we mean by evil; and in this way it can understand any such good thing either as *"eligibile vel fugibile"*: that is, as fit to be taken or to be left. But reason cannot envisage the perfect value, *i. e.,* welfare, from the point of view of evil or of any defect, and thus man of necessity wills welfare, and he could not will to be unhappy or to be miserable. But since choice has to do not with the end, but with the means, we have no choice of the perfect value or welfare, but only of particular values. Man, accordingly, is not forced, but free in his choices (1–2, q.13, a.6).

Choice or selection presupposes thought, for this metaphysical reason:

We saw that choice follows the judgment of reason on what should be done. Yet there is a good deal of uncertainty about what should be done because actions run into specific

CHOICE OF MEANS

and contingent cases, and these are so changeable as to be uncertain. Now, in doubtful and unsettled questions reason ventures no judgment without a previous inquiry, and so there must be this exploration before reason says what is to be done. It is this scrutiny that we call deliberation. Hence, Aristotle in his *Ethics* (bk.3) says that choice is a desire of something which has been considered beforehand (1–2, q.14, a.1).

Some will certainly object to this and say that deliberation is out of place in a study of the moral or free act, because to deliberate is plainly the business of reason. Yet this would be to miss the essentially mixed character of the activity which we describe.

When the acts of two faculties are inter-related, there is in each something of the other, and either could be named from the other. Now it is plain that the act of reason as director of the means, and the act of the will which tends to the means at the suggestion of reason, have an inter-relationship. Hence, in this will-act or choice there is evidently something of reason, that is, there is the order; and in deliberation, which is an act of reason, there is something of the will: first, by title of the matter, for we deliberate on what we should do, and also by title of motive, because in willing the end, we begin to think about the means. Aristotle says in the *Ethics* (bk.4, ch. 2) that choice is an intelligent desire, to show that intellect and will concur in it, and John Damascene (*De Fide Orthod.*, 2, c.22) says that deliberation is a desire that keeps informed, to make it clear that deliberation belongs in a measure to the will, on which inquiry is founded and from which it arises, and also to the intellect, which conducts the inquiry (1–2, q.14, a.1, ad 1).

We may say that deliberation takes on a still more precise aspect when we study the voluntary act called consent, which goes with it and sanctions it. The center and substance of deliberation is an activity of the intellect. As such, it finds in itself the principle from which it arises and the conclusion to which it comes. Its point of departure may be a simple sense perception: a bit of bread, let us say, or some filings of iron. But it may also be a universal principle of either the theoretical or the practical order: *e. g.,* thou shalt not steal, or man cannot live without food. These are principles of deliberation, precisely because there is no room to deliberate about them. As for the outcome of deliberation, this is given us by the first means that we must accept if we care to reach the end (*ibid.,* a.6). But this purely intellectual conclusion of an action done on the will's account is normally completed by an acceptance or consent in which the will takes the leading rôle without a rival.

To consent supposes the application of one of the senses to some object. And the function of the senses is to know present things, whereas the imagination can form images of objects even in the absence of the imaged objects. And intellect, for its part, gets hold of universal notions and seizes them in both the presence and the absence of the individual objects. Now as the act of the conative faculty is a kind of

CHOICE OF MEANS

inclination toward the thing itself, presented in thought, this very application of our conative power to the thing, when the power fastens upon it, is given the name of sense, as if it had some sort of experience of the thing on which it fastens, in so far as it is satisfied with it. So it is said in the first chapter of the Book of Wisdom: "Think of the Lord in goodness." In this sense, to consent is an act of the conative faculty (1-2, q.15, a.1).

This act of consent is situated at a fixed point in the economy of the willed act, and because it has to do only with the choice of means, we may not allow it a direct bearing on the end. If we could, we should destroy the plan of this complex edifice.

Consent means the application of a conative movement to something that is at the disposal of the one applying it. In the practical order, we should put first the perception of the end, secondly, reflection on the means, and lastly, the desire of these means. Now, desire tends naturally to the end of ends; so that the turning of the conative activity on this end, once it is perceived, has not the nature of consent, but simply of will. Yet, when there is question of things which are means, and as such exist only in view of the end of ends, these means are matter for deliberation; and there can be consent with regard to them as often as the movement of desire is applied to the judgment which closes deliberation. A conative movement towards an end, however, does not apply to deliberation, but deliberation rather applies to it, because it presupposes a desire of the end; whereas desire of the means presupposes a deliberation already concluded (1-2, a.15, a.3).

Preceded by deliberate consent, choice in its turn is prolonged by the putting to work or the use of what the will needs to carry out the sentence just given. This action seems to be effected particularly by the powers of the soul, the members of the body, and the exterior instruments which the will employs to serve its purposes; but the action belongs to the worker and not to the tool which he uses. Thus it is the will that puts all the other powers to work, and to it properly belongs the business of employing them (1-2, q.16, a.1). So we may add a new link to the chain of operations which binds together our free activity, though it is important to note that here we are rather at the nearer end of another chain attached to the first. To perceive the good, to will it, to deliberate on the means of attaining it, and to consent to the result of this deliberation, to choose at last the means which this consent points out—here is a series complete by itself, one which we might regard as finished: the integral willing of the end includes the willing of the means. With use begins a second free activity, which certainly derives from the first, but instead of tending to will, as the other does, this tends precisely to take possession of the willed thing (*ibid.*, a.4). From this new point of view, the will commands acts through the organ of reason which puts the order into a formula.

To command is an act of reason, but it presupposes an act of the will. To realize this, we must remember that the acts

CHOICE OF MEANS

of will and of reason interact on each other, because intellect reasons on what is to be willed, and the will decides to reason. An act of will is preceded by an act of reason, and vice versa. And as the influence of the preceding act continues to make itself felt in the act following, it sometimes happens that a particular act of the will exists only according as there subsists virtually in it something of an anterior act of reason, as we said of use and choice; and, conversely, an act of reason exists only as there subsists virtually in it something of an act of the will. To command is essentially an act of reason; for he who commands orders him whom he commands to do something, by suggesting it or indicating it to him, and such ordering, no matter how it is done, is the work of reason. Now reason can suggest or point out in two ways: first, absolutely, and this intimation is expressed in the indicative, as when we say to anyone: This is what you are to do. But at other times reason suggests something to a person in a compelling way, expressed in the imperative: Do this. The first of the soul's powers that leads to the doing of things is the will, as we have said (q.9, a.1). And as a second mover moves by commanding, this is done in virtue of the will. It seems, then, that to command is an act of reason, but presupposes an act of the will, and in virtue of this the intellect proceeds at the command which the will gives to carry out the act (1–2, q.17, a.1).

This command goes just before the execution or doing of the act, and the action in turn utilizes the means selected for the end; there is almost nothing in soul or body that the will cannot employ in view of the end. It uses, first, the will itself, for it can will that we will. It makes use also of reason, as it can command us to reflect, to pay attention, to give or withhold assent in all instances in which conclusions are not evident. It uses even the sense appetite, so far at any rate as our desires and impulses are under the control of reason, which in its turn comes within the purview of the act of will. It also employs, with the exception of the internal organs of vegetative life, at least the exterior members which obey the sense powers of the soul, and which, by way of them, obey reason (*ibid.*, q.17, a.6-9).

Such is the scheme according to which human acts are built up. They show an almost unlimited complexity in their elements, so that they can be combined to fit every conceivable formula and have every kind of repercussion on each other, since the will can consent to its own choice and consent to its consent, and use itself to give consent or to make a choice, and so on and so on indefinitely (q.16, a.4, ad 3). They also have a oneness of substance from the human soul whence they arise, and from the reciprocal order putting them together and ranking them above and below each other (q.1, a.4), and most of all from the end of ends, which guarantees a unity of principle to all these acts born of itself, and points them back towards itself as their origin.

Chapter III

MORAL VALUE AND DISVALUE

We know now what a human act is, but we do not yet know what gives it precisely the moral quality of a good act or a bad one. And perhaps it would embarrass us "to ground morals," that is to offer a just reason for this dual qualification, unless we kept in mind the perfect continuity which makes morals one with metaphysics. It is by integrating man with a system of beings and with the metaphysical laws of action that we have found the specific law of his activity. So, it is by taking moral value as an instance of value in general, and not by supposing *a priori* that it is an irreducible datum and a quasi-miracle, that we shall give it place and relevance in the elements of metaphysics.

What is value, quite aside from moral prepossession? It is an aspect of being. There is nothing that could justify the apparition of value at some point in human thought or in the scheme of things, if it were not present from the beginning. That which is, is; in as far as it is itself, it is one. So far as it is knowable (and all that has being can be an object of cognition), it is true. So far as desirable (and all that has being can be an object of desire), it is good. The same is true of the human act. It need not put on a new quality and arise no one knows whence, to become good or bad. It need not even become one or the other: it is good in the measure in which it is, and bad exactly in so far as it does not exist. Let us lay down the principle, and then follow up concrete cases of it in their intricacy and detail.

We would say of good and evil in actions just what we say of good and evil in things, because anything acts itself out: such as it is, such it does. Now, each thing has as much of value as it has of being. As indeed we said in the Prima Pars (q.5, a.3), good and being are in a sense synonymous. Only God has the whole fulness of his being in a unified and simple way, whereas the fulness of being proper to each particular thing hinges on many relations. It may turn out that some of these have being from a certain point of view, and yet lack that fulness which belongs to them: for instance, the fulness of human being requires that it be made up of body and soul and gifted with all the powers and instruments of knowledge and action, and if a man lacks any of these, he has not the fulness of human being. Therefore, the more of being a man has, the more he has of value, but, contrariwise, in the measure in which he lacks something of the fulness of his being, in that measure he lacks good and is called evil. Take the example of a blind man: he shares goodness from the fact that he is alive, yet it is an evil for him to be without his sight. But if anything were without entity or goodness, you could not say that it was good or bad. And as the nature of good requires the very plentitude of being, if anything lacks what belongs to the fulness of its being, we would say that it is not good in an absolute, but only in a relative sense, namely, in so far as it exists: yet it can be called a being purely and simply, and only relatively a non-being, as we said in an earlier book (1, q.5, a.1, ad 1). We would also say of every action that, so far as it possesses being, so far it contains good, but in the measure in which it lacks anything of the fulness of being due to a human action, just so far it lacks good and deserves the name of evil. Say, for instance, it falls short of the amount that reason fixes or is out of place, and so on (1–2, q.18, a.1).

This is the principle that we submit for the grading of moral acts. We have now to work out its consequences. The words quoted a moment ago from St. Thomas give us a hint of the essential factor needed for an action to have fully the character of a human action. It is not enough that it be done by man, for man does not always act as man. It must be aimed at an object fit for him in view of his nature. An animal fathers a monster; this is because his nature has gone wrong. A man brings his actions to bear on an object which is not properly his object; this also means that his way of acting has got off the track. Thus an action has its full quality of human action when it strives for an object which man should seek, and then too, *eo ipso,* it is good. On the other hand, an action has not its whole character of human action when the object which it aims at is not what the "form" of man requires, and then also, *eo ipso,* it is an evil action (1-2, q.18, a.2). There are, therefore, two kinds of actions: human or good actions and non-human or evil actions; and we may know them by the fact that the former point toward an object suitable for the nature of man, while the latter do not. And what is the nature of man and the "form" which makes him man? It is reason.

In the practical order, we know good from evil by a reference to reason, because, as Dionysius says in his work on *The Names of God* (part 4), the good of man is to conform to reason. And, conversely, that is evil which is out of line with reason. In fact, what is good for each thing is whatever goes with it according to its form; and what is evil for it, is that which is foreign to the order of its form. It is patent, then, that the difference between good and evil, in relation to the object, has a direct reference to reason and lies in the fact that the object is or is not harmonious with reason. For acts are termed human or moral in so far as they obey reason (1–2, q.18, a.5).

Let us state now, in less metaphysical terms, the relation set up between the human will and its objects. Whatever the will aims at, is its end; and as we have distinguished two points of application of the free act, the one interior (which is the act of willing), and the other exterior (the carrying out of the decision), so we shall distinguish two ends of the will, one interior, the other exterior; but we shall always keep this latter in a subordinate place.

Acts are called human in so far as they are free, as remarked above (q.1, a.1). Yet in a free act there is a double act, namely, the inner act of the will and the exterior act. And each of these two acts has its object: properly, the end is the object of the inner act of the will, while the end of the exterior act is its object. Consequently, just as the exterior act gets its rating from its object, so the interior act of the will is ranked from its end, which is strictly its object. Now, everything that enters into the domain of the will plays the part of a form with regard to that which is in the domain of the exterior act, for the will in acting uses the members as tools. Nor have exterior acts any moral quality, except in so far as they are free. If, therefore, we look for the species of the human act in its form, we find it in its end; but if we seek it in its matter, we find it in the object of the exterior act. Aristotle says (*Ethics,* bk.5) that he who steals so as to commit adultery is more an adulterer than a thief (1–2, q.18, a.6).

We thus come back to the interior act by which the will aims at the end and picks the means in view of the end, as to the very source of morality. We must, therefore, apply our analysis to this, in order to determine fully the conditions of the moral life. First of all, because the fitness of the object to the power of willing limits the goodness of the act, the object of will must be set before the will by reason.

As we have remarked, goodness of the will turns in a very exact sense on its object. And this object is offered to the will by reason. Indeed, the good known by the mind is the goal suited to the will, whereas the good of sense or of imagination is not adapted to the will, but to the desires of the senses, because will can tend to the universal good which reason knows, whereas the hunger of the senses tends only to this or that good grasped by the faculty of feeling. For this reason, goodness of the will depends on reason in the same way that it depends on the object (1–2, q.19, a.3).

On the other hand, it is clear that the agreement of an object with human reason is not a one-way relation, and the nature of reason concurs to fix it as much as, and more than, the nature of the object, for an object is an object only from a faculty which understands it. But from whence does reason come? It is certainly a reason which is human in a precise sense, that is to say, supplied with everything needed in order to know; yet we cannot fully analyse its functions without seeing that it bears the mark of its divine origin. Primordially, the human intellect is as a blank slate, on which nothing is written. Hardly, however, have the first sense perceptions been felt, when the intellect forms universal ideas—the idea of being, for instance, and of principles, such as the principle of causality. Whence comes this readiness to conceive the universal and the necessary, whence comes it to the mere faculty of knowing a specific and contingent being? It can come only from God, from whom the natural light dwelling within the human intellect has the power to form, beginning with sense experience, notions and principles like the divine ideas. Each act of intellectual knowledge thus brings into play a light whose power arises from a transcendent origin.

And what is true in the order of knowledge is equally true in the order of action; for it is one and the same intellect that we call theoretic when it seeks truth in order to know it, and that we call practical when it seeks good in order to do it (1, q.79, a.11). Beginning, then, with our first sense experiences, we build principles of action as we work out principles of knowledge (*ibid.*, q.12), and these principles, by their very necessity and universality, are witnesses to the eternal and divine law from which they come (1–2, q.19, a.4). The agreement of the object with the will, which is the human and moral mark on acts, is now transferred to the agreement of the object with the bidding of conscience, itself an application of the first principles of action, which, for their part, are only human reflections of the divine law. How can this harmony of the object with reason and with the law of God be made sure of? By the subjection of the will to reason. If reason, in a hypothetical case, is right, and the will does not follow it, the will is plainly in the wrong, and it is equally so if, when reason is mistaken, the will refuses to follow it.

In an instance of indifferent acts, the will which breaks with a reason or conscience that is out of line, is in a sense bad, on account of its object, on which we know that goodness or badness of the will hinges. Certainly not on account of the object taken in its proper nature, but only so far as it is then perceived by reason as a good to be done or an evil to be left undone. And as the object is what reason proposes to the will, as we have said (q.8, a.1), from the fact that any object is offered by reason as evil, the will, in taking a step toward that object, bears an evil mark. And this is true not only of what is indifferent, but also of that which is in itself good or bad. In fact, not only what is indifferent can wear the quality of good or evil, but even what is good can put on a character of evil, or what is evil, a character of good, because of the way in which reason understands it. For example, abstinence from fornication is good, and the will never starts toward this good of abstinence except as offered to it as a good by reason; if then such abstinence should be offered as evil by an unreliable mind, the will would aim at it as an evil and, therefore, be itself evil, for it would will something which is not an evil in itself, but which accidentally becomes an evil because of the way reason sees it. Thus, to believe in Christ is good in itself and necessary for salvation; yet the will purposes this only according as reason suggests it. This is why, if reason were to offer belief in Christ to the will as an evil, the will could accept it only as an evil; not that it is an evil in itself, but accidentally it would be an evil, because of the way reason views it. And consequently, Aristotle in the *Ethics* (7, c.9) says that he who does not follow right reason is truly incontinent, but that, incidentally, so is he who does not follow reason, even though it be on a wrong scent. It must be said, then, that if the will is out of step with reason, whether the latter be true or false, it is always evil (1-2, q.19, a.5; *cf. De Veritate,* q.17, a.4).

It is the same in the inverse instance, in which reason is deceived, but the will follows it. Certainly,

MORAL VALUE AND DISVALUE   87

if there is question of those errors which are willed or which are due to an inexcusable ignorance (we have spoken of this in q.6, a.8), the will remains evil. But this is not so if the ignorance creeps into the act without a censurable neglect (1–2, q.19, a.6).

Let us recall our analysis of the voluntary act and of that movement of purpose which carries the will toward its end by way of the means used. We thus reach the conclusion that, in moral acts, goodness of the will turns especially on goodness of purpose. To follow reason, true or false, is really to be guided in the direction of the end which reason sets up and to employ the means only in view of the end. If, therefore, good and evil depend on the object, and if it is the purpose which points all toward this, it is necessarily the purpose which first orientates actions toward either good or evil. In every instance in which a purpose is bad, the action of the will also is wholly bad; for you cannot do good while you see it as bad, if that doctrine is correct which says it is the object known by the intellect that specifies the act. But if, on the contrary, the purpose is good, certainly it does not displace the inner act of the will which is to follow it, nor of the exterior act which is to carry it out; but it goes over in some way upon them when they are produced and it communicates to them something of its own merit (q.18, a.8, and ad 1). The purpose, therefore, is not the whole of the willed act, and this is why the quality of will which is added, and of the exterior act which prolongs them, borders upon the quality of the purpose; yet it is as the form of the interior and the exterior act of the will, and for this reason, though we do not always merit so much as we aim to merit, we often merit more than we will and more than we do.

And at the same time we remark how the goodness of an act depends on its accord with the divine law.

> If indeed the goodness of the will depends, as we have said, on the purposing of the end, and if the end of ends for the human will is the absolute value or God, as we said earlier (q.1, a.8), the human will, to be good, necessarily must advance toward that absolute value. And this value has first and immediate reference to the divine will, of which it is the proper object. Besides, as that which is primary in each genus is the measure and norm of everything that enters into that genus, and as, on the other hand, nothing is right or good except as it comes up to its own measure, it is required that the will of man be good, *i.e.,* in harmony with the will of God (1-2, q.19, a.9).

This moral system thus puts into place at the outset the concept of "ought to be," for if this ought to be is not inscribed to begin with in that which is, no artifice of dialectics can put it there. To discover what each thing ought to be or to do, it is enough to state the definition of that thing and to ask it to realise itself. The Thomistic moral system also handles the concept of the "intentio" or purpose, noting that the problem of good and evil cannot receive a single and unilinear solution. Morals follows the psychological description of the human act, and because this is complex, an act will be thoroughly good only if it is good in each of its elements. A moral act has goodness in the sense that it is an act, and value through the reality of its own substance. Secondly, it should be a human act, that is to say, the willing of an object in accord with reason. Besides, it should take account of circumstances, for the object is to be conformed to reason not merely in a general way, but in the particular instance in hand. This interior act of the will should also be completed, if there is opportunity, by the exterior act which carries it through. Accordingly, this moral system, though based wholly on purpose, does not reduce the morality of the act to that of the purpose that animates it. For if the purpose is bad, the will and the exterior act will inevitably be also bad; but if the purpose or the end is good, it remains still to choose means which are not unworthy of it and which, if possible, are exactly suited to it. And when the means are chosen and the act is willed, it still remains to transfer this will by an act which does not lodge ridiculously on this side of the first purpose and which, if it can be, is precisely adapted to it. The purpose thus permeates all the elements of the voluntary act, but it does not replace them.

And it is because the human act, in order to be

good, must meet its definition squarely, that the full guarantee of its value is in God. Man does well in so far as he acts as man, and there is nothing better for him to do than to act as man in order to act as God wishes him to act. In brief, the human act is a rational act; but the natural light of reason is only the interpreter of eternal truth in the theoretical order, and of eternal law in the practical order. Thus every transgression of the orders of human reason is a transgression of the divine law and every bad act is a sin (q.21, a.1). By the mere fact that they are referred within our reason to the divine law, our good acts become worthy of praise and merit, and our evil acts blamable and condemnable in the eyes of God (*ibid*). For this reason, revelation introduces no break of the continuity in our inner life, either in the order of knowledge or in the order of action, because all the promptings of a right conscience are beforehand commandments of God.

Chapter IV

LOVE AND OTHER EMOTIONS

We have described the quality of acts of the will as acts belonging to man. However, a being does not necessarily do the acts which it alone is to do, and this is the case here. Man acts strictly as man when he acts freely; though remaining a man, he can act as an animal. He can do this the more from the fact that he truly is an animal, though a thinking one. Now the science of morals arises from concrete acts done by real men in a set of given circumstances; it is the whole man, therefore, spirituality and animality combined, that must be sketched in order to arrive at a moral science. The emotions of the soul form precisely those acts of man which are not exactly human, but common to man and brute What in general are the emotions? Which are chief among them? What problems do they set for the science of conduct, and what features do they give our moral life? Here are the main questions which the presence of animality in man's essence puts to rational research.

1. THE EMOTIONS IN GENERAL

What is an emotion? It is an activity which consists in the soul's undergoing something. Now to undergo or suffer, in the broadest sense, means simply to receive; but in the most precise sense, it means essentially to bear; that is to say, to receive an action which must imply a certain suffering and loss. When it is a question of words, it is up to us to follow accepted usage. We shall accordingly employ the term emotion for the whole gamut of meanings which goes with it, that is, to mark any passing from better to worse, such as sadness, and any passing from worse to better, such as joy. But we shall always suppose: (a) that in the proper sense an emotion never belongs to the soul as such; (b) that, consequently, it belongs to it only in so far as the soul is joined to a body; (c) that being the repercussion in the soul of a changed state in the body, it subjects the soul to a law of change which is not its own, but the body's; (d) that this law is that of corporal movement, the specific character of which is that what is moved abandons one place or state and passes over into another place or state; (e) that an emotion of the soul, strictly understood, supposes that the soul is obliged to leave one state to enter into another, and that it is subject. In a word, when the soul as such acts, it yields nothing, even when it receives, for it can receive without giving up anything: as in the instance of the intellect and the acquisition of knowledge, when new facts are added to old ones. When the soul acts as united to the body, it cannot receive anything without subjection, because the states of the soul, instead of being added

THE EMOTIONS IN GENERAL

together, replace each other, just as bodily movements do, nothing of which, except the echo, is kept in the soul. And this is true, no matter in what sense the action be done, and whether it be done by soul to body or by body to soul, provided, of course, that the action is common to both elements of the human composite.

For anyone who takes the word emotion in its correct sense, that which is incorporeal cannot feel an emotion. The one thing that could of itself experience an emotion proper to it is the body, so that, if an emotion, properly so-called, should affect the soul in any manner whatsoever, this could be only in so far as the soul is united to the body, and hence by accident. Now the soul is united to the body in two ways: first by title of form, so far as the soul gives being to the body which it vivifies; and second, by title of mover, so far as it carries on its activities through the body. And in each way the soul is subject to the emotions by way of accident, though in different fashions. In fact, in a being made of matter and form, action comes from form and emotion from matter. This is why emotion begins with matter and does not touch the form, so to say, except by accident. But no one feels any emotion unless something acts upon him, because all emotion is the effect of action. We may, therefore, say that the emotions of the body belong indirectly to the soul in two ways. First, in the sense that emotion begins with the body and rises to the soul, which is united to the body as its form, and it is any bodily feeling whatsoever. Thus when the body is wounded, the union of body and soul is enfeebled, and the soul itself, which is joined to the body according to the condition of the body, suffers by accident. Secondly, in the sense that the emotion begins in the soul in so far as the soul is the mover of the body, and so enters the body. This is called an animal emotion, and we have plain instances of it in anger, fear, and the like; for they can be produced only if there is perception and desire on the part of the soul, from which a modification of the body results, just as there can come from the activity of an agent a change of a movable thing under all the relations in which this movable thing is subject to the activity of the agent. And when the body is modified or altered in this way, we say that the soul itself undergoes this in an accidental sense (*De Veritate,* q.26, a.2).

Evidently we have yet to learn why and how the soul can feel such emotions, or on its own account can provoke organic disturbances in the body of which, in its turn, it bears the recoil. If we wish to go back to the metaphysical principle on which the solution of the problem definitely hinges, we shall have to study the whole order of beings. To suffer, to feel—is to undergo, or, yet more broadly, to receive. God, who is pure act, receives nothing, and therefore experiences no emotion. But as soon as we leave God, we leave behind unmixed actuality; the most perfect angel has some potentiality, and there is, therefore, something which he has not, but could receive. Coming down from the level of the angels, we meet the human kind; and the lack of actuality which widened and widened as we descended from angel to angel, is yet more visible when we reach the human intellect. We know, of course, that the human mind has no innate ideas and that it must receive the whole content of its knowledge from without. Let us go on down to the interior of man himself: his faculty of knowing depends on the object, but his faculty of desiring depends first on the idea which is made from objects and, beyond that, it depends on the objects themselves. Because the desire of man does not reach things then except by way of ideas which he gets from them, it is doubly dependent and still more passive than intellect. Yet, if rational desire is more passive than reason, sense desire is even more passive than rational; for the first is dependent only on the idea of what is a good for reason, while the second depends on what is a good for the soul as united to the body, all of whose needs have their immediate echo in the soul. Desires of this kind thus presuppose not only objects and perception of objects, but, far more, the perception of objects known as good by the soul, though they are not the proper good of reason, and it is in this most passive part of the soul that the emotion is most at home. Hence, *emotion is a modification which results accidentally in the soul from the fact of its union with the body and the seat of which is in sense desire.* How are we to tell one emotion from another and to classify them?

Let us turn to this sense desire in which the emotions seem to be begotten. We have three names, sensuality, sense desire or, more technically, sense conation, for this one thing, namely, *desire born of a sense perception of that which is of interest to the body*. This desire translates itself at once into a movement which can be effected in two directions. When it takes an object agreeable to the body, or gets away from a painful object, the movement accomplished to seize it or to flee it is attributed to a faculty which is given the name *concupiscibile;* but when it resists an object to destroy or neutralise it, we attribute it to a faculty which bears the name of *irascibile*. These two technical terms are explained by the fact that concupiscence (or strong desire) is the type of movement which leads us toward pleasure or makes us flee pain, and that anger (*ira*) is a kind of violent reaction to opposition.[1] As we are here in the presence of two distinct faculties, the emotions relevant to each constitute a distinct genus, those of the first kind pointing to the pleasurable or the painful, while those of the second have for object all that is hostile or, as we say in face of the difficulty which it presents, all that is arduous.

The emotions of the first and the second type belong to different species. In fact, as the several faculties have different objects (as we said: 1, q.77, a.3) it must be that the emotions of the faculties are related to different objects and that, as a consequence, and *a fortiori,* the emotions of the various faculties differ in species. There must indeed be a greater difference in the object to diversify the faculties in a

[1] These terms of St. Thomas are often translated literally, but they are ambiguous in English. Maher, in his famous *Psychology,* leaves them in the Latin, but with their meaning explained we prefer to call them the emotions of the first and the second group. —Tr.

THE EMOTIONS IN GENERAL

specific way than to diversify emotions and actions. Just as on the sub-human level diversity of genus results from a diversity in the potentiality of matter, but diversity of species from a diversity of form in the same matter, so in the acts of the human soul the acts which belong to different faculties will be not only of different species, but even of different genera, while the acts or emotions which concern different special objects within the one common object of one power will differ only as the species of that genus.

If, therefore, we wish to know which emotions belong to this or that kind of desire, we must study the object of each faculty. Now we have just said that the object of the faculty in the first case is the sense good or evil taken absolutely, that is to say, the pleasurable or the painful. But as it necessarily happens that the soul sometimes has some difficulty or puts up a fight either to make sure of some good or to escape an evil of this pleasure-pain kind, it is so far in some way raised above the animal's facile power. So, good and evil, as a little bit hard and uphill, are the object of the faculty of the second kind of emotion. Whichever emotions look to good or evil in an absolute way are in the field of the pleasure-pain faculty, and these are joy, sadness, love, hate, and the like; and whichever emotions have to do with good or evil as hard or arduous, as anything that is taken or missed with some difficulty, belong to the other faculty, and these are boldness, fear, hope, and the like (1-2, q.23, a.1; *De Veritate*, q.26, a.4).

With the main distinction of the two genera of emotions once made, we may introduce subdivisions according to their species by beginning with a dual basis of classification, one of which holds for the two kinds of emotion, the other for the second group alone.

In the emotions of the soul we run across a double contrariety—one coming from the contrary objects, that is, from good and evil, and the other resulting from the contrariety of the two movements by which one nears or is kept at a distance from the same object. Now, in the first groups of emotions we find only the former kind, the kind that arises from the objects, whereas in the other we find both.

The reason for this is that the object of the pleasure-pain appetite, as noted, is good or evil without qualification. But the good as such cannot be a point of departure, but only a point of arrival. Nothing indeed shuns the good as such, but, on the contrary, all desire it; and in the same way nothing wants evil as such, but all flee it. And, therefore, we can never come to evil as a good, but only use it as a starting point. So any pleasure-pain emotion (for instance, love, desire, joy) that takes a look at the good, is as it were for it, but every emotion (such as hate, aversion or fleeing from evil, and sadness) that sees evil is against it. In this type of emotion, then, there can only be contrariety due to the fact that one is near to, or far from, the object.

The object of the other kind of emotion, however, is the sense good or evil, not now taken absolutely, but, as we have said, as difficult or hard to get. Now when a good is difficult or arduous, it causes us to tend towards it as good, and in this sense it arouses the emotion of hope; but if it is too far away from us by reason of being arduous and difficult, it begets a feeling of despair. And likewise an evil that is arduous causes us to avoid it as evil and turns into the emotion of fear; but just because it is difficult, it warrants our striving for it and offers us the occasion of being freed from subjection to evil; and the emotion tending to it is boldness. Thus we find in the second kind of emotion, first the contrariety which results from the contrariety of good and evil, for example between hope and fear, and also that which comes from being close to, or far from, the same objective; as, between rashness and fear (1–2, q.23, a.2).

To show how complex this problem is, we need but to subordinate the classification to the facts and to show how impossible it is to deduce the facts from the classification. Let us add that there is at least one emotion that in no way allows a contrary. Anger really supposes a struggle against an evil already present; and if we wish to seek a contrary to it by distance from this evil, we run into sadness, which is of the other group; and if we seek its contrary in the opposition of good to evil, it is plain that, by substituting a present good for an irritating evil, we stir up the feeling of joy, which also belongs with the first group. We, therefore, cannot create the contrary of anger, and the only way to escape from it is to calm oneself (*ibid.*, a.3). If we make allowance for this notable exception, it will be possible to draw up a complete classification of the emotions, proceeding with the contruction of pairs and, except for anger, joining to each emotion its opposite.

Emotions are distinguished by their active causes, which causes are the objects of a soul's emotions, and the difference between the active causes can be studied from two points of view: first, according to the species or nature of these active causes themselves, as fire differs from water; and secondly, according to the diversity of the faculty which acts.

Now the diversity of the active cause or mover, so far as there is question of its power of moving, can be understood in emotions of the soul by analogy with natural agents. Every mover in some way either draws that which he moves to itself, or repels it from itself. If we take first the instance of its drawing the moved thing to itself, it produces three effects. In the first place it gives it an inclination or fitness to tend towards the mover, as a light body situated on a high place does, when it confers lightness on the body which it begets, and through this lightness the inclination or fitness to stay in the high place. Secondly, if a generated body is outside its proper place, it causes it to be brought into that place. Thirdly, it causes it to rest in that place, once it is there, for the cause which makes one rest in a place is the same as that which makes it come into the place. And repulsion is to be understood in the same way.

Now, in movements in the conative part of the soul, value is as an attractive force and disvalue as a repellent force. Primarily, then, value begets in the faculty of desire an inclination, a fitness, or a co-natural affinity for value, which have the marks of the emotion of love, and corresponding to it, in the camp of evil, is the emotion of hate. Secondly, if value is not yet possessed, it gives desire a start towards acquiring the value which is loved, and this constitutes the emotion of desire. The evil opposed to this is estrangement or aversion. Thirdly, when the value is won, it gives desire a certain repose in the good which has been attained. This turns into delectation or joy; evil, on the other hand, gives sorrow or sadness.

THE EMOTIONS IN GENERAL

If we go on now to the other group of emotions, there is supposed first a certain fitness or tendency to seek good or to fly evil, which is related to good or evil in an absolute sense. But in the field of a value that is not yet attained, it begets hope and despair; with regard to imminent evil it engenders the emotions of fear and boldness. With regard to the good already possessed, there is no emotion of the second kind, for in this case the character of arduousness, of which we have spoken, is not encountered; the emotion of anger results, on the contrary, from the actual presence of evil. It is plain, therefore, that there are three pairs of emotions of the first type, namely: love and hate, desire and aversion, joy and sadness. Parallel to these are three of the other kind, namely: hope and despair, fear and audacity, and anger, which alone has no contrary emotion. There are, then, eleven different emotions in all, six in one group and five in the other, and all emotions of the soul are subsumed under these (1–2, q.23, a.4).

Each of these eleven emotions arises in a specific way. Because the second imply the first, the first of the emotions is the first of the *"concupiscibile,"* that is, love; and the second is its contrary, that is, hate. Next are desire of the loved object and aversion from the hated one; then hope of the desired good, and despair of it. Hope in its turn fosters rashness, and despair of winning causes fear. Anger may succeed rashness to beat down whatever stands in the way of realizing one's earnest wishes, and at last joy and sadness are left as emotions resulting from all others, in the sense that they mark the soul as at peace in the enjoyment of the object which it loves, or disquieted over not being able to get possession of it (q.25, a.3). Four of these emotions are commonly taken as the main ones: joy and sadness, because they are the last and stand at the end of every emotional disturbance; hope, because the term of the emotions belonging to the first group (I love, I desire, I hope); and fear, because the term of the emotions of the other group (I hate, I flee, I fear).

There is one question left relative to the emotions in general: Are they good or bad in themselves, and whence have they the quality of moral good or evil which people attribute to them? To answer this question we need invoke no new principle, and for elucidation it will suffice to recall what a moral act is. An act is moral or properly human in so far as it is willed. But the emotions in themselves are not willed, the proof of which is that the animals have feelings, but no morality. The emotions as such, therefore, are neither good nor bad. But for the same reason it is clear that any emotion can become good or bad once it is integrated, in a rational being like man, with willed acts which are themselves good or bad. Thus we settle the famous controversy between Aristotelians and Stoics on the question whether all emotions are morally evil.

On this question, the Stoics and Peripatetics were of different opinions, for the Stoics said that all emotions are bad, while the others held that emotions under control are good. Now this disagreement, though in word it seems serious, in reality amounts to little or nothing, when one studies the meaning of the respective positions. For the Stoics did not keep sense and intellect distinct, nor therefore sense desire and rational desire. Hence, they could not tell the emotions of the soul from habits of will, nor give ranking to emotions of the soul in the sense appetite and mere movements of will in the rational appetite, but called every conative rational movement "will" and gave the name of "emotion" to any movement which went beyond the limits of reason. Cicero, in the third book *De Tusculanis Disputationibus,* calls all emotions "diseases of the soul" and from this definition argues that those who are diseased are not in health (*non sani*), and those who are not in health (*non sani*) are without feeling or senseless (*insipientes*), and that the insensate are insane (*insani*).

The Peripatetics on the other hand gave the name emotion to all movements of sense appetite and, therefore, judged good those emotions ruled by reason and evil those that get away from the government of reason. The result was that when Cicero (*op. cit.*) found fault with the Peripatetics for their approval of controlled emotions, his reason was that all evil, even though slight, is to be avoided; his whole specious argument being that, just as a body, when moderately sick, is not in health, so this control of the diseases or emotions of the soul is not health; for the emotions are not called diseases or disturbances of the soul unless they get beyond the control of reason (1–2, q.24, a.2).

Let us now go on, keeping in mind our description of the moral act. The conclusion on which we insisted was that an act of such a complex structure as a human act could not be completely good—we should almost say, completely successful, from the moral point of view, unless each element in it was what it ought to be. Accordingly, we not only do not bring against the emotions the exclusion which a morality of "good will," as that of Kant, urges, but, on the contrary, we have the duty to requisition the emotions in order to give them the moral quality which they naturally lack. They are a kind of morally indifferent animal stuff within us and it is our duty to humanise ourselves fully by working reason into them. We have not only the right, therefore, but also the duty to have experience of the emotions, provided they are good; and they are always good when they come from an act of reason rather than run away with it.

Because the Stoics thought every emotion of the soul evil, they were consistent in claiming that an emotion cuts down the value of an act. For when a good is mixed with evil, it either becomes less or ceases to be; and what they said would be true, if we were reserving the name of emotions of the soul to the disorderly stirrings of the sense appetite and took them as perturbations or diseases. But if by emotion we mean simply any movement of the sense appetite, then the perfection of human value requires that the emotions themselves be controlled by reason. Indeed, since human good resides in reason as its root, this good will be more perfect the more it is extended to all that constitutes man. For example, it doubtless belongs to the perfection of moral value that the acts of the body be under the control of reason, and consequently, since the sense appetite can obey reason, as we have said (q.17, a.7), it belongs to the perfection of the moral or human act that the very emotions of the soul should be controlled by reason. Therefore, just as it is better that man should both will good and realise it by an external act, so it is of the perfection of moral value that man should direct his whole self, not merely his will, but also his sense appetite, towards it, as it is written (Psalm 83): "My heart and my flesh have rejoiced in the living God," taking the word heart for rational desire and the word flesh for sense desire.

To the objection that whatever slows up the judgment of reason lessens the moral quality of an act, the answer is that the relation of the emotions of the soul to the judgment of reason is twofold. First, they can precede it; in which case, as they darken the judgment of reason on which the value of the moral act depends, they do cut into the goodness of the act; for it is more praiseworthy to do an act of kindness from a judgment of reason than from the mere feeling of mercy. Secondly, they can result from the judgment of reason and they do, in two ways: first, by a kind of superabundance, when the superior part of the soul is intensely moved toward something, the inferior part of the soul follows the movement; and the consequent emotion in the sense desire is a sign of the intensity of the will, and so indicates a greater moral value. And again, by way of choice, that is when man judges and reasonably chooses to be affected by some emotion which, with the help of sense desire, gives him power to act more promptly, and then the emotion adds to the value of the action (1–2, q.24, a.3, c. and ad 1).

Let us consider the human emotions one at a time, both those of the first and those of the second type, beginning with the queen and mother of them all, that is, with love.

II. EMOTIONS OF THE FIRST TYPE

The first two emotions which we meet of this variety are love and hate. It is at once evident that love is rightly classed with the faculty of desire, because it is the source of the movement directed toward the desired end. In fact, it is the affinity of the will with a certain value and the complacency which the will takes in it that begets love; therefore, love is this first onset felt by the soul at the touch of an object which it knows to be intimately allied to it, and towards which it goes in order to lay hold of it and to enjoy it (1–2, q.26, a.2). That is to say, love is an emotion and the basis of desire. But there are two degrees of love, and the difference in their moral value is such that it is important to keep them distinct.

As Aristotle says in the second book of his *Rhetoric* (c.4), to love is to will good for some one. If this is so, then the movement of love tends towards two things, namely: towards the good which one wills for anyone, whether for himself or another; and towards him for whom he wills the good. With regard to the good which one wills, there is love of desire; but with regard to that for which he wills the good, there is love of friendship. And this division supposes one term prior to the other; for what is loved with a love of friendship is loved absolutely and for itself, whereas what is loved with a love of desire is not loved absolutely and in itself, but for another. For just as *ens per se* is simply that which has being, whereas relative being is that which exists in another; so good (convertible with being), taken simply, is that which has goodness, but that which is the good of another is a relative value, and consequently, the love by which anything is loved for its own good, is love simply; but the love by which anything is loved for the good of another, is a relative love (1-2, q.26, a.4).

If this is the nature of love, what causes it? The good and the beautiful, as known to reason. We have said that a kind of affinity or spontaneous complaisance of the lover in the loved is its origin. If this affinity is merely perceived by the senses, the love thence born is a sensual love; but if it is known by intellect, the resulting love is a spiritual love of the good; and if this knowing of the good becomes a source of satisfaction for thought, the love which results from it is a spiritual love of the beautiful, for the good is that which satisfies desire, while the beautiful is that which, even when seen, is satisfying to us. Yet, though recognition by the intellect is necessary in order that love be spiritual, love is not measured by the knowledge we have of the object.

Not all that is required for perfect knowledge is needed for perfect love. Knowledge is related to reason, whose work is to distinguish between things which really are one, and to compare and in some way unite distinct things; and so a perfect knowledge supposes that we know one by one all that is in a thing, for instance, its parts, its powers, and its properties. But love is in the faculty of desire, which regards a thing as it is in itself. For this reason a perfect love asks only that a thing be loved just as it is known in itself. It may turn out, then, that a thing is more loved than known, because it can be perfectly loved, though not perfectly known. Plain evidence of which is observed in the realm of the sciences, for men love them for the summary knowledge which they get from them; they know for instance that rhetoric is a science that helps them to persuade, and this is what they love in rhetoric. We may say precisely the same of the love of God (1-2, q.27, a.2, ad 2).

We now understand what place love has among the emotions—a place that is necessarily the first. Any emotion of the soul implies a certain movement of the soul towards an object, or a repose in this object, whose likeness to and kinship with the soul causes the soul to rejoice in and to be satisfied with it. Love, therefore, is at the root of each emotion, and as we shall everywhere find its effects linked with those of the others, a description of its effects is at once required.

The first and most direct effect of love is union. If it is a question of love of desire, the lover experiences a desire to effect a real union with the beloved object which he needs for himself; in the case of a love of friendship, the union is no longer real and material, as in the preceding case, but it is nevertheless immediate, for it is love itself that is the bond and union, the friend being for the lover only another self (1–2, q.28, a.1). Hence, we may say that they who love each other are no longer in themselves, but each is in the other, by a kind of attachment or, more properly, a kind of inherence.

This effect of mutual inherence can be understood with regard to the faculties both of knowledge and of desire. In relation to the faculty of knowing, we say that the beloved is in the lover because the beloved remains in the lover's thought, in the sense of the Epistle to the Philippians (c.1): "For that I have you in my heart." The lover, too, on his part truly enters by thought into the beloved, in this sense, that he is not content with a superficial knowledge of the beloved, but tries to know in an intimate way each quality of the one he loves, as the Holy Spirit, which is the love of God, says (Cor., 2, 10), he "searcheth all things, yea, the deep things of God." In reference to the faculty of desire, we say that the beloved is in the lover because he remains in his affection by a sort of complacency: whether the lover rejoices in him and his good points when he is present, or desires him and tends toward him by the love of desire in his absence, or toward the good which he wishes for the loved by a love of friendship. And he does this, not for any esoteric cause, as when one desires a thing for the sake of another, or wills a good for some one on account of some third thing, but he does it with an inner complacency in the beloved object. We may speak, then, of *an intimate love* and even of the *bowels of charity*.

On the other hand we may say that the lover is in the beloved, in one sense by a love of desire, and again by a love of friendship. Indeed, the love of desire does not rest with attaining an external and superficial enjoyment of the beloved; but it seeks to possess fully that which it loves, by going, so to speak, to the interior of it. And in the love of friendship, the lover is within the beloved in the sense that he regards the ups and downs of his friend as his own, so that it seems that it were to himself that these good or bad things come in the person of his friend, and that it is he who is affected by them. Thus it is the way of friends to will the same things, and to be sad and to rejoice over the same things, as Aristotle says both in his *Ethics* (bk. 9) and in his *Rhetoric* (bk. 4). And so the lover, by taking his friend's goods as his own, seems to be in the beloved as if made one with him; and by the contrary fact that he wills and does for his friend as for himself, in some way seeing his friend as one with him, the beloved thus is the lover. And thirdly, in case of the love of friendship, this mutual inherence may be understood in a third sense: love is shared; for friends love mutually, and will and also do good to each other (1–2, a.28, a.2; *cf.* 3 *Sent.,* 7, q.1, a.1).

This mutual inherence of lover and beloved gives us a chance to explain the other effects of love. For instance, one grasps the fact that its ultimate aim is ecstasy, for the lover, when he truly loves, is literally out of himself; one sees that zeal is the normal effect of love, for zeal is enviousness to get hold of the good which we love, or to be rid of those who dispute it; that love is a beneficent and preservative emotion, because it always wills good and perfection; that love is also the prime mover of all our actions, because he who acts does so for the good which he desires and loves. And so we again come into touch with the first source of all action and of all being, God. He creates because of love, and the movement by which He loves Himself in things like Him is, on a metaphysical view, their own movement. It is because he is the first Good and the first Love that all movement tends to some kind of good and so represents a movement of love, conscious or unconscious, towards God.

Standing over against love is hate, which is the second emotion in this group. This is the contrary of love and is opposed to it, point for point. As the object of love is good, that of hate is evil, that is to say, the immediate perception of an essential inconsistency between that which one loves and some specific object. It is love, therefore, that causes hate, for one must love a thing before hating its contrary; and as an effect cannot be stronger than its cause, love cannot possibly fail to excel hate. So, too, as love has good for its object, nothing that is good in itself can be the object of hate; no one, therefore, can hate himself, unless this be without knowing it and because he is deceived as to his true nature; and no one can hate truth as such, for it is good in its essence. Yet we can detest this or that truth as contrary to our desire in given circumstances (*ibid.,* q.29). Let us go on now to the second pair of love-hate emotions: to desire, which we so classify in the instance of sense desire, and to aversion.

The way in which the end, or the good, moves is not the same when the good is present and when it is at a distance. When present, its effect is to cause us to be content with it, and when absent, it induces us to tend towards it. For this reason, if we take an object agreeable to the senses and regard it so far as it is, so to say, adapted and shaped to desire, it causes love. But considered as absent, and as drawing desire toward it, the effect of it is desire. And taken in so far as it brings repose by its presence, it begets pleasure. *Concupiscentia,* therefore, is an emotion specifically different from love and from pleasure; but to desire this pleasant object rather than that causes movements of *concupiscentia,* which show only individual differences (1–2, q.30, a.2).

Some desires or tastes are natural: these are desires for what belongs to animal nature, as nourishment, drink, and rest. The emotion which carries us towards these objects is *concupiscentia* in the proper sense, and is as much the animal's as it is man's. Other desires, however, take us toward objects which we think of as good and agreeable, not because they are indispensable to our nature, but because our thought reports them as desirable. These emotions more properly deserve the name of cupidity; and they are proper to man, for it is distinctive of man that he represents to himself values beyond those that his nature demands. Now it follows of itself that the taste for natural value is necessarily finite and limited, for we cannot wish an infinity of food at one time; yet at least we can want, indefinitely, new kinds of food and drink, and

DESIRE AND AVERSION

in this way natural desires are, so to say, insatiable. As for desire of goods not needed by nature, they are plainly infinite in all senses, for we control such desires by what reason tells, and our reason never wearies of conceiving beyond that which we already have (*ibid.*, a.4).

Aversion, the emotion opposed to desire, is not of any great importance, and as it has for its object an absent evil, people very often confuse it with fear (a.2, ad 3). Yet it is not fear in the strict sense, any more than desire is hope. At present we merely note its place, though we are not required to analyse it.

The last two emotions of the first variety—pleasure and sorrow—are of decisive importance. First of all we remark that pleasure is certainly an emotion; for we have said that every movement of the sense appetite is an emotion; and pleasure is the movement started in the sense appetite when the animal is in a state which suits its nature and of which it is aware. If the good whose acquisition motivates this pleasure is a natural good, and if it is a good which consequently has been the object of what we have just called desire or "concupiscence," we term this emotion a pleasure in the strict sense. But if the good is such only for reason and accordingly has been the object of what we have named cupidity, the emotion is called joy. And so the animals, because they lack reason, only have pleasures, but never joys; we, on the contrary, who have reason, can experience joys, and are even capable of turning pleasure into joy. Man, then, is a rational being who can have pleasurable feelings to which his body is a partner, but who can also do agreeable actions which are only in the realm of will and thought. Which satisfactions are greater for him, those that come from activity of spirit, or those that arise from bodily emotions?

Pleasure is born of our union with a value which is suitable for us, when that value is known and felt. Now in the workings of the soul, especially of the sense and intellectual life, we must remember that because they have no transition to an external stuff, they are acts or perfections of the doer, as, for instance, to know, to feel, to will, and so on. For actions which do go over on any external matter are rather acts and perfections of the matter which they transform, since movement is an act which the mover starts in the movable thing. Thus, the actions of the sense and mental life of which we have spoken are in themselves a certain good of the doer, but as, besides, they are known by sense and by intellect, a pleasure is born of them, and not only of their objects. If, therefore, we compare pleasures which we take in the actions themselves, that is, in the knowledge of them by sense and intellect, there is no doubt that intellectual are much greater than sense pleasures. The truth is, we take more pleasure in knowing a thing by comprehending it than by seeing it, for first, the intellectual knowledge is more perfect, and it is also better known, because intellect is more capable of reflecting on its own knowledge than is sense. Besides, intellectual knowledge is more precious to us, for there is no one who would not be willing to lose his bodily sight rather than his intellectual sight and to be without the latter, as are beasts and madmen, as Augustine says in the fourteenth book *De Trinitate*.

If, therefore, we compare intellectual pleasures to the sense pleasures of the body, taking them *in themselves and absolutely speaking,* spiritual pleasures are greater. We prove this by a study of the three conditions required for pleasure, namely: the *conjoint* good, that to which it is *united,* and our *union* with it. In one word, value for the spirit is in itself greater than value for the body, and it is loved more by us, as is evidenced by the fact that men abstain from bodily gratifications so as not to lose honor, which is a spiritual good. Besides, the intellectual part of the soul is much nobler and knows more than does the sense part. Add to this that the union of the soul and its object is closer, more perfect, and more firm; closer, because sense stops at the outer accidents of things, whereas intellect goes to the essence, for its object is being or *quod quid est;* more perfect, because the union of the sensed with sense supposes change, which is imperfect act; thus, sense pleasures are never at any moment all they could be, but always imply something which is gone by and something waiting for consummation, as is plain in the instance of pleasures in food and sex, whereas pleasures of the spirit occur without change, and are there at once; more firm, because objects of sensual delight fall to pieces and soon cease to be, whereas spiritual values are not subject to decay.

Nevertheless, considered *with regard to ourselves,* the pleasures of the body are stronger, for three reasons. First, because things of sense are better known to us than are things of intellect; second, because sense pleasures, being emotions of sense desire, imply a bodily modification, which does not occur in spiritual delight, unless by a kind of repercussion of the higher desire on the lower; third, because bodily pleasure is sought as a kind of remedy against the needs and afflictions of the body, which take their toll in certain sadnesses; and consequently bodily pleasure, coming unexpectedly out of sadnesses of this kind, is felt more and is more welcomed than spiritual joy, which, as we shall see (q.35, a.5), has no contrary (1–2, q.31, a.5).

If we apply the same principle in comparing sense pleasures to one another, we shall see that they also form a hierarchy, but in a different way—according to the dignity of the pleasure or its intensity. From a practical point of view, touch is the most useful sense, but sight is the most noble.

By reason of its usefulness, the pleasure of touch is greater than any other sense pleasure, but on the ground of the knowledge gained, the pleasure of vision is the leader. So if we wish to compare sight and touch, we shall find that, in an absolute sense, the pleasure of touch is higher, so long as we stay within the limits of sensual joys. It is plain that the natural in any being is also the strongest thing in it; pleasures of touch are precisely of this kind, as the natural desires, *e. g.*, for food, sex, and so on, tend towards them. But if we study these pleasures in the light of the fact that sight serves the mind, then the pleasures of sight are superior, in the same measure as pleasures of the intellect are above those of the senses (*ibid.*, a.6).

We have yet to ascertain the cause of this pleasure and its main effects. Because it supposes that we are conscious of possessing a good suited for us, its cause is free accomplishment of an activity adapted to our nature (q.32, a.1), and, as a consequence, the doing of all that is natural to us (comprising in our "nature" the nature of others whom, because of the friendship we bear them, we no longer mark off from ourselves; a.6), is a source of pleasure for us. As for the effects of pleasure, these are not easy to define, because we can use only material figures to describe inner states which are not material. We may say, however, that pleasure has for its chief effect a kind of enlargement of the soul, which widens to gather in the good of which it becomes aware (q.33, a.1). So, pleasure guides an act, done by a power of the soul, to its full achievement. For the act done by the soul is at once a good in itself, but pleasure gives it the added good of appeasement of desire in a good at last attained. And this perfection ends by overflowing on the performance of the act itself, for one does better what he does with pleasure, bringing to the doing of it all his resources and attention (a.4). Let us add, too, that pleasure, as we have proved for the emotions in general, is, morally speaking, neither good nor bad in itself. As an end and perfection of the act, pleasure is worth what desire is worth: it is good, if the desire which it feeds rests in an object conformed to reason; it is bad if the object in which the desire, whether higher or lower, rests, is out of accord with the demands of reason (q.34, a.1).

We turn now to the last of these emotions, which is sorrow. This is the opposite of pleasure, and is outlined as the presence of an evil, plus the conscious perception of its presence (q.35, a.1). Just as courage of the soul is distinct from pleasure, sadness of soul is distinct from sorrow of the body (a.2), and both the one and the other originate, as all the emotions do, from love; but they derive from it by way of hate. For the first of the emotions is love, which is born in the soul from contact with the good; the second is hatred of evil, which, of course, arises from love, and it is through hate that sorrow over present evil also makes its way up to love (q.36, a.2). As for its effects, sorrow or sadness is a veritable disease. Begotten of a nearness to that which nature abjures, sadness impairs nature in every way, weakening our power of apprehension (q.37, a.1), weighing down the soul (a.2) by opposing the pleasure which enlarges it, enervating all its operations (a.3), and harming the body itself, whose vital functions it contradicts, to such a degree that sometimes it stifles the use of reason and even drives men into melancholy and mania (a.4). Because sadness and sorrow are diseases, they must be nursed, and the specific remedy for them is the contrary emotion, *i. e.,* pleasure or joy.

Pleasure is a kind of resting of desire in a suitable good, whereas sadness comes of something at variance with desire; and, therefore, among the conative movements, pleasure is

PLEASURE AND SORROW

related to sadness as rest is related to bodily fatigue, which arises from attempting a work that is naturally too much for the body. Indeed, sadness implies that the power to desire is in some way worn out or ill at ease; just, then, as rest of the whole body is the remedy for any exhaustion, from whatever source it comes, so pleasure is the cure and alleviator of sadness, no matter what its nature or source (1–2, q.38, a.1).

Nothing in the line of soothing remedies is to be despised; not tears, which ease the soul and hinder it from centering itself on the evil; not sleep, baths or the other cures which correct the effects so unfailingly produced in the body by this emotion (a.5); not the sympathy of friends, who thus prove their love for us and pour joy into our hearts (a.3); and, above all, not the most powerful of palliatives.

As we have said, it is in the contemplation of truth that the supremest joy lies; and, as was just said, all delight sweetens sorrow. This is why contemplation of truth moderates sadness or sorrow, and this it does the better if one is a more perfect lover of wisdom. Here, then, is the reason why men who contemplate divine things and future blessedness rejoice in tribulation. Better yet, this is why people find joy even in the midst of bodily torment, as did the martyr Tiburtius, who with his bare feet trampled on burning coals and said, "It seems to me that in the name of Jesus Christ I tread upon blown roses" (*ibid.,* a.4).

Though it is in essence a sign of evil, sorrow, like the other emotions, can be turned into good. For it is good and even praiseworthy to be saddened over evil that is done, and by adding evil to the evil which it accompanies, it makes this still more detestable; which effect gives sorrow a kind of utility. With it we complete our study of the first group of emotions, and go on now to an examination of the second.

III. EMOTIONS OF THE SECOND TYPE

For the six emotions of the first group we have only five of the second, and we may remember that this lack of balance comes from the fact that anger stands alone without a mate. The five are hope and despair, fear and boldness, and anger. No one doubts that hope is an emotion, but it is so easily confused with desire that some might hesitate to put it into the second class. Yet it is so far from blending with desire that it presupposes desire, and it is through the intermediary of desire that hope, like all the emotions of this group, is joined to the first of all emotions which is love.

The kinds of emotions are known by their objects, and we have four conditions to take into account in studying the object of hope. First, the object should be a good; strictly speaking, there is no hope except of the good; this is the way in which it differs from fear, which has to do with evil. Second, the good should be a future, for one does not hope for what one already has, and in this sense hope is distinct from joy, which is of a present good. Third, it is required that the good be hard to get, obtainable with difficulty, since we never say that anyone hopes for a thing of meager worth or for what he can get in an instant. Just here is its note of difference from desire and longing, which are for a good that is truly future; hence desire belongs to the first group, and hope to the second. This good, though hard to get, should still be attainable, as no one hopes for what is wholly out of his reach, and it is on this point that it diverges from despair. It is plain, then, that hope differs from desire, as the emotions of the second class differ from those of the first. Hope presupposes desire, and, as we have remarked (p. 101) all the emotions of the second group imply those of the first (1–2, q.40, a.1).

The essentially emotive quality of hope is seen in the fact that it is in evidence even among the animals; we might almost say, among senseless bodies. But action is in some sense disunited (*décomposé*) in the animals, as they are led by instinct to a good whose suitableness for them is known by another. It will be useful for us to reflect on the deep metaphysical unity which this idea supposes in the structure of the universe.

The inner feelings of animals can be known from their external behavior, which makes it clear that the brute animals experience hope. For instance, if a dog sees a rabbit or a bird too far off, he does not start for it, as if he had no hope to catch it; but if the prey is close to him, he goes for it as if with a hope of seizing it. Now, as we have pointed out (q.1, a.2), the sense desire of animals, and even the natural desire of senseless things, follow the understanding of some mind, as does the desire of an intelligent being, which desire is called "will." But there is this difference—that the will is aroused by the knowledge of an intellect joined to it, whereas the activity of natural desire is ruled by knowledge in a mind which is separate from it and which originates the action. It is the same with the sense desire of brutes, because they act by the light of a native instinct. So in the actions of the animals and the movements of natural things a process goes on much like works of art, and in this way [we know] there is hope, and despair also, in brute life (1-2, q.40, a.3).

Despair is the opposite of the first emotion of the second group, and on this title it falls into second place. But this is as far as the contrast of this pair of emotions is of the same sort as that of preceding pairs. Emotions of the first class are set over against each other in the sense that, as a rule, to a movement of the soul towards good there corresponds a movement away from evil, and so it is solely a difference of objects that makes these emotions distinct. But emotions of the second type may be contrary to each other, though the object never changes its nature, and simply because desire is for or against one and the same object. Such is precisely the way with despair, whose proper object, like that of hope, its opposite, is not an evil, but a good.

We have said (q.23, a.2) that two types of opposition are possible in changes. One kind is the result of approaching different termini, and only this kind can occur in emotions of the second group; for instance, this is the way love and hate

DESPAIR

are opposites. A second kind arises from approaching towards or receding from one and the same terminus, and is evidenced among emotions of the second class. The object of hope, let us say, which is a good that is hard to get, does attract, it has that nature so far as we see the good as possible of attainment, and hence hope implies a tendency and approach towards that good; but if the good is thought impossible to get, it turns us away, because, as Aristotle says in his *Ethics* (3, c.3), when people come to what cannot be done, they just give up. It is in this light that despair sees its object: it supposes a yielding, and is contrary to hope, as retreat is to advance (1–2, q.40, a.4).

Viewed in its causes, hope, especially, is an emotion fed on experience, because, as we gain experience, we grow better able to act and more sure of ourselves. Also, we become experienced by thought as well as by action, and by the use of our minds we see that it is possible to do things which pure empiricism would not let us attempt. On the opposite side of the fence, of course, experience can cultivate despair; but, to make a long story short, it is not doing, but thinking, that can dishearten us, and thus experience gives us two motives for hope against one for despair. This emotion of hope rises strong in the hearts of young persons, "because they have everything ahead and little or nothing behind them, and as memory is of the past and hope of the future, they have not much to reflect on, but live in great hopes. . . . So, too, those who have not known rebuff or run into obstacles, readily think they can do anything, and they are of vivid hope." We may add that drunken men are in the same class, for they are as hotheaded as youths and no more given to thought, and so hope is ready with them and they never have a doubt (a.6).

The effect of hope, then, is to spur our activity and though, like every emotion, it is caused by love, in its own turn it is a cause of love.

Hope may look to either of two objects. It can have the hoped-for good as object, but because this good is hard (though possible) to get, it may happen that what is difficult, is possible for us, not through our own, but through others' efforts; in such cases hope turns toward the means through which the good becomes possible to us. In so far, then, as hope regards the goods we hope for, it is caused by love; for there is hope only of a value that is desired and loved. But when hope has to do with the means that makes a value possible to us, it is caused by love, and not the other way round. For as soon as we hope that values can come to us through some one, we take steps toward him as our good, and we begin to love him; though from the fact that we love anyone we need not hope to get anything from him, unless indirectly, so far as we believe that we also shall be loved by him. To be loved by anyone, then, causes us to hope in him, and our love for him is caused by the hope or trust which we put in him (1-2, a.40, a.7).

The next two emotions of the second kind are fear and boldness. Fear has all the qualities of an emotion in a high degree: it is felt, it is in the sense

FEAR AND BOLDNESS

appetite, and it is related to an evil. No element, therefore, is wanting to it. Since the object specifies an emotion, the proper object of fear is exactly the opposite to that of hope: a foreseen evil which is hard to face, and which we feel we cannot stand if it does come, though we have yet some hope of escaping it.

A man fears a coming evil that is so far beyond his power that he cannot prevent it. But like human value, a human disvalue may be studied either in man's own activity or in external things. A disvalue has two fearful aspects for man's own doings: work is a burden to nature and brings on *laziness,* as when a man flies from his job through fear of heavy labor. Again, some nameless evil hurts our reputation: in the case of fearing infamy for an act we are about to commit we are *ashamed* to do it, and if we have already done the wrong, we feel *confusion*. On the other hand, the evil which is in external things can be beyond a man's power to withstand in any of three ways. First, because of its bigness, as when a person sees some huge evil and cannot judge the consequences of it; the result is *astonishment*. Second, because of its unusualness; that is, an evil that we are unused to is put before us, and so it is immense in our eyes; the result here is that we are *dumbfounded,* our imagination is so far beyond its experience. Third, because of its unexpected character we cannot possibly provide against it, and then the fear is called *anxiety* (1-2, q.41, a.4; *cf.* q.42, a.2, the last lines).

If we try further to identify the causes of fear, we find two main ones. The first evidently is love, for we fear an evil solely because it takes from us a value that we love. The second is a lack or default of the power and resources needed to thrust back the evil that is upon us and that is about to separate us from the value that we love. As for the effects of fear, there are four: a drawing in, or a kind of taking in sail; then it drives us to ask advice, it makes us tremble, and changes our way of acting. Let us examine the first of these effects.

In the emotions of the soul, the movement of the conative faculty takes the rôle of formal principle, just as the change of the body takes that of material principle. These two elements are suited to each other, and the bodily change is like a conative movement, and corresponds to it. Now as to the movement of desire, fear works in this a sort of retrenchment or contraction, because, as we said, fear comes from imagining that some evil is threatening us and can hardly be driven off; and that anything be hard to thrust aside is the result of a lack of power. And the weaker any power, the fewer objects it reaches, and so from imagination, which starts fear, there follows a drawing in of desire. We can notice this in the dying, whose nature has little force and draws away within itself; and also in towns where the citizens get afraid and fly from the outskirts and go downtown as far as can be. Analogous to the withdrawing, which is the way of animal desire, there follows in cases of fear a withdrawing of the heat and blood of the body to the interior (1–2, q.44, a.1).

From this first effect of fear there comes as a natural result the second, which is a trembling or trepidation.

FEAR AND BOLDNESS

We have just said that fear starts a contraction or withdrawal from the outer to the inner parts of the body, and thus the extremities become cold. So a trembling sets in, caused by a loss of the grip which holds the several members steady, the chief difficulty being a lack of heat, which, as is noted in II *de Anima,* is the instrument the soul uses to move the body (*ibid.,* a.3).

At such a time men are especially minded to ask advice and to be taught by others the surest way to escape the dangers threatening them; in fact, fear forces them to consult themselves also or look into themselves in their striving for a favorable outcome of the situation. Yet fear is an evil counsellor, because it makes the feared things loom bigger and more redoubtable than they really are; fear urges reflection, but falsifies it (*ibid.,* a.2). The fourth main effect of fear, namely, the influence it has on our action, is more complex.

The causes of a man's activities are the soul, which is a relative first mover, and the members of the body, which are its instruments. An activity, of course, can be hindered by a failure of either the tools or the hand that uses them. As for the members of the body as instruments, fear by its nature always slows up their operation, because of the chilling which it effects in the extremities. As for the soul, a moderate fear, which does not greatly disturb reason, is a help to effective action, because it causes alertness and makes a man reflect and attend to what he is doing. But when fear becomes excessive and upsets reason, it gets in the way of even the soul's activity (*ibid.,* a.4).

The opposite of fear is *boldness* or *audacity,* which is the fourth emotion of the second group. Like its contrary, its proper object is evil, but whereas fear flies from evil, because it doubts any near victory over it, boldness turns on it and attacks it with the aim of triumphing over it (q.45, a.1). Here, again, a reverse movement, with regard to the same object, outlines the opposition of the two emotions. If we ask now by what thread boldness mounts up to love, evidently it is by hope that it is at first suitably attached. The truth is, audacity supposes a hope of reaching around and downing the peril that menaces, for to give up hope is to fear the difficulty which would have to be conquered to win the good one hopes for. This is why, in spite of its heroic look and the high deeds it can in certain instances inspire, boldness does not rise above an instinctive kind of hope and remains not a virtue, but an emotion; it differs from courage by the whole distance that separates sense from reason.

As boldness is one of the movements of sense conation, it is in tow to perception on the part of our faculty of feeling. But the faculty of feeling makes no comparisons and no inquiry into the particulars of an event; rather, it sizes them up instantly. And as it sometimes happens that so quick a perception does not permit a discernment of all the difficulties in a situation, one may take a bold step and march upon the danger, and then, when one has had experience of the danger itself, one feels it greater than he had thought, and gives up the undertaking. On the other hand, reason first runs over everything that may help to lighten the load, and, therefore, brave men, advancing on danger in the strength of a reasoned judgment, seem at first to lack driving power, for they are not passionate, but go ahead armed with the needed deliberation. When they are in the thick of danger, however, they do not crash into any unexpected thing; indeed, sometimes they find the dangers less than they had supposed, and hold out better in their efforts. We may add that it is to accomplish the good of virtue that brave men face danger, and no matter how great the perils, this will of the good remains in them. But the over-bold act only from the impression that first gave them hope, and shut their eyes to fear (1–2, q.45, a.4).

We have yet one emotion, which is the last of the second type and of all the emotions; this is anger. We recall that it is alone, but this is because, making up for its difference from the four preceding emotions, anger unites in itself the two movements of diverse kinds which up to the present we have found divided into pairs among the emotions. It stands by itself, then, only because in some way it is double and counts for two.

An angry man seeks to avenge himself on some one, and for this reason the movement of anger tends in two directions: first, to the very vengeance which he wishes, which he hopes for as a value, and in which consequently he takes delight; but it tends also towards him on whom the man wishes to take vengeance as towards a being who is his own contrary, and is poison to him, and who enters, so far as he is concerned, the ranks of evil. This means that a dual difference is to be kept in mind between anger and love, or anger and hate. The first is that anger always looks to two objects, whereas love and hate sometimes heed only one; this is the case, for instance, when we say that a man loves (or hates, for that matter) wine or some such thing. The second difference is that the two objects which love keeps before it are both good, for if the lover wills the good of anyone, it is because this one is like himself. And the two objects which hate eyes have an evil look about them, the hater willing evil to someone because this latter is not in agreement with him. For its part, anger views one of its objects in the light of value, that is, in the light of the vengeance which anger desires, and the other in the light of disvalue, and this object is the undesirable man on whom it would take vengeance. And so anger is an emotion that, we may say, is compounded of contrary emotions (1-2, q.46, a.2).

What we may call this general character of anger (*potest ira dici passio generalis, in quantum ex concursu multarum passionum causatur*) is just what makes it less serious than such a feeling as hate. It is less set and, though more impetuous and violent, is quickly cloyed when it gets a chance to inflict on its enemy the chastisement it desires. But hate is insatiable as it were; it wishes not the evil of punishment on its enemy, but evil purely and simply, and consequently, this emotion knows no measure. We might in a sense even say that anger aims at good, as one of its two acts is good. Thus it is with good reason that Augustine likens anger to a straw and hate to a beam, as we shall be convinced by comparing the two.

Just what an emotion is, and just what it does, is known from its object. Now the object of anger is the same as that of hate, for just as he who hates wishes evil to him whom he hates, so he who is angry wishes evil to him at whom he is angry. But their procedure is not the same. He who hates wishes his enemy evil as evil, but the angry man does not wish evil as such on him against whom he is angry, but only so far as he discovers in evil a sort of good quality, looking at it from the point of view of vengeance. That is why we have said that hate means the application of evil to evil, while anger consists in the application of good to evil. It is plain, too, that to desire an evil which we think is justified, has less of the nature of evil than to will anyone evil purely and simply; indeed, to will anyone evil as justified, could even be an act of the virtue of justice, if done in obedience to the bidding of reason. Anger is bad only because, in taking vengeance, it does not heed what reason urges. It is clear, then, that hate is worse and more serious than anger (1–2, q.46, a.6).

If we examine anger in its roots, we always find an unjust act directed personally against him at whom one is angry (q.47, a.1). This act is inspired by a lack of respect that one has for the offended person, and this basic sentiment can appear in any of three forms: *contempt, rivalry,* and *insult.* In the last analysis, these are the motives to which anger can always be traced. For if we could suppose that the injury done us is caused only through ignorance, we should suffer from it, but we would not be provoked. And when we notice that, while anyone has hurt us, he is himself lashed by a storm of emotion, we feel less angry than if he who injured us did it of set purpose (q.47, a.2). It is thus the deliberate scorn that hurts us, and it does it the more cruelly because we see in such a sentiment a radical negation of our value as men. Also, we may say that the higher a man's value, the more it naturally increases the occasions of his being chafed, his very superiority making more unjust the contempt of which he is the object (a.3).

As for its effects, we must remember that a just anger is pleasant to feel and the best remedy for the sadness which the injuries urging us to revenge have done us. The satisfaction it affords the irritated man is complete when he achieves an effective vengeance, but even without that the bare hope of revenge is agreeable, as is the pleasure of often thinking of what we strongly desire (q.48, a.1). All the same, anger occasions the gravest physical troubles and the most violent outward manifestations because of the heat which it works up in the blood and the boiling over that results, and for the same reason it affects the use of reason. For though reason does not employ any bodily organ in order to think, it needs sense perceptions as the content out of which it draws its ideas and it needs all the members of the body as instruments to carry out its orders. But the undue heat which anger imports into the heart, which is the center of life, leads to a general perturbation of every function and every organ; and, though in an indirect manner, it slows up the free working of reason.

Chapter V

THE INNER PRINCIPLES OF MAN'S ACTION

We began by outlining the moral end toward which human acts tend when they are what they ought to be (ch. 1, "The Master Value"). We tried to make it clear that actions are human so far as willed, and we then described the inner make-up of an act of the will (ch. 2, "Structure of the Human Act"). With a knowledge of what the terminus of an action is, and also what its structure is, we were able to show that the suitableness of the elements within an act to their objective permits us to qualify the act as good, and their unsuitableness to stamp it as evil, and that the degree of its moral character follows the degree of this adaptation (ch. 3, "On Moral Value and Disvalue").

Thus we marked off the most general conditions of an activity which is truly human, and hence moral. We still had to pass from these conditions to the concrete detail of acts. Now, among the acts which a man does, some are not strictly his, but only in so far as he is an animal. They are "natural," and not properly human, and hence are outside morals and can become good or bad through the use a man makes of them. We proceeded to describe and rank them, and we pointed out how each of them arises (ch. 4, "Love and Other Emotions"). From now on, the field of our study will no longer be general conditions of morals, but the direct principles which preside over our moral acts.

These principles are of two types: those that are within the human being, or *interior principles,* and those that rule the acts of human beings from without, or *exterior principles.* Among the interior we put the virtues in the first class, and link with their study that of the vices contrary to them. The exterior principles which we shall study are the several moral laws; man does not make them, but they are imposed on him from without, and he should guide his actions by them.

I. VIRTUE

A thorough sifting of the inner principles of human acts would suppose that we consider not only the principles that are specifically required for developing the moral life, but also those implied or presumed by them. From this point of view, all a man's active powers work together to effect a moral act. The soul, of course, is not, like God, a pure act, hence we cannot find in it any operation or power of operating that essentially belongs to it. In other words, the human soul, because it has not its existence from itself, necessarily receives all that it is. Hence, even when it occurs in a being and is defined by it as a form of an organized body, it is not capable of drawing from itself the faculties it needs to carry on its many functions, but it must receive them, and this is why, since it does not draw them out of its own essence, the powers of the soul are really distinct from the soul itself. These faculties or active powers given to the soul, or form of the body, so that it can do other things besides being the form of the body, plainly make up the immediate inner principles of all our acts (1, q.77, a.1), including our moral acts. Because of their very general character, however, the study of them is not specifically to the point in morals, but goes back to the science of the soul, which describes senses, intelligence, and will one by one.

Yet if we view the soul as equipped with its faculties, we shall be constrained to posit other inner principles of action, and these, though not exclusively the property of moral acts in the strict sense of the term, nevertheless develop on the field of morals as on their chosen ground, and they are hardly separable from a qualification of good and bad. These are the virtues. In fact, the problem which we have just posed as to the essence of the soul, is put in analogous terms of its faculties; they certainly have not of themselves the determinations needed for going at once into action; some *inner principles,* half-way between faculties and acts, must of necessity enter in. For if the human soul with its powers were wholly in act, as God is, it would lack nothing for action. If it were only a particular natural form, as those of bodies which are at once all that they can be, it would need nothing further for the exercise of its activity. And if the human soul were a form of the same kind as the elementary forms, which are naturally inseparable from their qualities, it would always act like the elements, which are necessarily hot or cold, moist or dry. But the human soul is of quite a different nature, because of the universal indetermination marking the power to think with which it is provided. Take, for example, the intellect itself. It is assuredly by nature that the intellect can know everything and thus can become all things; yet it would never pass from its simple capacity of knowing to the concrete multiplicity of the particular facts which it knows, if it did not in the beginning get hold of the first principles from which it receives a primary determination and which it goes on to employ as instruments. With the help of these principles, which it applies to the real, it proceeds to build up the sciences; and these in their turn are subordinated to each other and are more and more detailed until the intellect, enriched and rounded out with these specifications which it has taken on, becomes the progressive master of the unending minutiae of truths.

How are we to conceive of these particularizing principles that are acquired? Plainly, they are not faculties, for they are are added to the faculties which they suppose as given; hence they are only a kind of disposition to use the faculties rather in one way than in another. Yet, when one of these dispositions is fixed so as to form a lasting acquisition of the soul, it becomes truly a property of the soul, that is, something that belongs to it as a stable and characteristic quality. Technically, we name each of these properties, acquired and kept by the soul, by the Latin word which translates the idea of a permanent possession: *habitus* (1–2, a.49, a.1). These acquired principles evidently are needed in order that the soul can apply its faculties to the doing of moral or any other acts; these, then, are the moral habits which we are going to study. We first show that virtues are habits.

A *virtue* is a perfection added to a faculty of the soul. The perfection of anything lies chiefly in the relation of this thing to its goal, and as the aim or goal of a potency is act, we say that a potency is perfect when it is adjusted to its act. Now some potencies are of themselves adjusted to their acts, as the natural active potencies; that is why such natural powers merit in their own right the name of virtue. The rational powers, however, which are proper to man, are not set on just one activity, but are indeterminate with regard to many. But by way of habit they are determined to their acts as we said a moment ago. Therefore, the distinctively *human virtues are habits* (1–2, q.55, a.1; *cf. De Virt.,* q.1, a.1).

Besides, the virtues are dispositions set, not in a way of *being,* but in a way of *acting.* It is their *human* quality that demands this.

As we have pointed out, the very name of virtue stands for a certain perfection in a potency; and as there are two kinds of potencies, with regard to being and to acting, the perfection of each of them is called virtue. Yet potency as to being is of the order of the matter, which is potential being; whereas potency as to acting is of the order of the form, which is the principle of action, because each thing acts only so far as it is actual. Now, in the make-up of man the body is as the matter and the soul is the form. So far as the body goes, man has nothing that the other animals have not, and it is the same with those powers which are common to soul and body. Therefore, only the powers which are proper to the soul, that is, the rational powers, are uniquely man's. So the *human* virtue of which we speak cannot belong to the body, but singly to the soul; and human virtue is accordingly related not to being, but to action. It is thus of the essence of a human virtue that it be a readiness set for action (1-2, q.55, a.2).

Not only should this disposition make straight the paths for a certain kind of action, so that the virtue we speak of may be genuinely human, but it should likewise be a *good* disposition, in order that, in a word, it may be a virtue. And since the virtues are fixed dispositions, giving the faculties of the soul their full expression, it is always for the good of the soul that we have them, and they themselves may be good. Hence, we can in a measure explain and justify the celebrated definition got up from several texts taken from Augustine (chiefly, *De Libero Arbitrio*, 2, c.19): Virtue is that good quality of the mind by which we live rightly, which no one uses ill, and through which God works in us, without us (*in nobis sine nobis*). Leaving aside the last part of this definition, which applies to virtues infused by God into the soul—that is, the supernatural virtues—we may say:

This definition takes in the whole meaning of virtue, even though we omit the last part, and it belongs to every human virtue. As we have noted, a virtue rounds out a potency relative to its perfect act; but the perfect act is the end and aim of the potency or of the being which acts, and, therefore, virtue should make good both this potency and the agent. That is why, in the definition of virtue, there is something relating to the perfection of the act and something relating to the perfecting of the power or being which acts.

If we study the perfection of the act, two conditions are required, namely: that the act be right, and that the habit cannot become the principle of any contrary act. Indeed, the principle of good or bad acts cannot in itself be the perfect principle of a good act. The virtuous habit should be the principle of a good act, but in such a way that it cannot possibly become a bad act. . . . The first of these conditions is laid down by the words: *by which we live rightly,* the second by these: *which no one uses ill.*

If we look at virtue from the other side, that is, in so far as it makes him who possesses it good, there are three things to attend to: the subject itself, and this is set off when we say: *of mind,* because there cannot be any human virtue except in that which belongs to man as man. Secondly, the perfection of the intellect; and this is indicated by the word *good,* because we call good that which is controlled in view of its end. Thirdly, the manner in which the virtue is inherent in one, and this is indicated by the word *quality,* for virtue is not an emotion, but a habit. Now all these elements unite in virtue, whether it be a moral, an intellectual, or a theological virtue, and whether it be acquired or infused. As for what Augustine adds, that God works *in nobis sine nobis,* this has to do only with infused virtue (*De Virtut.,* q.1, a.2; *cf.* 1–2, q.55, a.4).

Granted that the human soul is the place where virtue resides, the question arises, whether virtue dwells in the very substance of the soul or in its faculties. It seems clear, at first sight, that the proper subject of virtue should be the faculty which it determines, for it is the perfection of a faculty, and that which is the perfection of a faculty ought to be in that faculty. Moreover, we have said that virtue is a disposition for action; and this disposition is in the faculties which act and not in the very substance of the soul. We know also that virtue makes a being ready for what is better for it; and the better for any being is its own end, and it is only by use of its faculties that a being can reach its end (1–2, a.56, a.2). However, a difficulty remains: The faculties are not substances, and the virtues are only qualities; hence there must be some substance to bear a virtue, and since the faculties are not substances, it cannot be they that support the virtues. How are we to solve this difficulty?

We answer: the relation of subject to accident must be one of three. First, it affords it a support, for accident does not stand by itself, but is borne by a subject. Second, their relation is that of potency to act, for subject yields to accident as potency to the active principle, and so we give to accident the name of form. Third, it is the relation of cause to effect: for the principles of the subject are of themselves the principles of the accidents. If we speak of the first cause, an accident cannot be the subject of another accident; since in fact no accident stands by itself, it cannot serve to support anything else, unless, perhaps, we say that it supports another accident in so far as it is itself supported by a subject. But from the other two points of view, one accident can serve as a subject with regard to another, as transparency does with regard to light and a surface with regard to color; and one accident can also be the cause of another, as moisture is of taste. It is in these last two senses that we say, an accident is the subject of another accident, because the subject is found to receive one accident through the intermediary of another. This is quite as true as when we say that a faculty of the soul is the subject of a habit. The fact is that habit stands in the same relation to the faculty of the soul as act does to potency, since a faculty is not determined by itself, but by habit to this rather than to that. It is also through the first principles of the faculties of the soul that acquired habits are produced. It must be said, then, that the faculties are subjects of the virtues, because the virtues inhere in the soul by way of the faculties (*De Virtut.,* q.1, a.3).

We have to inquire now in which faculties of the soul we find the chief habits which rule over the performance of moral acts, and we shall see that these habits are essentially at home in the will, or

VIRTUE

in all the other faculties of the soul, so far as these depend on the will.

In each thing, virtue is judged by its relation to the good, because it is the virtue of a thing, as Aristotle says (2 *Ethics*) that makes good both what has the virtue and whatever it does. Thus, virtue in a horse is what makes him a good horse, a good traveller carrying his rider well, which is the work of a horse. If a habit is a virtuous one, this is because it is directed towards good; which may occur in either of two ways, either materially or formally. It happens formally, if it goes on towards good, but not seen as good. Now good, taken as good, is the object of only the conative part of the soul; for the good is what all desire. It is thus the habits in the conative part or those dependent on the conative faculty that are formally aimed toward the good, and this is why they have in a high degree the nature of virtue. As for those of the habits that are neither in the conative part nor dependent on it, they can, of course, be materially headed towards what is good, but not formally and under its nature of good; hence we may call them virtues in some sense, yet not in so proper a sense as the other habits.

The intellect, both speculative and practical, can be perfected in two ways by a habit. First, absolutely and in itself, in so far as the intellect precedes and in a manner moves the will; secondly, in so far as it follows the will and carries out its act, we might say, at the behest of the will; for, as we have noted, intellect and will imply each other. Habits which are in either the speculative or the practical intellect in the first way, may be regarded as virtues in a sense, yet not in the strict sense, and it is only in this strict sense that intelligence, science, and wisdom are in the speculative intellect, and that art is in the practical intellect. We say indeed that a man is intelligent or wise from the fact that his intellect is fully ready to know the truth, which is the value or good of intellect. And though this truth can be willed, in so far as man wishes to know truth, all the same it is not from this aspect that the habits we mentioned bring us any perfection; for though a man have knowledge, this does not cause him to will to study the truth, but only enables him to do so; and for this reason the study of the truth itself is not knowledge in so far as willed, but in so far as directed towards its object. And it is the same with art in the field of the practical intellect, for art does not give a man this perfection of willing to achieve a work that satisfies the rules of art, but only the knowledge and ability to do it.

As for the habits which are in either the practical or the speculative intellect when intellect follows will, they approach closer to virtue because, equipped with them, man no longer has simply the power and knowledge for right action: he also has the will to do. We see this in faith and prudence, though in different senses. Faith gives the speculative intellect a perfection by making it obey the will; as, for instance, the act of faith by which man assents to what is above human reason precisely because he wills to do so. This is what Augustine says (*Tract. in Joannem,* 26) that man can believe only if he wills to believe. Faith, then, is in the speculative intellect, so far as this is subject to the command of the will, just as temperance is in our desires, so far as these are obedient to the order of reason. This is why, when there is belief, the will commands the intellect, not only as to exercising the act, but also as to specifying the object: because of an order of the will the intellect gives assent to a particular belief; just as when a temperate appetite tends towards this or that means, it is because the means has been decided upon by reason. Prudence for its part is in the intellect or the practical reason (see below, p. 155), for the will determines not the object, but only the end; and as for its object, it is prudence itself that seeks it, since, if we presuppose the end, which is the good chosen by the will, it is prudence that goes in quest of the means by which this good can be won and kept.

Thus we see that the several habits of intellect have different relations to the will. For certain of them have no utter dependence on the will, unless as to their use, and even this is but by accident, because the use of such habits as science, philosophy, and the arts, depends differently on the will than on these habits themselves. Thus man is by such habits not made able to will to use them well, but only to use them.

We have a second kind of habit of intellect which does depend on the will, in the sense that it receives its principle from it, for in the realm of doing it is the end which is the starter. Prudence is such a habit. A last type of habit receives from the will even the specification of its object; faith is an instance. And though all these habits may be called virtues in some sense, this name nevertheless belongs most perfectly and properly to the two last. But it does not follow that they are the most noble or the most perfect of all habits. (*De Virtut.*, q.1, a.7; *cf.* 3 *Sent.*, d.23, q.1, a.4; 1–2, q.56, a.3).

To resume: If we take the word *virtue* in its proper sense, as a virtue is always a principle of action, and the immediate principle of action is always the will, a virtue properly speaking can reside only in the will. And if virtue be in some other faculty than the will, as in the intelligence, this is only so far as that faculty is moved by the will. When the act of the intellect is fully specified by the will, as in the case of faith, the habit of the intellect wholly realises the meaning of virtue. When the act of the intellect receives from the will at least the specification of its end, which is the good willed by a right will, the habit of the intellect is a genuine virtue; as in the case of prudence. And when, as a last type, the habit in question simply makes the intellect capable of acting well without in any way specifying it to perform good actions effectively, it is a virtue but indirectly, because concerned only in a round-about way with action and the will.

We see now the relation which the master faculties of man, intellect and will, have to virtue. Without intellect, there is determinism and no choice possible in the realm of action; hence the agent in such case acts always in the same way and does not need any complementary habit or virtue. But if intellect is the necessary condition where there is to be virtue, it is not its habits that are the virtues; and if there are any virtues, they are not intellectual, but voluntary. We remark this clearly in instances in which the virtue lies in a faculty of the soul which is neither the intellect nor, in proper language, the will. Take for example courage as an emotion of the second kind and temperance of the first. These are very noble virtues, but they can be in the emotional life only of a man, and not of an animal, for these two types of emotions of the soul are immediate sources of action, and can produce virtues in the genuine sense of the term; they have no need to receive the specifications of it except in the measure that, shot through with intelligence, they themselves share the indeterminism of that faculty (1–2, q.56, a.4). *A virtue then is a settled habit of doing good, and the proper subject of it is the power of choice in an intelligent being.* How are the virtues acquired? Are they natural to us and innate, or are they acquired step by step?

We have a natural fitness for knowledge and virtue; but in their perfect form they are not natural to us. This is the better opinion, because just as when there is question of natural forms, the virtue of natural agents is not at all hostile to them, so when there is question of the acquisition of knowledge, it is by study and exercise that the virtue maintains its efficacy. Still, it must be kept in mind that in a given subject fitness to receive the perfection of form can be twofold. First, according to its passive power only, and it is thus that there is in the matter of air a fitness for the form of fire. Secondly, according to both its passive and active power, and it is in this way that a fitness for health is found in a sick body; because the body is able to receive health. It is in this last-mentioned sense that man has a natural aptitude for virtue, partly by reason of the nature of his species, since aptitude for virtue is common to all men, and partly by reason of the nature of the individual, since some are more fit for virtue than others.

To grasp this truth, it is necessary to know that three faculties of man can serve as the subjects of virtue: the intellect, the will, and that of the conative emotions, which are divided into three classes. Now we must, in some measure, give an account of each of these subjects both as to its fitness to receive virtue and as to the active principle of virtue that is in it.

We know, of course, that in the cognitive part of the soul there is, first, the possible intellect, which is in potency with regard to all intelligible things, the knowledge of which forms cognitive virtue; and secondly, the active intellect, whose light makes things actually intelligible. Among these things some are immediately known by man, are known from the outset without study or research. These are the first principles, not only of a speculative kind, as: *the whole is greater than any part,* or the like, but also of the practical sort, as: *evil must be avoided.* These facts are naturally known and are the principles of any and all knowledge that we can acquire by study, whether to speculate or to do. Similarly, in the case of the will, it is plain that there are natural principles of conduct; for the will tends towards the end of ends by a natural inclination; and in the practical order the end takes the place of natural principle, and so the inclination of the will is as an active principle with regard to every disposition acquired in the exercise of the affective part of the soul. It is clear that the will itself, as power of choice among means leading to an end, is suspectible of a habitual inclination toward such or such means. As for the emotions, they are naturally capable of obeying reason, and it is this fact that makes them naturally susceptible of the virtue achieved in them in the measure that they are habituated to follow the good of reason. And as all these dispositions to virtue result from the nature of humankind, they are common to all men.

There exists another type of disposition to virtue, resulting from the nature of the individual, and because of it this or that man is temperamentally inclined to a particular virtue. This inclination is good, indeed it is a beginning of virtue; and still it is not perfect, because a perfect virtue would imply the rule of reason well established. And therefore, in defining virtue, we say that it chooses means *according to right reason*. And if anyone should follow inclinations of this kind without the discernment of reason, he would often sin and so, without the help of reason, this beginning of virtue does not form a perfect virtue. But it is necessary to say something of it as well as of the preceding virtues, for if we come down from universal principles to conclusions, it is by an inquiry of reason; and it is due to the work of reason that man is brought from a desire of the end of ends to the means fitted for that end. And it is reason also that, though it commands any of the emotions, subjects itself to them.

It is clear, therefore, that the concurrence of reason is required for virtue to be entire, whether it be a virtue of the intellect or of the will, of emotions of one kind or of another. And here is what its consummation consists in: that the disposition to the virtue which is in a higher faculty be applied to the virtue of the lower part. For example, man is made fit for virtue of the will by the disposition to virtue which is in his will and also by that which is in his intellect; and he is made fit for the virtue that is in the emotions by the beginning of the virtue that is in them, and also by that which is in the higher faculties: but not vice versa. It plainly follows that reason, the highest of the faculties, concurs for the attainment of each of the virtues, . . . and so the perfection of virtue comes to man not from nature, but from reason (*De Virtut.,* q.1, a.8; *cf.* 1–2, q.68, a.1).

We have now in a measure rounded out our definition of virtue, including in it all the required conditions. A virtue is a *settled disposition,* in other words, a habit; its home is in a faculty of the will, or in any faculty that holds from a voluntary one; it belongs only to an *intelligent being,* who is capable of determining himself to his acts; it has its origin in *a natural germ,* but it comes to full bloom only by the *help of reason,* which forms and in a sense imprints in the lower faculties a right disposition, without which the acquired disposition would not be a virtue.

II. CLASSIFICATION OF THE VIRTUES

There are three kinds of virtues: intellectual, moral, and theological. Those in the second class form the proper object of our study, and it is on the classification of them that we shall chiefly dwell. Still, the moral virtues are incomprehensible so long as we are ignorant of the intellectual, at least one of which is their necessary condition; and we should get a false idea of the moral virtues if we did not know of the existence of the theological virtues needed to bring them to their perfection.

In the intellect itself it is proper to distinguish between a speculative and a practical function. If we take first its speculative function, it will seem to us as being, by definition, unconcerned with anything practical and active; as such it cannot be the seat of genuine virtue, since the virtues, strictly speaking, are dispositions for action. The intellect, as speculative, can have only the virtues which are from a good kind of being and not those which cause us to act from these good dispositions. But at the same time it furnishes the properly free virtues with matter on which to apply themselves. To have knowledge is a virtue of the speculative intellect; to contemplate truth by using this knowledge is, on the contrary, a moral virtue. It is thus necessary, first to have those virtues which are only from a manner of being, then to be able to exercise the contemplative virtues, which are the highest and rule the activities of the others.

The habits, or ways of being acquired and maintained lastingly by the intellect, are three. There is *intelligence,* which consists in the possession of the first and immediately evident principles of knowledge, such as the principle of contradiction and its derivatives. Second, *science,* which consists in the possession by the intellect of the conclusions of such or such a particular branch of study, the knowledge of which is not immediately evident. Third, *wisdom,* which consists in the possession by the intellect of the most universal principles and of first causes, and under these are ranged the principles of each specific science. We see at once that these three intellectual virtues are not only distinct, but also hierarchical, and that the two others are subordinate to wisdom. Science, in fact, depends on intelligence, since the sciences are built up in part out of the first principles of knowledge; but wisdom contains both intelligence and science, because it consists in the possession of the final findings of the sciences and at the same time of the first principles on which these conclusions depend (1–2, q.57, a.2, ad 2). Wisdom is thus the highest intellectual virtue, and whoever has it, has the others.

But if we consider the practical function of the intellect, and keep in mind the part which it plays in the elaboration of voluntary acts, we distinguish three principal moments: deliberation (p. 74), judgment (p. 75), and command (p. 76). Here again there is not one of these operations that we cannot become capable of doing, and of doing better; each of them, therefore, can become the object of virtue. And certainly, to deliberate and to judge are, rightly speaking, acts of the speculative intellect; yet they are subordinate to ends that are immediately practical. To be able to deliberate well is to possess a virtue which we may call *good counsel,* in the sense in which we say of certain persons that they are good counsellors. To be able to judge well, whether following natural reason or common law, is to have that virtue which we mean when we say of a man that he has *good judgment.* There remains a third virtue, *prudence,* which is by far the most important of all, and alone of the intellectual virtues cannot be dissociated from the moral.

The difference between the natural and the rational virtues is that a natural virtue is determined to one single thing, whereas a rational virtue conditions several things. Now, in order that a rational or an animal desire be inclined towards an object, it is necessary that this object be known; for when the inclination to an end is not preceded by knowledge, it is that of a natural appetite, as of a heavy body which tends downward. Hence, though there must be a known good to serve as object of either animal desire or rational desire, when this good is always the same, there can be a rational inclination in the appetite and a natural judgment in the faculty of knowledge, as is the case with the animals. And as in fact they carry on only a few operations, on account of the weakness of their active principle, which has but a limited field of action, there is a uniform value for all animals of the same species; this is what causes their desire to tend to this good by natural inclination and causes them to pass, in virtue of their power of knowing, a natural judgment on a value that is proper to them and is ever the same. It is this natural judgment and this natural desire that cause every sparrow to build her nest in the same way and every spider to spin her web in the same way, and we can observe the same thing among other animals. Man, however, performs many different operations, because of the dignity of his active principle or soul, whose power in a sense (*quodammodo*) reaches to the infinite. And this is why a natural desire of the good and a natural judgment are not enough for man, if he is to act rightly; he must be farther directed and perfected.

It is by a natural desire that man is inclined to seek his

own good. But man's good takes very different forms and can consist in any one of several things. Accordingly, it is not possible that man should have a natural desire for such a determined good as would satisfy at once all the conditions required for being his good. Indeed, his good varies in many ways, according to the diverse circumstances of persons, times, places, and the like. And for the same reason a natural uniform judgment is not enough for seeking a good of this kind, but it is necessary that man be made fit to search out and pass judgment on his own goods (with all the conditions which make them desirable in determined circumstances) by use of reason, whose business it is to make a comparison among several objects. Now, to do this, reason, without a habit to perfect it, is as speculative reason would be if it had no habit of science. It could not do it, except poorly and with difficulty. Just as speculative reason, therefore, should be rounded out by the habit of a science, so that it be capable of judging correctly of the circumstances relevant to it, so the practical reason should be completed by a habit so as to be able to judge correctly what is good for man to do in each particular instance. We call this virtue prudence. Its home is the practical reason. It perfects all the moral virtues of the conative life, each of which begets an inclination of desire towards a determined kind of human value. For example, justice begets an inclination towards that value which makes for equality in all the circumstances of social life; temperance, towards that good which forms the mastery of our appetite; and so on, for each of the other virtues. Now all this can be done in many different ways and is not done in the same way by all. Hence, to set up a right way of doing it, requires a prudent judgment. So it is from prudence that all the other virtues get their rightness and perfection; and this is why

CLASSIFICATION OF THE VIRTUES 155

Aristotle says in the second book of his *Ethics* that it is right reason that determines the just medium in moral virtue. And as it is to this rightness and this rounding out of their perfection that all habits of the conative powers owe their quality of virtue, it follows that prudence is the cause of all the virtues of the conative powers; and they are called moral only in so far as they are virtues (*De Virtut.*, q.1, c.6).

In view of these facts it is evident that prudence is an intellectual virtue, and that without it none of the moral virtues would realise its own end, and as prudence itself supposes a knowledge of principles, these two intellectual virtues are necessary conditions of all the moral virtues.

Prudence is a virtue very much needed in human life. To live well means to act well. And to act well does not depend solely on what one does, but also on how he does it, that is on what he does in virtue of a right choice and not from mere impulse or emotion. On the other hand, choice has to do with means, and rightness of choice requires two factors: namely, an end which is what it should be, and a means in harmony with this end. As for what the end should be, man is suitably disposed by the virtue which perfects the conative part of his soul, the object of this being value or end. But as for the proper means in view of this end, man should be disposed directly by a habit of reason, because deliberation and choice, dealing with the means, are acts of reason. As a consequence, there necessarily should be in reason an intellectual virtue, so that reason is perfected by squaring itself as it must with the means. This virtue is prudence. Prudence is thus a virtue necessary for living well (1–2, q.57, a.5; for the relations of art to prudence, see *ibid.,* a.4).

We must not let ourselves be led astray by a false analogy between prudence and art. Prudence is not an art of producing virtues which, once produced, can subsist without it, as the works of art survive the art and the artist who made them. Art is reason made capable of producing objects exterior to it, and art introduces into these objects that perfection which they will henceforth possess. Prudence is reason made capable of knowing how we must act, and so it does not have to do with finished works, but with doing. The result of art, therefore, is the beauty or excellence of the work of art. The result of prudence is not the goodness or perfection of the man who so possesses it that he could dispense with prudence once he is enriched with its effects; its result is the goodness or the perfection of the very acts performed by the man. This is why we have said that prudence is necessary if a man is to live well; because to live is to act, and prudence is the lasting regulator of our actions.

If we go on to consider the moral virtues, we shall see them marked off from the intellectual, first, in the way the two kinds are formed. Not all philosophers admit this distinction, because not all conceive properly the relations of the faculties of the soul to reason. Socrates, for example, taught that reason

CLASSIFICATION OF THE VIRTUES 157

rules the body as a despot rules his subjects. If this were true, we should have no need of other virtues beyond those of reason; he who had prudence and the science of intellect would never commit any fault, and no fault would ever have any cause but ignorance. We know, however, that reason does not command the other faculties as slaves; it is an enlightened monarch who gives directions to free men. The conative part of the soul is notably a master in the use and specification of its acts; it therefore requires its own virtues, which are not mixed up with prudence or the other virtues. Consequently, intellectual and moral virtues are two distinct classes (1–2, q.58, a.2 and 3) and there cannot be more than the two, because there are but two principles of human acts: intellect (or reason) and will.

Viewing them in a general way, let us see, first, what part the moral virtues play as controllers of our activity. We shall note at the outset that they condition intellectual prudence, and that prudence conditions them. For prudence is a good disposition, which gives the intellect a chance to choose the means in view of the end; but it is desire, perfected by its moral virtues, that judges of the end and decides what ought to be (*ibid.,* a.5). A prudence exercised on a desire minus moral habits would be exercised then on a desire enslaved by its passions and would place the virtue of the intellect at the service of a morally evil cause. In fact these two orders of virtue, which we have specifically distinguished, work together through the intermediary of prudence.

In the second place, we shall note that the moral virtues are in contact, and as it were at blows, with the emotions. For the two of them register at the same office—the conative side of the soul. Not that there is between the emotions and the virtues the incompatibility supposed by the Stoics; we have pointed out the source of that error (p. 104). But certain virtues are applied to the emotions as the remedy is applied to the disease which it is designed to cure, or as the virtues are applied to the faculties which support them and which they direct and use. Of course, it is necessary to grant that not all the virtues are related to the emotions, for we have a rational appetite or will, and the virtues of the will—justice, for instance—have to do, not with the emotions, but with the activities of the soul (1-2, q.59, a.4). Yet even when virtue does not directly apply to emotion, it accompanies it, and so, contrary to the view of the Stoics, there are no perfectly virtuous acts unless man is quite fully concerned in them.

If we call *disordered affections* emotions, as the Stoics did, it is plain that there is perfect virtue without emotions. But if we call *all the movements of sense desire* emotions, it is clear that those moral virtues that are related to the emotions as their proper matter, cannot exist without emotion.

CLASSIFICATION OF THE VIRTUES 159

The reason is that otherwise moral virtue would result in making sense desire wholly useless; and the part of virtue is not to cause the faculties subject to reason to cease from the exercise of their proper acts; it is rather to cause them to carry out the orders of reason through the use of their proper acts. It follows, therefore, that, as virtue disposes the members of the body to the exterior acts they should do, so it fits sense appetite to accomplish its proper and orderly acts.

If, on the other hand, we study the moral virtues, which are related not to the emotions, but to activities, they can exist independently of the emotions. The virtue of justice is of this kind, for it applies the will to its proper act, which is not an emotion. It is none the less true that from the act of justice there results, at least in the will, a joy which in the beginning is not an emotion, but if it is developed for the perfection of justice, manages in some way to flow over from joy to the sense appetite, because, as noted before (q.17, a.7), the lower powers follow the movement of the higher; and the more complete this overflow, the more emotion it arouses (1-2, q.59, a.5).

We should pause, however, at this first distinction between the points of application of the virtues, to make out the two principal classes of moral virtues, and we therefore leave the general consideration of virtue to attempt a classification of the latter. At the outset, let us put down as the first group of moral virtues all those that have to do with action. In one sense, all of them share more or less the nature of justice, for to act well is always to give everyone his due. But in another sense they are distinct from one another because we do not owe the same to everyone and for the same reason. For example, to give to God what is His due, is religion; to give our parents their due, is filial piety; and, on the other hand, to return a favor, is gratitude, but to pay a debt would not be. Thus the grouping of all the virtues that deal with action and that govern our special relations, is formed by the many specific virtues ranked, because of their kinds, under the one virtue of justice.

Thus the first class of virtues is built up. But there remains a second group: the virtues which have to do with the emotions. We might at first be tempted to make the virtues correspond to the emotions by applying each of them to a particular emotion. Yet this is the one method that would halt our progress, for a single virtue is enough to moderate two contrary emotions, such as fear and boldness, because virtue takes up precisely a middle position; and one single virtue is enough to repress two emotions directly deriving from each other. We shall, therefore, put temperance against the emotions of the first kind, courage against fear and boldness, and so for the other virtues. But because the ranking of the moral virtues that have to do with the emotions does not always follow the grouping of the emotions, such classification is impossible; we know only that it will be complex and that it will refer simultaneously to several different principles: subjects, emotions, or objects of virtues. By combining

THE CARDINAL VIRTUES

or substituting the three principles for one another, St. Thomas restates the ten moral virtues that are related to the emotions and are given by Aristotle in his *Ethics* (bk. 2): *Courage,* which moderates fear and boldness in the second type of emotion; *temperance,* which moderates too strong a desire for goods known by touch and relating to the conservation of the individual or the species; *generosity,* which tempers our desire for the bodily goods perceived by an inner faculty; *magnificence,* which tones down the vehement desire and hope for money; *honor,* the very name of which expresses the desirable quality of the object; *magnanimity,* which carries us on in the hope of winning a difficult honor; *meekness,* which mollifies the emotion of anger; *affability,* which consists in showing ourselves agreeable with others, in word or act, in serious matters; *sincerity,* which consists in showing ourselves, in words and acts, just as we are; and lastly, *playfulness,* a virtue which makes us agreeable in games and pleasant exercises (1-2, q.60, a.5). Among all these virtues, whether of mind or character, four stand out from the others. These are the so-called cardinal virtues: *prudence, temperance, fortitude,* and *justice.*

We can number things by beginning with their formal principles or with their subjects; and in either way we find four cardinal virtues. For the formal principle of the virtues of which we speak is the good of reason. We may view this good in two ways: first, so far as it lies in thought and reasoning, and we then have a principal virtue which we call justice; secondly, in the sense that a reasoned order is put into things: if it is introduced into activities, we have justice, but if it is introduced into the emotions, we should have to name two virtues in order to give an account of the twofold repugnance of emotion to reason. For emotion in the first place can impel to some act contrary to reason, and it is needful that the emotion be repressed; then the virtue gets the name of temperance. But emotion can also keep us from doing what reason prescribes, as fear turns us away from danger or fatigue, and it is then necessary that man be made firm in what is reasonable, lest he should run away; and the name of the virtue in this case is fortitude. And when we glance at the subject of the virtues, we find like ones, and an equal number of them. For there are four subjects of the virtue of which we are now speaking: first, reason taken in itself, which prudence perfects; then, that which only shares reason, and this in its turn is subdivided into three kinds: the will, which is the subject of justice, emotions of the first type, which form the subject of temperance, and of the second type, which form the subject of fortitude (1-2, q.61, a.2; *cf. De Virtut. Cardinal.*, q.1, a.1; see below, p. 176).

These virtues are named cardinal virtues because they are in a sense the hinges (*cardines*) on which all others turn, and because the others presuppose them. For every virtue that effects good in the name of reason is related to prudence; every virtue that directs our activity towards the good relates to justice; every virtue that tempers the emotions is in the field of temperance; and every virtue that makes

THE THEOLOGICAL VIRTUES 163

the soul firmer against emotion is close to fortitude. These, then, are the basic moral virtues; but they are not the highest virtues, for the theological in turn perfect and crown them.

The study of the theological virtues as such certainly has nothing to do with the competence of the moral philosopher and, as their name shows, they belong to the theologian. But though moral science may not take the description of them for its object, it cannot be polished off without postulating them. When we define the sovereign human value, we see plainly that man's essence implies a demand of the infinite which no human good can meet. Hence the two kinds of happiness, distinct though co-ordinate, the nature of which we have described and which we ranked in hierarchical fashion (p. 41). Now, it is clear that if it is of the essence of man to be meant for an end beyond that which his essence can realise, it is necessary that fit means be given him, or he will despair of ever attaining it. Therefore, just as ethics requires, for strictly philosophical reasons, a religious morals to round it out, so the intellectual and moral virtues need the theological virtues to crown them and to carry on to perfect achievement the work they have begun.

Man is perfected by virtue for doing the acts which lead him to happiness, as is evident from what precedes (q.3, a.5). But human happiness or felicity is of two kinds; one kind is proportioned to human nature, that is to say, man can attain it by the mere principles of his nature; whereas the other is a happiness which exceeds man's nature and which he can reach only by divine help by a sort of participation in the divinity. In this sense it is said that, through Christ, we are made *"partakers of the divine nature"* (2 Pet., c.1). And because this happiness exceeds the limits of man's nature, the natural means which man uses for acting as well as he can are not enough to direct him to this aforesaid happiness. It is necessary, therefore, that other principles be superadded to man, so that he be conducted to supernatural happiness, as natural means lead him to his natural goal, though even this is not independent of God. These extra principles are called theological virtues, because they have God for their object, in the sense that they turn us properly towards God, because they are given us only by God, and, lastly, because they are known to us only through Holy Scripture, in which God reveals them to us (1–2, a.62, a.1; *cf.* 1–2, q.65, a.2, and 3 *Sent.,* d.33, q.1, a.4).

With *faith,* which perfects our minds by giving them habits of the truths to believe; with *hope,* which perfects the direction (*intention*) of our wills by pointing them toward their supernatural end as something accessible to man; and *charity,* which spiritually changes our wills by attaching them to this end, we attain the full reach of the human soul, thoroughly fitted to work with effectiveness for the attainment of the master value. The bases of the edifice, vaulted over with supernatural gifts and beatitudes, are thus laid down wholly; and we shall pause a moment to take a look at the foundation of the building. First, the intellect viewed in its theoretic function, with its virtues of knowledge, intelligence, and wisdom; then in its practical working, with the habits of art and skill, the virtue of prudence and the related virtues of judgment and good counsel. Afterwards, desire, studied in its rational form with the virtue of justice, which perfects the will; and in its sense form, with the ten virtues of fortitude, temperance, generosity, magnificence, magnanimity, love of honor, meekness, affability, truth, and playfulness. Lastly, there comes a supernatural perfection which brings faith to the intellect, and hope and charity to the will, so as to make man capable of his high destiny. Such is the soul wholly equipped—"*expedita,*" as the Scholastics say. We have now to see the soul love and act, to see it acquiring and developing the several virtues, uniting them and putting them to work.

III. THE LIFE OF VIRTUE

In defining virtue we have noted that it always implies an original disposition of the subject brought step by step to its full development through the exercise of reason. This conclusion is the same for every moral virtue properly so-called, excluding, of course, the theological virtues which are not acquired by reason, but are infused into the soul by God, and also excluding whatever moral virtues God may infuse into us to make ready the ground for the theological virtues with which he aims to crown the moral (1–2, q.63, a.3). Let us consider, then, a merely human moral virtue, won little by little through repeated acts conformed to reason, and let us ask how it works. Its proper and constant effect will always be to outline the middle road that an act should take so as to be morally good.

From what has been said (q.55, a.3) it follows that by its nature a virtue disposes man to the good, and that the peculiarity of moral virtue is that it perfects the conative part of the soul with regard to some determined object. The measure and rule of the movement of desire toward the desirable is reason itself. On the other hand, the value of all that is measured and ruled lies in being brought into conformity to its rule, as the value of a work of art is to obey the rule of the art; and evil for an object of this kind consequently consists in being out of harmony with its rule or measure, which lack of harmony comes of the object's exceeding its measure or not living up to it. This is easily seen in all objects which are ruled and measured, and it appears that the good of moral virtue consists in a squaring up with reason as measure. But it is plain also that the midway between overdoing and underdoing is the agreement or conformity; so it follows, no less plainly, that moral virtue takes the middle of the road (1–2, q.64, a.1; *De Virtut.,* q.1, a.13).

This middle way, however, cannot be settled by an abstract rule that gives us a definitive estimate in one word; for in the degree that moral research approaches its ideal limit, that is to say, the determination of the detail of particular acts, it is itself particularised so as to be fitted to all the circumstances defining the nature of each act in its individuality.

In the case of actions and passions, means and extremes are fixed only by taking account of circumstances. There is, therefore, no reason why a thing could not be extreme for a virtue in one circumstance and yet be the middle way and reasonable in other circumstances. And this is precisely what does happen in (the virtues of) magnificence and magnanimity. For if we consider the absolute quantity of that toward which the magnificent or the magnanimous man tends, we shall qualify it as extreme and the limit; but if the same matter is studied in the light of other circumstances, it will have a medium look, for virtues of this kind justly tend towards the maximum, and reasonably so, that is to say, where and when on some good ground they ought to do so. However, it would be an excess to tend toward the limit when we should not, or where we should not, or if for some good reason we should not; and it would be a deficiency if we did not tend toward this extreme where we should and when we should. And so Aristotle says in the fourth book of the *Ethics* that magnanimity is assuredly at the extreme, but since that is where it should be, it keeps the mean (1–2, q.64, a.1, ad 2).

In relation to what is reason to fix this mean? Will it have to consider something of the thing, or rather something that seems such to it through relation to the subject who acts?

We may call the mean of reason that which reason determines in any matter, and in this sense the mean of every moral virtue is a mean of reason, since, as we have just shown, moral virtue consists in the mean conformed to reason. Now it can sometimes be that the mean of reason is equally the mean of the thing (*medium rei*), and then the mean of moral virtue ought to be the mean of the thing, and this is the case in the virtue of justice. But sometimes the mean of reason is not the mean of the thing, but a mean fixed in reference to us; and this is the kind of mean found in all the other moral virtues. The reason is that justice rules the acts which have to do with exterior things, where right should be established in itself and absolutely; for, as justice gives to each one his due, no more and no less, the mean of reason is one with the mean of the thing. The other moral virtues, however, are concerned with interior emotions, in which this right could not be set up in the same way, because with regard to the emotions men are not the same. And, therefore, when it is a question of the emotions, right reason should be determined in relation to us, who are affected by these emotions (1–2, q.64, a.2).

We may add that what is true of the moral virtues in a proper sense, is true equally of the intellectual virtues, and especially of that virtue of the practical intellect which we have said rules all the moral virtues, namely, prudence. For as to the speculative intellect, its object or proper good is truth; and the measure of truth is none other than the thing which it expresses. If intellect misses this object by running over or under, it misses at one stroke its middle way, its good and its object. As for the practical intellect, its proper good is that which appetite truly ought to desire, and, taken in relation to its object, it is in this object again that its measure is found; but once the practical intellect has laid hold of the object, this becomes the measure of desire for it. Rightness of reason, consisting in the just mean, is thus also found to be the rightness of the moral virtue which reason rules, reason itself, measured by its object, becoming in turn the measure of virtue (*De Virtut.*, q.1, a.13).

Let us take up now a new problem, that of the relation and interconnection of virtue with virtue. Its practical importance is considerable, for on the solution which we shall give to it will depend the method which we are to follow in the acquisition of virtue, and to solve it for the cardinal virtues is to solve it for all the dependent virtues.

Moral virtue may be regarded either as perfect or imperfect. In its imperfect form, a moral virtue, such as temperance or fortitude, is merely an inclination in us to do a good act, and this inclination may be from our nature or it may be the result of habit. Taken in this sense, the moral virtues are not linked together; for we notice that such or such a person who by his native disposition or habit would be ready to do a work of charity, is not so prepared for a life of chastity. Now perfect moral virtue is a permanent disposition which inclines us to the doing of a good action, and if we view the moral virtues in this way, it must be said that they are inter-dependent, as indeed almost anyone will admit.

We may give two reasons for this, following the different ways in which the cardinal virtues are distinct from one another. For, as we have said (q.61, a.3 and 4), there are some who divide them according to the general properties of these virtues. They admit, for example, that discretion is a part of prudence, right of justice, moderation of temperance, and firmness of courage; and they admit this, whatever the content of these virtues may be. The connection of virtue with virtue is thereby readily evident. For there is no praising firmness as a virtue, if it lacks moderation or right or discretion, and so on for the other virtues. And this is the meaning of their connection given by Gregory in the twenty-second book of his *Morals* (ch.1), where he says that if the virtues be disjoined, they cannot be perfect virtues, because that prudence which is not just, temperate, and courageous, is not genuine; and so, too, of the others. Augustine likewise gives an argument of this kind in the sixth book *On the Trinity* (ch.4).

Others draw a line among the cardinal virtues according to their several contents, and take the view that Aristotle took of their connection in the sixth book of the *Ethics* (ch.12). As we said earlier (q.58, a.4), a person cannot have any moral virtue without prudence. For it is the way of this virtue to make a right choice; and in order that choice be right, it is not enough that there be an inclination toward the legitimate end which the possession of moral virtue fixes, but a person must directly choose those things that lead to the end, and these things have to do with prudence, which is counsellor, judge, and master of the means. On the other hand, one could not have prudence if he had not the several moral virtues; because prudence is a right knowledge of what to do (*recta ratio agibilium*), and it proceeds from the ends of

THE LIFE OF VIRTUE

actions as well as from its beginnings, and to these ends we are directed only by the moral virtues. Just as we cannot have a speculative science without a knowledge of principles, therefore, so neither can we have prudence without the moral virtues. The plain conclusion is that the moral virtues are linked together.

As for the objection that we can practice one virtue without practicing the others, it is to be said that some moral virtues are limited to lifting us to the level of common duties, that is to say, those that are met ordinarily in every human life. Man, in this order, should bring himself to the practice of all the moral virtues and, if he does all well, he will acquire the habits of all virtues at once. But if he goes to work to master the matter of only one of these virtues, and neglects that of another, for instance, to get the better of anger, but not of lust, he will attain a certain settled way of controlling his temper, yet this disposition will not truly be a virtue, since prudence, run over by sensuality, will then be behind time. So too the natural inclinations cannot become perfectly virtuous where there is no prudence. Other moral virtues, however, raise man above the common level, such as magnificence and magnanimity. And as occasion is not usually offered to all for practice in the matter of these virtues, we can have the other moral virtues without actually having these, that is, without having them effectively acquired. All the same, if one has gotten possession of the other virtues, he almost has these too, and he has them virtually. For when we have practice and become adept at generosity in little gifts and little expenses, then, if there is any cash left over, we shall acquire the virtue of magnificence at the cost of little exercise. So the geometrician with a modicum of study gains a knowledge of a conclusion on which he had never reflected, for we say that we already have that which we easily achieve. And this is the dictum of Aristotle in the second book of his *Physics:* when very, very little is lacking, it is as if nothing were lacking (1–2, q.65, a.1 and ad 1; *cf. De Virtut. Cardinal.,* q.1, a.2).

The relation which we have just established holds only for the moral virtues, and thus only for the virtues won by exercise; we should have to draw up a different formula to solve the problem of the interconnections of the theological virtues. For we must not be unmindful that the theological virtues, infused by God into the soul, are the only perfect virtues, because only they direct man in view of the end of ends, whereas acquired virtues are but relative virtues, since they prepare man only for the good things that serve as steps toward this end. There is a difference in kind, then, between these two classes of virtue, and this is why we may practice the natural moral virtues without the theological and supernatural ones. Many pagans practiced the former without receiving the others, and this experience is enough to decide the question (1–2, q.65, a.2). As for the interconnection of the theological virtues, the problem is simple. The addition of these virtues to the moral virtues is a direction of our actions to a final supernatural end. Now it is the virtue of charity that attunes the will to this end, and we cannot receive charity from God without at the same time receiving faith and hope, as we cannot

THE LIFE OF VIRTUE

lose charity without at the same time losing the other two virtues. On the other hand, faith and hope enjoy in a way the rôle of virtues preparatory for charity and beget each other, so that we can receive faith without as yet possessing hope and hope without possessing charity. The proposition holds only if the case is of these virtues in an imperfect form, when hardly meriting the name of virtue; for without charity they miss their proper end and do not go through with their acts as they should. To sum up: there is no necessary connection between the realm of the moral and that of the theological virtues, but we cannot have the theological virtues without having the moral. And within each order of virtues, we can well have the rough outlines of the lower virtues without the higher virtues, but we cannot have any virtue in its perfect form, nor the highest virtues which crown the others (as moral justice or divine charity) without having all at once. It is true that we thereby suppose the existence of hierarchical degrees among the virtues, and this is the hypothesis that we must now examine.

From the point of view of the specific difference of virtue from virtue, the need for putting them into hierarchic form is at once apparent. For it is reason that gives man's acts their quality of genuine human good; but the virtue which perfects reason as to what should be done is prudence, and, therefore, prudence is superior to all the moral virtues, which share the rule of reason only through it. For the same reason justice surpasses the other virtues of will as the most rational, and courage, which is in the field of the second type of emotion, excels temperance, which is in the first (*cf.* q.66, a.1). Besides a virtue taken in itself can be more or less perfect in different individuals, or in the same individual at different times. The virtuous life has not that rigidity which the Stoics imagined, and there can be virtue without there being absolute virtue. The degrees due to habit and the point which a virtue has reached, the more or less excellent natural dispositions, the more or less penetrating clearness of reason, the more or less abundant gift of grace, should always be taken into account by the moralist who wishes to describe the complexity of virtues. Only by supposing all things equal and taking the vantage ground of absolute value, are we in a position to introduce a set hierarchy of the many virtues. Their order will be like this: the intellectual virtues absolutely excel the moral; the highest moral virtue is justice and the highest intellectual virtue is wisdom. We shall try now to establish this position.

The kind of virtue depends on the object, as was said before (q.54, a.2). This is why, in absolute terms, the noblest virtue is that which has the noblest object. And it is plain that the object of reason is nobler than the object of desire. For reason seizes something of the universal nature of things, whereas desire tends to them in their particular being. As perfecting reason, then, the intellectual virtues are essentially nobler than the moral virtues, which perfect only desire. Yet if we regard virtue from the point of view of action, then moral virtue is the nobler, because it perfects desire whose function it is to move the other powers to act, as we have seen (q.8, a.1; p. 64). For since virtue is the perfection of a capacity, the word "virtue" means the source of action, and consequently, the moral virtues merit the name of virtue better than do the intellectual, though in an unqualified sense the intellectual are the nobler (1–2, q.66, a.3).

On the strength of this principle we shall rate justice as head of the moral virtues and, by the intermediary of the two cardinal virtues of fortitude and temperance, shall subordinate to it all other virtues.

People, strictly speaking, regard as the most excellent, that virtue in which the good of reason is most resplendent; and in this sense justice excels all the other moral virtues, as nearest to reason in both its subject and object. First, in its subject, because justice resides in the will, and the will is a rational appetite, as we know from what was said (q.50, a.5). Secondly, in its object or content, because it has to do with operations which rule not only a man himself, but his conduct toward others, and this is why it is said in the *Ethics* (bk.5) that justice is the most illustrious of the virtues.

If we go on to the other moral virtues, those having to do with the emotions, the good of reason shines out the more in each, the greater the objects towards which there is a movement of desire subject to reason. Now the greatest value a man possesses is life, on which all else depends. And therefore courage, which subjects the movement of desire to reason in everything bearing on life and death, holds first place among those moral virtues that rule the emotions, though it is ranked below justice. That is why Aristotle remarks in his *Rhetoric* (1, c.9) that the noblest virtues are essentially those that are most honored, for a virtue is a power that does good, and this is why we especially honor the brave and the just, the virtue of courage being useful in war, and the virtue of justice in both peace and war. After courage, temperance gets the highest rating, because it subjects desire to reason in everything that has to do immediately with life, either for the individual alone or for him in relation to the species, that is, in matters of nourishment and sex. So these three virtues, together with prudence, are the main ones and the most worthy (1–2, q.66, a.4).

We still have to settle the place of prudence. It would evidently be first, since it is the first of the cardinal virtues, if we could class it with the three moral virtues of justice, fortitude, and temperance, over which it presides. But properly it is the keystone of the edifice of moral virtue. We must, therefore, compare it to the virtues of the intellect, and we are then constrained to subordinate it to wisdom. For if the grandeur of virtue is measured by the grandeur of its object, no virtue can surpass that which considers the supreme and first cause, God.

Since prudence looks to human things, and wisdom to the cause of causes, it cannot be said that prudence is a greater virtue than wisdom, unless, as is said in the *Ethics* (6, c.7), the greatest thing in the world is man. It must be said then,

THE LIFE OF VIRTUE

as it is said in the same passage, that prudence does not command itself, but that the contrary is rather the case; for "the spiritual man judgeth all things, and he himself is judged of no man" (1 *Cor.,* c.2). Prudence does not meddle with the very high matters which wisdom studies, but it commands affairs subordinate to wisdom and prescribes how men should act to arrive at wisdom. Hence, prudence or political virtue is here the servant of wisdom, for it leads to it and prepares the way for it, as the porter keeps the gate for the king. Besides, prudence studies the means of attaining happiness, whereas wisdom considers the very object of happiness, which is the highest knowable thing. If, then, the study which wisdom directs toward its object were perfect, there would be perfect happiness in the exercise of wisdom; but as the exercise of wisdom in this life remains imperfect as to its chief object, which is God, the act of wisdom is a kind of outline or sharing of the happiness to come; and so this act of wisdom is nearer happiness than prudence (1–2, q.66, a.5, ad 1 and 2).

Such is the ideal system of the virtues, with the order and required connection ranking them and tying them together in their perfect form. And even in the approximate realisations of them which the living of a moral life affords us, the relations as defined are respected. A virtue never grows up isolated in the human soul or dies there, but the complete system of the virtues is either enriched or impoverished, yet each virtue remains on the rung of perfection proper to it. The fingers of the hand are unequal, but they all grow at once without their proportions being changed; the virtues, though they are more or less noble, wax strong and wane, but they do not, any more than the fingers, change their proportions (q.66, a.2, c.). To say that two men are equally strong but one of them is more prudent, is to forget that the strength of the other lacks prudence and that consequently he is weaker. The moral life has the perfect cohesion of an organism whose elements are at once integral and ranked or ordered.

IV. ON FAULTS AND SINS

Virtue, as we have defined it, is essentially *ordered* towards the doing of good acts. *Disordered* acts and those which are not related to their end as they should be, are given the contrary name of *sins*. Moreover, virtue is in itself a *good* disposition, independent of the works which it does. The evil quality opposed to it goes by the name of *malice*. Lastly, virtue is above all a habit, an acquired and set disposition, and what is directly opposite to it as habit is called *vice*. Sin then is an act contrary to the act which produces virtue; malice is the quality contrary to the quality of virtue; vice is a habit contrary to the habit which builds up virtue. That is to say, the study of vices amounts to taking the direction reverse to the study of the virtues, by pointing out that vices are dispositions contrary to nature and reason, which is the peak of human nature, as virtues are dispositions conformed to the order of nature and to reason. This is why St. Thomas does not stop to give a general definition of them, but brings the whole weight of his effort to bear upon the study of the evil acts which the vices give birth to, and these evil acts are sins.

An evil human act is what we call a sin. To be human, this act must be voluntary; and to be evil, it must violate, first, the rule of reason and, in addition, the law of God (1–2, q.71, a.6). With the genus of sin thus defined, we can classify sins according to the different objects to which they are related. Some consist in the disorderly enjoyment of spiritual values (fame, praise, and so on) and are called spiritual sins. Others consist in the disorderly enjoyment of corporal and natural values, which are tangible, and these will be named carnal sins (*ibid.*, q.72, a.2). These objects themselves can, furthermore, be divided differently according as a sin of either the spiritual or the carnal type violates the law of God, or the law of society, or the law of human reason.

As we have just noted (q.71, a.6), sin is a disorderly act. Now the order which man should fulfill is threefold: first, with regard to the rule of reason, in the sense that all our actions and reactions should stand by the rule of reason; secondly, with regard to the rule of the divine law, according to which man should direct himself in every affair. If man were by nature a solitary being, these two orders would be enough; but as he is by nature a social animal, as is proved in the *Politics* (1, c.1), a third order is needed to direct man in relation to other men with whom he must live. Now of these three orders, the second contains the first and goes beyond it. For all that is contained within the order of reason is contained within the order of God himself, but certain things that are within the divine order are above reason, such as the truths of faith or the duties which are owed to God alone. So he who sins in such matters is said to sin against God, as does a heretic, or a sacrilegious or blasphemous person. Likewise, the first order takes in the third and goes beyond it, because in all our relations with our neighbor it is first required that we control ourselves according to the rule of reason, though in particular instances we follow reason in matters which concern ourselves only and not our external activity, and sin is then called a sin against ourselves, such as gluttony, lust, or extravagance. In other cases, however, sin involves relations with our neighbor, as in theft or murder. Plainly, they are not the same objects that we are concerned with in our relations to God, our neighbor, and ourselves. Hence, the distinction of sins comes from that of objects, the upshot of which is their specific divisions. So this distinction of sins is properly a distinction of the several kinds of sins; and the virtues also, of which the sins are the contraries, are put into different classes because of this same difference. For it plainly follows from what was said earlier (q.62, a.1-3) that the theological virtues direct man with regard to God, temperance and fortitude with regard to himself, and justice with regard to his neighbor (q.72, a.4).

We may now say summarily that what distinguishes the kinds of sin is their different motives, and consequently their objects, since it is the object that motivates them. From this there also result, as

FAULTS AND SINS

from their chief and primal cause, the degrees of seriousness which enter into sins.

Sins differ in seriousness in the same manner as one sickness is more serious than another. For just as health, as a value, lies in a kind of balance of the animal secretions so as to accord with the nature of the animal, so virtue, as a value, consists in a sort of harmony between the human act and the rule of reason. Now, plainly a sickness is more serious when the equilibrium required among secretions is altered by the lack of proportion of a more essential principle; thus disease is more dangerous in the human body when it arises from the heart, which is the propeller of life, or from an organ near the heart. It must, therefore, be that sin is graver when the disorder concerns a principle that has a higher place in the order of reason. Now reason orders everything in the line of human acts from the point of view of the end, and as a consequence, the higher the end that a sin looks to in human acts, the graver is that sin. On the other hand, it follows from what we have said (q.72, a.1) that the objects of acts are their ends, and this is why seriousness in sins is measured by the difference in their objects. For example, it is clear that exterior things are ordered in view of man as their end, and that man in turn is ordered toward God as his end, so that a sin which attacks the very substance of man, such as murder, is graver than a sin that deals with exterior things, such as theft, and that sin which we commit immediately against God, as unbelief, blasphemy, and the like, is yet more serious. And within the order of each of these sins, one sin will be graver than another according as its object is more or less important. As sins are specified by their objects, the difference in seriousness as measured from the nature of their object is the first and main difference, because consequent upon their species (1–2, q.73, a.3).

From this distinction all others flow more or less directly, because if the seriousness of sins increases with the dignity of the virtues which they contradict, it is because virtues, like vices, are distinct from each other in function of their objects. For the same reason, spiritual sins, if we suppose other things equal, are more serious than carnal sins. The latter imply a movement of turning towards the body, whereas the former imply a movement of turning away from God. And for the same reason, circumstances change the meaning of sins to the degree that they change the nature of the object they deal with and bring more relevant principles into our actions; as fornication becomes adultery, or theft sacrilege. The condition of the person against whom we sin, or the dignity of him who sins, also enters into these circumstances, just as do the extent and complexity of the evil caused by our unworthy actions.

If we ask in which powers of the soul sin can be, it will appear at once that as a willed act it can be in any power of the soul capable of causing such an act, directly or indirectly; therefore, first, in reason, which as a final court judges the acts we are to do, in view of the divine law (q.74, a.2 and 3); in sense desire, which should be subject to the orders of reason; in the will, which is the immediate source of our activity, of our bad acts as surely as of our good ones. It is in each of these three seats of sin that we must seek its causes, and mainly in reason, which is the principle giving our acts their proper quality of humanness. The intellectual vice which keeps the road open to sin is ignorance. We ask, then, what is ignorance?

Ignorance is not the same as nescience, because this latter means that a thing simply has no knowledge (every being that lacks a knowledge of certain things can be said to be nescient or not to know them), whereas ignorance implies a privation of knowledge, that is, a lack of knowledge of something one is naturally capable of knowing. And there are things we are bound to know, namely, those things without a knowledge of which we cannot do in a fitting way the acts we should do: thus, everyone in general is bound to know what must be believed and the universal precepts of right, and each one in particular is bound to know what has to do with his station and its duties. There are other matters that we could know, but are not generally bound to know, such as the axioms of geometry or some particular laws. It is clear, then, that whoever neglects to have or to do what he is bound to have or to do, sins by omission, and this is why ignorance of what we are bound to know is a sin of neglect. We do not, however, impute negligence to a man for not knowing what he cannot know. Such an ignorance is called "invincible," because, however we may try, we cannot overcome it, and ignorance of this kind, since it is not willed and not within the power of the will to remedy, is not a sin. It follows that invincible ignorance is no sin. As for the ignorance which we could overcome, this *is* a sin if it concerns what we should know; otherwise, it is *not* (1–2, q.76, a.2).

If we suppose that ignorance is vincible, but that it really exists, that it deals with something we are not bound to know, and that it keeps from us such a circumstance of the act that we would not do the act if we knew the circumstance, the effect of such ignorance is to make the act really involuntary. And in fact we then do one thing, though we think we do another. In such teaching as that of St. Thomas, in which the willed act is based on the rational knowledge of the possible ends that desire could embrace, the voluntary quality of acts that are done is in rigorous proportion to their rationality. As for measuring in each particular case the degree of ignorance which is mixed with the act, and the resulting degree of freedom, this is plainly a complex task, and we cannot formulate *a priori* any but general directions for it.

Just because every sin is willed, ignorance can cut down the sin just as far as it cuts down the freedom of the act; but if ignorance does not restrict freedom, it in no way lightens the sin. And certainly the ignorance which excuses outright from sin because it takes away freedom, does not merely make the sin less, but does away with it. On the other hand, an ignorance that does not cause, but simply accompanies sin neither decreases nor increases the sin. The only ignorance that can lessen sin is that which is the occasion of sin, yet this is not a blanket excuse from sin. It may be, first, that the ignorance, directly and in itself, is willed, as when one of his own will remains ignorant of something so that he can the more freely sin; such an ignorance seems to increase the voluntariness and the sin, for it is the attachment of the will to the sin that makes one willing to bear the evil of ignorance so as to have the liberty to sin. But sometimes the ignorance which causes sin is willed not directly, but indirectly and by accident; for instance, when a man is not willing to trouble himself with studies, and the result is that he is ignorant, or when he wills to take an immoderate sip of wine, and the result is that he gets drunk and lacks discretion. Such ignorance does lessen freedom and, therefore, the sin; for when a man does not know that a thing is a sin, we may not say that his will directly and of itself commits the sin, but only as a by-product, and there is then less contempt and, as a consequence, less sin (1–2, q.76, a.4).

Let us now proceed to the causes of sin in sense desire. One recalls, of course, that the part of the soul that perceives sense goods by the aid of the body and at the reckoning of the body is the proper place of the feelings. And feeling can exercise an indirect influence, if not a direct one, on the will; for all the powers of the soul run their roots into the unity of its substance, in such a way that when one of the emotions is wholly engaged in an act, the others are obliged to slacken theirs, or at least it makes no effort to help them (q.77, a.1). We may easily prove this by examining the influence which feeling can have on the knowledge possessed by reason.

The opinion of Socrates, as Aristotle reports it in the seventh book of the *Ethics* (c.2), was that knowledge can never be overcome by the emotions; whence he concluded that all virtue is knowledge and all sin is ignorance. There is a measure of reason in this view, for the will looks always toward good, at least the apparent good, and never does the will choose evil, unless that which is not good somehow appears as good; and therefore, the will never tends toward evil, if there be no ignorance or error on its part. Whence it is written in Proverbs (c.14): "They err that work evil." Yet it is a fact of experience that many act in a way contrary to what they know, and we can confirm the point on divine authority. We have for example the word of St. Luke (c.12): "And that servant who knew the will of his lord, and prepared not himself, and did not according to his will, shall be beaten with many stripes"; or the word of St. James (c.4): "To him therefore who knoweth to do good, and doth it not, to him it is sin." And so Socrates had a clear-cut reason for his opinion.

It is of importance to make a distinction here, as Aristotle teaches in the *Ethics* (bk.7, c.3). For as man is directed to right action by a twofold knowledge—universal and particular—the lack of either is enough, as was said (q.76, a.1), to put a stop to correctness of both will and action. It may happen that a person has a general knowledge of some matter, for instance, that no one is to commit any act of fornication, but does not know that this act in particular, which is fornication, is not to be done; and this is enough for his will not to follow the universal knowledge of reason on the point. We should remember, too, that there is nothing to hinder one's having correct knowledge of a particular case, and not merely of a general principle, and still not thinking about it in fact,

FAULTS AND SINS 187

and it seems not difficult for a man to do the opposite of that which he knows, but to which he gives no actual thought. And that a man should not consider in particular what he habitually knows, occurs sometimes from mere lack of attention, as when a man who knows geometry does not take time to reflect on the conclusions of geometry, if he has to think of them all at once and impromptu. And if sometimes he does not reflect on the knowledge which he has, it is because of some hindrance, as, for example, an exterior occupation or some bodily ailment.

It is precisely for this reason that he who is in an emotional state does not reflect specifically on what he knows in a general way, for the emotion interferes with his thought. Emotion so hinders in three ways: first, by a kind of distraction, as we have just explained (q.77, a.1) ; secondly, by a contradiction, because emotion generally inclines to the contrary of what in a broad way we know is to be done; and thirdly, by a kind of physical perturbation, in consequence of which reason is as it were bound and kept from freely doing its work. It is in this last way that sleep or drunkenness, by the bodily change which they induce, impede the use of reason. And it is plain that, in certain instances, the same effect follows from the emotions, because when these are most intense a person loses all control of reason and very many, when too much in love, are led to do witless things. This is the way that emotion draws reason to judge, in a particular case, against the general knowledge it has of what should be done (1–2, q.77, a.2).

Emotion in such instance plays the part of a kind of infirmity. For though, in a healthy soul that has a normal balance, all the powers ought to be subject to the guidance of reason, in a soul whose emotions are not controlled, it is reason that is dependent on sense desire. Self-love, by which each of us wills his own good, is disorderly; it wills sense values and temporal values, and it carries on as if the higher values existed for the sake of the lower. It is not that self-love as such is bad, since it is a fitting thing and it is natural that a person should love himself; but he must love himself with an orderly love and will the good that is becoming to him. But all love of self that departs from order implies the preference of man to God, and this is the very definition of sin. A disordered love of self is thus at the bottom of all sin. Yet if it is the emotions that disorder love, and if the emotions are a disease, we may believe that they decrease the seriousness of sin and excuse it. We have still to make an inquiry on this point.

The one cause that can wholly excuse from sin an act that is evil in its nature, is whatever makes it perfectly involuntary. If there is any emotion that makes the act following it quite involuntary, that emotion is an excuse from the sin; otherwise, not a total excuse. On this subject, two points are to be considered. First, an act may be voluntary either in itself, as when the will goes directly for the object, or by reason of its cause, when the will goes for the cause, but not for the effect, as is evident in the instance of a man who gets drunk and to whom, in consequence, we impute as voluntary all that he does in the drunken state. Secondly, we should draw a line between what is directly voluntary and what is but indirectly so. That upon which the will moves

FAULTS AND SINS

is directly voluntary; and that is indirectly so which the will could but does not prevent. Therefore, we must keep several different cases distinct. Sometimes an emotion is so strong that it fully overbears the use of reason, as it plainly does with those whom love or anger makes delirious; and in such case, if this emotion was voluntary from the beginning, the act is imputed as sin, being voluntary in its cause, as we just noted in the example of the drunkard; if, however, its cause was not voluntary, but natural, as when sickness or some such cause throws us into so strong a feeling as quite to overturn the use of reason, the act becomes involuntary, and is altogether excused from sin. But in certain instances the emotion is not such as totally to break off the use of reason, and then reason can thrust the emotion aside by giving itself to other thoughts, or prevent it from realizing its effects, since the members go to work only with the consent of reason, as we remarked some time ago (q.17, a.9). Accordingly, emotions of this kind do not wholly excuse from sin (1-2, q.77, a.7).

The third and last interior seat where there resides a cause of sin is the will. Just as the intellectual cause of sin *par excellence* is *ignorance,* and as its great sense cause is *emotion,* so its supreme voluntary cause is given the name *malice,* or, to use the complete expression of St. Thomas, *certain malice.* The meaning of this is as follows. To sin by certain malice is not to commit evil through ignorance nor under the urge of violent passion, but by the deliberate will to choose evil instead of good. That this disorder occur, it is necessary that a permanent vicious disposition, otherwise called a habit, incline the will toward the evil act, as the habits which are virtues incline it toward well-doing. Each time, then, that a habit, or a permanent and acquired disposition, is the cause of the evil act which the will chooses, we say that the sin is committed with a malice certain of its deed and fully responsible for its choice. Yet the reverse is not true. While every evil act chosen by a vicious disposition is of certain malice, there are some acts of certain malice that are not born of a vice. We can do some acts conformed to virtue without being virtuous, and we can equally commit some evil acts without falling into the vice to which they correspond, for virtues and vices are habits, whereas an isolated act is not a habit. It will thus be necessary to work out, as we proceed to do, a list of the interior causes of sin.

The will associates differently with good than it does with evil. Because of its very nature, this power of the soul is inclined to the good of reason, as to its own object, and that is why we say that every sin is against nature. In order that the will be inclined to evil in its choice, therefore, something more is needed. For sometimes the evil occurs because of a defect of reason, as when a man sins through ignorance, and sometimes through an onset of sense desire, as when he sins through feeling. In neither of these cases, however, does one sin with certain malice. For there is sin of certain malice only when it is the will itself that moves its very self to the evil. And this can be done in either of two ways.

The first is this. A man has, let us say, a disposition that is ruined and inclined towards evil, so much so that in his disposition some evil is in a sense suited to him and is like himself; the result is that the will tends to this evil as towards a good, because of itself each thing tends toward what is fitting and proper for it. Now, depraved dispositions of this kind are either habits acquired by a custom that turns into nature, or they are diseased dispositions on the part of the body, as those persons have who feel a natural inclination towards certain sins because of a natural weakness of the body. The second way is this. The will of itself tends toward some evil because that which would say nay to the will is removed. Suppose, for example, that a man keeps from sinning, not because sin displeases him, but because he hopes for eternal life or fears hell-fire, so that if the hope were deadened by despair, or the fear by presumption, he would sin without check and with certain malice. It is plain, then, that the sin which is committed with certain malice always presupposes a certain disorder in a man, but that this disorder is not always a vice, so that it is not needful that every one who sins with certain malice sin by reason of a vice. (1-2, q.78, a.3).

Sin that is committed with certain malice is in every way the gravest of sins. For, first of all, sin lies chiefly in the will, and never is the will more fully responsible for its act than when of itself it commits the act, as is here the case, instead of committing it through ignorance of the intellect or some feeling of the senses. Besides, feeling passes and ignorance is easily corrected, but vice is a disposition that gives way but slowly; it is even a quality which is in a sense permanent. Vice is to emotion what a chronic disease is to the momentary paroxysm of a fever which seizes the sick man only at intervals. Let us add in particular, also, that the vicious man is badly disposed with regard to the very purpose of his moral acts, whereas the emotional man perhaps is turned away from his good resolve only for the moment while the emotion lasts. The principle of morality is undermined in the first, but left standing in the second, the one giving up, and the other only interrupting, his excellent project (*ibid.*, a.4).

With the study of vice, and of the consequent sin, we have completed our study of the inner principles which preside over the doing of our good and bad acts; and now, in line with the scheme we laid down as a preamble, we proceed to study the several moral laws, that is to say, the exterior principles by which human acts are to be controlled.

Chapter VI

LAW ON THE HUMAN LEVEL

The theologian knows an exterior source of the evil acts of man: it is the devil, whose solicitation leads us into sin. He knows just as well an exterior source of good acts: it is God, whose grace is a sufficient help against temptation and a remedy for the troubles of a nature weakened by sin. The philosopher also knows an exterior source of good actions, and his reflection can understand this principle, though here as elsewhere reason and nature in the long run find within themselves an inner need of going beyond themselves. This principle or source is law, which regulates and obligates our activity from the outside. This outer character of law, however, brings no heteronomy into the moral life, for law is of precisely the same order as reason, the inner principle from which human activity gets its human and, therefore, moral character.

Law is a rule or measure of action, and it brings man to act or keeps him from acting. The word *law* is from *ligare*, to bind, because it obliges one to act (*lex, ligare, obligare*). Now the guide and standard for human activity is reason, and this is the first principle of man's action, as follows from what was said earlier (q.66, a.1). For it is reason that arranges things for an end, and, in Aristotle's view (*Ethics,* 7, c.8), the end is the chief director in what is to be done: but in any class or group whatever the main or chief thing is the measure and standard in that group: as, for instance, unity in the matter of numbers and the first motion in the matter of physical movement. So law is a function of reason (1-2, q.90, a.1).

In what sense does law belong to reason? Evidently, it belongs to practical reason, and within practical reason to the end of ends, which is the one principle capable of binding man's will in each individual act. And the end of ends, as we saw (p. 37), is vital welfare or happiness, and thus law is a rule that obliges us in view of conducting us to happiness. It is not always the same as the specific reason whose practical work is to regulate our actions for our welfare, for reason directs a person's acts for his own welfare; but this individual lives in society and is a member of the body politic, and, as is always the case with groups, he is directed in view of the whole of which he is a part. This or that man's reason, though qualified to guide his actions for his welfare, is not, therefore, qualified to shape them for the good of the community to which he belongs, and to subordinate them to it. Here is the basis of the *exteriority,* so far as the individual is concerned, of the principle which obliges his activity. Law, then, will express the demands of reason ordering the individual's life in view of the common good of his group and speaking from the outside in the name of that group.

In its first and main sense law means an arrangement for the common good. But to manage things for the common good is the work either of the whole group or of its representative. So, to pass a law is the business either of the group or of some public person who has charge of the group, since to guide to a goal is always the right of him of whom it is the proper goal (1–2, q.90, a.3).

Law may become an inner principle of our actions, therefore, and it should do so, but it is within us only as a sharing of a principle promulgated from the outside. This is why no private person can make a law or constrain us, but can only caution, urge, or at the most enjoin. The father commands in his household, but he does not make the law. "For just as the individual is one of the family, so the family is a member of the city or state, which is the rounded community, and this is why, just as the good of one man is not the end of ends, so the good of each family is for the good of the whole settlement, which is a perfect group; he who rules a family, therefore, can give precepts and orders, but they have not the force of law" (*ibid.*, ad 3). Summing up all these marks of law, we obtain the following definition: *Law is an ordinance of reason promulgated for the common good by one who has charge of the community.*

We shall go at once to the sources. What is the biggest community? The universe. And who governs it? God. What, then, will be the original and broadest of all laws? The *eternal law* of God.

Law is simply a dictate of practical reason given by the ruler of an independent community. This makes it plain that if, as was shown (1, q.22, a.1 and 2), the world is ruled by divine providence, the entire universe is governed by divine reason. And so the very basis of the government of things, resident in God as in the king of the universe, has the nature of law. And as the divine reason is an eternal concept, and not one of time, as Proverbs says (c.8), so a law of this kind should be called eternal (1–2, a.91, a.1; *cf. C.G.,* 3, c.115).

The eternal law is thus simply the eternal reason of God, seen as law-giver for all works, acts, and movements done by created things, whatever these be (q.93, a.1), and, in consequence, it is the primal source of all other laws.

As we have seen, law supposes a mind directing activities to their end. Now in all actions it is required that the power of a secondary mover be got from the power of the first mover, for the secondary agent does nothing except as started by the first agent. So in governors. The nature or plan of government is got from the first ruler and given to others. Thus the outline of what is to be done in the state is passed on, at the king's word, to the lower officials. In art we have a like procedure; the design, which is the architect's, is carried out by craftsmen and manual laborers. Since the eternal law is the supreme ruler's plan of government, all plans of

LAW ON THE HUMAN LEVEL

government done by lower rulers must be derived from the eternal law. These governmental plans are laws additional to the eternal; thus all laws, so far as they have a part with right reason, are based on the eternal law. That is why Augustine says (*De Lib. Arb.,* c.6) that nothing in the laws of time is just or legitimate that men do not work out for themselves from the eternal law (1-2, q.93, a.3).

If we try now to define the field in which this law applies, we shall see that it takes in all that is not eternal and uncreated like itself, in a word, all that is neither itself nor God. The totality of creation, therefore, of both free and determined things, is subject to the eternal law, but things that have not intellectual knowledge are not subject in the same way as those that have reason. The former are subject to the divine law written into the structure of their being, but they do not recognize it (*ibid.,* a.5). Man, on the contrary, is subject not merely to the law of God, but to the prescriptions of this law, that is, to the knowledge which he has of it. Hence, man's subjection to this law is twofold: first, as a natural being he is subject to the overruling of providence as is all creation; then, as a being with mind and capable of sharing in an interior notion of this exterior divine law which rules him. The perfectly good man is he who is a perfect subject of the divine law and always acts in accordance with it; and men are evil or bad just so far as, knowing the divine law and keeping it poorly, they tend to avoid it. Their attempts make only a show of success, however, for what the wicked man does not observe of the eternal law, he must make compensation for in the form of chastisement, so that his account is quite strictly squared in the end (*ibid.*, a.6). We shall see in what way the other laws derive from this primary law, and first what is this eternal law.

A law can be a rule and measure in either of two senses: first, as in the ruler and measurer; again, in the ruled and measured; because so far as anything has a share in a rule or measure, so far it is ruled and measured. Since all things that are subject to divine providence are regulated and guided by the eternal law, as is evident from the preceding article, it is plain that all things have some part with the eternal law, in so far, that is, as they have from its impress an inclination to their specific activity and their specific ends. Now the rational creature, as well as others, is subject to divine providence, but in a more excellent way: it becomes itself a partaker and dispenser (*particeps et providens*) of providence; it looks out for the welfare of itself and others; the eternal reason, through which it has a natural inclination to its due activity and its goal, is shared in it. Such sharing of the eternal law by the rational creature is called the *natural law*. Hence when the Psalmist, having said (Ps.4): "Offer up the sacrifice of justice," adds, as if speaking to those who want to know what are the works of justice: "many say: Who showeth us good things?" and he answers: "The light of thy countenance, O Lord, is signed upon us." What we may call the light of natural reason, by which we discern what is good and what evil, a function of the natural law, is simply the imprint of the divine light in us. It follows that the natural law is a sharing of the eternal law in a rational creature (1–2, q.91, a.2).

Our business now is to study the content of this law. We can safely infer it from the rôle which the natural law plays as chief regulator of our activity. As all knowledge derives from first principles intuitively known to us, so all desire of the means derives, directly or not, from our inborn desire of the end of ends; and since it is the natural law that directs us towards the goal of the universe, it is from this law that the original direction of all our acts comes (*ibid.,* ad 2). But the bearing of specific means on the end of ends is far from being simple and clear, for the particular reason that each power of the soul will turn towards that end according to the individual light in which it sees it, and so the universal natural law which directs us towards God is broken up or diversified, from our point of view, into several subordinate natural laws.

In an absolute sense, being is the first thing the mind knows. Similarly, good is the first thing that comes within the range of the practical reason, whose end is action. In fact, every agent acts for an end which has the nature of good. The first principle of practical reason is that it is founded on the good; it may be defined: The good is what all desire. This, then, is the first precept of the law: Good is to be pursued and done, evil is to be avoided; and on this all other precepts of the natural law are based, namely, that all that is to be done or avoided is in the realm of the prescriptions of the natural law, and the practical reason naturally knows them as human values (or disvalues). But because value or the good has the nature of an end, and evil or disvalue the contrary nature, all those things to which man has a natural inclination are seen in the natural light of reason as good and to be sought and worked out, and their opposites are seen as evil and to be avoided. According to the order of natural inclinations, therefore, is the order of precepts of the natural law. Man has, *first,* an inclination to good or value in line with the nature which he has in common with all substances; that is, every substance strives for self-preservation according to its kind; and in keeping with this inclination those things that conserve human life are in the field of the natural law. *Secondly,* man has a natural urge to some more special values, in which urge he is one with other animals; and on this score we say that those things are of the natural law which nature teaches to all animals: such as the union of male and female, the training of the offspring, and so on. *Thirdly,* man tends to a good or value in keeping with his rational nature, which good is distinctively his own; for instance, he has an inborn impulse to know the truth about God and to live in society; and so the several matters needed to carry out these most human tendencies belong to the natural law: namely, that man avoid ignorance, that he take care not to offend others with whom he must live, and so of whatever is pertinent (1–2, q.94, a.2).

While manifold in its specific determinations, the law of nature is one with the oneness of the primary precept, which we have said contains all others, and it is one also from the fact that it is the same for all

LAW ON THE HUMAN LEVEL

This is why natural rights are the same for all peoples. One may, of course, ask how it is that usages and customs are so different in different countries, and how it is that men with the same human nature draw from the same principles of the natural law conclusions that are so basically different. It is because of the difference between the sciences and speculative reason, which relate to law as universal and necessary, and the moral and practical reason which relate to law as particular and contingent. The principles of the natural law are the same in all countries and among all peoples, and the most general deductions from them are usually the same among all. But the farther we come down toward more and more specific prescriptions, the more the chances of error in the deduction increase; interest and sentiment enter in, evil dispositions interfere with thought, so much so that, though a man sets out reasoning from principles of natural law, he comes to will acts that contradict it (*ibid.*, a.4). This is why the natural law, which is one for all men, seems manifold and discordant among different individuals. It is unchangeable in itself, and its principles cannot be torn from the heart of man, but it appears variable and is sometimes obfuscated by error in its application to details.

Besides the divine law which embraces all laws, and the natural law which is its immediate application to a group of beings, we have *human law,* which undertakes to cut down the interval between the universal principles of nature and the endless multiplicity of specific instances (1–2, q.91, a.3). The special laws enacted on the authority of kings or the groups whom they represent do not add anything to the content of the natural law; they only define that content and make it more precise, so that those who do not know how to observe it or are unwilling to do so, should find worked out and imposed for their acceptance a deduction which draws from the universal principles of the law of nature the particular conclusions required by the social life. St. Thomas well notes what we may call this pedagogic character of the positive law and remarks that it is a necessary educator because of the inadequate morality of men who are still young and because of the danger that may come to the social peace of persons ill disciplined. The well trained and upright man has no need of the law, as he is already in accord with it, but it is indispensable for the welfare of the social body taken as a whole, for it is the law that brings to reason those whose own reason is not a guide to them.

There is in man a natural aptitude for virtue, but he must have some discipline to reach the perfection of virtue. Indeed, we see as much in the fact that a man must work to obtain the necessities, food, for instance, and clothing; he has from nature a beginning of what he needs, that is, a mind and hands, but not the complete equipment, as have the other animals to which nature has given sufficient covering and food. Now for such discipline and work a man is not readily sufficient to himself, because the perfection of his virtue mainly consists in keeping himself away from unwarranted pleasures, to which men are strongly prone, and especially the young, with whom discipline is more effective. And so it is needful that men get from others this discipline through which they advance in virtue. As for those youths who are ready for excellent living because of a good natural disposition or because of custom or a divine gift, a father's care and advice are enough. But because there are some heedless young fellows who are ready for wrong-doing and cannot easily be moved by words, it is necessary that they be protected from evil by force or fear, so that they may at least cease cutting up and let others live in peace, and that in this way they may by custom come to do voluntarily what at first they did through fear, and thus become virtuous. Now, a discipline of this kind that checks through fear of the penalty is a discipline of law, and laws must be made for the sake of human peace and excellent living; because, in Aristotle's comparison (*Politics,* 1, c.2), as man, when he is perfect in virtue, is the best of the animals, so, when he breaks with law and justice, he is the worst of them, because he is armed with reason, as the other animals are not, to fight against concupiscence and ferocity (1–2, q.95, a.1).

The other qualities which we may allow to human law come from this essential character. First, human laws look in principle to general situations and not to specific instances; for the means should be proportioned to the end, and as the end which human laws have in view is the common welfare, that is, the good of the group made up of many persons engaged in different activities at different times, it is needful that laws be made for the whole duration of the community and the mass of citizens composing it (*ibid.*, q.96, a.1). Civil laws then do not condemn absolutely all vices; not, of course, that they approve any vice, but human law is promulgated in view of civil order and is interested only in what immediately concerns that order, or at any rate does not rigorously proscribe vices unless they directly attack that order. Also, because they are meant to apply to the whole civil body, they should be adapted to the average of the citizens in that body, and not to some tiny little minority of an élite.

As Isidore of Seville says in his *Etymologies* (bk. 5, c.21), a law should be possible, from the point of view both of nature and of the custom of the country. Now a faculty or power of action proceeds from an inner habit or disposition, the proof of which is that the same thing cannot be done by him who has not a habit of virtue and him who has, just as the same thing is not possible to a boy and to a grown man. So the same law is not to be passed for children as for adults, because many things are allowed in children that are punished, or at any rate found fault with, by law in grown persons; and a good deal is let go in imperfect men that is not borne with in the most virtuous. Human law, of course, is made for the generality of men, the most of whom are not of consummate virtue, and therefore, it does not prohibit all vices, from which the excellent keep themselves in any case, but only the worse vices, which it is possible for the majority of people to avoid, and mainly those that are a nuisance to others, for if these were let go, human society could not be kept together: human law forbids, for instance, murder, theft, and so on (1-2, q.96, a.2).

We have defined human laws and their nature, but have still to consider two serious problems: How far do these laws obligate a person's conscience? and: In what cases and on what grounds is it allowable to change the laws of the State or to pass over certain details of them? We shall begin by examining the first question, and shall see that three main conclusions force themselves on our minds: any law, so far as it is just, binds conscience; the law is imposed on all; but it is less the letter than the spirit of the law that is imposed on us.

Some of the laws that men make are just and some are not. As for just laws, they have a binding force in conscience from the eternal law whence they derive, as Proverbs (c.8) says: "By me kings reign, and lawgivers decree just things." Laws are regarded as just, first, *from the end,* that is when they are directed to the common good; secondly, *from their author,* that is when the law that is passed does not exceed the authority of the legislator; third, *from the form,* that is when a proportionate and equitable burden is imposed on subjects for the general good. For since the individual man is one of a group, a man's existence and whatever he has are of the group, as the existence of the part depends on the whole. For this reason nature inflicts injury on the part to save the whole. So laws that distribute burdens equitably are just and bind in conscience.

Unjust laws are of two kinds. First, they may oppose human welfare by contradicting the requirements just mentioned: from the point of view of the *end,* if any ruler, say, should pass laws imposing burdens on the people and making rather for his own vanity or aggrandizement than for the public good; or of the *authority,* if a man legislates clearly beyond the power given him; or of the *form,* if burdens, though for the common good, are inequitably imposed. These are not laws, but acts of violence or tyranny; as Augustine says (*De Lib. Arb.,* 1, c.5), an unjust law is no law. We conclude that such laws do not oblige anyone's conscience, unless perhaps to avoid scandal or rioting, in which case a man had better yield his own right, as St. Matthew says (c.5): "If anyone force thee one mile, go with him other two, and if a man take away thy coat, give him thy cloak also." Secondly, laws may be unjust as opposed to religious values, as the laws of tyrants prescribing idolatry or any such thing against divine law. No one may observe such laws, because, as we read (Acts, 5, 29), "we ought to obey God rather than men" (1–2, q.96, a.4).

As for the second conclusion, that law obliges all, a difficulty may claim our attention. The law is made for the good of the many and ought to apply to each person of the many with three possible exceptions that are really only apparent. A man is bound to obey only the law of his country, for the law of a group of which he is not a member is not his law. An inferior officer cannot force on us a law from which a superior dispenses us, for the former acts lawfully only on a mandate from the latter. Lastly and particularly, the law is for all, but it *compels* only the wicked. In this connection we remark: "Virtuous and just men are not under the law, but only wicked men, for anything forced and constrained is contrary to the will, but the will of good men is in agreement with the law, and the will of bad men is out of agreement with it; so not the good but only the evil are under the law" (*ibid.*, a.5). As for the third point, about interpreting the letter of the law, this matter should be handled in the same way and related to the fundamental notion of legality. Every law is enacted for the general good of the people who support it, and it is its usefulness that measures its lawfulness.

It sometimes happens that an observance serves the good of all in a majority of cases, but that in some instances it is terribly burdensome. Because the legislator cannot foresee every individual case, he passes the law in line with what ordinarily happens and keeps in mind the service of the public; and if it so happens that the observance of the law is injurious to the common weal, the law is not to be observed. Take the example of a besieged town; a law is passed that the gates should remain closed, and this is useful and for the general good in most instances; but there might be a case in which the enemy would harass the citizens keeping the town, and it would be calamitous for the town if the gates were not opened. In such a fix the gates should be thrown open, contrary to the letter of the law, but to protect the general good, which is the purpose of the lawgiver. It is to be kept in mind, however, that if the literal observance of the law has not an element of immediate danger, which should at once be remedied, it is not the business of everyone and anybody to interpret what is useful and what not useful for the group; rather, it is the function of the rulers, who have authority to dispense from the law in such cases. It is when peril suddenly arises and allows no delay for recourse to a higher officer, that the necessity itself carries the dispensation with it, for necessity knows no law (1-2, q.96, a.6).

The reader certainly perceives at this point how to settle the second problem that had arisen: May we ever change a law? Made for the good of all, laws should be fitted to the needs of those whom they govern, they should be perfected and keep step with the changing needs of the men who uphold them.

Human law is a dictate of reason to direct human action. There are two reasons why such a law may justly be changed: one on the part of reason, the other on the part of the men whose action the law regulates. As for the first, because it seems natural for human reason to advance step by step toward perfection, we see in the speculative sciences that those who were the first to philosophize left us imperfect works which their successors elaborated with great perfection; and it is the same in the life of action. Those who first tried to discover what is useful for the generality of men were unable to study out the whole problem at once by themselves, and left institutions in part achieved and full of defects; but those who came after them did the work over and left institutions that are less inadequate from the point of view of human welfare. Secondly, on the part of the men whose activities the law regulates, a law may justly be changed because of changed human conditions, for in different circumstances different conditions are expedient for the people. Augustine offers this example (*De Lib. Arb.*, I, c.4): Suppose a people is well ruled, is not frivolous, and is very careful to protect the general good: it is quite right that the law should allow such a people to elect their own officers and in that way carry on their civil affairs; but if the same people become depraved and sell their votes and turn the government over to villainous fellows and rascals, it is just to take away from the people the power of giving honors, and to leave it to the discretion of a few good men (1-2, q.97, a.1).

From the fact that the law should be changed when there is a chance to better it, does it follow that it should be changed as soon as people see the possibility of bettering it? In a sense, yes; otherwise we should be contradicting the principle which we meant to apply. But the notion of betterment ought not to be understood of the law in the abstract and in itself, but of the situation of the men subject to it. Changes in the law ought to have as a result not the betterment of the law, but the betterment of the real situation of the people. In most such cases an attitude wisely conservative is to be recommended.

As we said a minute ago, human law is correctly changed when the change provides for the public welfare. Change of law, however, precisely as change, is a kind of hindrance to the common weal. This is because custom is a great help to the observance of law. This is so true that what is done contrary to the common custom, though it is of small consequence, seems a serious matter. When a law is changed, the constraining force of the law, so far as custom is undermined, is cut down, and for that reason human laws should never be changed unless human welfare gets back in some other direction as much as it loses in this. And this may happen, either because some great and very plain advantage comes from the new statute, or because it is exceptionally necessary, or because the accustomed law contains a manifest inequity, or its observance is exceedingly mischievous. So the jurist Ulpian declares (*De Constit. Princ.,* l, 1) that, in making new laws, there must be an evident gain for giving up the legislation that for a long time has seemed just (1–2, q.97, a.2).

This practical conservatism of St. Thomas, based on the dictates of justice, is a kind of presage of analogous formulas and conclusions found in Montaigne and afterwards in Pascal. But the inspiration animating it is very different in the intellectualism of Thomism and in the scepticism of the *Essais*. If custom is respectable and beneficent in the eyes of St. Thomas, it is not merely as custom, it is only so far as it concretizes and condenses a sort of practical judgment of reason which, though not cast into a worded formula, teaches by the reiterated acts of many people the actual agreement of those acts with what the people take to be good. That is also why custom can go so far as to be the basis of new laws. The intellect that sets up laws does not show itself simply in words, but also in deeds; this is so true that the inner movement of the will and the concept of reason may be expressed in many exterior and repeated acts of many men witnessing to the fact that an old law no longer answers to the needs of the actual situation, but has become useless and must be reformed (a.3, c. and ad 2). Thus the people have the right to take their own customs as law, as in the instance of a free people who enjoy the legislative power; and farther, the repeated acts done by the subjects of a ruler show by the fact of their repetition a character that is not accidental and is therefore reasonable and, when accepted in fact by the ruler, they take on the force of law.

With the definition of human law, general morals rounds out the description of the most immediate exterior principle of moral acts which the thought of the philosopher can reach. If it is not given to reason to go farther by itself, it may at least mark off the place that transcends it and remember that the exigency of going farther is written within its own nature (see p. 163 and p. 35). Reason is a faculty capable of the infinite and it requires a transcendent and infinite end for us: "because man is meant for eternal happiness, an end out of proportion to his natural human powers, it is necessary that, besides the natural and the human law, he be directed to that goal by a law divinely given" (q.91, a.4). Such precisely is the divine law. It comes to the aid of reason and frees it from the uncertainties which it suffers even in the realm of the natural law;

it penetrates to the inside of consciences to direct their interior, which human law does not reach, and it guides man in view of his supernatural goal, which is God.

Part Second

THE MORAL LIFE IN PRACTICE

Up to this point we have studied in a general way the virtues, the vices, and everything that is comprised in the domain of morals. But we must now turn back and consider them again, this time in a particular way. The reason is that, so long as they remain general, ethical studies have not their full utility, since they need in the end to prescribe what men are to do, and because human actions are in the domain of the particular.

If we look at them one by one, ethical problems are of two kinds: first, those we shall examine at once (ch. 1–5) have to do with the study of such or such particular virtue or that vice which is contrary to it; the others, which we shall investigate in a later place (ch. 6) are concerned with the various states, that is, the situations in which men in fact are and the kinds of life they can lead.

Chapter VII

LOVE OF OUR NEIGHBOR

If we attempt to classify the virtues which flow from general ethics, we see that they range themselves under seven chief ones: three of which are theological—faith, hope, and charity; and four are cardinal—prudence, justice, fortitude, and temperance. The study of these theological virtues, supernaturally infused into us by God in view of ends which also are supernatural, is not within the philosopher's field as such; but as their name indicates, they belong to the theologian. This is not to say, however, that life can disregard them, or that the moralist can lawfully ignore them; for though moral science is formally distinct from theology, the man who in the concrete leads an individual moral life will lead it differently according as he does or does not subordinate it to a supernatural life. Thus in a scientific architectonic order which arranges all in line with Christian wisdom, theology includes morality, but morality does not therefore include theology. From this it follows that a complete exposition of morals, properly speaking, does not require a study of the theological virtues, and yet the theological virtues are the necessary condition of a complete moral life. We think it needful then to point out first, the place held by this keystone of the moral life, and especially of that one virtue that keeps in place all the others, namely, charity.

Charity is in its essence a "love of friendship," that is to say, in line with the distinction we made above (see p. 106), a love by which we wish good to another. To wish good itself is a "love of concupiscence," and no one would pretend to entertain friendship for the good things of which he experiences a desire; one can love wine or horses, but he cannot have them for friends. If, then, we are to have friendship, it is toward the very person to whom we wish this good that our sentiment should go: "besides, there must be a love on both sides, for the friend is a friend to his friend; such a benevolence can never in fact be without a certain communication, and as there exists between man and God a communication by which He gives us His happiness, this communication must become the basis of a certain friendship." The precise love on which this communication rests is charity, and it plainly follows that charity is a kind of friendship between man and God (2-2, q.23, a.1). And it is for this reason that charity seems to us the most sublime of all the virtues. "Human acts are regarded as good in the measure in which they are guided by the standard which they should meet; and since human virtue is the principle of good acts, it necessarily follows that it consists in coming up to the standard of human acts.

Now the rule of human acts is twofold, as we have seen earlier (p. 84): human reason and God. But it is God who is the primal standard, since human reason itself ought to be guided by that model; and since it is the proper nature of the theological virtues, of which God Himself is the object, to come up to this original standard, they excel the moral and intellectual virtues, the nature of which consists in measuring up simply to human reason. For the same reason, that one among the theological virtues themselves should be chief which most directly reaches God. And that which exists of itself is always more sublime than that which exists through some other, and from this point of view faith and hope reach up to God only in so far as we receive from Him knowledge of the true or possession of the good, whereas charity attains God himself as the end in which we rest, and not as that through which we attain something else. This is why charity surpasses faith and hope, and, as a consequence, all the other virtues, precisely as prudence, which in itself measures up to reason, excels all the other moral virtues, which come up to the standard of reason only in so far as it allows them to determine the just means in actions and in the human emotions (2–2, q.23, a.6).

If this is so, for all the greater reason we have in this supreme virtue the source of all the acts of charity that a man can perform. This reciprocal friendship of man and God cannot in reality be limited to the divine being taken in itself; it extends necessarily to everything that comes from the divine being and in some way shares from Him that which it is. To grasp the need of such a conclusion it is enough to recall the relation which binds us always to the good of those whom we love. When a man is our friend, with the same friendship that unites us to him we love his children, his admirers, and everything that belongs to him on any title. And farther, we may love our friend with an affection so deep that we come to love his for the sake of him, even though they offend us and hate us (*ibid.*, a.1, ad 2). Thus, the charity we experience toward God, thanks to the gift of God Himself, spontaneously becomes the spring of our love for men, inasmuch as they derive from God and belong to Him (*ibid.*, q.25, a.1). Hence the hierarchy of our acts of love is evident to us, at least in its basic principle. There will be excluded from our love, first, all creatures not capable of engaging with us or with God in this friendship on which charity rests. And these, to be precise, are creatures devoid of reason. How indeed would we wish their good, since they are not rational and free and as a consequence, not capable of using our love? Besides, how would there be between them and us that interrelationship on which friendship depends, since they are without the reason through which we could have part with them? And, as a last word, how would charity, itself based on the sharing of an eternal beatitude, unite us to beings unqualified for an eternal beatitude? We could only love irrational creatures, then, with a friendship or charity which is figurative and takes them in by indirection, that is to say, in so far as we desire to conserve them for God's honor or man's good, but not directly and for themselves (2–2, q.25, a.3). But once you grant this principle of exclusion, we may say that the love of man for God naturally takes in everything that can associate with him and share in his happiness.

How shall we pass from this universal principle to the hierarchy of the acts of charity which it is permissible to build up? Plainly by a classification of these acts according to the more or less immediate kind of relation which binds them to the first charity whence they come. There is, therefore, an order in charity, and this order is based on the relation of the love with which we love each being to the first source of this love, which is God (2–2, q.26, a.1). Let us apply this rule to the most outstanding cases on which the moral experience invites us to reflect, and first to the relation between the love we owe to God and that which we owe to our neighbor.

Every friendship has to do, in the first place, with the object in which the good upon the sharing of which it is founded chiefly resides. Now we just saw that the primary source of all charity is happiness, because it is in it that those who love each other have inter-communings; and since it is in God that happiness directly dwells, evidently it is God that we must love chiefly and directly with a love of charity. Hence, God is the object *par excellence* of charity, because He is happiness itself, whereas the love we have for our neighbor comes from a derived charity so far forth as he, like ourselves, shares in this happiness which is God (q.26, a.2). For the same reason every man ought to love God more than himself (a.3) and, within himself, he should love his soul more than his body, because he loves his body by reason of the happiness which it shares in only an indirect way. This love of the body should, moreover, express itself in a constant endeavor to purge the body of all contamination and to minister in the soul's work, which is the attainment of complete joy in God (2–2, q.25, a.5). A question which it takes more penetration to answer is, whether man ought to love his neighbor more than himself. As a matter of fact, God has spoken to us— "Love your neighbor as yourself" (Levit., 19, and Matt., 22). It seems, then, that the love we feel for ourselves should be taken as the model to be imitated in the love of others, and that, as a consequence, the love of ourselves would be superior. In strict truth, the first source of all love is God; man loves himself only in relation to God, and he loves his neighbor even more indirectly still, and only in so far as he is associated with his neighbor in the enjoyment of the same good (namely, God). It follows plainly that if we keep as center of reference the primal charity on which all other charity is founded, the love we have for ourselves goes before and directs the love we should have for our neighbor. Evidence that well ordered charity begins at home lies also in the fact that no one should yield to the commission of a sin so as to free another from the sin, for sin hinders us from sharing in complete happiness (2–2, q.26, a.4) and this latter is the *raison d'être* of charity. But it would come out far otherwise if we were to compare the love which we allow our own bodies to that which we give our neighbor. For if we love our neighbor as linked to our love of God, and so, too, to our happiness, we ought to love his soul, as sharing directly in this happiness, more than our body, which has only an indirect share in it (a.5).

If we next consider "our neighbor" in relation to the multiplicity and diversity of beings which make him up, still finer gradations of charity can be predicated. Since, as a matter of fact, charity consists in wishing the good of others for the love of God, we should feel in reference to others a degree of charity proportioned to that of the good which we ought to wish them. And at this point there is an important distinction between the nature of the good we wish others and the intensity of the internal act with which we wish it to them. If one takes the first point of view, it is clear that our charity would wish the same good to all beings, without distinction; our love, because it wishes that all men share the same blessedness, wishes that they all share God. Besides, from this point of view, our charity would not admit other degrees in the welfare of our neighbor than those which come necessarily from his actual attitude toward the sovereign good; that is to say, a charity that loves others only because God's love wishes that these others, whoever they be, share in blessedness in a degree corresponding exactly to their merits. How, indeed, could we love others with a view to God unless we were to put before all else a love of God's justice, since God wishes that better persons share more fully than others in his blessedness? If, however, we take the second point of view, that of the intensity of the act by which we love our neighbor, it is a wholly different matter. Though we do not cease to desire that the justice of God be fulfilled and that the better be better rewarded, we cannot fail to wish that the better be also our nearest associates, to like it that more of welfare accordingly come to those who have to do more with us, and to love them with a more intense charity (q.26, a.7). Let us try to study out the order which charity should have in this domain that is so complicated and so full of thorny problems.

The first question that arises in this connection is the following: Should we put before all other love that which we bear the members of our own family? Strictly speaking, we should say yes, for no other tie is so intimate or so fixed as that of blood. We shall remark, however, that in particular given circumstances some accidental bonds can and should come before the bond of blood. The broadest formula that serves as a rule in cases of this kind is that which bids us to put before all others the bond corresponding to the real and actual circumstance. For instance, when it is a question of a relationship in the natural order, we should put first those joined to us by a bond of blood; when it is a question affecting the civil order, we should put our fellow-citizens before everyone else; and when a war breaks out, we should give first attention to our comrades in arms. And in fact custom gives spontaneous confirmation to this view; for at a marriage one invites and gives the place of honor to his parents, whereas in a civic ceremony parents come after the official delegates (2-2, q.26, a.8). In a word, the love we have for parents remains in itself the deepest love, but other friendships can step in ahead of it and effectually take possession, because of what is peculiar to each of them.

If we go now into the very heart of the family, we shall find there a gradation of charity, yet the degrees of it can be reversed according to the point of view under which we study them. Thus, the father is a greater good to the son than the son is to the father, for the father holds towards his son the place of God. But if we view the matter under the aspect of the experienced feeling and its intensity, father loves son more than son loves father, for the father loves himself in the son, who is a part of his very self and is loved from his birth, that is since long before the son could know and love the father (a.9). In like manner the husband regards his parents as worthy of a love more deferential than that which he has for his wife; but the feeling linking him to his wife will be that of a closer union, since he and she are not two, but one flesh; and this is why, though he has left his parents to live with her, he will nevertheless, when circumstances demand it, put the obligations he has toward her second to those he has to his parents (a.11). As a last parallel, and this is probably the instance in which appears most clearly what a difference separates the order of service from the order of feeling, benefactors merit to be loved by those whom they assist more than they love these latter, and yet they often love them more than they themselves are loved, a fact that Aristotle accounts for in several ways.

In the first place, the benefactor takes the one he serves as his own work, and he effectually speaks of his protégé as of his own creation; this is because, as a matter of fact, he has put into him, by his benefactions, something of himself. It is himself, then, that the benefactor loves in the one he benefits, as the poet loves his poems, for everyone loves himself, and does not find anywhere a better thing than what he himself does. And one may suggest a second reason. Man naturally loves to contemplate his own good; the one served sees in his benefactor only a good useful to him, whereas the benefactor sees in the one he helps a good that is an honor to himself; now utility passes, and honor remains, in such a way that the protégé is agreeable to the benefactor long

LOVE OF OUR NEIGHBOR

after the benefactor is useful to the protégé. Besides, we esteem what has cost us some effort, and as it costs us more to give service than to receive it, we love those who benefit us less than those whom we benefit (a.12).

These remarks, which are of a purely psychological kind, permit us to see at once why charity is not a moral virtue, but a virtue that transcends the scheme of morals. In themselves, all these movements of the soul through which we attach ourselves to our kin and wish them well, are no other thing than emotions of the soul, and we have already met them in this connection. What is the apex of love to which natural beings can reach? The most intense, if not the most noble, is maternal love. It is mothers who are the greatest lovers, observes St. Thomas. Yet such a love is less a virtue than an emotion through which the mother clings to her child as to that one of all values that is most inseparably conjoined to her. So for the other attachments we have spoken of, for it is clear that the benefactor is attached to the one whom he benefits as to a boundless source of inner satisfactions, or as to the mirror from which his own goodness is reflected. All these movements of soul are, therefore, natural, and it is because they are natural that a transcendent principle must enter to raise them up to the rank of virtues. Charity, as the sharing in us of divine grace, does not take the place in our soul of the origin of these movements; it is always we who love, and as our will remains the origin of love, it has the merit of it; but charity points our will towards God and directs in view of this supernatural end all the acts which this will does (2–2, q.23, a.2). It comes then to gather up, to put in place, and to make holy that which of itself does not properly speaking get beyond the order of nature.

This statement allows us to grasp the reason why the theological virtues rule the moral life of man and, without ever being able to shut him up within their limits, lead him to perfection. Indeed, the movements of the soul which charity transforms, if they are considered apart and in themselves, never can rise from the order of natural affections or passions to that of virtues. And certainly they cannot raise themselves to the dignity of supernatural virtues, for nature has nothing in it that allows it to stand up above itself and to bring it about that what is good for it become good and of merit in the sight of God. Only God can crown it with this grace and make it "acceptable." Now he makes it such by a virtue, that is a settled disposition to do good; and as the good of which there is question is not included in the order of nature, the power which makes it acceptable cannot come from nature or belong to it, and it is for this reason that charity always transcends the order of morals. But for the same reason only this supernatural charity can transform into moral virtues what with us were at first only emotions. Mother loves child, citizen loves fellow-citizen, soldiers love their comrades in arms: affections coming from nature, normal affections, legitimate and good in themselves because conformed to the spontaneous movement of a right will, yet they are not moral virtues and cannot in any instance become moral virtues. They are not moral virtues, for the reason that the mother (for instance) needs no fixed disposition got by practice and strengthened by custom to come to love as she should the child she has brought into the world. Likewise, the son doesn't go into special training to acquire a love of his father; and the citizen, born in a town, reared among its people, used since childhood to the manners, language, and moral code of his fellow-citizens, is without any bidding inclined to love them, and it takes no effort of his to be able to do this. With charity entering now to add itself to our moral life, it will but cause the love naturally rising from the mother's heart for her child to become a virtue, and it simply puts this love in a place suitable to it in an order which is not the order of nature. It cannot, therefore, cause what is not a moral virtue to become a moral virtue, but it can make a supernatural virtue of it (1–2, q.23, a.3, ad 1), and this charity transforms and re-orders that which could not of itself reach so far as the moral world. Grounded upon God as on its proper object, charity really shuts out all false virtue that is turned only towards man: the prudence of the greedy man who sells himself for gain; the justice of the grabber who fears he might lose an advantage; the temperance of the miser who only fears spending something; the courage of the miser who is strong to work, but only to get rich. As for the true moral virtues, they are made perfect by subordering their ends, good in themselves, to the highest end and supreme value, which is God.

Let us study now in the last place the natural inclinations and emotions themselves. These become fit to put on, through charity, a worth from the supernatural virtues that they could not put on in the order of morals. So charity, with God as the goal of human life, enters into it from above and wholly transfigures it, and for this reason we may say that charity is the soul of all the virtues.

There is in human life also, as a kind of crucial experience, a point of discernment, a parting of the ways, between what is of nature and what is of grace. This is the gospel precept to love our enemies. "If you love them that love you," Christ says, according to St. Matthew, "what reward shall you have? do not even the publicans this? And if you salute your brethren only, what do you more? do not also the heathens this?" (v, 46). Now this does not mean that it is not good and morally commendable to salute our brothers and to love our friends. Nay, it is certainly better to love our friends than our enemies, for love has the good for its object, and a friend, by the fact that he is a friend, is better than an enemy, in whom only hate is encountered; a friend

LOVE OF OUR NEIGHBOR

is thus an object more suited for love than is an enemy. But if on the other hand we consider *the reason* why we love the one and the other, then the love we have for our enemies puts on a character that is exceptionally worth while and even unique; it enters into that charity of which Pascal said that it is "of another order," a higher one, for "there can be other reasons than God why a man should love his friends, but God is the only reason man can have for loving his enemies." And we can easily appeal to God as the highest reason for loving those who love us, for our friendship for them is quite transfigured. But as the power of fire is known by the fact that it takes hold one by one of materials that are more and more difficult to burn, so the strength of our love for God is known by the fact that it reaches to and embraces objects that are the most difficult to love (2–2, a.27, a.7).

If we look at it in itself and in the supernatural effects that go with it, charity will appear to us as particularly laden with two of the most charming fruits that it can produce, a spiritual joy free of all sadness which the presence of the loved good gives, and a perfect peace, which everyone desires, but which is not found except in God (q.28, a.1, and q.29, a.3). Simply as moralists we should study charity in these transformations that it brings from above into our moral life and in the beneficent effects that it works there.

When we look at it from this point of view, the

field that it chooses to work in is that of mercy and succor of the poor, two fresh opportunities for us to be specific and exact with concrete instances of the order of grace and the order of natural morals.

Taken in itself, compassion is not a virtue. We will what is good for us, we naturally detest what is contrary to us; face to face with the evil our neighbor is suffering from, we get a painful and even a sorrowful impression, because our neighbor is part of ourselves and because in an indirect way we feel hurt by the evil under which our neighbor labors. To speak exactly, compassion is just an emotion of the soul, a view confirmed by the sudden, unwilled and unreflecting character of this impression which we experience. Now the non-volitional movement which disturbs us and which can even get us to lean toward some spontaneous gesture of compassion, is in some souls brought together by reason and is judged, ordered, and justified by it; it then becomes one form of the virtue of justice, and this reasoned mercy induces us to resettle the unfortunate person in the property to which, though injustice of some kind has deprived him of it, he has a right (2–2, q.30, a.3). Supernatural charity goes farther yet and does every last thing; for it takes this virtue, or even this mere feeling of a naturally good soul (*ibid.,* ad 4), and makes of it a Christian work *par excellence* in what concerns man's duties to his neighbor. Man's love for God certainly rules the whole Christian life, but immediately after the love of God comes the love of our neighbor in God, and then, as a consequence, the Christian virtue of mercy, which, for the love of God, relieves men of the evils from which they suffer (*ibid.*, a.4, ad 1).

This is to say also that well-doing and succor of the needy, which are effects and outer manifestations of charity, follow mercy in the changes which grace works in it. To do good to those whom we love is a natural turn, for so far as we love them, we include them in the love we bear ourselves. But reason makes a virtue of this sentiment by regulating and guarding it to the end that our well-doing is directed first to those nearest us, in this way intending that we should do each one the kindness relative to the order according to which he is immediately associated with us: to our parents we do the kindnesses of family life; to other citizens, those of civic life, and so on for the others (q.31, a.3). Yet well-doing gets its full reward only by subordination to the highest of the supernatural virtues, and it is not unreasonable that the act of giving alms, a concrete materialization of the virtue, is commonly called the doing of a charity. Alms-doing indeed, taken with all the elements that define it, consists in giving something to the poor, in compassion and for the love of God (*ibid.*, q.32, a.1). Alms are of two kinds: *corporal* alms, which are realised in the seven works of mercy and are a remedy for poverty of body; and *spiritual* alms, which are realised in prayer for our neighbor's soul, in education to take away poverty of thought and intellect, counsel to guide in a practical way the uncertain mind, in consolation to lighten the sadness brought on by emotions, and in brotherly correction to chide one effectively for his faults so that he will correct them (*ibid.*, q.32, a.2). Then, too, order and discretion come in, introduced by reason. For instance, it is clear that, in an absolute sense, spiritual alms is better than material alms; however, we are not to make use of silly methods, such as trying to succor a famishing man by teaching him philosophy: it is much better to feed the dying man than to teach him (*magis est pascendus moriens quam docendus*). It is equally clear that we ought to help all the poor people whom we can help, by denying ourselves things we do not need, and even things that sometimes, with too great indulgence, we think we do need; though we must make judicious choice and take account of every given circumstance. What remains common to all these acts of alms-giving is God's love, which is their soul and which lifts them up from mere movements of our natural pity into deserving acts of charity.

Chapter VIII

THE PRUDENT MAN

Prudence, we have noted, is a cardinal virtue whose court is in the practical reason. Because of it we are able to make out which means the will should take to reach its ends. On this virtue, then, lies the charge of guiding the doings of the other three great virtues, for it tells each of them what it is to do in order to act conformably to reason (2–2, q.47, a.7). If we study it in its concrete activity, as we are now to do, it seems to us that it makes itself known in a series of intellectual qualities which we may say make up the integral parts of it.

The prudent man is first of all a man of good memory, for prudence rests on experience, and experience comes to be a storehouse of remembered things by the help of which we can make our present life benefit by our past. The memory we speak of here is evidently not the mere power of recalling things, though this is the basis of it; rather, it is the art of keeping with care those memoranda that one may later have need to consult. The virtue of prudence neglects nothing that can make our actions more easy and orderly, not even the mnemotechnical processes that help us the more readily to fix memory: association with sense images, which are easily retained because the sensible is the proper object of our knowledge, and only abstract ideas are hard to keep in mind; the putting of our ideas into order, in such a way that we recall one thing through another; reflection and meditation when the importance of things is such that we want to remember them, that is to say, on the one hand, impressing them strongly on ourselves by an initial effort of the attention, and on the other by going over them often and naming them so as to preserve a memory of them (2–2, q.49, a.1). Then again, intelligence necessarily plays a part in the virtue of prudence. Here what is in question is not intellect as a power of the soul to perceive the first principles of knowledge, but a certain quality of the intellect. As a faculty of the soul, the intellect takes for granted universal principles, and these become the majors of our moral syllogisms: *we must do evil to no one*. But prudence has for its object to determine what must be done in such and such a case in order not to do evil to anyone. Thus the difficulty is to find in each particular human instance the minor of the syllogism, the *now this would be to do evil* . . . In a word, conformably to our definition, prudence has the business of finding means so that the general end, never to do evil to anyone, may in a given case be realised. This is why prudence requires in the intellect a kind of divining quality, which quality will permit the intellect to formulate correctly the *particular principle* of moral action in each set of circumstances. And there is here more than a natural aptitude, there is a special fitness to be acquired, as a kind of training to find out the means dictated in any particular instance (*ibid.,* a.3). In acquiring these qualities, he who wishes to become prudent will neglect none of the means: in the presence of those better informed he will be docile and always ready to be instructed (a.3); he will learn the art of reasoning closely, so as to make no errors in his deliberation (a.5); he will be watchful to take all circumstances into account (a.7) and will be cautious, so as not to let that act go awry; but, most of all, and this is the great art of the prudent man, he will be able to foresee the future. Prevision is hazardous, since it has to do with future contingencies and no science can be made of these, yet it is so necessary a thing that its very name is in some sense identified with that one of the virtues that it serves. Prudence is foresight, that is to say, prevision of the way acts and events will come to pass from the moment the end is willed until, by way of the means that prudence presently chooses, the willed end is reached (a.6, c., and ad 1).

Let us examine this virtue at work in the large field that belongs to it. No one doubts that it is at home when it attempts to rule the individual moral life, for this is its proper use, and therefore St. Thomas does not insist on it. But it is important to give evidence of its remarkable extension bringing under its control the whole of social life, and it is yet more important to see why prudence becomes a virtue more and more perfected in the measure that its purview expands and its authority widens out. We shall grasp this clearly if we reflect on the fact that it is the virtue of governing well, and especially on the fact that it is the virtue of exercising authority well in that form of government that is best of all, namely, the monarchic form.

It is the part of prudence to govern and to lay down the law, and so wherever there is a special way of government and legislation, there is also a special corresponding instance of prudence. Now it is clear that he whose business it is to govern not merely himself, but a self-sufficing community, as a city or a State, does function as governor of a particular perfect system. Government indeed is more and more perfect when it is more general, and can take a wider scope and make sure of remoter purposes; and so prudence in an especial and completer way is a mark of the king, whose work is to rule State or city, and for this reason we think that the knowledge of how to govern is a kind of prudence (2-2, q.50, a.1).

Yet it is also a mark, and no less a mark, of prudence to know how to give obedience to government and to submit freely in view of the good of the State. We have a name for this virtue. It is "civic virtue" and it is a virtue just as suitable to subjects as the other is to kings.

The slave's activity is obedient to the master's orders; he yields to the one commanding him, yet he does not yield as do inanimate and senseless things, for these are moved by an outsider. In fact, beings that have no life and no reason are moved from without, and are not themselves properly agents at all, because they lack the mastery of their acts, which lies in free will; and so rightness of governance is not theirs, but belongs to those who put them into motion. Men are different from these. Men, even when enslaved or in any way subject, are acted upon indeed by the commands of others, but in such a way that they act on themselves by their own free will; and thus there is needed in them a certain uprightness of being, so ruled that, though they obey others, they direct themselves by a kind of prudence, called "civic" (2–2, q.50, a.2).

This pivotal virtue can be and ought to be particularized further so that it comprises in a detailed way the objects which enter its purview.

Now, as a matter of fact the nature of the object, whether it be studied in general or in particular, in whole or in part, gives the diverse objects and the diverse virtues, and this diversity causes one virtue to be more important than another. For instance, it is quite plain that the family stands intermediate between the individual and the city or State, for as the individual is part of the family, so the family is part of city or State; and as we have seen that prudence in the broad sense, as governing the individual, is not the same as civic prudence, we also see that the economy of the household is necessarily different from both (*ibid.*, a.3).

For the same reason we add to the three preceding kinds of prudence a last type, that of the leader of an army:

> Works of art and of reason ought to be conformed to the works of nature, which were begun by the divine reason. Now nature tends to these two ends: first, to rule every single thing in itself, and secondly, to resist external things that attack it and might destroy it. To these ends, nature gave to animals not only a power of desire, so that they are led to those things that are adapted to their welfare, but also a pugnacious tendency, so that animals stand off their enemies (see p. 96). Hence, in those things that are reasonably done, there should indeed be a civic prudence, to put in their places things making for the common good, but there should also be a military prudence, to turn aside any aggression from enemies (*ibid.,* a.4).

With prudence studied thus in its various aspects there go three closely linked virtues, and we should give these their due here and look at them in particular. First, there is what we call the *virtue of counsel,* that is to say, the virtue that enables us to deliberate well. It is immediately subordinated to prudence, but should not be confused with it.

The distinctive mark of virtue is that it has to do with an action and that it makes this action good. And so, where there are different acts, there are differing virtues, and especially is this true where the nature of the goodness in the acts is not the same. For if there were the same nature of goodness in them, then diverse acts would appertain to the same virtue: thus the goodness of love, and of desire, and of joy depends on the same act, and therefore all these belong to the same virtue of charity. But acts of reason are different according as the intended effects are different, and there is not just one unvarying goodness in them. For it is one thing that a man be a good counsellor, another that he judge precisely, another that he make good laws; which is evident from the fact that a man may have one of these qualities without the others. It must be, then, that there is a virtue of good counsel fitting a man to consider matters carefully, and another virtue, namely, prudence, that enables him to frame laws successfully; and as counsel is meant for commanding, as an end of more importance than itself, so good counsel helps prudence, which is the higher virtue, without which there would simply be no virtue, as there are no moral virtues without prudence, nor any other virtues without charity (2–2, q.51, a.2).

The vice which in general is the opposite of prudence goes by the name of imprudence, and that which in particular is the opposite of good counsel and is most often the cause of trouble and error in deliberating is *precipitation*. This term is doubtless a metaphor taken from the sense world to express a purely interior movement, but it does express it. To be precipitate is, literally, to go head first into an abyss, that is to tumble instead of taking life easily step by step.

Well, the peak of the soul is reason, and the base is work done by the body; and there are midway steps, which we are to come down in an orderly way: there is memory of bygone things, knowledge of present ones, adroitness in looking into the future, reason to compare thing with thing, and docility to respect the opinions of one's elders. These are the several steps one takes in deliberating well, and if anyone is hurried into action by impetuosity of will or of passion, and runs across these stages, he will be guilty of precipitation; and since disordered reflection is a kind of imprudence, the fault of precipitation evidently comes within the content of imprudence (2-2, q.53, a.3).

Now, in going into such detail on the acts that serve the virtue of prudence, we show the need of strengthening, by a related action, an operation that is at once even more important than deliberation: namely, judgment which gives prudence reason to command and concludes deliberation. By judgment we do not end abstract speculations in the field of the sciences, but we decide what is to be done in a particular case. Because experience is full of evidence that many learned men have not got good sense, we are dealing here with a virtue that is specific and distinct.

Good sense gives correct judgment not merely in speculative matters, but in the particular actions that are the concern of prudence. That is why the Greeks gave the name σύνετοι to those possessed of this virtue, that is to say, judicious men, or again εὐσύνετοι, men of good sense, while those that had not this virtue were called ἀσύνετοι, foolish men. Now, wherever there are different acts, coming even from different causes, there certainly must be different virtues; and it is evident that the good quality of counsel and the good quality of judgment are not reducible to the same cause: for there are many persons who deliberate a great deal, yet they are not of thoroughly good sense, because they cannot judge rightly. For example, in the speculative sciences there are men who are good research students, because their reason is quick to run over all aspects of a question, probably by gift of the imaginative power to conjure up varying images readily, and yet because of some fault of intellect they are incapable of a correct judgment; and this is chiefly the result of common sense taking a wrong turn and forming a wrong judgment. And so besides good counsel we need the virtue of good judgment, or what we have called good sense (2-2, q.51, a.3).

The fault opposed to this virtue is the same as that opposed to the third virtue connected with prudence, namely, perspicacity. This latter virtue, like common sense, is related to judgment, but it is a judgment that is to be exercised in exceptional circumstances, where mere common sense is not sufficient. Nature acts in determined ways, and anyone who predicts the growth of a seed has reason to predict a normal growth, yet sometimes he is fooled and it is an unforeseen monster that is born. And he who could judge not only with an eye to the ordinary laws of nature, but in view of divine providence, would understand that this derogation from nature's ordinary laws must be effected according to broader laws known to God only. The man of good sense is he who can judge the normal situations of the moral life by the use of the general rules of conduct; but there are extraordinary circumstances, in which a departure from the habitual rules of conduct is required to satisfy higher and universal laws, and it is the virtue of perspicacity that gives it to judgment to discern these laws (2–2, q.51, a.4). The fault opposed to both good sense and perspicacity is lack of consideration, that is neglect to think over what ought to be thought over in order to form a correct judgment (2–2, q.53, a.4).

All the faults we have spoken of are obstacles to the several operations that we thought needed to lead to the good judgment a prudent man ought to pass. Still, the proper end of prudence is not judging; it judges only to impose laws, and even to do this is not enough: it is likewise necessary to keep to the laws one has prescribed. Here again, therefore, a fault would be a menace to prudence, and this time in the very permanence of its proper act. This fault is inconstancy.

Inconstancy means a backing down from the proposed good that one has set himself to, and the source of this weakening always lies in the conative powers. For one falls away from the good first intended only because of something inordinately pleasing to him. However, this foregoing is not completed without a fault of reason, the fault of abjuring what it had rightly accepted; and because the failure to withstand passions that could be withstood comes from the feebleness of that power that does not hold firmly to the good as conceived and proposed, inconstancy, so far as yielded to, is a fault of the intellect. Yet since all rightness of the practical intellect has to do in some way with prudence, so all lack of this rightness belongs to imprudence. And so inconstancy, so far as yielded to, is a mark of imprudence; and as precipitation comes from a defect in the act of counsel, and inconsideration from a defect in the act of judgment, so inconstancy comes from a defect in the act of command, and a man is said to be inconstant from the fact that reason fails to order those things that have been considered and judged good (2–2, q.53, a.5).

To finish up this practical study of prudence, we have still to study a whole series of sins which consist much less in directly contradicting prudence than in imitating, nay, we might say, in parodying it. It will be enough to name, as an example, the prudence of the flesh, to understand at once what a deformation this sin causes in the virtue of prudence, by ordering all our actions in view of the good of the body instead of ordering them, as prudence would, in view of the Sovereign Good (*ibid.*, q.55, a.1). But we much less easily perceive what a disguise other vices, such as craft and guile, impose on prudence.

Craftiness consists in putting on manners that are not sincere, but seeming and pretended, in order to achieve an end, either good or bad. Now the putting on of such manners can be studied in two ways: first, as the very thinking out of such ways, and this matter belongs properly to craft, as indeed the working out of the right way to a legitimate end is a part of prudence. Secondly, we can look at the putting on of these manners from the point of view of carrying them into execution, and this is the work of deceit. Therefore, deceit is in some sense the fulfilment of craftiness, and is really an offshoot of it (2–2, q.55, a.4).

Fraud in its turn comes within the same category, for it is simply a species of deceit. As a matter of fact, we might give the name deceit to the whole procedure for putting craftiness into action, when it is a matter of words or deeds; the name fraud means more properly a deceit that is translated into acts (a.5), but it is a deceit and is amenable to the same definition. On the contrary, it is harder to mark off the difference between the real virtue of prudence and mere care for temporal things, which resembles prudence in certain of its aspects.

Anxiety or care supposes an effort made to obtain something. Now we evidently apply more effort where we have fear of failing, but where we are sure of achievement, we are scarcely anxious. With so much prefaced, we may say that anxiety over temporal things can be illicit in three ways. First of all, from the point of view of the things of which we are over-careful: if, that is, we seek transitory things as an end; and it is in this sense that Augustine says in his book *On Monastic Works* (ch. 26): "When the Lord said: Be not solicitous for your food nor for what you shall put on, He said this that we might not keep our eyes on these things and that we might not do for the sake of these things what we are commanded to do by the Gospel teaching." Secondly, solicitude for temporal things can be illicit because of excessive zeal given to get a hold of temporalities that draw a man away from spiritual concerns, where his chief service ought to be given; and so St. Matthew tells us (xiii, 22) that the care of this world choketh up the word. Thirdly, from the point of view of a superfluous fear, when, namely,

THE PRUDENT MAN

a man is afraid that, though he do what he should, he will not have the necessaries; which fear is for three reasons debarred by Our Lord: first, on account of the greater benefits, that is to say, body and soul, divinely given man without any solicitude on his part; second, because of the help God gives the animals and plants according to their nature and without any concurrence on the part of man; third, because of divine providence, the ignorance of which was the only thing that brought the pagans to put their main trust in the search for temporal goods. And so Augustine concludes that our solicitude should principally be for spiritual values, and that we should be confident that, if we do what we ought to do, temporal goods will come as we need them (2-2, q.55, a.5).

In this way we have also solved the problem of whether we are to be anxious for the morrow:

No work can be virtuous unless it have an entourage of proper circumstances, one of which is an appropriate time, as is said in Ecclesiastes (c.8): "There is a time and opportunity for every business." And this holds not only for exterior works, but also for interior solicitude. Indeed, with every season there goes a care proper to itself: in summer we have the work of the harvest, in autumn the vintage, and if anyone were taken up in mid-summer with worried thoughts of the vintage, he would burden himself uselessly with a work that belongs to a later date. Hence, Our Lord forbids this care as too anxious, saying: Be not solicitous for the morrow, and adds: the morrow will be solicitous for itself. That is to say, it will have its own cares which will be trouble enough for the mind; as indeed this saying shows: Sufficient for the day is the evil thereof (2-2, q.55, a.7).

Chapter IX

EVERY MAN HIS DUE

The specific object of justice (*justitia*) is what is just (*justum*), that is to say, in case of a settlement that which right (*jus*) demands. Now the right which justice looks to is divided into natural and positive. That justice be satisfied, the relation of equality between different persons interested in the same act must be guaranteed. This equality may be of two kinds. Let us suppose, for instance, that it is a matter of an exchange of products. We might manage the exchange first without taking account of anything but the products exchanged, each man giving precisely as much as he received, and this would be natural right. But we might regulate the exchange by a pact or agreement, whether it be private or public and made known by the ruler, and this would be an example of positive right (2–2, q.57, a.2).

The written law is only the formulation of these two rights, but the code has a different relation to each of them. For the code contains the natural law, but does not make it, and it is not from the law that the code gets its force, but from nature. With positive law it is another matter; for the code does not merely contain the positive law, but besides makes it and gives it the force of law (*ibid.*, q.60, a.5).

Whatever be the nature of the law under consideration, we would say with the jurists that justice is "the steady unceasing will to give to every man his due" (*ibid.*, q. 58, a.1). As a will governed by reason and enriched by the purpose to do good, justice is manifestly a virtue—a fact that we have shown earlier in another connection. We may even say that it is in some sense a universal virtue, because we have seen that its work is to fix the right expedient in all actions dealing with external things (see p. 138; *cf.* 2–2, q.58, a.5 and a.6). Yet it is no less in its place when it sees to the maintenance of right, that is, to the natural or positive equity that ought to regulate the relations of man to man.

The vice of injustice is the contrary of the virtue of justice, and is the point-for-point negation of it. So far as justice manages the individual's relations to the public in a way conformable to the requirements of law and subordinates him to the common welfare, it is given the name of legal justice, and the sin of disavowing this justice is called illegality. And so far as justice takes care of the inter-relations of individuals within a community in a way conformable to the requirements of law, it gets the name of particular justice. The sin opposed to this justice is injustice pure and simple, and because of this sin an individual wants to have more, in matters of riches and honors, than the just share that he has a right to, and in the case of burdens and labors he wants less than his just share (*ibid.,* q.59, a.1). One will notice that because the vices, like the virtues which they oppose, are set dispositions to act in a particular way, we do not regard as strictly unjust a man who may have given others more or less than their due through a mere inadvertence or under the influence of anger momentarily disturbing his judgment. The man marked by the sin of injustice is he who freely chooses an inequity contrary to right, just as he exhibits the virtue of justice who freely chooses an equity consistent with right. For whoever freely chooses injustice, chooses it just because it pleases him, and it pleases him just because it has become a habit, therefore a vice, with him (*ibid.,* a.2). Now that is certainly a serious vice which denies at once the natural law and the law of God, and, by the bare fact that it tends to our neighbor's harm, breaks down within us charity, which is the keystone of the whole edifice of virtues.

Just as the proper object of justice is right, so the proper act of justice is to say what is right, in a word, to judge. And for a judgment to be licit, it should fulfil three basic conditions: arise from a just inclination, proceed from someone who has authority to make it, and be given according to right reason, which is the guide of justice. Let any one of these three conditions be lacking, and the judgment ought to be taken as bad and not permissible. If it is at fault for having contradicted the rightness of justice, it is a perverse and unjust judgment; if the fault is a lack of authority in him who pronounces, it is a usurped judgment; and if the trouble is that it is passed on little known matters, and more on faith and simple conjecture than on a sound basis, it is a rash judgment (*ibid.*, q.60, a.2), or perhaps it is merely a suspicion. Nothing is more common than this last kind of injustice, but nothing is more complex than the causes from which it proceeds.

A suspicion, as Cicero says, is a persuasion of evil, but a persuasion resting on slight indications, and this notion has three different sources. First of all, in the fact that he who so judges is himself evil, and because he is conscious, we may say, of his own malice, he easily has a bad opinion of others, as indeed Ecclesiastes says (c.10): "The fool when he walketh in the way, whereas he himself is a fool, esteemeth all men fools." Secondly, in the fact that he who passes such judgment is ill affected towards others: for when a person condemns another, or hates him, or is angry with him, or envies him, the least signs are enough to get him to think evil of the other, it being the way of people to think readily what they want to think. Thirdly, it comes also from long experience, and for this reason the Philosopher tells us (*Rhetoric*, 2, ch.13) that old men are extremely suspicious because they have had much experience of others' defects. Now, the first two causes of suspicion go with and show forth a perverse affection, whereas the third narrows the ground for suspicion, since experience makes for certitude and this is anything but suspicious in nature. At any rate, suspicion is never without some wrongness, and the farther suspicion goes, the more wrong it is. Suspicion itself has three grades: first, a man may begin for flimsy reasons to doubt the goodness of some one. This is a slight matter, for it goes with that human adventure without which life itself is not carried on, and so says the ordinary commentary on the First Corinthians (c.4): "Judge not before the time." The second step is this: on slight warrant, a man makes up his mind for sure about another's badness, and if this judgment be in a serious matter, it is a serious sin, because it involves contempt of one's neighbor; whence the same Gloss says: "If because we are men we cannot avoid all suspicion, we should at least withhold our judgment, that is to say, our final and set opinions." The third stage is when a judge proceeds to condemn a man on mere suspicion. This directly contradicts justice, and in consequence is a mortal sin (2–2, q.60, a.3).

With justice so defined, we begin the study of the parts that make it up, that is, first of all the study of its two principal kinds: commutative justice and distributive justice; then the study of the virtues that are linked with and complete justice.

1. COMMUTATIVE AND DISTRIBUTIVE JUSTICE

The distinction between the two basic kinds of justice is closely tied up with the distinction we have drawn between legal justice and individual justice. This individual justice looks to one private person, a person who has within the community only such a place as any one part occupies within a whole. And if we study one of these persons in reference to the other, we find a simple relation between private persons, and relations of this kind are governed by commutative justice, the regulator of exchanges set up between man and man. But we may study the relations established between the whole and its parts, that is to say, the order that portions out to different individuals what is coming to them in common. Relations of this type are ruled by distributive justice, which sees to it that each member of the community gets out of the common fund a part proportioned to and due to him (2–2, q.61, a.1). In either case, justice remains faithful to its definite function, which is to guarantee the happy medium and to maintain equity between the two parties in question; though, of course, this equity is not of the same nature, whether it is a matter of commutative or of distributive justice.

Distributive justice consists in giving something to a private person, on the principle that what belongs to the whole, is due to each part. And what is given is naturally so much greater according as the part holds a more important place in the whole. For this reason, in distributive justice just so much more is given to anyone out of the common goods as that person has a higher ranking in the community. In an aristocracy the rating is according to worth, in an oligarchy according to money, in a democracy according to freedom, and so on, for any other kind of régime. And so in distributive justice the line of demarcation is not taken as an equality of thing to thing, but a certain proportion of things to persons; that is, so that as one person is more important than another, the thing that is given to one person is greater than that given to another. This is what Aristotle says (*Ethics,*

5, c.3) that such division is a geometrical proportioning, in which the equality is not based on quantity, but on fitness. Thus we say: 6:4::3:2, because in each instance the proportion is of one and a half, the larger number containing the smaller one wholly and half again; however, there is no equality between the quantities by which each larger number exceeds the smaller, for six is two more than four, whereas three is only one more than two.

In exchange or trading we pay a particular person something in consideration of some other thing that we have received from him. This is most evident in buying and selling, in which there is at once the nature of exchange. In these cases it is needful to get a balance of thing with thing, in such a way that whatever a man has that is not his own, he is to return to the other whose it is; and so an equality, a kind of arithmetical mean, is struck, that is, in relation to the two extreme quantities the division is even. Five, for instance, is the arithmetical mean between four and six, for it is one above four and one below six. If two persons in the beginning had five each, and one of them got one from the other, the recipient would have six and the other four: it would then be justice for them to return to the mean, and one be taken from the man having six and given to the other who has only four; each will now have five, which is the mean (2-2, q.61, a.2).

Let us examine, one at a time, those vices that can endanger the virtues of distributive and commutative justice. In what regards the first kind of justice, the capital sin to be avoided goes by the name of *human respect*. The basic principle of distributive justice consists in giving to every member of a group the share of things that is coming to him according to his place in the group. But human respect, or respect of persons, begins to vitiate shares every time we let some other line of demarcation than this rule decide the part going to each individual.

We may suppose, as an instance, that it is a matter of giving someone a professor's honors and duties. If distributive justice is observed, this man has a claim in exact proportion to his learning, for it is his learning which marks out his place in the social hierarchy in relation to the order of teaching. To act justly in such case is to take into account just the learning of the candidate; on the contrary, to take into consideration his person is to be guilty of human respect, that is to say, to have regard to something that is not the one rightful reason we can have for conferring this dignity on him: his wealth, for example, or the ancestor that relates us to him. Here we may define "person" in a general way as being: any other condition than the legitimate cause for the attribution of a good in question. This means that persons necessarily vary with cases, and that a condition that involves respect of persons in a given case may be lawful or even required by justice in another. It is a matter of respect of persons if we take lineage into account in bestowing a prelacy, but it is not such if we take inheritance into account in making a will, and the crime of which we speak appears only when it comes in to falsify the proportions (2–2, q.63, a.1). Still, this is not to say that it is always easy to indicate the point at which this crime begins, for the right that fixes the individual's share in the group's goods is rarely a simple matter. Since we have taken the instance of honor and of public duty as examples, we may note that honor is testimony given to the virtue of one whom we wish to pay deference to, but that public honors often are addressed less to what men are than what they represent. A prelate, no matter how bad he might be, is deserving of honor as representing God; our parents and teachers have a right to respect, not only on their own merits, but as sharers of the dignity of Him who is father and master of all things; old people, too, have a claim to honor, because age raises at least the presumption of virtue. It is true that this sign is sometimes deceptive and that, as the Book of Wisdom says (c.4), "venerable age is not that of long time, nor counted by the number of years . . . a spotless life is old age." As for riches, well, it may be necessary to pay them some tribute because of the standing they give to a man in a community; however, one would be guilty of respect of persons if he took into consideration anybody's riches and thought much of him on that account (q.63, a.3).

If we look next into the sins opposed to commutative justice, they will seem numerous indeed and varied, because of the many different ways in which exchange between persons can be carried on.

EVERY MAN HIS DUE

Some of the exchanges made between persons and presided over by commutative justice are voluntary and some are not. There is involuntary exchange whenever anyone uses another's property or person or work against the other's will. This can occur in secret and by fraud, or in the open and by violence; and in either case the injury can be done either to the property, or to the person, or to a related person. When it is a matter of property, and one gets away in secret with another's goods, we call the act *larceny;* when the act is done in the open, it is called *rapine*. When a man himself is taken, either his person or his dignity is endangered. When his person is in question, he is taken secretly to be killed treacherously, or perhaps clubbed or poisoned; when he is taken openly, he is killed openly, or thrown into prison, or flogged, or in some way mutilated. His dignity is attacked secretly by false witness or detraction or defamation or the like, and openly by accusation before a court, or by public insult. One can be wronged also in someone related to him, for instance, in his wife, by the act of adultery, or his servant, who may be induced to desert the master, and either of these actions is usually done in secret, though they can also be done openly. And so for all related persons, injustices of all kinds can be committed on each of them exactly as on the central person. Still, adultery and the seduction of servants are injustices directly on these persons themselves, though because servants are in some way owned (*possessio quaedam*) by the master, the seduction of them is a kind of theft.

Exchange, however, is voluntary when one gives something to another. And if he simply gives his own goods to the other though not obliged to do so, it is not a question of justice but of generosity. For a free transference has nothing to do with justice, unless in so far as there might be something owed in the case. There could be such debt in any of several ways. First, a man may simply turn over something to another as pay for something of the other's, and this is what goes on in buying and selling. Secondly, a man may give something to another and allow him to use it, but with the duty to return it; and if he gives him the use of it gratis, the exchange is called *usufruct* in the case of things that produce some fruit, and a loan (*mutuum, seu commodatum*) in the case of things that do not fructify, such as money, furniture and the like. If the use is not given gratis, it is called *renting*. Thirdly, a man may give another something that he is to get back, and not that the other is to use it, but to keep it for him; and this is called a *deposit,* or *security,* when one pledges his property or himself in trust to another. Now in all actions of this kind whether voluntary or not, the manner of settling is the same: the two parties have a claim to equal return; and so every one of these cases is in the field of the one kind of justice, namely, commutative (2–2, q.61, a.3).

It is not difficult to make out that, among these acts where another's good is concerned, some correspond to vices, such as murder, that dispose of another's goods without his consent. Not that every destruction of any kind of life is a crime against justice, for the individual exists only in view of the whole of which he is a part, and every time that his destruction is useful to the good order of the whole, it becomes a legitimate thing. Man may, then, without scruple sacrifice plants to feed animals, and animals to nourish himself, for this is a use of them in view of their normal end (q.64, a.1). He may even put an evil-doer to death, because a man of this kind is a nuisance to the whole community, and the ruler or the judge representing him only sees, as he should, to the health of the community by cutting off its diseased parts, as we cut off gangrenous members from the body. But it goes without saying that no private person has authority to do this, save in a case of legitimate self-defence, and that the priest least of all should soil his hands with blood.

For two reasons, a priest may not kill anyone. First of all, he is chosen for the ministry of the altar, whereon is represented the Passion of Christ brought to death. Now, as St. Peter says in his First Epistle (c.2), Christ did not return blow for blow, and it is not fitting, therefore, that the cleric should strike or kill, for the servant ought to imitate his master, according to the saying of Ecclesiasticus (c.10): "As the judge of the people himself is, so also are his ministers." Another reason is that the ministry of the New Law is entrusted to the priest, and in that law there is no penalty of death fixed or of any physical mutilation (contrary to the Old Law, whose priests and Levites might chastise and put to death); and in order to be a fit minister of the New Testament, he ought to keep away from such things (2–2, q.64, a.4).

Suicide is a crime of the same order, for it not only destroys the charity with which a man is bound to love himself, but it disposes, as if it belonged to him, of a life that in reality belongs to God. Man's free will extends to all the acts of his life, yet not to that life itself, for he has received that, and it is rightly His only, from whom man has life, to deliver man from afflictions in time and to let him enter a happier life (q.64, a.5, ad 3). To mutilate a man, to harm him, to take away his liberty without cause, is to commit an injustice, for it is to dispose against his will of the integrity or freedom of his person, which does not belong to us. Besides, in these cases, as in that of homicide, a penalty may for any valid reason be lightened, and a judge may, therefore, chastise and imprison the guilty man, and may put him to death, and a father may chastise the son whom he has the business of educating, though he is not allowed to harm his health or person.

All the crimes that we have just mentioned affect our neighbor in a personal way, but there are others that affect his goods or the things that he possesses. The fact that such vices exist, plainly supposes the lawfulness and rightness of proprietorship, for if there were no lawful ownership it would be no injustice to seize what men claim they possess. Now it is a natural right for man to have some exterior objects and to make them his own. All things are from God, but man is God's image precisely because he has reason and thus can dispose as he wills of the material world. This is why God in the creation said: "Let us make man to our image and likeness: and let him have dominion over the fishes of the sea." Besides, it is a good thing and useful to the general welfare for the individual to have some property that belongs to him, and this arrangement need not prejudice the communal goods that are to remain in the hands of the whole group.

In the matter of exterior goods, man has two privileges. The *first* of these is the power of getting, and getting rid of. Under this heading, it is lawful for a man to have some things of his own. This is even necessary for human life, for three reasons. In the first place, a man is more careful to look after things that belong to him alone than things that belong to everyone or to many: for people keep out of the way of work and leave community jobs to someone else; and this is just what happens where, for instance, there is a plethora of servants. A second reason is that human affairs are kept in better order if everyone is given charge of something that belongs to himself, and there would be confusion if everyone was to take care of everything, indiscriminately. Thirdly, man's status is kept more peaceful in this way, and everyone is content with his own things; and indeed we see that among those who own something in common and with no division lines, trouble quite often arises. The *second* privilege that man has in exterior goods is the use of them. Yet in this matter man should not retain exterior goods as his own, but as everybody's; that is, so that in case of necessity he can the more easily share them with others. So the Apostle says to Timothy (I, vi, 18): "Charge the rich of this world . . . to give easily, to communicate to others, to lay up in store for themselves a good foundation against the time to come, that they may lay hold on the true life" (2–2, q.66, a.2).

Such is the natural and social basis of the right to property. It is clear that any act derogating from

this right is a fault, and that any fixed disposition to derogate from it is a vice. This is why we have classed robbery and larceny, which is a secret form of robbery, among the sins of injustice. Yet this is also why any apparent theft ceases to be theft when it legalizes itself as a last resort on the same ground that proprietorship itself rests on, that which would seem a theft then becoming, in virtue of this principle, a lawful appropriation.

As a matter of fact, what exists by human law cannot repeal or restrict any part of either the natural law or the divine law. Now the order fixed by Providence is that lower things should be arranged so as to serve human needs. And so in dividing these things and appropriating them, as allowed by human law, no obstacle is to be placed to man's being served by them. And therefore things in which some persons superabound ought by natural law to go to the sustenance of the poor. Hence St. Ambrose says (*Serm. de Tempore,* 64) : "This bread which you store belongs to the hungry, these clothes which you hide away belong to the poorly clad, this money which you bury in the earth is for the ransom and freedom of afflicted people." Of course, as there are many who are in need and as the same goods cannot help all of them, the free disposition of his own goods is left to every man, so that he may assist the unfortunate. Still, there are cases of such urgent and plain necessity that the suffering persons may to relieve the immediate need take whatever comes to hand, as, for instance, when life is in danger and one cannot do anything else. A person may then lawfully use another's goods to supply his wants and seize upon such goods, either in public or private, without really committing either theft or larceny (2–2, q.66, a.7).

Howsoever frequently injustice may be committed, either against persons or things, we may say that its chosen field is still what men properly call justice, that is to say, it is justice that the courts ought to give. There is no party to a case whom this vice does not dog: the judge, the plaintiff, the accused, the witness, the lawyer in his plea, all are exposed to fall into it. The gravest fault that can menace a judge, who is a public person dispensing justice in the ruler's name, is the temptation to do his work as a private person: to judge someone not within his jurisdiction, to condemn on knowledge obtained as a private person, and not on what the trial reveals to him or his own research reveals to him in a lawful way, to condemn a man whom he knows to be guilty, but whom no one accuses—these are confusions between man and judge which justice is meant to avoid (q.67). As for the accusation, it is not merely a right, it is a duty every time that an evil that has been committed threatens to cause damage to either the spiritual or the material good of the community. But the accuser should first of all be bound to show incontestable proof of what he says, and if he cannot do it, his duty is to withdraw (q.68). If he goes too far, especially in bad faith, the accuser becomes a calumniator, guilty of a criminal act in his turn, and the judge may inculpate him.

A person may proceed with an accusation only when he is absolutely sure of the matter and when there can be no possibility of ignorance of the facts. Yet it does not follow that everyone who brings a false accusation against another is a calumniator, but only he whom malice incites to bring such accusation. In fact, it might happen that one would accuse another through lightheadedness, that is, one might too easily believe what he had heard, and this would be an instance of temerity; or he might, because of some excusable error, go on to accuse; all of which matters should be left to the prudence and discernment of the judge, who will not condemn of calumny a person whom puerility or some pardonable mistake has led to make a false accusation (2–2, q.68, a.3, ad 1).

The accused naturally thinks first of defending himself; yet he has no right to do so at the expense of truth.

It is one thing to keep silent about a truth, it is another to affirm a falsehood. The first is permitted in some cases, for no one is bound to tell every truth, but only those truths that the judge may and ought to demand according to the regular legal form: for instance, when a man's crime is abroad and infamous, or the indications of it are external and plain, or when the trial is well advanced. But to advance an untruth is in no case allowable for anyone. Now one can proceed to what is allowable either in a lawful way adapted to the end desired, and it is prudent to do this; or in a way that is not licit and not fitted to the proposed end, and this is what a wily fellow, full of deceit and trickery, would do (see above, p. 243). The first way is praiseworthy, the other is vicious. The accused then may defend himself by saying nothing about a truth which he is not bound to avow; for example, by not answering questions that he is not obliged to answer, and to do this is rather a prudent evasion than self-defence by chicanery. However, he is not permitted to lie or be silent about any truth he is bound to tell, or to use any trickery or fraud, for this would amount to a lie and to self-defence by deception.

Sometimes (some might object) the accused may defend himself by deceit, since according to civil law anyone is allowed to circumvent his enemy in a lawsuit; but to defend oneself so is most deceitful, and therefore the accused commits no sin when, in a criminal case, he defends himself by deceit. In answer we may say that human law leaves unpunished actions which are sins in the judgment of God, as for, instance, fornication. In fact, human law does not demand of man virtue of every kind, which is for the few only and cannot be shared in by so great a crowd as human law is designed to take care of. Still, for a man to be unwilling to commit a sin in order to escape death, which faces him in a criminal case, is a mark of perfect virtue, for of all terrifying things death is the most terrifying (Aristotle, *Ethics,* 3, c.6). And so if a guilty man does mislead his enemy in a suit, he sins by getting him to do wrong; but civil law has no penalty for this sin, and it is so far said to be licit (2–2, q.69, a.2, et ad 1).

If we inquire into the rôle of the witness, we see that it does not raise fewer or less thorny difficulties. To bear witness in favor of an accused person whom one knows to be innocent, is strictly a duty. Every man is bound to do it if asked, and he is bound to do it spontaneously if he is not asked. On the other hand, no one is required to witness against an accused person in order to bring against him charges of which no one suspects him and which the regular course of justice has not revealed against him. Still less is a man bound to give testimony to aid the accuser to prove a case he has not made a success of, for a person is not obliged to make an accusation if he cannot prove it; "and even if danger menaces the accuser, we need not trouble ourselves about him, for he has gotten himself into this predicament, whereas the accused is menaced and exposed to danger in spite of himself" (q.70, a.1). As for evaluating testimony, we may say that there is no absolute rule. A human action is particular and may or may not come to pass; but there is no science of the particular; let a person then dispose of one or two or a thousand witnesses, he will ever have only a probability, never unquestionable certitude. However, this is no reason for making little of the probability that the testimony of two or three witnesses gives, nor for arguing that three witnesses are not better than one. Three allow for a beginning, a middle and an end, that is, for a final confirmation of the agreement arrived at by the first two witnesses. True, this agreement does not always exist, and it is hard to know in what measure people must secure it.

When the disagreement among witnesses is on crucial circumstances that might change the nature of the case—for instance, the time or place or the chief persons concerned—the testimony is of no force, because if they are in disagreement on such matters, it seems that their testimony is individual and as if they witnessed to different cases. Thus, if one says that an event occurred at such and such a time or place, and another assigns another time and place, they seem not to speak of the same event. Yet it does not weaken the testimony for one to say he does not remember the time or place and the other to name a precise time and place. And if the witnesses for the accused and the accuser are in complete disagreement on the main points, and are equal in number and character on both sides, we ought to decide in favor of the accused, for a judge should be readier to pardon than to condemn, except perhaps in certain cases in which the accused has the advantage to begin with. But if the witnesses on both sides are in dissent, the judge will follow his own good sense in settling which party is to get the decision, though he will, of course, take into account the number of the witnesses, their reputation, the favoring circumstances, the standing of the case, and so on. A man's testimony is rejected if when he is asked about what he has seen or knows he contradicts himself, but not if there is some disagreement in his answer on matters that he gives an opinion on or has heard rumors of. But if there is discrepancy in what he says about some circumstance not bearing on the very substance of the matter in hand, for example, whether it was clear or a little cloudy, or whether a house was painted, or the like, this does not throw his testimony out, for men usually do not bother much about such things, which easily slip out of mind; nay, some lack of agreement on such matters, as St. Chrysostom says (*Homil. in Matt.*, 1), makes testimony the more credible, since a full concord in all such things, even the least, would make us suspect that the answers were prearranged. Still, once the witness is heard, the matter is left to the prudence and discernment of the judge (2-2, q.70, a.2, ad2).

There remain now the lawyers, whose business, very often, is a mighty delicate one. They practice a profession, and have a right therefore to a just salary (*ibid.,* q.70, a.4). Absolutely speaking, they are not obliged to offer their services to the poor man, even though he is in need, for this is a work of mercy and, like any alms, is obligatory only on certain conditions, such as, if the poor man is in urgent need of legal help and there is no one in a better position to give it to him. On the contrary, if the need is not urgent or if this poor man could be assisted by a lawyer who is of near kin to him or who is better off, it is a good work indeed to defend him, but not an absolute duty. Otherwise, we should be bordering on the conclusion that lawyers ought to put their own work aside in order to serve the poor. Let the lawyer then be charitable; let him besides have the requisite qualifications for practicing his profession: skill in presenting his client's defence, an ear to learn accusations and a tongue to refute them, a reputation for honesty above suspicion, for he who cannot answer for himself can still less answer for others; let him above all things have the honor that will keep him from ever defending a case that he knows to be unjust, for thus he would make himself an accomplice of the injustice which he is employed to defeat (*ibid.*, q.71).

Whatever be the form that injustice may put on, whether it be crimes properly so called, or injuries less directly against persons, such as insult, scorn, slander, calumny or mockery, the specific remedy for the evil committed is the same: *restitution*. This word means that one is given back a possession which belongs to him, and which he has given up voluntarily in the instance of a loan or a deposit, or of which he has been dispossessed in spite of himself in the instance of an injustice (*ibid.*, q.62, a.1). In cases in which restitution cannot be made by giving back the very object that was taken away or destroyed, at least its equivalent must be given. This happens when a man's honor is attacked or the members of his body are maimed, and compensation should then be fixed with due attention to the circumstances of the parties, by a just man chosen as arbiter (*ibid.*, a.2, ad 1), and without prejudice to the penalty that the guilty man may have coming to him for the moral fault he has committed (a.3). The demands of restitution are absolute, if we take the point of view of moral justice, and it is this absolute character that allows us to fix *a priori* the conditions according to which restitution ought to be made. Everyone who has not only committed, but protected injustice, or in any way taken part in it, is bound to restore and repair in the exact measure in which he was responsibly tangled up with it: for example, the person who commands an unjust act is evidently answerable for it; and so is the accomplice without whose consent the act could not have been done, the recipient of stolen goods who hides them away, and even the monarch whose business is to see that justice is respected in his domain, but who lets evil-doers multiply, as if the revenues he enjoys were not meant precisely to give him a chance to uphold justice (*ibid.*, a.7). And the man guilty of injustice or the accomplice in it ought not only to make restitution, but he ought to do it at once, for it is no less reprehensible to keep what is another's than to take it.

II. THE VIRTUES ASSOCIATED WITH JUSTICE

It may at first blush seem unusual that there should be virtues connected with justice, that is to say, tied up with it, and that these nevertheless do not strictly belong to it. Yet the fact is explained if we take into account the twofold demand that should be met in order that there be a virtue of justice: to give to another what is due him, and in such a way as to build up an equality that has been torn down. From this point of view we may say that every virtuous act done in relation to another person has to do more or less immediately with the virtue of justice, though we find that there is no justice properly speaking when the action in question has not for its end the rendering to someone what is due to him, or when it cannot give it to him in such a way as to re-establish equality. Hence, there are a great many virtuous actions that are just because they set up the relation that ought to exist between the one who does them and the one whom they are meant to help, but yet not completely just because they do not pay an out-and-out debt or really establish an equality. We have a typical instance of this second kind in the virtue of *religion*. To be religious is to give to God what is due Him, and it is, therefore, to do a just work. Still, how can we give back to God what is due Him? The Psalmist says (Ps. 115): "What shall I render to the Lord for all the things that he hath rendered to me?" So far, therefore, the virtue of religion is only an incomplete justice. *Filial devotion*, by which we give our parents the reverence that is due to them, is of the same order, for we cannot hope to balance in this way what they have done for us. Examples of the first kind could easily be cited in great numbers. For though there are absolute legal debts in relation to our neighbor, a debt when it is simply moral is far less definite, and a person can hardly speak of justice in the strict sense of the word. It is thus that we owe truth to others, and that others owe us an acknowledgment for the good turns we have done them. In the same class are generosity, affability, well-wishing, peace, and a score of virtuous attitudes that make our conduct what it should be with regard to others, but resolve into actions whose debt-outline is scarcely traceable (2–2, q.80, a.1).

Let us take up first the virtue of religion. It is a special virtue, since it has its special object, which is to give God the honor that belongs to Him; and it is a moral virtue, though it has a theological aspect.

Religion is the virtue that gives God the worship due to Him. Two things are to be studied in religion: one of these is what religion offers to God, that is to say, worship, and this in relation to religion has the rôle of matter or object; the other is the person, namely, God, whom we worship in religion. Now, the acts by which we worship do not come so near to God as does a human act of faith in God. We may indeed say that God is the object of faith, not simply because we believe God, but because we believe in Him; whereas, to give to God the cult due to Him is limited to going through a ceremonial worship, such as sacrifice offered or the like, in His honor. Thus it is plain that God is not taken as the matter or object of the virtue of religion, but as its end; and religion is, therefore, not a theological virtue whose object would be the ultimate end, but a moral virtue which is concerned with the means to be used in gaining this end (2–2, q.81, a.5).

It follows from the nature of things that, if religion is a moral virtue, it is rightly the first of all moral virtues, for its immediate and direct object is the honor of God. The form we can most easily

VIRTUES ASSOCIATED WITH JUSTICE 271

see under which it is expressed is worship, that is, one or more exterior acts in which the body necessarily takes part. But its deepest form is devotion, or the act by which the soul itself is dedicated and given over wholly to God. Let us then, in the first place, examine the interior acts which inspire and rule the virtue of religion: namely, devotion and prayer, which is its expression.

Devotion engenders in the religious soul two effects that are readily noticeable: an accidental sadness born of seeing our soul habitually kept so far from God, and an essential joy born of the sentiment which this soul knows in actually coming near to God. And this twofold effect of devotion shows us at once the twofold source from which this virtue is fed.

The extrinsic cause of devotion, the main cause, is God. St. Ambrose says of Him (*Comment. in Luc.,* ch.9; from *Et conversus* . . .): "God calls whom He judges worthy, and whom He chooses He makes religious; and if He had wished, He would have made the Samaritans, who had no devotion, to be a devout people." Yet there should be an intrinsic cause on our part, which cause is meditation or contemplation. For devotion consists in an act of the will by which man gives himself with readiness to divine worship; and any act of will is born of an intellectual reflection that goes before it, since it is the intellectually known good that is the object of the will. Augustine says in *De Trinitate* (14, c.8) that "will is born of intelligence." It is required, then, that quiet forethought be the source of devotion, and it is through such forethought that man is led to give himself to divine worship. Two considerations lead to this end. One of them is God's goodness and His benefits; which is thus expressed by the Psalmist (Ps. 72): "It is good for me to adhere to my God, to put my hope in the Lord God;" and this first consideration begets in us the love which is the proximate cause of devotion. The second consideration is of our own failings, because of which we need to lean on God, as the Psalmist says: (Ps. 120): "I have lifted up my eyes to the mountains, from whence help shall come to me. My help is from the Lord, who made heaven and earth." This bars out presumption, the vice of trusting to our own strength and not yielding to God (2–2, q.82, a.3).

Now for the other interior act by which religion is expressed. Prayer, of course, is good and really required for the perfection of this virtue. It is good, because metaphysics shows us that things are not governed by a blind necessity or by any divine caprice, but by divine foresight and planning; hence we may pray, not in order to change the unchangeable plans of God for us, but in order that by our acts we may fully effect the order prearranged for us by God (q.83, a.4). The act of prayer is needed also because it is essentially a request made to God by man to obtain from Him whatever we require, and because this human acknowledgment of our own poverty is an indispensable beginning of the virtue of religion (a.5). We should, therefore, pray, and when we hardly know what to ask of God, it is enough to observe the following rule: we should ask in our prayers whatever we ought to desire: namely, first, spiritual goods for ourselves, our friends, and even our enemies; then, material goods too, but only so much of them as may be a help in gaining the Sovereign Good of the soul, to which they should remain subordinate.

The exterior acts of religion come next in order, and we may say first that their necessity is based on man's very nature.

If we give glory and honor to God, we do it not for His sake, for He is already full of His own glory, and nothing can be added to it by any creature. We do it rather for our sake, because to reverence and honor God is to submit our minds to Him, and our perfection lies in this act. For anything is perfected so far as it yields to what is above it: the body so far as it is animated by the soul, and the atmosphere so far as it is illumined by the sun. Now, for union with God the human mind needs to be led on by sense things, because the invisible things of God are understood by the things that are made (*Rom.* c.1). This is why in divine worship we need some corporal things, so that by them as by signs the mind of man is awakened to spiritual acts and conjoined to God. Thus religion supposes interior acts as its principal ones and as having to do directly with the virtue of religion, but it also supposes exterior acts as secondary and as meant to be aids to the interior (2–2, q.81, a.7).

The chief of the exterior acts are these: adoration, by which our bodies bow down before God as our minds are humbled before Him in devotion (q.84, a.2); sacrifice, which is not merely a Christian custom, but more a duty of natural law known by all peoples and based on man's desire to signify and confess his dependence on a higher being, as soon as he begins to think on the problem of his own poverty (q.85, a.1); and lastly the vows, by which a religious person obliges himself to live a better life and to settle himself in it according to the quasi-material formula of the spoken words he uses to bind himself (q.88, a.1).

The other virtues linked with justice are those that bind man not merely in relation to God, but also in relation to certain other men. Obedience, for example, causes man's will, by its submitting to a superior will, to reproduce the subordination of natural inferior forces to the higher forces which God has expressly willed as Orderer of the world (q.104, a.1). Gratitude, too, is close to justice, because it brings us to give to God, to parents, and in general to benefactors, what we owe them for the good things we have received from them (q.106, a.1). Like obedience, it rests on the analogy that the moral order is to be enforced if we would maintain the natural order willed by God. Every effect naturally points back to its cause as that which is its purpose and *raison d'être,* and whoever receives a benefit is so far an effect of the benefactor, since he would not be wholly what he is if he did not have the gift he has received; he should, therefore, turn toward him in some way to acknowledge his dependence, and this is why God, as the cause of all things, turns

VIRTUES ASSOCIATED WITH JUSTICE

them all back toward Himself (q.106, a.3). One of the most charming and vital virtues connected with justice is truth. It is a virtue, for it is good to speak the truth, and whatever makes us do good is a virtue. And it is a kind of justice, in the sense that it pays off a sort of debt, if not a legal debt, at least a moral one that all of us contract toward our neighbors by the very fact that we live in society. This debt or duty is the manifestation of truth.

Because man is a social being, one man owes to another that without which human society could not go on. And men could not live together unless they had towards one another a confidence founded on the mutual telling of the truth. Thus the virtue of truth takes on in some ways the character of a debt (q.109, a.3, ad 1).

Truth is only one virtue, but there are many vices opposed to it: lying, double-dealing, boasting, which makes us represent ourselves as better than we really are; irony, a subtler vice that makes us dissimulate and unjustly rate down our own strength with the aim of deceiving others on what we are (q.113, a.1). And as truth-telling means that we give others what the exigencies of social life require in the realm of thought, so affability is our means of meeting those same exigencies in the realm of manners: by it we say and do what is fitting and prescribed, not by the law of the land, but by the rules of civility (q.114, a.2).

Chapter X

THE MAN OF VALOR

We now take up the study of fortitude as the third cardinal virtue. We should recall that this name "cardinal" is given to the four virtues that possess in an eminent degree the general characteristics required in all virtues. One of these marks undoubtedly is a firmness in our way of acting; and this firmness flows directly from fortitude, so that this virtue is in some degree integral with all other virtues. So it is said to be a cardinal virtue, and it ranks next after justice in the hierarchy of these four virtues.

Augustine says (*De Trinitate,* vi, c.8): "In those things whose greatness does not consist in size, to be great simply means to be excellent." A virtue, then, is so much greater as it is the more excellent or good. And what in particular is man's good? Dionysius says it is the good of reason (*De Div. Nom.,* iv, 4). Now prudence, as the perfection of reason, essentially possesses this good. Justice, too, employs this good in so far as it is the business of justice to make reason king in all human affairs. Other virtues also help to preserve this value by so tempering the emotions that they do not turn man away from the rational good. If we take these two last

THE MAN OF VALOR

(fortitude and justice) in their order, fortitude has first place, because fear of imminent death is the greatest thing in the world to turn man away from the rational good. Next comes temperance, because all pleasures, and especially those of touch, keep man from the good which reason prescribes. And that which is of the essence of virtue is more important than what is only a help to virtue, and this latter, the help, is better than what serves, in a negative way, to clear out obstacles. That is why the main cardinal virtue is prudence, the second is justice, the third is fortitude, and the fourth temperance. After these come the other virtues (2–2, q.123, a 12).

As we have just pointed out, the proper object of fortitude is to clear out of virtue's path any obstacle that feeling opposes to virtue, especially the feeling or emotion of fear, and most of all that particular and agonizing fear which the peril of approaching death inspires. Whoever can do the greater can do the less. The man, then, who is capable of overcoming the fear of the most terrible of bodily evils, is of course able to win against the fear that all other evils might bring upon him. Here we have the reason why the virtue of fortitude is best seen in the presence of death, yet not every danger of death is equally fit to show forth this virtue.

We have said that fortitude strengthens man's spirit against the greatest of all perils, namely, death. Still, as fortitude is a virtue, and as the essence of virtue is to tend always to good, it follows that, if man is brave and faces the danger of death, it must be in order to seek a certain good. Yet the danger of death occasioned by sickness or a storm or an assault from robbers or any such thing does not menace man directly as a seeker of some good; on the contrary, the danger of death brought on by war is a direct peril to man as a seeker of a particular good, that is, in so far as he defends the common good in a just war. And a war can be just, in either of two senses. First, in a general way, when two armies face each other in the field. Secondly, in a particular way, when a judge or even a private citizen does not flinch from a just judgment though he fears the sword over his head or some other deadly peril. It goes with the virtue of fortitude then, to make a man courageous of soul before the dangers of death that may be imminent indeed in common warfare and also in the particular attacks to which we may stretch the name of war. We must, therefore, grant that courage has to do properly with the danger of death to which war exposes us; but the brave bear themselves well in face of deadly danger from any other cause, for there is no danger of death that man may not encounter for the sake of virtue: for instance, he may go to help a sick friend and not run from the danger of a deadly infection, or keep on a journey in the interests of some pious business and not turn aside through fear of shipwreck or robbery (2–2, q.123, a.5).

It follows that the proper effect of the virtue of courage is to resist rather than to attack.

In matter of fact it is harder to resist than to attack. There are three reasons for this. In the first place, a man needs to resist only when invaded by one stronger than himself; for he who attacks does it because he is the stronger, and it is harder to fight a stronger man than a weaker one. Second, he who resists knows the presence of danger, whereas he who attacks regards danger as in the future; and certainly it is more difficult to stand firm in present dangers than in view of future ones. Third, to hold out takes a longer time, whereas a person can attack with one sudden onrush, and it is harder to stay a long time waiting than to go swiftly into some arduous work (2-2, q.123, a.6, ad 1).

We come now to determination of the courageous act *par excellence,* which is also the most perfect act. It is martyrdom. That it is the very type of the courageous act will appear later in a particular manner; for it is an act of virtue, since it strengthens man in the good, and it is a virtuous act in a supreme degree, since it strengthens him before the danger of death that confronts him in the particular battle called persecution (q.124, a.5). But it remains to notice in what sense martyrdom is at the same time an act of the highest perfection.

There are two ways of looking at an act of virtue. The first has to do with the class to which the act itself belongs, and its relation to the virtue which immediately produces it. In this sense we may say that martyrdom, which is the taking of death as one ought, is not the most perfect act of virtue. In fact, to suffer death is not in itself an act of virtue, but only when it is done for some good, which good itself is founded on an act of virtue, as, let us say, faith in God, or love for God; so this act of virtue, as it is the purpose of constancy in the face of death, is better than this constancy.

The second way of looking at an act of virtue is concerned with the first motive of the act, and this motive is love of charity; it is chiefly in this light that an act makes for perfection of life. As the Apostle says (*Col.,* c.3) : *Charity is the bond of perfection.* Now among all the acts of virtue martyrdom is the best demonstration of a perfect charity. For one shows more love for a thing, the more he contemns some other loved thing for it and is willing to suffer more grievous things for it. And it is evident that of all the goods of the present man most of all loves life itself and, on the contrary, hates death most, particularly a death borne with bodily torments: through fear of which, says Augustine, even the brute animals give up the greatest pleasures. In this sense it is plain that martyrdom is a more perfect act in its kind than other human acts, since it is the mark of the highest charity, as St. John says (c.15) : "Greater love than this no man hath, that a man lay down his life for his friends" (2–2, q.124, a.3).

The vices which are a denial of the virtue of fortitude are three: timidity, inability to fear, and overboldness. Timidity is that which keeps us back in the face of a danger that reason bids us to face; it is the very contrary of courage.

In every instance fear comes from love, for a person fears only the contrary of what he loves. And love, for its part, is not in any determined genus of virtue, or of vice either, but ordered love is included in every virtue, since a virtuous person always loves the own good of virtue; and disordered love is present in every sin. For from a disordered love comes wrong desire. So a badly ordered fear is included in every sin: the miser fears the loss of his money, the intemperate man of his pleasures, and so on. But the main fear is of the danger of death. That is why we say that the disorder begot of this fear is opposed to fortitude, which means above all the braving of death, and that the main vice opposed to fortitude is timidity (2-2, q.125, a.2).

As for the inability to fear, though it might seem praiseworthy at first sight, it is no less vicious than the other. The truly brave man is not the heavy, senseless stock that, knowing nothing, can fear nothing. Nor is he the fellow who, caring little, has little fear of losing; nor yet he who, settled in pride and presumption, does not fear that any danger can ever menace what he loves (q.126, a.1). The really brave man is he who loves what he should and who fears what he should and when there is reasonable ground for fear, but who sets himself against this fear and turns upon the danger (*ibid.*, a.2). There is, then, a midway between him who fears too much and him who does not fear enough, and this course is not timid, not unflinching, and let us add, not brazen. We know that audacity is an emotion (see p. 128). Like all emotions, it is good when regulated by reason. It may be a good thing to take the field when the time is ripe for doing so and when some threatening danger must be cleared out of the way; but boldness is an evil when it goes to excess, shows a lack of moderation in the exercise of fortitude, and when it opens the door to needless and untimely invasion

(2–2, q.123, a.3, and q.127, a.2). Virtue goes over into vice every time that the good yields to evil by a violation of the promptings of reason.

Related to the cardinal virtue of fortitude are four virtues that share its nature, but do not fully realize its definition. These are magnanimity, magnificence, patience, and perseverance. Magnanimity may not be classed with fortitude, nor are the two of the same degree, for the difference between them is that between standing unmoved before death, heedless of one's life, and giving proof of the kind of grandeur that magnanimity implies (2–2, q.129, a.5). Yet it is a virtue of the same class as the other, and when it is guided, it is in some sense the contrary of fear.

By its very name, *magnanimity* supposes a soul fit to strive for great things. Now we can study a virtue in two lights: first, in relation to the matter with which it deals, or on which it acts; second, in relation to its proper act, which lies in using this matter in a fitting way. And as it is mainly in view of its act that we define a virtue, a man is called magnanimous chiefly because he has a spirit inclined toward some great deed. But if we look at the grandeur of this act itself, it in its turn seems to us to be twofold, according as we take it either in a certain perspective or as absolute. An act may be called great either relatively or absolutely. It is called great in the former sense though it employs something cheap or of ordinary value, but makes the very best use of it; and that act which makes the very best use of the very best thing is called great simply or without qualification. The things that men use are exterior things, and the greatest of these is honor; for we have seen (q.103, a.1 and a.2) that it is a very near neighbor of virtue and indeed a kind of present witness to some virtue, and also that it is given to God and to all best things, and that men lay aside everything to win honor and avoid shame. And because the greatness of the magnanimous soul is judged directly from the greatness of his acts, as his strength is gauged from their difficulty, it follows that magnanimity has to do with honors (2–2, q.129, a.1).

For the same reason we say further that, as an unavoidable consequence, this virtue tries for the greatest honors, but, in a way suggested by reason, moderates the hope we have of them. Here again virtue lies in taking a middle road, for it is an excellent thing to aim high and to desire and value one's own honor, which, after virtue, is most worthy of our efforts; but it is an excellent thing only if we desire no more than the highest honor reason tells us we are worthy of (*ibid.*, a.3, ad 1). At the same time we see that, without being in a proper sense identified with the virtue of fortitude, magnanimity is yet related to it and dependent on it, for honors are hard things to get, even though one be worthy of them; he must have firmness of soul, not, of course, so much as to face death, but enough to stand out against the obstacles that block his way to the rewards which he thinks are his due, and enough also to think himself worthy of them and therefore able to hope for them (*ibid.*, a.5). It is a tight rope that this virtue walks, for to believe ourselves able to reach what is above our heads, is presumption; to believe ourselves worthy of an honor not in line with our true merit, is ambition; to like honors won on false titles or as seen by man's fallible mind or for any other end than God's honor or man's good, is vain or empty glory. Yet to be incapable of so much as wishing the honor to which one has a right in God's view, which one can win before God as he ought and for the purposes he ought, is pusillanimity, littleness of soul, the very etymology of which is at odds with greatness of soul or magnanimity.

It is the etymology of the name which gives us light also on the essence of the second main virtue linked to fortitude, namely, magnificence. The question here no longer is that of *being* a great soul, but of *doing* great things, or at any rate of extending oneself to do them (2-2, q.134, q.2, ad 2). Thus magnanimity is great because of the objects which it aims at, but magnificence derives its greatness from what it does, and also from the way in which it does it. It is in the realm of doing, *i. e.,* of producing, and is a virtue proper to the artist, whom it predisposes to realize works that are great in their dimensions or precise in their matter. It is one of the virtues, we should add, that can most poorly do without exterior goods; the magnificent man is he who has wherewithal to give and who knows how to give.

The mark of magnificence, as we just said, is to aim at doing some great thing. And to do any great thing proportionate costs have to be borne, for no one does things on a grand scale without heavy expense, and for this reason magnificence knows how to foot big bills so that important works be done as they should be. Now, to pay out is to part with money, and some men are such that their exaggerated love of money keeps them from doing this; and so the expense itself which the magnificent man incurs in doing a splendid work may be taken as the content of magnificence, and so, too, may the money which he pays out to meet this expense, or even his moderated liking for money, which does not get in the way of the large cost (2–2, q.134, a.3).

Magnificence is so truly a virtue that a vice makes its appearance as soon as the virtue is lacking: littleness or incapacity to give up the necessary sum for his undertakings. This is the vice of the man who is wanting in magnificence; and prodigality or a readiness to lavish without aim the resources one has at his disposal, is the fault of the man who by his overdoing misses the virtue of magnificence.

We have two other lordly virtues related to magnificence. These are: patience and perseverance. Patience is not precisely the same thing as fortitude, for it does not mean withstanding the fear begot of danger of death, yet it is strictly analogous to it. That is, it supposes a holding out against any sadness or depression that is not of so strong a nature as the fear of death, but that could run us off on a detour from the good mapped out for us by reason. And perseverance, we might say, is the fulfilment of all true fortitude, and in a way is simply the continuance of its effects.

Virtue looks to what is good but not easy to attain, and where there is a definite kind of difficulty or of the good to be won, there can be a special virtue. Now, the pursuit of virtue gets goodness, and labor too, from two sources. In the first place from the kind of act done, and this depends in turn on the nature of the object in question. Secondly, from the length of time, for the fact of sticking for a long time to a difficult problem has a special knottiness of its own, and this is why to keep on and on at a good until one completes it is the mark of a special virtue. And so, just as temperance and courage are particular virtues, for one moderates the pleasures of touch (which in itself is not easy) and the other checks both the fear and boldness that come in company with the danger (which checking also is hard work), so perseverance is likewise a specific virtue and its business is to be constant in these or other virtuous enterprises as long as is necessary (2-2, q.137, a.1).

We must not confuse perseverance with constancy, which is another virtue linked with fortitude. The two have not the same difficulty to overcome. What perseverance withstands and provides us against, is the length of time that we must keep up our effort, whereas constancy arms us for the most part against the obstacles and hazards which might get in the way of our purpose to do good (*ibid.*, a.3). This latter virtue is thus not so directly related to courage as perseverance, because the difficulty that comes of length of time is more at the center and within the act of virtue than the one that comes from exterior hindrances.

We note, too, that perseverance occurs, as do all virtues, at a temperate half-way point between the two excesses of softness and obstinacy. A lazy man breaks with a good cause as soon as any difficulty arises, even though this difficulty could be conquered. An obstinate man will not give up a resolution once it is made, even though he be unreasonable in holding to it. So, stubbornness clings to a scheme longer than it should, and softness lets go sooner than it should, but perseverance, unlike either, persists just as long as it ought, and that is why we consider it a virtue.

Chapter XI

THE PRACTICE OF SELF-CONTROL

In the study of temperance we come to a new object in relation to which it is defined. This object is sense pleasure and strong carnal desire. The strict business of temperance is to keep these in check. We might be even more precise and, taking the path that we followed in defining the virtue of courage, try to find which pleasures and which desires it should most of all moderate. The truth is, this is one of the four cardinal virtues, and it certainly has to do with a difficulty that is big and bound up with, not to say inherent in, the very nature of the human beings that we are (2–2, q.141, a.7). What is this difficulty?

The field of temperance is strong desire and sense joy, as that of fortitude is fear and rashness. Now, as the express object of courage we took the apprehension and presumption associated with the greatest of all evils, those that put an end to nature herself, that is, the perils of death. In a like manner temperance ought to be concerned with desires of the delights that are strongest of all. And because delight goes hand in hand with natural functioning, the more natural the functions with which they are linked the stronger are the delights. Now, among animals, the most natural of all actions

THE PRACTICE OF SELF-CONTROL

are those by which individuals survive by the help of food and drink and those by which the species is preserved through the union of male and female. It is accordingly with the delights of eating and drinking and of sex that temperance properly deals, and as pleasures of these kinds depend on the sense of touch, it follows that temperance pertains to the pleasures of touch (2-2, q.141, a.4).

As objects inferior to the foregoing we give second place to the delights of taste and also those of the senses of smell and sight, which latter may overlap those of touch and make them the more attractive. All these pleasures are, therefore, subjected by the virtue of temperance to a fixed rule, which determines the use of them, and this rule is found in the purpose of the pleasures which it has the work of keeping moderate. Their proper purpose, of course, is to make sure of the life of the individual and that of the species. This, then, will be the rule of temperance: to take of the goods and pleasures of touch just the amount that the needs of life require (*ibid.*, a.6). Thus we find this virtue equidistant between two contrary excesses: insensibility and intemperance. The former sins by default and by crushing desire; this vice exists, and there is no need to confuse it with what is merely a just moderation.

Anything that is contrary to the order of nature is bad. Now nature has associated pleasure with the functions necessary for the life of man, and this is why the order of nature demands that we use pleasures of this kind just as much as is needful for the preservation of man, whether in the life of the individual or of the species. If anyone, therefore, should so far fly from pleasure that he would pass up things necessary for the conservation of nature, he would sin as flying in the face of the order of nature; and this would be an instance of the vice of insensibility. Still, we must note that sometimes it is worthy of praise and even needful, for the sake of some cause, to deny oneself the pleasures that go with actions of this kind. For instance, some people abstain from pleasures of food and drink, or of sex, for the good of their health. Others find it necessary to refrain from many dissipations in order to hold their jobs; penitents who want to build up strength of soul practise abstinence from pleasures as a kind of diet, and persons who aim at contemplation and try to be free for divine things should turn aside from the delights of the body. Nor do any of the aforesaid groups fall into the vice of insensibility, for they all act in a right and reasonable way (2–2, q.142, a.1).

The intemperate man sins by an excess that is the contrary of insensibility. He lets himself be carried away in the pursuit of pleasures that are tempting to the senses, especially by those that allure the sense of touch. Looked at from one point of view, the vice of intemperance would appear as worthy of some indulgence, for in the long run it is simply a criminal disorder of inclinations that in themselves are rightful and natural. But in reality it is a particularly low vice that merits censure through and through; in fact:

Condemnation seems to be the opposite of honor and glory. Honor should go to excellence, as glory to any striking worth. And if so, intemperance is blameworthy for two reasons. First, it is completely out of accord with human excellence, since it looks only to the delights that we have in common with the animals; and indeed it is said (Psalm 48): "Man when he was in honor did not understand; he is compared to senseless beasts, and is become like to them." Second, intemperance is all out of step with man's nobility and beauty, because the delights after which the intemperate run are those in which the light of reason is little seen, and yet it is from this light that the whole grandeur and beauty of virtue arise. Such pleasures, then, are as slavish as any can be (2–2, q.142, a.4).

We see at once that the virtue of temperance takes in, as an integral part of itself, a virtue that is its invariable companion. This is modesty. Whoever loves the moderation that reason brings into our pleasures, detests at the same time the disorder that intemperance sets going, and it is this shame that we call modesty. In a like way temperance supposes and implies the virtue of honor. Though honor, taken in itself, has a much wider extension than has temperance in the strict sense, it is most closely related to the latter. For temperance has the work of bringing our lowest and most humiliating tendencies within the reign of reason, and this it could not begin to do without honor, which is the very taste for spiritual beauty brought into our lives by the rule of reason.

The specific applications of the virtue of temperance are many, because it has many pleasures to moderate and many ways of moderating them. Abstinence, for instance, or the mastery of self in the use of food so as to keep in line with the demands of reason. Fasting, which is a particular act for the exercise of the virtue of abstinence and which is therefore bound up with it. These restraints are excellent and effective ways of checking the opposed vice, known as gluttony, under whatever form it shows itself: fondness for rare and costly dishes, a studied way of preparing them, too large an amount of nourishing food, rapacity and speed in the gourmand's style of eating—how many wrong steps reason chides and the virtue of temperance sets itself to put right. And what is true of food, is just as true of drink. Sobriety has for its purview a measured use, and drunkenness is its direct opposite. Besides, this virtue and this vice are truly of a kind distinct from those that neighbor on them and are like them; the truth is that nothing is so directly and so out and out contrary to the practice of reason as excess in the use of intoxicating drink, so much so that we have here a special problem that menaces the reign of reason and a special remedy meant to take care of it. We may go even farther and note down the persons who are in a particular way obliged to sobriety.

Any virtue can be seen in either of two lights. First, there are vices which it debars and strong desires which it keeps

THE PRACTICE OF SELF-CONTROL

in leash. Then there is the purpose which it serves. So the need of a virtue is particularly felt by a person for either of two reasons. In the first place, he may be remarkably prone to the passion which this virtue muzzles, and to the vices which it destroys. Seen thus, sobriety is peculiarly required in youths and women; because youths are full of vigor and warmth and desire of pleasure, and women are not forceful enough in mind to resist pleasures, and that is why, according to Valerius Maximus (bk. 2, c.1), the Roman women in the olden days used not to drink wine. Another reason why sobriety is demanded more in some persons is that it is needed more for the work they have to do. Wine taken immoderately gets very much in the way of thought and judgment; and so sobriety is rigorously a duty for old men who to teach others need rational vitality, for bishops and all ministers of the Church, who ought to give their minds all the time and devotedly to spiritual concerns, and for rulers of whom wisdom is expected in the governance of the people (2-2, q.149, a.4).

The contrary of sobriety is drunkenness, the outward signs of which are easily known; the ethician looks at this vice from several distinct points of view.

Drunkenness is a fault that lies in the immoderate use and enjoyment of wine, and might occur in any of three ways. In the first instance, a man might not know that he was taking too much or that the stuff was intoxicating, and he might get drunk without sin. Second, a man might know that he was drinking heavily, but think that the liquor could not make a man drunk, and his drunkenness would not be grievously sinful. Third, one might know that he was drinking too much and that the drink was strong, and yet be more willing to get drunk than to give up the cup. Such a person is a real drunkard, because acts are not classified as moral and immoral when the doer does not intend them, but only when he does definitely intend them. In such case intoxication is a grievous sin because the man, knowing what he is doing and willing to do it, cuts himself off from the use of reason, whereas it is only by the use of reason that we take any virtuous path and leave sin on the detour. He sins seriously by exposing himself to the danger (2–2, q.150, a.2).

By the same token we see how to solve the mooted problem of knowing whether intoxication is an excuse for the one who commits a crime while in that state. Plainly, since the drunken man has not the use of reason, he does not know what he does at the moment he does it, and so his drunkenness does help to excuse him. But it fully exonerates him only in the instance of that chance intoxication of which we first spoke and which in itself is not a fault. On the other hand, if a man gets drunk of his own accord and then commits a crime, he is responsible for putting himself in the way of committing it, though the fault itself is lessened because not directly chargeable to his will.

We may add that what abstinence and sobriety are to the use of food and drink, chastity is to sex pleasure, always with this difference, that an absolute abstention from the pleasures of the table is something that the needs of nature cannot stand, whereas one can entirely refrain from this second kind of pleasure. Perfect virginity can be kept, and is so far from being unlawful that it is quite commendable, for the reason that it very well qualifies man for the highest form of life accessible to him.

What is vicious in man's acts is whatever rides full tilt against right reason. Now right reason is willing that a person use a means in the measure in which it serves its end. And as Aristotle says (*Ethics,* 1, c.8), values for man are of three kinds. The first are external, as, for instance, money; the second are for the welfare of the body; the third are spiritual values, among which those of a life of contemplation are higher than those of a life of action, as the Philosopher contends in the *Ethics* (10, c.7) and as Our Lord also says (St. Luke, c.10): "Mary hath chosen the better part." Of all these values, the external serve the bodily; the bodily are rated in view of the spiritual; and among spiritual values those of a life of action are subordinated to those of a life of contemplation. The work of right reason, then, is to use external good things so far as is expedient for the body, and to use the other values in their places. If, for the sake of bodily health or to seek truth, a man should let certain values pass which otherwise it were well to possess, he is not vicious, but a man of reason. And if anyone gives up bodily pleasures so as to be the freer for contemplating truth, his choice squares excellently with reason. This is what devoted virgins do; they abstain from sensual delectation to have more freedom for contemplating divine truth. So the Apostle says (I Cor., c.7): "The unmarried woman and the virgin thinketh on the things of the Lord, that she may be holy both in body and in spirit. But she that is married thinketh on the things of the world, that she may please her husband." Virginity therefore is not blameworthy, but quite praiseworthy (2–2, q.152, a.2).

Yet perhaps some people will protest that virginity is an open contradiction of the law of nature, which God sanctioned when, to make sure of the survival of the race, he gave the command to individuals: Increase and multiply and fill the earth (*cf. Genesis,* c.1). We grant that it is a fault against the law of nature if anyone brings his own individuality to nothing by wholly refusing food. Is not, then, the refusal to beget a like fault? Is it not to act contrary to the maintenance of the race?

The response to this is that every precept involves a duty, but that duties are of two kinds. There are duties to be fulfilled by this one person, and he cannot omit them without sin. But there are duties to be borne by a group, and no one of the group is held to carry out such duties: they are necessary indeed for the group, and no one is able to do them; yet they are completed, provided one person does this, another that. Now the command to eat, given man by the law of nature, must needs be carried out by each one, otherwise the individual could not survive. Yet the order to reproduce the species is given to the whole human race, which, of course, is duty-bound to physical reproduction, but also to spiritual progress. The needs of the human race are, therefore, sufficiently taken care of when some take up the work of carnal generation; others abstain from it and have leisure for contemplation of divine things in view of the welfare and adorn-

THE PRACTICE OF SELF-CONTROL

ment of the entire human family. The same principle holds in an army; some protect the supplies, some give signals, some go into battle, and in this way the total obligation is on the group and could not be borne by one (2-2, q.152, a.2, ad 1).

The vice that stands over against chastity is sensuality, which in its strict sense is defined as having chiefly to do with sex pleasures. This vice makes its appearance as soon as such pleasures are in any manner or degree turned aside from their purpose, which is the preservation of the race through generation. Few vices sound the tocsin among the powers of the soul for so far-reaching and thorough a disorder.

When the lower powers are strongly set on their objects, the result is that the higher faculties can no longer function, or do so only in a disordered way. Now, in the vice of sensuality the baser appetite, that is, lust, does strive most eagerly after its object of pleasure by a vehemence of passion and delectation. What comes of this is that sensuality runs a disorder through the nobler powers of reason and the will. But any action supposes four steps. The first is an act of simple understanding, which sees some goal as a good, but sensuality stays this act, as is said in the Book of Daniel (c.13): "Beauty hath deceived thee, and lust hath perverted thy heart;" it fathers a mental blindness. The second stage is a mapping out of the road we must take to reach the end, and this act also is bothered by lust; whence the saying of Terence in *The Eunuch* (1, c.1) where he speaks of voluptuous love: "If an affair is beyond reason and measure, you cannot guide it by any plan;" at this point lust begets hurry, which means the absence of aim, as was said earlier (see p. 239). The third turn is a judgment of what we must do, and this is likewise hindered by sensuality; as Daniel says of old voluptuaries (c.13): They have turned away their minds, that they might not remember just judgments; the result is a lack of thought. The fourth step is a reasoned command of what we are to do, and this is blocked by sensuality, which keeps men from doing what they know they ought to do; inconstancy is born now; so Terence wrote of a man who said he was going to give up a woman friend (*l.c.*), "One false little tear will put a stop to these words of his!"

So far as the will is concerned, two disordered acts result from lust. One is desire of the end, and here enters a love of self in the disordered pleasure that is wanted, and a hatred of God because He forbids the pleasure that is sought. The other is attachment to the means, so that one has an affection for life here and now and wants a sensuous enjoyment of it, and he loses hope of a future life, because when a person is too much given to carnal delights, he takes no care to attain spiritual ones, but has a distaste for them (2-2, q.153, a.5).

We just saw which virtues are implicit in temperance and the vices that make war on it. We must next study the virtues that, while not to be exactly called temperance, are within it almost as parts of it, are at any rate its neighbors and have something of its nature. There are three of these: continence, forbearance, and modesty.

If one were to take the term *continence* in an unrestricted sense, as some do, the virtue meant would

THE PRACTICE OF SELF-CONTROL

be the same as the virginity of which we have spoken. But to be exact, continence is something other, something less. It is a kind of quality, and not a virtue out and out. The really chaste man has the mastery over the movements of his physical self; one who is only continent has to labor more or less to control them and is not able to get a full captaincy over them. The effort is worthy of praise and credit; he is a good man in the sense that he struggles against evil; but his virtue is not perfect, because in a soul in which consummate virtue has its kingdom, no passion should ever rise up violently against the orders of reason. One sees how deserving continence is when it is lacking. The incontinent man is not rooted and fixed in evil as is the intemperate person who has a set disposition to do wrong and is satisfied to give himself up to passion, yet he lets himself be stirred by a strong passing movement toward evil, which though he at once repents, he had a duty to resist (*ibid.*, q.156, a.3). The main results of continence are in its opposing sense desire under two of its most basic and passionate forms: anger and lust; the leading effect of incontinence is to make us yield to them.

We may take *forbearance* as a second virtue in the field of temperance. We must show how this is like and how it is unlike meekness. The meek man is able to cool down within him the fiery anger that rouses him; the man of forbearance has power to cut down the penalties that an overcharged justice might prompt him to inflict (*ibid.,* q.157, a.1). The two of them have this common mark of virtue, that they are ruled by reason, for it is not by any blind sentiment that the meek and the patient man rein in anger or lessen chastisement, but because of a sane judgment condemning this resentment and discipline as excessive (q.157, a.2, ad 1). These qualities are called virtues by a stretching of the sense of that word; their contraries are anger and cruelty. We inquire first what anger is, taken precisely as a vice.

As we remarked earlier (see p. 129), the word *anger* in its proper meaning refers to one of the emotions, and every emotion of sense desire is good so far as ruled by reason, but if it breaks with the rational order, it is bad. Now reason can rule anger in either of two ways. The goal sought is revenge, and when this is aimed at in a reasonable way, the desire which starts such anger is praiseworthy, and we speak of a righteous anger. But if this desire for revenge in any way breaks through the bidding of reason, the arousing of anger is vicious; for instance, when one desires to have a man punished who does not deserve it or does not deserve so much, or does not have him punished according to lawful order and for the right purpose, which is the upholding of justice and the correction of the fault; in such instance, anger is vicious. The second way of ruling anger has to do with its degree. It supposes that the movement of anger does not get too hot, either within or without; so that if the bounds of moderation are passed, the anger, though for a just revenge, will not be without sin (2-2, q.158, a.2).

The essential thing in cruelty is a kind of hardness and a rigorous feeling that shuts out every inclination to lighten the penalty inflicted on guilty persons. It is not at odds with that mastery of self which keeps reason from going beyond what is justly the limit in fixing a punishment to be imposed, but with that sweetness of spirit which we have named forbearance and which brings the judge to soften a little an austerity that is perhaps excessive (q.159, a.1, ad 1). We should not confuse cruelty with a relish for ferocity, a species of brutality that takes a bestial pleasure in making people suffer and gloats over the torture inflicted on a victim. The reasonable course is then twisted, because instead of punishing to straighten out a fault, it is done to see people suffer. So long as you are merely cruel you are guilty of a malice that is still human, but when you take pleasure in a thirst for blood, you lower yourself to the level of the brute.

The third of the virtues joined to temperance is *modesty* or moderation in the use of pleasures that are less than those of touch. It is not the least fruitful or happy in its effects on our moral life. We have noted that pleasures of touch are the bounded range for the virtue of temperance, and if there is needed a special virtue for the most intense physical delights, one is needed for the less intense. Modesty is just such a virtue, no matter under what form we may study it. For instance, it is undoubtedly true that we have an appetite for honors and for everything that is great, so much so that we must have the virtue of magnanimity to maintain the desire in the face of the vice of despair. To keep that ambition from the contrary vice, which would hurry us, through lack of moderation, to ever more lofty aims, must we not have another virtue? This is the work of modesty: to give us balance at the correct point; and so it is called humility. Briefly, then, we may say that humility is the dress that modesty wears in order to manage our hopes (2-2, q.161, a.4) and that its contrary is pride, the first of all sins and the most serious kind of sin. As we already know, any sin has a formal and a material element. The material part is the movement by which man gives himself to some limited value, the formal is the movement by which man turns away from the unchanging value or God. Now humility in its perfect form means man's yielding to God, and pride is a refusal to submit to God and His law; so it is that pride is the first of the sins, because we may say it substantiates the definition of sin.

In any classification, that which is of itself comes first; and we have just seen that the act of turning away from God, or the formal principle of sin, belongs to pride *sui juris,* but to other sins only as a consequence. It follows that pride is by its nature the first of sins and for the same reason the font of all other sins (2-2, q.162, a.7).

This is wholly a natural doctrine, but it agrees with the thought of the Church, which regards original sin as a sin of pride. The promise of the devil: "You shall be as gods, knowing good and evil," begot in the mind of the first man a disordered desire to be like God, that is to say, to be able to make out by the force of his own nature what ought to be good or evil for him and by his purely natural resources to attain a position for doing this good or avoiding this evil (q.163, a.2). This was a sin of great gravity, nay, the gravest of all sins, if not in its matter, then at least in its effects and because of the state of perfection of those who committed it.

The study of original sin, which was a toosufficient desire of a knowledge more than human, brings us by a natural path to a form of modesty that men of intellect run the greatest danger of forgetting: the virtue of limiting curiosity. It supposes a good understanding of nature; indeed:

This virtue (*studiositas*) is concerned with the taste and desire for knowledge, and only in an indirect way with knowledge itself, for we must judge differently of the very knowledge of truth and a thirst or zeal to know truth. Knowledge of truth is generally a good thing, but it can in an accidental way and as a consequence be evil; for example, some get proud over knowledge of truth, as is said (1 *Cor.,* c.8): "Knowledge puffeth up;" and some men use knowledge of the truth to commit sin. Of course, the desire or ambition to know truth can be either right or wrong. It is wrong, for instance, every time that a man is desirous of a knowledge of the truth for the evil he can get out of it; such are those who drive themselves in the conquest of knowledge so that they may plume themselves over it, persons described by St. Augustine (*De moribus Eccl.,* 21): "There are men who lay aside virtue and know not God or the majesty of that nature that remains ever the same, and who think they do something great if they inquire with the greatest curiosity into that universal magma that we call the world, but pride gets such a hold on them that they come to think they live in the heavens about which they argue." The zeal of those also who study only in order to sin is vicious; as Jeremias says (c.9): "They have taught their tongue to speak lies, and have labored to commit iniquity."

The desire to know the truth can be perverse in a second sense. The desire itself may be ungoverned, in any of four ways. It may be that a less useful study turns us into a detour from the main road that we should travel. Thus St. Jerome says (Letter 146, "On the Prodigal Son"): "We notice that priests close up the Gospels and the Prophets, and read comedies and sing the love songs of the Bucolics." Secondly, it may be that some try to learn from forbidden masters. This is evidently true of those who beseech the devils to show them the future; it is curiosity, but superstitious; whence St. Augustine says (*On the True Religion,* 4): "I do not know whether philosophers are not kept from the Faith by the vice of asking curious questions of the demons." Thirdly, sometimes a man wants to know the facts about creatures, but does not link this knowledge to its lawful goal, which is a knowledge of God; as Augustine remarks (*l.c.,* 29): "In the study of creatures an aimless and perishable curiosity is not to be employed, yet there must be a measure of inquiry in view of unchanging and imperishable things." Fourthly, a zeal to know is on the wrong scent when the truth in question is beyond the range of the human mind. As men we very easily make mistakes. Hence the saying of Ecclesiasticus (c.3): "Seek not the things that are too high for thee, and search not into things above thy ability, . . . and in many of God's works be not curious;" and, afterwards: conjecture on things above their understanding "hath deceived many, and hath detained their minds in vanity" (2–2, q.167, a.1).

This is the same as the last of the six points of advice given by St. Thomas to Brother John for earning the treasure of wisdom: "Seek not things that are above your head." That is, Do not try for what you cannot reach. For all the greater reason we should modestly check our curiosity in the world of purely sense knowledge, which, more than intellectual acquirement, should be kept as a servant to our final purpose.

There remain the expressions of modesty which are quite exterior and well known. They show themselves in one's carriage and dress. Undoubtedly, modesty in food and clothing is a virtue, for these matters depend on our will, and hence should be subject to the law of reason (q.168, a.1). And what reason chiefly asks is that everyone bear himself and attire himself as becomes his sex, person, and work. Let a woman take trouble to please her husband as she should, but go no farther. Let women who are unmarried and do not wish to marry or have not the chance, be not anxious to impress anyone. Let each person conduct himself as any sensible man would expect of him in the light of who he is and what his position is; and let this rule stand for all occasions: whether one is busy, or at rest, or at play. For it is foolish and therefore bad to be unable or unwilling to divert oneself, and it is really a vice to be troublesome to oneself and to hinder others from playing if they have fun at a game. Yet be sure of it, to play too much would be worse than not to play enough, for amusement in life is like salt in cooking: a little is enough. Still, we must know how to take it.

To keep himself fit, a man needs to rest his body. He cannot work all the time, because he has just so much strength, and this is equal to just such and such tasks. It is the same with his soul, whose energy has its limits and is suited to definite labors. So when it spends itself on work beyond its capacity, it has to toil and gets tired; this is particularly true in spiritual labor that uses the body, as when the intellect works through the bodily organs. But sense goods are values connatural to man; and so when the soul rises above the sense world, and attends to the thought world, animal fatigue is born, whether he is engaged with work of the practical or the speculative reason. And that fatigue is greater if he aims at contemplation, for in this he is more detached from the sense order; though in some exterior undertakings of the practical reason the physical labor is greater, yet in either case the man who wears down himself more, is he who works more intensely with his mind.

Now as a fatigued body is rested through physical quiet, so a fatigued soul needs to be eased by mental quiet. As we said when we studied the emotions (see p. 118), pleasure is a rest for the soul. So the remedy for a tired-out soul is

THE PRACTICE OF SELF-CONTROL

first to break the strain that work of mind entails, and then to appeal to pleasant delight.

We read in the *Sermons of the Fathers* (c.24) that some people were horrified one day at finding St. John the Evangelist playing with his disciples. John asked one of them who had a bow to draw the arrow, and when he had done this several times, asked him whether he could keep it up. The man said that if he were to keep it up the bow would break. Then St. John replied that man's soul also would break down if it were kept under a constant strain. Here is the necessity of using once in a while those words and actions called games: they have no other aim than to please the soul, yet they serve as a kind of rest for it. And this is the teaching of Aristotle, who says (*Ethics,* 4, c.8) that to play is to rest.

It is quite needful, therefore, to have a spirit of play. But there seem to be three particular points to be avoided. The first and main one is that we are not to seek recreation in words and deeds that are dirty and mischievous; as Cicero said, there is a kind of joke that is low, wanton, shameless, and foul. The second matter is to take care that the poise of the soul is never wholly lost; in the words of St. Ambrose: "We must be careful that while we rest our minds we do not lose our balance, which is a kind of focal point for our good deeds;" and of Cicero: "As we give children not carte blanche but leave to play only decent games, so even in games the uprightness of our minds should be like a light." Our third care should be that sport, as all human actions, be in keeping with the persons and time and place and other circumstances; that is, that it be worthy, as Cicero remarks (*De Officiis,* 1) of the time and of the man.

Well, such questions are planned and guided by reason, and any habit that functions in a reasonable way is a moral virtue. Play, then, can be a virtue. It is the virtue which Aristotle named the *spirit of play* (see p. 161). We call playful (εὐτράπελος: literally, versatile and ready) those persons who endeavor to give an amusing turn to what is said or done, and because this virtue checks a man and makes him moderate at games, it is listed under modesty (2–2, q.168, a.2).

With this we close the detailed study of the cardinal virtues. What we have still to do in order to round out applied ethics, is to define and grade the several ways of life in which men are expected to practise these many virtues.

Chapter XII

THE AIM OF GROUP-LIVING

In inquiring into the conditions for the growth of the moral life, we need to give attention first to man in society. We said earlier that man is a social animal and gave proof of this. Other animals have by nature everything they require to live alone: a coat of hair or feathers to cover them, teeth, horns, or claws for attacking, or at least speed to make their get-away and defend themselves. Man has not any of these, and if we suppose him living in isolation, he is unable to get himself the equivalent of them by his own power. So he must band with others, so that he may do something of their work, and they something of his. The necessity of association arises also from the need of acquiring knowledge. The beasts know by a kind of inborn instinct which of many things are good for them and which harmful, but man has to learn this discernment of objects and this science of their fitness by reasoning from principles. This science cannot be the work of one man, but requires a social organization. The practical question is, How can a society be organized, and, more than that, how should it be organized?

The possible forms of society are three: monarchy, aristocracy and democracy, and each of these stands over against a form which is the breakdown of itself: tyranny, oligarchy, and demagogy. Monarchy is the government of the people by one man, and its corrupt form (tyranny) is the oppression of all or some of the people by one man. Aristocracy is the ruling of the people by a small number of first-rate men, and the debased form of it (oligarchy) is the oppression of all or a part of the people by a few; it means rule by a tyrannous few. Democracy (*politia*) is the just control of the State by a large group, as by the military, for instance, and it miscarries into demagogy (*democratia*) or the oppression of one social class by another, as when the common people abuse their numerical power and oppress the monied caste; this amounts to tyranny by the crowd.

Of course, we have no mind to choose any of the tyrannous kinds, but it is in order to ask which of the three just forms of government is best.

An answer that will hold for every case cannot be given to this question. Rome is an instance of a nation that for a time had a monarchic government, but this degenerated into tyranny. We might expect the people to oust the tyrants and through very horror of such a régime set up an aristocratic reign of the consulary type. Or better, such a turnover might become the signal for an unbelievable renewing of vitality, and in fact we know from Sallust that this is what really took place.

THE AIM OF GROUP-LIVING

It often happens that men who live under a king are sluggards about doing anything for the general good, for they know that such efforts bring them nothing, but serve him who holds the property of the community under his thumb. When, however, they see that public funds are not in the grip of one man, they care for them not as if they were another's, but each one looks after them as if they were his own. Experience shows that one city of this kind, ruled over year after year by a governor, sometimes gets more done than a king, who has three or four cities, and that light services asked by a king are done less willingly than the heavy burdens which the people themselves impose. This was the practice during the growth of the Roman republic. For the people bore military conscription, and when there was not enough money to pay the army, they put their private fortunes at the disposition of the public, and even the Senate itself kept back nothing except the gold ring and stud which each one wore as insignia of his office. But the people were worn out with incessant quarrels that turned into civil wars, and in the course of these the liberty for which the people had so greatly struggled, slipped out of their hands and fell into the clutches of the emperors. In the beginning these rulers did not want to take the name of kings because the Romans hated it. Some of the emperors were of royal bearing and were devoted, and they looked out for the common welfare; due to this fact the Roman State held together and spread out. Yet many of them who were tyrannous toward the people, and weak and cowardly toward the enemy, brought Rome down to nothing.

The Hebrew people took a like course. At first they were governed by the Jews and were snatched at by the enemy from every side, for each one did only what looked good to his private self. At the prayer of the people, God gave them kings, but these were wicked men, who turned the people away from thè worship of the one God and brought them down at last into slavery.

Thus we are always between Scylla and Charybdis. Either we fear the tyrant and in doing so forego the very excellent form of government which is the monarchic, or we have a great care for this kind of government and run the risk of its lapsing into tyranny (*De Regimine Principum*, i, 4).

The trouble we have of making a choice becomes all the more real when the seriousness of the chance taken grows, and this occurs *pari passu* with the superiority of the régime for which we are inclined to cast our vote. The corruption of the best ever gives us the worst. So, which is the wiser course: to rest content with not being very good for fear of becoming very bad, or, in spite of everything, to aim at the better and to let the less good take care of itself? The alternative is not so absolute as it looks at first blush, and we can get a good grasp of the matter by outlining the reasons which make monarchy the best type of government.

A king is a man who governs a city or a province in view of the general welfare of its people. Even so, we may ask, which is more for the good of that town or district, to be ruled by one man or by several? For an answer we have to inquire into the aim of the ruler to work for the good of the ruled. He is like the captain of a ship whose undertaking is to keep his charge safe through storms at sea and bring her into port in good shape. Now the good or welfare of an as-

THE AIM OF GROUP-LIVING 313

sociation or group lies in its being one and at peace, for if it has not peace, the purpose of its social life is missed, and the people, divided within itself, becomes burdensome to itself. The ruler of a people should look, therefore, to making sure of harmony and peace. And he has no more right to think twice whether the people subject to him are to have peace than the physician has to decide whether he shall cure his patient. For no one should debate about the end which it is his business to serve, but only about the best means to reach it. The Apostle Paul, when he had commended the oneness of the believing people, said (*Ephes.*, c.4): "Be careful to keep the unity of the Spirit in the bond of peace." A régime will be the more useful, the more certainly it makes for unity and peace, since we say that a thing is more useful when it more certainly leads to its end. And as the great source of heat is a body that of itself is warm, so it is evident that what is one in itself, can better effect unity than what is manifold. The rule of one, then, is more useful to the people than the rule of many.

. . . Besides, the way things are in nature is best, for nature takes the best road at every turn, and in nature the general form of government is unitary. One member, namely the heart, moves the other members of the body, and one power of the soul, that is, reason, is chief and chairman. The bees have only one queen, and in the whole universe there is just one God as maker and ruler of all. This is a reasonable arrangement. For the many derive from one. And if things of art imitate those of nature, and if the better a work of art is, the more it is like nature, it must be best that the human many be governed by one.

Experience gives the same verdict. Towns and countries not ruled by one man have quarrels and agitation and little peace, so that the complaint that the Lord made through Jeremias seems true of them (c.12): "Many pastors have destroyed my vineyard." Whereas places and cities ruled by one king enjoy peace, justice is at home among them and they have plenty of everything. That is why the Lord promised as a gift that His people should have one head and that there should be only one prince among them (*De Reg. Princ.,* i, 2).

Certainly the hazard remains of falling into tyranny which, as the contrary of the best, must be the worst (*ibid.,* i, 3). Still, we are to keep in mind that tyranny is not a danger peculiar to monarchy. Oligarchy and demagogy are also tyrannies and, though a coterie or a crowd is in the saddle, are not always a less load to bear. When we say that the tyranny of one man is the worst type, we are thinking of unmitigated tyranny, for as just one man employed in the rôle of king to further the public interest is the surest warrant of civic happiness, so one man engaged as a tyrant in exploiting the people for his own profit is the source of the most frightful political evils. But really it is not often that we have such a tyranny. Most frequently it is limited to the fleecing of a few families or a large or small group of citizens; the welfare of only a section of the people or town is implicated, and the others are left in peace. However, when government is in the control of a few corrupt and tyrannous men, the trouble is with the government itself, and it quite upsets the equilibrium of the whole city or nation. On top of this, govern-

THE AIM OF GROUP-LIVING 315

ment by a few more often begets tyranny than government by one man, because of the jealousies that arise among them and rouse one to put the others out of the way. We conclude, then, that in ordinary instances monarchy is beset with fewer dangers.

When we face two evils we should choose the less. Now, on the one hand, we have the better type of government with a slight risk of its becoming the worst and most complete kind of tyranny. On the other, we have governments that are not so good to begin with and that run the risk of becoming tyrannies, the least of which would disturb the good order of the entire State. If, then, the only reason for not choosing the better régime is fear of tyranny, and if tyranny is even more to be feared in the less good régimes than in the better, there is no reason for not choosing the better. We consequently make our choice of government by one man (*ibid.*, i, 5).

If royalty is selected, a king has to be chosen and instructed in his duties. Though it is the intention of the people to intrust its guidance to one man, it does not at all follow that the people should commit itself into the hands of the first comer. On the contrary, the preference ought to be given to a man whose disposition warrants the hope that he will never turn into a tyrant. And if, in spite of their precaution, he becomes one, they will do well to bear with him while he is bearable, for we often exchange a bad tyrant for a worse. Then, if at last they are brought to the extremity of getting rid of him, they should be careful not to resort to violence and assassination, but rather imitate the patience of the early Christians toward their persecutors, the Roman emperors, and try to proceed in a legal way to get the tyrant to resign, for the people who choose kings always have the authority to deprive unworthy and tyrannous ones of their office (*ibid.,* i, 6).

What, as a matter of fact, is the surest guarantee that people can have against a tyrant? That the heavy burden of royalty have as companion the hope that it will be fitly repaid if it is well borne. Kings are men, and if they know that a just monarch is rewarded and the injustice of a tyrant is always punished, we may hope that they will not let themselves become vicious. And what will this reward be?

Some, notable among them Cicero, have urged that princes be nourished on gold and glory. Now, there is no doubt that glory is a reward becoming a prince, and even necessary for him, and that he has need of money to meet the many expenses which his office throws upon him; a prince without honor and without resources is not a prince. Yet we see that even in these quite external matters a good king is better provided for than a tyrant, for tyranny never lasts long, it costs dearly in armies and police, and it leaves after it, instead of honor, the memory of an accursed name (*ibid.,* i, 10).

Rewards of this kind, however, are not fit to give princes courage and steadfastness to conduct themselves as good kings, and there would be some im-

THE AIM OF GROUP-LIVING 317

propriety in the people to expect kings to live by these things. The fact is, a king who wants to win a name and to grow rich will more often succeed by depending on his subjects, raising armies, and carrying on wars in which his people sometimes lose everything except liberty. And we have shown above (p. 36) that no reward on earth is enough to fulfil the lawful desires of any man. How, then, could honors and riches satisfy the desires of a king, at least when we leave out of the picture the heavenly honors reserved by God for his elect?

It is in this last sense that it is correct to say that honor and glory are a king's recompense. For what earthly and passing honor could be like this honor, that man should dwell with God and be His associate, that he should be ranked as a son of God and have inheritance with Christ in the kingdom of God? With admiration and desire of this honor King David said (Ps. 138): "Thy friends, O God, are made exceedingly honorable." And what human glory or praise is comparable to this, which falls not from the tongue of a flatterer or deceiver nor is dependent on a mistaken notion of man, but comes from the inner witness of conscience and is confirmed by the witness of God and His promise to recognize in the sight of the angels and the glory of the Father those confessing him? They who seek this glory find it and receive a human glory that they do not seek; take, for instance, Solomon, who not only received from God the wisdom that he asked for, but was given glory above other kings.

We may add that he who does his royal duty in a worthy way will win a particularly high place in the celestial kingdom. If bliss is the reward of virtue, great bliss should normally be the reward of great virtue. Now the consummate virtue is that which makes a man capable not only of directing himself, but also of guiding others, and the more men he can put and keep on the right course, the more his virtue, as a man is admitted to have a body of more power if he can down more adversaries and lift heavier weights. It takes an added virtue to govern a family as well as oneself; how much more, then, to rule a town or a kingdom? To administer the kingly office well is thus the sign of a superior goodness, and it should have an outstanding reward (*De Reg. Princ.,* i, 8 and 9).

We now suppose a prince of note, deeply conscious of the duties of his trust, keen and desirous of bearing himself well and worthy of such a recompense. In what light will he see his duties as sovereign? We have said before that the ideal work of art is like nature. Royal government is but one instance of government, and has models to follow in nature. Let a king inquire, then, how soul governs body, how reason rules the soul or, better, how God directs the world, and he will know how to go about his work. If he takes God's providence as pattern, he will find a twofold task: to found kingdoms, cities or institutions as God creates, and to look after his people and guide them to their end, as God rules the world and directs it to its end. In the matter of building he will imitate the remarkable work by which God separated the elements, made each thing distinct, and gave it its proper place. We shall, therefore, see the king choose a place that is healthful and flowing with natural resources, pleasant to live in, safe from enemies, if it is a town; and if it is a kingdom, he will also have to choose the sites for towns, camps, schools, areas for the soldiers to drill in, roads for commerce, and so on. He will have to see that everyone is settled according to his status and that each serves according to his ability; that, once the location of the court is fixed, he who is judge is most just, and once the church is built, men who are really worthy are the priests. And in the matter of government he will notice that God guides the world by directing all beings to their ends, and he will try above all to conduct his subjects to theirs. What is this end, and can only he reach it?

A person ought to pass the same judgment on the end of a whole group as on the end of each one in it. If, then, the end of a man is a good within himself, the ultimate end of the governance of a people is to get and make permanent within itself such a good. On the supposition that this ultimate end of man, individual or social, were physical life and health, the king ought to be a physician; if it were money, a financier should be chosen king; if the chief value that the people could attain were science and truth, the king should be a professor. But it appears that the aim of a social group is to live good lives, since men form groups in order to live well, something that a man living alone could not do. Excellent living, then, is the goal of human association.

The evidence of this is that only they who have the common job of living well are parties to a social unit. Indeed, if the sole objective of society were to subsist, then animals and slaves would be citizens of the State; if it were to pile up shekels, all those who do business together would belong to the same commonwealth. Since, however, a man of virtuous life is meant for that higher end which lies in fruition with God, the end of the social group must be the same. We would say, therefore, that the ultimate aim of society is not merely that men should live together in virtue, but that this good life should be the path they take to arrive at the enjoyment of God.

If such an end can be reached by a purely human virtue, the business of the king is to direct men to that end. The truth is, we give the name *king* to the man who stands at the very tiptop of human government. And a régime is more excellent when its aim is higher. For a man who has the final objective as his goal always has command over the men who handle the tools helpful toward that end, as the sea captain who is getting ready for a trip outlines for the builder what kind of ship he will have fitted out for the undertaking, or as the townsman who needs a weapon tells the gunsmith what kind of a weapon to make for him. However, to rejoice in the sight of God is not an end attained purely by human virtue, but by divine favor, as the Apostle says to the Romans (c.6): "The grace of God, life everlasting." So it is by divine rather than human guidance that we make our way to that goal.

The king of such a realm, therefore, is more than man, he is God, Our Lord Jesus Christ, who by way of introduction to heavenly glory makes men the sons of God. The government that has been given to Him will not fail. Indeed, Holy Scripture calls Him priest but also king, in the words of Jeremias (c.23): "A king shall reign, and shall be wise." It is from Him that the royal priesthood derives. And what is more, all believers in Christ, as they are His members, bear the name of kings and priests. But the spiritual realm must be distinct from the earthly, and the management of this kingdom is given not to the kings of the earth, but to priests, and mostly to a supreme priest, the successor of St. Peter and vicar of Christ, the Pope of Rome, to whom all kings of the Christian people should be subject, as to Christ himself. We know that anyone who has charge of a work has a right that those helping to realize it be at his command and under his orders. The way with pagans was that both priest and the whole divine cult served for the conquest of temporal values, which made for the general welfare of the people, and as the king had to take care of the people, it was natural that priests were subject to the kings. And in the Old Law earthly goods were promised to a faithful people not by the devils, but by the true God, and thus priests were subject to kings. In the New Law, however, the priest is higher, because the values towards which he directs men are spiritual, and for this reason kings ought to be submissive to priests in the kingdom of Christ.

At the same time we see how admirable are the paths trod by Providence when in the city of Rome, which God foresaw as the future central home of the Christian peoples, the custom grew little by little of having the civil rulers obedient to the priests. So Valerius Maximus reports: "Our City thinks that all other things ought always to be put second to religion, even those things by which she wishes to show honor to the supreme civil power. Emperors do not hold back from a share in the service of the altar, convinced that they will have a mastery of human affairs if they are good and faithful servants of the divine power." And because the religion of the Christian priesthood was slow to bloom in France, God let the pagan priests of Gaul or Druids give laws for all

Gaul: you may read of it in a book that Julius Cæsar wrote, *De Bello Gallico* (*De Reg. Princ.,* i, 14).

Such seems to us the ideal structure of a humanity wholly formed after the requirements of Christian ethics: at the top of the pyramid is the Pope, the vicar of Christ, who directs all the people to the final and supernatural goal of mankind, that is, to God. Beneath the Pope a group of monarchies, whose kings are ranked next to him and at the same time each of them rules his own people. King should be subject to Pope, because he controls his kingdom only in the interests of the common good of his subjects, and this good lies finally in a spiritual realm that is the Pope's. A king ought to recognize the limits of his jurisdiction: his government helps to prepare men for an end which it is not sufficient to secure for them. In a word, this preparatory work is his proper work, and is the basis of the rightful power that a king has over his people. With a respect for the law which God has given and the Church teaches, the king shapes the present life of the people in view of a future blessedness, making sure by law of a regard for virtue and affording a chance to practice it by the maintenance of peace, whence flow order and prosperity (*ibid.,* i, 15).

Thus, subject in a humble way to minor officials, then to greater ones, then to kings, and at last to the Supreme Pontiff, who is at once head of the Church and of humanity, individuals, groups, and

THE AIM OF GROUP-LIVING

States are ranked in hierarchical order under the master objective of all social living, which is the same as the goal of all moral life, of the whole life of reason, the whole order of nature, and which we call God.

We may now take some one individual, at any place on this pyramid, and inquire how he ought to live. Two kinds of life, neatly distinct, offer him a choice: a life of contemplation or a life of action. Man is said to be a rational animal, and reason can have either of two aims. Either it is free for contemplation of truth, without other end than this contemplation, and then a man leads the contemplative life; or reason seeks the truth, so that man may know what he ought to do, and this is the active life. Briefly, to keep separate the two functions of reason, namely, theory and practice, is to define at once the only two sorts of life that a reasonable creature may lead (*Sum. Th.*, 2–2, q.179, 1 and 2). Is it necessary to choose, and if so, how is one to choose?

Certainly, if we suppose a wise man who has already chosen the better part and uses the lesser good for the sake of the better, no incompatibility exists between the active and the contemplative life. Quite the contrary. The active life can be and ought to be a powerful help to the contemplative when it takes the soul's passions in hand, puts them in order, tranquillizes them, and leaves the field free for contemplation (*Sum. Th.*, 2–2, q.182, a.3). It is nevertheless clear that, from an absolute point of view, the two kinds of life are essentially incompatible: a person cannot think for the sake of thought, and at the same time think for the sake of action, and it would be yet more impossible to have leisure for contemplation while one goes into action. Therefore, a man must choose and cast his vote for the better life. Doubtless, that is the contemplative life, and as proof it is enough to define this life.

We are speaking now of that form of the contemplative life which man can attain. The difference between an angel and a man is this (see Dionysius, *On the Divine Names*, 7, c.2) that an angel grasps the truth by a simple intuition, man by beginning with many data, comes to understand a truth. So the contemplative life (of man) has one act in which he finally is perfected, that is, the contemplation of truth, and in this it has unity; but it has many acts by which it comes to that final act. Some of these have to do with the learning of principles with the aid of which a man proceeds to the contemplation of truth, while others have the business of deducing from these principles the truth that he seeks to know. But the full and rounded act is the contemplation itself of the truth (2–2, q.180, a.3).

It is not difficult to specify the farthest goal of the contemplative life and to show its greater excellence by the way the active life is subordinate to it.

A thing is relative to the contemplative life in one of two ways: by a primary or a secondary claim, *i. e.*, a preparatory one. The thing that primarily belongs to the contemplative life is contemplation of divine truth, for this is the goal of all

THE AIM OF GROUP-LIVING

human life. That is why Augustine says (*On the Trinity,* 1, c.8) that "contemplation of God is promised us as the end of all our acts and the everlasting perfection of our joys." It will be perfect in the future life, when we see God face to face, and it will make us altogether happy. At present we practise contemplation of divine truth in an imperfect way, we look as through a glass and in a dark manner; yet this is some kind of beginning of happiness: it begins now and will continue in the future. And does not the Philosopher say (*Ethics,* 10, c.7 and 8) that our ultimate felicity is in contemplation of the greatest knowable object? The works of God lead us, as by the hand, to an understanding of God, as it is written (*Rom.* i, 20): "The invisible things of God are clearly seen, being understood by the things that are made."

So a study of God's works belongs in an indirect way to the contemplative life: it guides man to a knowledge of God. Augustine says (*On the True Religion,* ch.29): "An inquiry about creatures should not be idle and passing curiosity, but a step toward lasting and eternal things."

It follows that we may classify the four stages of the contemplative life in the following way. First, the moral virtues. Second, intellectual acts that are not contemplative. Third, contemplation of the works of God. Fourth, which rounds out all the others, the contemplation of divine truth (2–2, q.180, a.4).

Take the case of a man who is earnest about moral perfection and has chosen the better of the two kinds of life that are open to us. He has got to choose a life-state in which to work out that better way. Plainly, men are in conditions that are socially unlike. And we do not wish to say merely that some are rich and some poor, some famed and others unknown, for these are variable individual differences that are subject to frequent upsets. A "state" (*status*) is a settled mode of living, quite or nearly inseparable from the person. It is first of all the free or the servile status of the individual. Basically, there are just two states of life, whether civil or spiritual, namely, slavery and freedom (2–2, q.183, a.1). Since our quest is the perfect moral life, we need not be preoccupied with a choice between civic slavery and civic liberty; these are matters that bear on the life of action, and we have cast our vote for the spiritual life of contemplation. We, therefore, turn to the higher order and make this distinction within it.

We have remarked that any state is either servile or free. And in spiritual matters there are just two kinds of servitude and two of freedom. One is a slavery of sin, the other a slavery of justice; and one is a freedom from sin, the other from justice. This is plain, in the Apostle's words (*Rom.* c.6): "When you were the servants of sin, you were free men to justice. . . . But now being made free from sin, you have become the servants of God." To live in bondage to sin or to justice is to have an habitual leaning either to evil by vice and sin, or to good by the virtue of justice. Likewise, to be free from sin is to stand unconquered by the tendency to sin, and to be free from justice is not to be faced away from evil by a love of justice. And because man's reason by its nature inclines toward justice, and sin is contrary to nature and reason, the freedom from sin, and the associated bondage to

THE AIM OF GROUP-LIVING

justice, is a veritable liberty. Indeed, through both of them man tends to the good proper to him. A bondage to sin on the other hand, and the accompanying freedom from justice, is out and out slavery; either one of these keeps man from what is his good.

It is a man's own doing that he is made the servant either of justice or of sin. The Apostle's words on the point are (*Rom.* c.6): "Whom you yield yourselves to obey, his servants you are whom you obey, whether it be of sin unto death, or of obedience unto justice." And as every human enterprise has a beginning, a middle, and an end, so the state of spiritual slavery or of freedom has three distinct periods. First, the condition of the beginners. Second, that of the proficients. Third, that of the perfect (2–2, q.183, a.4).

And so the end of moral endeavor, if looked at from the states of life, lies in the perfection of the contemplative state, and we return by this route to what the definition of the Value of values early taught us. The beginner lives the highest of the virtues, which is the theological virtue of charity (see p. 216). The perfect man, though he does not tend toward God with all his power, for our power for love is not wholly realized in this life, has at least a love that debars all serious sin or anything that might ruin the virtue of charity within him (*ibid.*, q.184, a.2).

We can readily see that the rounded whole of perfection amounts to keeping the two great commandments of Scripture: to love God with all our heart and our neighbor for the love of God. In these, as we read in St. Matthew, are the Law and the Prophets. All else is inescapably included. Fasting, vigils, prayer, chastisement of the body, the giving up of wealth, none of these is perfection, but all are instruments or means to perfection (q.184, a.3). What, then, is to be done that this inner moral perfection may become truly a state? Let it be fixed and made lasting by freely entwining itself with vows and promises to a rule of life. A man can be perfect though he does not bind his life to the state of perfection, but, alas! what a bother is the state of perfection to a man who is not perfect (q.184, a.4)! The moral life in its complete form requires both the man and the status, and this is the life of the religious contemplative. He is joined by a solemn vow to the most perfect kind of life, is faithful to it, and the settledness of his bounden state is like the unbrokenness of the beatific vision which is to be.

The conclusion does not take us by surprise. Once more, a last time, the problem of man's conduct, set by moral experience, has a full solution only in the realm of religion.

BIBLIOGRAPHICAL NOTES

A. The chief texts of Saint Thomas Aquinas dealing with ethics are these:

1. His studies on the *Sententiae* of Peter Lombard (1254–1256).

2. The *Summa Contra Gentes* (1258–1260), especially the Third Book.

3. The *Summa Theologica,* especially 1–2 (1269–1270) and 2–2 (1271–1272).

4. His studies of Aristotle's *Ethics* (about 1266).

5. His studies of Aristotle's *Politics* (about 1268), as far as bk. 4, lect. 6.

6. *De Regimine Principum* (1265–1266); incomplete.

7. *Quaestiones Disputatae de Virtutibus* (1270–1272).

We cannot be too urgent in recommending that the study of the *Summa Theologica* be given first place.

B. For material on the dates of the works of Saint Thomas, see P. Mandonnet, O.P. and J. Destrez, O.P., *Bibliographie Thomiste,* Le Saulchoir, Kain, 1921; the conclusions of the studies of P. Mandonnet are conveniently summarized in *Vie de Saint Thomas et ses Ecrits Authentiques,* pp. ix–xxi. To complete this collection we mention the excellent *Bulletin Thomiste,* mouthpiece of the Thomistic Society, published since 1924, and *Revue des Sciences Philosophiques et Théologiques* (Paris, Gabalda) which carries bibliographies and yearly indexes that are quite complete and serviceable.

C. For general introductions to the philosophy of Saint Thomas, the reader may consult:

1. A. FOREST, *Saint Thomas d'Aquin* (Collection: *Les Philosophes*) Paris, J. Vrin, 1923.

2. E. GILSON, *Le Thomisme* (mentioned above, p. 11).

3. Readers familiar with the thought of Saint Thomas at first hand will find a fruitful study in A. D. SERTILLANGES, *Saint Thomas d'Aquin,* 2 vols., Paris, Alcan, 1910.

(The English reader might also consult: D'ARCY, *Thomas Aquinas,* London, E. Benn, and Boston, Little, Brown, 1930; and GRABMANN, *Thomas Aquinas: His Personality and Thought* (tr. by V. Michel), London and New York, Longmans, 1928.—Tr.).

4. For Thomistic ethics the best single study is A. D. SERTILLANGES, *La Philosophie Morale de Saint Thomas d'Aquin,* Paris, Alcan, 1916; but we also highly recommend, as an introduction, the works of P. NOBLE, O.P., *La Vie Morale d'après Saint Thomas,* Paris, Lethielleux.

5. For Thomistic views on government, consult JACQUES ZEILLER, *L'Idée de l'État dans Saint Thomas d'Aquin,* Paris, Alcan, 1910.

D. As for the use of the present volume, we advise beginners to limit themselves to chapters i, ii, and vi, then to turn to the Second Part. Afterward they can return to the other chapters, which contain the philosophical basis for the system and might be too difficult at the outset. To dissipate fears, we note the following points:

1. Some books are clear at a first reading, but become less clear the more you think about them. Others are obscure at first, but become clear and ever clearer as you give more reflection to them. The great philosophers, and Saint Thomas is far from an exception, write this latter kind of book.

2. To see an author clearly, we must *explain texts,* that is: (*a*) learn his language, so as to use terms in the sense in which he uses them, and (*b*) initiate ourselves into the particular order in which he conceives and states his thoughts.

3. This order for Aquinas is analytic, in almost any instance which the reader finds difficult; that is to say, he states his thesis as if it were proved, and shows, often in the same phrase, the principle that does prove it. He goes so far as to let one phrase contain the thesis, the analytic proof, an illustrative example, and a confirmation of the thesis by reference to the part it plays in some other proof.

4. The reader will therefore have grasped and explained a passage, when he has (*a*) established the meaning of the technical terms to which the reasoning appeals, (*b*) reëstablished this reasoning in the synthetic order (from principles to consequents), and (*c*) separated from the reasoning the example that is there only to illustrate it.

5. Nothing is authentic on the thought of a philosopher—not the historian's study, nor the most painstaking translation—nothing, except the text of that philosopher, read in the language in which he wrote.

INDEX

Accident, *see* substance.
Accuser and accusation, 261-4.
Active life, the, 41, 323-4.
"Acts of man," 18.
Adoration, 273-4.
Affability, 275.
Aim is integrated with specific nature, 17; *see* end.
Albert the Great, 1.
Alms-giving—a charity, 231; educating as, 231-2; prayer as, 231-2.
Altruism, 218 f., 224.
Ambrose, St., 260, 271, 307.
Anger, 129 f., 299-300.
Appropriation of goods in necessity, 260.
Aristotle, 20, 22, 25, 29, 40, 42, 51, 53, 59, 64, 70, 73, 83, 86, 106, 110, 127, 143, 155, 170, 172, 186, 194, 224, 249, 251, 263, 295, 307, 325.
Art, 156; as imitation of nature, 313, 318.
Augustine, St., 39, 115, 130, 139, 140-1, 144, 161, 170, 206, 209, 244-5, 271, 276, 280, 304, 325.
Augustinianism, 7-9.

Baudin, Abbé, 11.
Benefactors, 224-5.

Bishops, and temperance, 293.
Boasting, 295.
Boethius, 51.
Boldness, 281.
Budé, Wm., 6.

Cæsar, Julius, 321.
Capital punishment, 256-7.
Cardinal virtues, 161-2; *see* temperance, fortitude, prudence, justice.
"Certain malice," 189-191.
Charity, 164, 172-3, 217; *see* love.
Chastity, 295-6, 299.
Chrysostom, St. John, 265.
Cicero, 103, 249, 307, 316.
Civic virtue, 236-7.
Compassion, 230-1.
Conation, 69; *see intentio*.
Contemplation, 41, 323-4; incompatible with action, 324.
Continence, 298-9.
Continuity, the, of Thomistic thought, 47-8.
Counsel, 138-9.
Courage, ch. 10; 174-5; of the miser and go-getter, 227-8.
Craft, 243.
Criteria, *see* standards.
Cruelty, 301.
Curiosity, restraint of, 303-5.

Damascene, St. John, 53, 73.
Death, fear of, 263, 277-281.
Deceit, 243, 262-3, 275.
Democracy, 209.
Devotion, 271-2.
Dionysius, 35, 82, 276, 324.
Drunkenness, 188-9, 292-4.

Educating, as alms, 231-2.
Egoism, 218 f., 224.
Emotions, ch. 4; in general, 91 f.; defined, 95; kinds, 96; reason and sin, 187-8.
End, ch. 1; 17, 319-320; end of ends, 19 f., 194; one final end, 20; same for all men, 22, 25; infinity of ends, 21; and morals, 21-2; as welfare or happiness, 194; moves to action, 65, 180-2; as principle of action, 61; and standards, 194; as chief director of action, 194.
Ethics, described, 19; empiric basis of, 26-7; the problem of, 16-18; the crucial problem of, 228-230; the basic principle of, 74, 77; and metaphysics, ch. 1; 15-16, 79; and God, 16; unity of ethical and material worlds, 57.
Extravagance, 285; *see* magnanimity, magnificence.

Faith, 144, 164, 172-3.
Falsehood, 244.
Fathers, Sermons of, the, 307.
Fear, affects the willed act, 58.
Fear, inability to, 281.
Ferocity, 301.
First principles of action, 199.
First principles of thought, 137, 148, 199, 234.

Forbearance, 299-300.
Foresight, 235.
Fortitude, ch. 10.
Fraud, 244.
Friendship, 219-220, 228-9.

Games, 306-8.
God, and ethics, 16; and will, 67; as first cause and last end, 20; as final cause, 15 f., 20, 322; as first mover, 20; imperfect knowledge of, 177; *see* transcendence, value.
Go-getter, his courage and prudence, 227-8.
Good, the, *see* value.
Good sense, 240-1.
Government, kinds of, 251.
Gratitude, 224-5, 274.
Gregory, St., 53, 170.
Gregory of Nyssa, St., 70.

Habit, 138.
Happiness, *see* value, end.
Honor, 27-8, 254, 283, 291, 316.
Hope, 164, 172-3.
"Human," 18, 60.
Human act, the, ch. 2.
Humanism, Christian, 2-7, 39-40, 48-9, 163-4, 228-9.
Human level, the, 17-19, 35-6, 53-4, 202-3, 211, 237, 258.

Ignorance, defined, 183; and sin, 183-7.
Inconstancy, 242-3.
Intellect, and science, 138; active and possible, 148; the condition of virtue, 146; *see* first principles of knowledge.
Intentio, 67; *see* conation.
Irony, 275.
Isidore, St., 204.

INDEX

Jerome, St., 304.
John, Brother, advice to, 305.
Judges, duties and faults of, 261-5; see "respect of persons."
Judgment, 240-1; conditions of just judgment, 248-9.
Justice, ch. 9; 174-5; defined, 247; kinds, 250 f.; as "reasoned mercy," 230-2.

Kings, training of, 315-8.
Kingship, of Christ, 320-1.

Lavishness, 285.
Law, ch. 6; defined, 195; a function of reason, 194-6; divine, 211-2; eternal, 196 f.; natural, 198 f.; human, 201 f., 208; and codes, 246; is for the group, 203-5; its development, 208-211; a guide and pedagogic, 202-3; compels only the wicked, 206-7; its binding force, 205-7; necessity knows no law, 208, 260.
Lawyers, 266.
Life of virtue, 165.
"Light of Glory," 46.
Limits of human powers, see transcendence.
Love, ch. 4; effects of, 109-111; mother love, 225; of neighbor, ch. 7; tested by love of enemies, 228-230.
Lust, 297-9.

Magnanimity, 167, 282-3.
Magnificence, 167, 284-5.
Martyrdom, 279-280.
Means (instrumental values), 70 f.
Meekness, 299-300.

Memory, and prudence, 233-4.
Mercy, 230-2.
Miser, courage and prudence of, 227-8.
Moderation, 301-2.
Modesty, 291; in dress, 305.
Monarchy, 312 f.
Montaigne, 210.
Morals, see ethics.
Moral good, value, see value.

Obedience, 274.
Object moves to action, 65, 180-2.
Order, see standards.
Orderer of the world, 10, 16-18, 23, 272, 274, 318.
"Ought to be," 88.
Ownership, private and public, 258-9; as natural right, 258.

Pascal, 210, 229.
Patience, 285.
Perseverance, 285.
Perspicacity, 241.
Playfulness, 306-8.
Pope, the, as ruler, 321-2.
Prayer, 271-3; as alms, 231-2.
Precipitation, 239.
Pride, 302-4.
Priests, 257; and temperance, 293.
Progress, a duty, 296.
Prudence, ch. 8; 155, 170-1, 174, 176-7; of the flesh, 243; the go-getter's, 227-8; as guide or norm, 233; see standards.
Pusillanimity, 284.

Rashness, 281-2.
Reason, see standards.
Religion, as a virtue, 269-270; and morality, 163; see transcendence.

INDEX

Renaissance, 5-6.
Research, qualifications for, 241.
"Respect of persons," 252-4.
Restitution, 267-8.
Revolution, 315-6.
Riches are for the poor, 260.

Sacrifice, 273-4.
Sallust, 310.
Sanction of morals, 10.
Scale of values, 175, 273, 280, 282-3, 295.
Scale of virtues, 173-7, 218-223, 237, 297.
Science, 137, 151-2, 241; gives tentative "laws," 241, 264; and the contingent, 235; is of the sensible, 42-44.
Self-control, ch. 11; *see* temperance.
Self-defence, 257; in court, 262-3.
Sensuality, 297.
Sex, 176, 200, 288-290, 295-7; *see* temperance, self-control.
Sin, 178 f.; causes, 185-6; its elements, 302; original, 302-3.
Slavery, 255, 326.
Sobriety, *see* temperance, drunkenness.
Social life, 194; its necessity, 309.
Socrates, 156, 186.
Solicitude, 244-5.
Soul, the, "expedita," 165.
Standards, 81-2, 88, 218-223, 231-2, 238, 239, 295, 307-8, 313; the middle way, 166; determined by reason, 167-9, 179-180, 193; determined by the "thing," 168-9; its dependence on us, 168; *see* prudence, scales of value.

State, its forms, 309 f.
State of perfection, 327-8.
States of life, 325-6.
Stoics, the, 158.
Substance and accidents, 141-2.
Suicide, 257-8.
Suspicion, as grounds of judgment, 249-250.
Syllogism, the moral, 74, 77, 234-5.

Temperance, ch. 11; and priests and bishops, 293; the miser's, 227-8.
Terence, 297-8.
Thomas, Saint, life of, 1 f.
Tiburtius, martyr, 119.
Timidity, 280-1.
Transcendence of man and reason, 33, 37, 43, 47, 211, 226-9, 322, 328.
Truth, 275.
Truth, the good of intellect, 144.
Tyranny, its forms, 310, 314.

Ulpian, jurist, 210.
Utopia, 318-9.

Valerius, Maximus, 293, 321.
Value, defined, 39, 40, 143, 199; is object of will, 16-17; as end, 19 f.; variability of, 201; absolute, eternal value, 228; the greatest value, ch. 1; 28 f., 37; money as greatest, 27; efficiency as greatest, 28; honor as greatest, 27-8; bodily as greatest, 30; pleasure as greatest, 31; happiness as consummate, 36-49; welfare as consummate, 72, 194; life as consummate, 175, 280; instru-

INDEX

mental, 70 f.; generic, 24; self-value, 23-4; for body, 115; for spirit, 115; of science, 41; emergence of, 79; limits of finite values, 112-3.

Vice, 178 f., 191-2; its nature, 248.

Virginity, 295-6.

Virtue, 135 f.; acquired, 147; definition of, 138-40, 147, 150, 178; belongs to the soul, 139; classification of, 150 f.; life of, 165; theological, 140-1, 172, 215.

Voluntary, 188-9; *see* will.

Vows, 274, 328.

War, just, conditions of, 278.

Wealth, as title to honor, 254.

Will, 61-2; moves and is moved, 64-5.

Willed act, the, 52 f.; affected by concupiscence, fear, ignorance, 58-60.

Wisdom, 176-7.

Witnesses, disagreement of, 264-5.

Woman, 293, 298.

GREAT BRITAIN

AND

THE ILLINOIS COUNTRY

1763-1774

KENNIKAT AMERICAN BICENTENNIAL SERIES
Under the General Editorial Supervision of
Dr. Ralph Adams Brown
Professor of History, State University of New York

To this Essay was awarded the
JUSTIN WINSOR PRIZE IN
AMERICAN HISTORY
for 1908

GREAT BRITAIN

AND

THE ILLINOIS COUNTRY

1763-1774

BY

CLARENCE EDWIN CARTER, A. M., Ph.D.,

KENNIKAT PRESS
Port Washington, N. Y./London

GREAT BRITAIN AND THE ILLINOIS COUNTRY

First published in 1910
Reissued in 1970 by Kennikat Press
Library of Congress Catalog Card No: 73-120870
ISBN 0-8046-1263-3

Manufactured by Taylor Publishing Company   Dallas, Texas

KENNIKAT AMERICAN BICENTENNIAL SERIES

PREFACE.

IN the present study my researches have been directed toward the discovery of the legal, political, and economic relations between Great Britain and the Illinois colony, and the political events in Illinois which illustrate some of those general relations. In addition to the Illinois settlement, the great West which was ceded to England in 1763 included other colonies of comparatively equal importance, the chief of which was Detroit. Whatever general principles, therefore, are ascertained with reference to the relations between the home government and the Illinois French apply equally to the whole West. In the discussion of the illustrative events, however, I have followed their course in Illinois alone.

In chapters I and III, both of which are in a sense introductory, no serious attempt has been made at original investigation. On certain points, however, I have sought to verify secondary authorities and harmonize conflicting statements by an examination of the sources. Chapter II deals with the legal position of the western settlements in the empire. Chapters IV and VII contain a narrative of events in Illinois from 1765 to 1774, gleaned entirely from hitherto unused manuscript material. The question of the economic importance of the West to the empire is discussed in chapter V. The various attempts to colonize the Illinois country by English settlers and the attitude of Great Britain toward such enterprises in general occupy chapter VI. This subject has been handled by previous writers, but considerable new material has been found which throws light on the colonizing movement, enabling one to disentangle the various plans.

The printed sources of value covering the period are few. Such collections, however, as the *Documents relating to the Colonial History of the State of New York*, the various editions of the works of Benjamin Franklin, and the *Reports on Canadian Archives* have been invaluable. The essay as a whole has been based, however, upon manuscript sources found in the various archives of the United States, Canada, and Europe. A personal search was made not only in the local archives of the State of Illinois, but in the libraries of the middle western and eastern States, as well as in the Public Record Office and the British Museum in London. In the last named places the bulk of the material was found.

I desire to express my gratitude for aid and encouragement to Professor Evarts B. Greene, in whose seminar in history at the University of Illinois this essay was begun, and especially to Professor Clarence W. Alvord of the University of Illinois, whose intimate knowledge of the field has been of material assistance throughout my study. I also wish to express my thanks for helpful criticisms of the manuscript to Professor Guy Stanton Ford of the University of Illinois, to President C. H. Rammelkamp and to Professor J. Griffith Ames of Illinois College, and to Professor Charles H. Hull of Cornell University, chairman of the Justin Winsor Prize committee. I owe an especial debt of gratitude to my wife and faithful amanuensis, without whose encouragement the essay would not have been completed in its present form.

CLARENCE E. CARTER.

JACKSONVILLE, ILLINOIS, *August 20, 1909.*

CONTENTS.

	PAGE
PREFACE	vii

CHAPTER I.
Introductory Survey 1

CHAPTER II.
Status of the Illinois Country in the Empire . . 13

CHAPTER III.
Occupation of the Illinois Country . . . 27

CHAPTER IV.
Five Years of Disorder, 1765–1770 46

CHAPTER V.
Trade Conditions in the Illinois Country, 1765–1775 77

CHAPTER VI.
Schemes for the Colonization of the Illinois Country, 1763–1768 103

CHAPTER VII.
The Struggle for a Civil Government, 1770–1774 . 145

DOCUMENTARY APPENDIX	165
BIBLIOGRAPHY	185
INDEX	201

Columbia College Library
Chicago, Illinois

CHAPTER I.

INTRODUCTORY SURVEY.

As a result of the treaty of Paris (1763) which added to the empire immense areas of territory peopled with savages and alien inhabitants, Great Britain was confronted with the momentous problem of readjusting all her colonial relations. At this time the necessity of strengthening the imperial ties between the old colonies and the mother country and of reorganizing the new acquisitions came to the forefront and led the government into a course soon to end in the disruption of the empire. Certainly not the least of the questions demanding solution was the disposition of the country lying to the westward of the colonies, including a number of French settlements and a broad belt of Indian nations.

The conclusion of the Seven Years' war saw a tremendous change in the relative position of France and England in North America: the former had lost and the latter gained an empire. The final struggle for supremacy was the culmination of a series of continental and colonial wars beginning near the close of the seventeenth century and ending with the definitive treaty of 1763. During the first quarter of the century France occupied a predominant position among the powers. Through the aggressiveness of Louis XIV and his ministers her boundaries had been pushed eastward and northward, thereby seriously threatening the balance of power in Europe. Until 1748 England

and Austria had been in alliance against their traditional enemy, and in the war of the Austrian Succession France had lent her aid to Prussia in the dismemberment of the Austrian dominions—at the same time extending her own power in the interior of America and India. These international struggles, however, brought no definite results: territorial boundaries had not been adjusted nor had the balance of power been satisfactorily settled. The growth of the power of Prussia under the leadership of Frederick the Great now became a most important factor. The aggressions of France soon ran counter to the course of the new national state and another conflict was inevitable. In the interval of nominal peace after the treaty of Aix-la-Chapelle in 1748, preparations were begun for another contest. The astute diplomacy of Kaunitz won France from her traditional enmity and secured that power as an open ally for Maria Theresa in her war of revenge.[1]

While the European situation was giving occasion for new alignments of the powers, affairs in America were becoming more and more critical between France and England. Here for over a century the two powers had been rivals for territorial and commercial supremacy. In North America the pioneers of France had won for her the greater part of the continent, the extensive valleys of the St. Lawrence and the Mississippi with all the land watered by their tributaries. The French claim to this region was based almost entirely upon discovery and exploration, for in all its extent less than one hundred thousand people were permanently settled. Canada at the north and the region about New Orleans on the extreme south contained the bulk of the population, while throughout the old Northwest settlements were few and scattering. Trading posts

[1] Perkins, *France under Louis XV*, II, 1-83.

INTRODUCTORY SURVEY

and small villages existed at Vincennes on the Wabash River, at Detroit, at St. Joseph near Lake Michigan, and at other isolated places. Outside of Detroit the most important and populous settlement was situated along the eastern bank of the Mississippi, in the southwestern part of the present State of Illinois, where about two thousand people were living.[2]

In contrast to this vast area of French territory and the sparseness of its population were the British colonies, with more than a million people confined to the narrow strip between the Alleghany mountains and the Atlantic Ocean. These provinces were becoming comparatively crowded, and many enterprising families of English, Scotch-Irish, and German extraction were pushing towards the mountains. Each year saw the pressure on the western border increased. The great unoccupied valley of the Ohio invited home-seekers and adventurers westward in spite of hostile French and Indians. By 1750 the mountain barriers were being crossed by constantly increasing numbers, and the French found their possession of the West and their monopoly of the fur trade threatened.

To prevent such encroachments the French sought to bind their possessions together by means of a line of forts extending from the St. Lawrence down the Ohio Valley to the Gulf of Mexico. It had indeed been the plan of such men as La Salle, Iberville, and Bienville to bring this territory into a compact whole and to limit the English colonies to the line of mountains. New Orleans and Mobile gave France command of the Gulf of Mexico and the Mississippi River; Louisburg, Niagara, and Frontenac

[2] Hutchins, *A Topographical Description*, ed. Hicks, 166ff; Pittman, *The Present State of the European Settlements on the Mississippi*, ed. Hodder, 84ff.

afforded protection to Canada against the English colonies. The weak point for France was the Ohio Valley, in the upper part of which Virginia and Pennsylvania settlers had already located by the middle of the eighteenth century. Céleron, who went down the Ohio in 1749, burying plates of lead to signify French dominion, warning English settlers and traders, and persuading the Indians to drive out the invaders of their hunting grounds, saw the inevitableness of the conflict. The American phase of the final struggle for colonial empire was to begin in this region.[3]

In the early years of the French and Indian war, the American counterpart of the Seven Years' war, Great Britain and her Prussian ally met with serious reverses everywhere, and it seemed probable that France would be able to hold her line of defence in America. The French colonies, however, were fundamentally weak. They were wholly dependent upon the mother country, and when the latter became absorbed in the continental struggle to the exclusion of her interests in the colonies defeat was inevitable. By 1758 the tide was turning in America; this, together with the victories of Clive in India and Frederick the Great at Rossbach and Leuthen, proved too much for the resources of France, and with the transference of the American struggle to Canada, and the capture of Montreal and Quebec, the war was practically at an end. In 1762 the financial condition of France became so desperate that Choiseul, the French minister of foreign affairs, was anxious for peace, and he found George III and Lord Bute, England's prime minister, ready to abandon their Prussian ally, and even to give up the fruits of some of the brilliant victories of 1762 which had brought Spain, a recent ally of France, to her knees.[4]

[3] Parkman, *Montcalm and Wolfe*, I, 39–67.
[4] Hunt, *Pol. Hist. of Eng.*, X, 23–40.

INTRODUCTORY SURVEY

The definitive treaty of Paris was signed February 10, 1763.[5] By its terms France ceded to Great Britain all of Canada and gave up her claim to the territory east of the Mississippi River, except the city of New Orleans, adding to this the right of the free navigation of the Mississippi. Spain received back Havana, ceding Florida to England in return. A few weeks before signing the definitive treaty, France, in a secret treaty with Spain, ceded to her the city of New Orleans and the vast region stretching from the Mississippi towards the Pacific. Thus was France divested of every inch of territory on the continent of North America.

The French colony in the Illinois country had been originally established to form a connecting link between the colonies in Louisiana on the south and Canada on the northwest. La Salle himself had recognized the possible strategic value of such an establishment from both a commercial and a military standpoint.[6] Even before any settlements had been made on the lower Mississippi, in 1682 he and his associates had attempted the formation of a colony on the Illinois River, near the present site of Peoria.[6] This, the first attempt at western colonization, was a failure. The opening of the following century saw the beginning of a more successful and permanent colony, when the Catholic missionaries from Quebec established their missions at Cahokia[7] and Kaskaskia, near the village of the Illinois Indians. They were soon followed by hunters and fur traders, and during the first two decades of the eighteenth century a considerable number of families

---

[5] Text of treaty in Chalmers, *Coll. of Treaties*, I, 467–483; *Documents relating to the Constitutional History of Canada, 1759–1791*, ed. Shortt and Doughty (Can. Archives, 1907), 73–84.

[6] Parkman, *La Salle and the Discovery of the Great West*, 312.

[7] Cahokia was founded in 1699 by the priests of the Seminary of Foreign Missions.

immigrated from Canada, thus assuring the permanency of the settlement.

Meanwhile the contemporaneous colony of Louisiana had grown to some importance, and in 1717, when the Company of the West assumed control of the province, the Illinois country was annexed to Louisiana.[8] Prior to this time it had been within the jurisdiction of Quebec. The Illinois country now entered upon a period of prosperity, many new enterprises being undertaken, notably the opening of lead mines. Shortly after its annexation to Louisiana, Pierre Boisbriant was given a commission to govern the Illinois country, and among his instructions was an order to erect a fort as a protection against possible encroachments from the English and Spanish. About 1720 Fort de Chartres was completed and became thereafter the seat of government during the French régime. In 1721 the Company of the Indies[9] divided Louisiana into nine districts, one of which was known as the Illinois district,[10] extending east and west of the Mississippi River between the lines of the Arkansas and Illinois rivers.[11] In 1731 Louisiana passed out of the hands of the Company of the Indies, and, together with its Illinois dependency, became

---

[8] Archives of the Ministry of the Colonies (Paris), series A, vol. 22, fol. 40.

[9] In May, 1719, the Company of the East Indies and the Company of China were assimilated to the Company of the West, the name of which was changed to Company of the Indies. Margry, *Découvertes*, V, 590.

[10] Winsor, *Narr. and Crit. Hist. of Am.*, V, 43.

[11] "Regulations for the government of the district", Archives of the Ministry of the Colonies, series B, vol. 43, fol. 103; Winsor, *Narr. and Crit. Hist. of Am.*, V, 43. The boundary between Canada and Louisiana during the French régime was approximately the 40th parallel. This left the French settlement at Ouiatanon to the Quebec government while Post Vincennes on the lower Wabash River was in Louisiana. Pownall, *Administration of the Colonies*, 192.

INTRODUCTORY SURVEY

a royal province.[12] It remained in this status until the close of the Seven Years' war, when that portion east of the Mississippi was ceded to England as a part of Canada.[13]

At the close of the French régime a number of villages scattered along the Mississippi River from near the mouth of the Kaskaskia northward seventy-five miles to Cahokia contained the population of the country. Kaskaskia at the extreme south was the largest town of the group, with eighty houses, five hundred whites, and about an equal number of negroes. Some seventeen miles north was Prairie du Rocher with a population of one hundred French and as many slaves. A short distance northwest of Prairie du Rocher, on the bank of the Mississippi, stood Fort de Chartres, surrounded by a little village called Nouvelle Chartres, where some forty families were settled. St. Philippe, five miles north of Fort de Chartres, contained twelve or fifteen families, and forty-five miles further north stood Cahokia with three hundred whites and eighty negroes.[14]

Most of the French people of Illinois came originally from Canada[15] although a few immigrated from France[16] and others were sent there from Louisiana by the Company of

---

[12] Winsor, *Narr. and Crit. Hist. of Am.*, V, 49.

[13] Treaty of Paris, section VII, *Can. Const. Docs., 1759-1791*, 86.

[14] Pittman, *State of the European Settlements on the Miss.*, ed. Hodder, 84-93. There is no detailed and satisfactory account of the French régime in print, with reference either to its political, social, or economic aspects. The works of Breese, Wallace, Brown, Mason, and others are entirely unscientific and unreliable. The recent discovery of a large number of papers bearing on the period will enable future scholars to reach more accurate conclusions. For a recent brief but judicious survey of the French, based largely on a study of documentary material, see Alvord, *Illinois Historical Collections*, II, xviii-xxv.

[15] Du Pratz, *Histoire de la Louisiane*, II, 296.

[16] *Ibid.*, I, 230-231.

the Indies.[17] There existed among them two classes, the "gentry" and the *habitant*, the latter being greatly in the majority. The *habitants* had belonged to the lower classes in Canada and possessed few of the social and intellectual attainments which marked their superiors. Occupied chiefly in the collection of furs or in the humbler duties of commerce, they came into close contact with the Indians, in whose company much of their time was spent. They not only associated with the Indians but many even married Indian girls.[18] Outside of the gains made in the peltry trade or their wages as boatmen their lives were not productive, and their scanty earnings were spent immediately upon returning to the villages. They cared nothing for agriculture and other settled pursuits, exhibiting in all their activities a total lack of initiative and of capacity to adapt themselves to settled life.[19] But the faults of the *habitants*, conspicuous though they were, differed much from those of the American frontiersmen. The frontiersmen had no respect for law and authority, while the *habitants* in general preferred to be guided by law in all their dealings.[20] Petty quarrels were frequent, but instead of ending them in a fight, recourse was invariably had to the courts. In their business transactions the assistance of judge or notary was always sought.[20]

On the other hand the "gentry", comprising the larger merchants and farmers, came from the better classes in Canada and France. They surrounded themselves with all the luxuries that could be brought from Canada or Europe. Some were able to claim nobility of birth,[21] and many were

---

[17] Bossu, *Travels*, 126.
[18] *Ibid.;* Du Pratz, *Histoire de la Louisiane*, II, 297.
[19] Volney, *View of the United States*, 338ff.
[20] Alvord, *Ill. Hist. Colls.*, II, xviii.
[21] *Ibia.*, xix; see also Du Pratz, *Histoire ae la Louisiane*, II, 297.

wealthy and influential. Some of the latter possessed capital before immigrating to Illinois, and others rose to prominence by industry and shrewdness. Among the more prominent were Jean Baptiste Barbau of Prairie du Rocher, the Bauvais, Charleville, Viviat, Lachance, and Cerré families of Kaskaskia, and the Sauciers, François Trottier, and J. B. H. La Croix of Cahokia.[22]

The government of the French was neither military nor paternal. Although the military commandant represented the king of France, he did not have all power, nor were the people subjected entirely to the will of the priest.[23] After 1717 the Illinois district was subordinate to the government of Louisiana. The civil government of the district was composed of a commandant, a commissary, a judge, a principal scrivener of the marine, a king's attorney, a keeper of the royal warehouse, a clerk of the court, deputy clerks, syndics, and notaries.[24] As a rule a number of offices were united: the positions of commissary, judge, and scrivener were held by the same person; and the duties of attorney and keeper of the royal warehouse were likewise combined. In addition to the officers already mentioned, each village had its captain of militia,[25] an important local executive officer appointed by the colonial authorities. His specific duties were to prepare the muster-roll of the parish and to enforce the decrees of the intendant of the council.[26] The syndic and the parish priest also had very

[22] Alvord, *Ill. Hist. Colls.*, II, xix-xx.

[23] Both views have hitherto been common to historians of the period. Pittman is largely responsible for the view that the people were subject to the caprice of the military commandant. Other writers have stated that the French were living in a kind of Arcadian simplicity, with no lawyers or litigation. An examination of the documentary material of the time indicates that both views are erroneous.

[24] Alvord, *Ill. in the Eighteenth Cent.*, 8
[25] Breese, *Early Hist. of Ill.*, 216.
[26] Munro, *The Seigniorial System in Canada*, 43, 73.

important local duties, especially with reference to the execution of the edicts of the village assemblies and the laws of the commons.[27] The French had in fact brought with them the organization of the village community and the system of land tenure which they had known in France. Each village had its common field divided into long narrow strips which the inhabitants cultivated, and the common, or pasture land, belonging to the whole community. The village assembly, meeting generally in the church-yard after mass, fixed the day for planting and harvesting, and all other matters relating to the common interest. If the business to be transacted related to the church, the presiding officer was the priest; otherwise the syndic presided at the meeting and saw to the execution of the decisions of the assembly.[28] The military commandant of the Illinois country was responsible to the governor of Louisiana, while civil officials were under the direction of the intendant.

All the land holdings of the French did not originate in the same way. The land acquired from the Indians was considered as belonging to the king's domain, which was disposed of in two ways.[29] At Kaskaskia and Nouvelle Chartres the king retained control of the land and granted it directly to the *habitants*[30] in *censive* holdings, but at Cahokia, St. Philippe, and Prairie du Rocher, large tracts were granted to individuals as seigniories, the title being similar to that of the benefice. The owners of these seigniories granted out smaller tracts to the *habitants* as

---

[27] Babeau, *Le village sous l'ancien régime*, *passim*, and Babeau, *Les assemblées générales des communautés d'habitants*, *passim*.

[28] Babeau, *Le village sous l'ancien régime*, ch. III.

[29] Alvord, *Ill. Hist. Colls.*, II, xxii, n. 2; Franz, *Die Kolonization des Mississippitales*, 201; Breese, *Early Hist. of Ill.*, app. E; Viollet, *Histoire du droit français*, 746ff.

[30] *Habitants* is here used in the broader sense of inhabitants.

manorial holdings which paid to the seignior an annual rent of a *sou* an acre. Cahokia and its lands belonged to the Seminary of Foreign Missions at Quebec, St. Philippe to the Regnaults, and Prairie du Rocher to Boisbriant, and later to Langlois.

The church is an institution which cannot be overlooked in any survey of the Illinois French. The people were so devoted to their religion that the church buildings were generally the most imposing edifices in the village. The parish priests at all times exercised the greatest influence over the lives of the people. No matter how debauched and lawless the *voyageur* became, the priest invariably recalled him to a sense of his dependence upon the church.

There were a number of parishes in the district: the parish of the Immaculate Conception at Kaskaskia, that of St. Anne at Nouvelle Chartres with its dependent chapels of St. Joseph at Prairie du Rocher and the Visitation at St. Philippe, and the parish of the Holy Family at Cahokia. The Jesuits governed the parish at Kaskaskia, where they owned a large plantation, a brewery, and some eighty slaves,[31] and the Recollect and the Sulpitian fathers ministered to the other villages. These parishes, together with those of the rest of Louisiana, were in the diocese of the bishop of Quebec.[32]

The relation of the Illinois country to Louisiana was economic as well as political. All of the trade of the upper Mississippi valley was carried on through New Orleans, and the southern colony often owed its existence to the large supplies of flour and pork sent down the river.[33] Although

---

[31] Pittman, *State of the European Settlements on the Miss.*, ed. Hodder, 85.

[32] Shea, *Life of Archbishop Carroll, passim.*

[33] Winsor, *Narr. and Crit. Hist. of Am.*, V, 53; Pittman, *European Settlements on the Miss.*, ed. Hodder, 95.

the inhabitants occupied themselves chiefly with hunting and with trading with the Indians, they yet raised a considerable amount of corn, wheat, and various kinds of fruit, which, together with cattle and hogs they frequently shipped to the New Orleans market.[34]

[34] Pittman, *op. cit.*, 93-95.

CHAPTER II.

STATUS OF THE ILLINOIS COUNTRY IN THE EMPIRE.

BEFORE entering upon the more detailed study of events in the Illinois country during the British régime, it seems necessary to examine certain general aspects of the subject in order to understand more clearly the significance of the period. The relation of that country to the empire, and the views held by contemporary British statesmen concerning its status are problems which naturally arise and demand solution. What was the nature of the government imposed upon the French in the Illinois country after the final occupation of the West? Is the prevailing opinion that the British government placed the inhabitants of those villages under a military government any longer tenable? Was the government *de jure* or *de facto*?

The treatment received by the settlements in the Northwest and West in general was fundamentally different in nature from that accorded other portions of the new empire. The treaty of Paris was signed in February, 1763, and the British ministry spent considerable time during the months immediately following in the formulation of a policy to be pursued towards the vast territories acquired in North America. In the summer of 1763 it became apparent that this policy must be determined upon immediately in order to pacify the minds of the savage inhabitants of the West who were rising in rebellion against the English. In

October, therefore, a royal proclamation[1] was issued, by the terms of which civil governments were created for the provinces of Quebec, East Florida, West Florida, and Grenada, and all the western territory outside the prescribed limits of these colonies, including a large portion of southern Canada of today, was reserved as a vast hunting ground for the Indian nations. No mention of the settled portions of the West, however, is made in the proclamation. It is therefore necessary to examine the official correspondence which immediately preceded the issuance of the proclamation, to find, if possible, what the directors of the British colonial policy had in mind.

When the proclamation was under discussion by the ministry in the summer of 1763, two opposing views with reference to the West were for a time apparent. It appears to have been the policy of Lord Egremont, at that time secretary of state for the southern department, which included the management of the colonies, to place the unorganized territory within the jurisdiction of some one of the colonies possessing a settled government, preferably Canada.[2] It was at least his aim to give to the Indian country sufficient civil supervision so that criminals and fugitives from justice from the colonies might be retaken. That he did not intend to extend civil government to the villages of Illinois or to any of the French inhabitants of the West seems clear, for his only reference is to the " Indian country " and to " criminals " and " fugitives from justice ".

[1] The text of the proclamation may be conveniently found in the *Annual Register*, IV, 208, and in *Can. Const. Docs., 1759-1791*, 119-123. For a discussion of the history of the proclamation and the origin of the various clauses, see Alvord, " Genesis of the Proclamation of 1763 ", in *Mich. Pioneer and Hist. Colls.*, XXXVI.

[2] Egremont to the Lords of Trade, July 14, 1763, *Can. Const. Docs., 1759-1791*, 108.

Lord Shelburne, president of the Board of Trade and a member of the Grenville ministry, and his colleagues were of the opinion that the annexation of the West to Canada might lend color to the idea that England's title to the West came from the French cession, when in fact her claim was derived from other sources; that the inhabitants of the province to which it might be annexed would have too great an advantage in the Indian trade; and finally that such an immense province could not be properly governed without a large number of troops and the governor would thus virtually become a commander-in-chief.[3] Shelburne then announced his plan of giving to the commanding general of the British army in America jurisdiction over the West for the purpose of protecting the Indians and the fur trade.[4] Lord Halifax, who succeeded Egremont at the latter's death in August, 1763, acceded to Shelburne's views. The proposed commission to the commanding general, however, does not appear to have been issued; for Hillsborough, who succeeded Shelburne as president of the Board of Trade in the autumn of 1763, favored a different policy. But there is nothing to indicate that Shelburne and his advisers had any thought of a government for the French colonies. No hint appears in the correspondence that the ministry had any idea of the existence of the several thousand French inhabitants of the West.[5]

[3] Representation of the Lords of Trade to the King, August 5, 1763, *Can. Const. Docs., 1759–1791*, 110–111.

[4] "We would humbly propose, that a Commission under the Great Seal, for the Government of this Country, should be given to the Commander in Chief of Your Majesty's Troops for the time being adapted to the Protection of the Indians and the fur Trade of Your Majesty's subjects." *Ibid.*, 111.

[5] They could not have been ignorant of the existence of such colonies in the ceded territory, for Sir William Johnson, who was familiar with western conditions, was in constant correspondence with the ministry, and such works as the *Histoire de la Louisiane* by Du Pratz, published in 1758, were doubtless familiar to English statesmen.

There remain one or two documents in which we might expect to find some reference to the government of the French settlers. The authors of that part of the proclamation of 1763 which provided for the reservation of the Indian lands and the regulation of the trade,[6] had in contemplation an elaborate plan comprehending the management of both in the whole of British North America.[7] It was left to Hillsborough, Shelburne's successor as president of the Board of Trade, to direct the formulation of the plan, which was finished in 1764. As the details of this program will be taken up in a later chapter,[8] it will suffice here simply to note the presence or absence of any provision for the French. The chief object of the plan was to bring about centralization in the regulation of the trade and the management of the Indians. In one article provision also was made for a certain kind of civil supervision. For the maintenance of peace and order within the reserved territory, the general superintendents and the commissaries at each post were empowered to act as justices of the peace, with all the powers belonging to such officers in the English colonies. They were to have " full power of Committing Offenders in Capital Cases, in order that such Offenders may be prosecuted for the same ; And that, for deciding all civil actions, the Commissaries be empowered to try and determine in a Summary way all such Actions, as well between the Indians and Traders, as between one Trader and another, to the Amount of Ten Pounds Sterling, with the Liberty of Appeal to the Chief Agent or Superintendent, or his Deputy, who shall be empowered

---

[6] See below, ch. V.

[7] Dartmouth to Cramahé, December 1, 1773, *Can. Const. Docs., 1759-1791*, 339.

[8] See below, ch. V.

upon such appeal to give Judgement thereon; which Judgement shall be final, and process issue upon it, in like manner as on the Judgement of any Court of Common Pleas established in any of the Colonies."[9] It is curious that no provision of this article applies in any way to the government of the French residing at the various posts.

Turning to another source, we find a document addressed directly to the inhabitants of the Illinois country, dated in New York, December 30, 1764 and signed by General Thomas Gage,[10] which was not announced in Illinois until the entry of Captain Sterling in October of the following year. This proclamation related solely to guarantees by the British government of the right of the inhabitants under the treaty of Paris: freedom of religion, the liberty of removing from or remaining within English territory, and regulations concerning the oath of allegiance make up its contents. Whether the inhabitants were to enjoy a civil government or be ruled by the army there is no intimation.

In contrast with the barren papers of 1763–1765 the documentary material after those dates proves so much more productive, that we are enabled to arrive at some pretty definite conclusions. Fortunately there were a few men in authority during that period who had considerable interest in the interior settlements, and who, from their official positions, realized the difficulties of the problem. General Thomas Gage, Sir William Johnson, and Lord Hillsborough are perhaps the most representative examples. Gage, who was commander-in-chief of the British army in America throughout the period under consideration, with headquarters in New York City, was in direct

---

[9] *Can. Arch. Report*, 1904, 244.

[10] *American State Papers, Public Lanas*, II, 209; Dillon, *Hist. of Indiana*, I, 93–94; see below, ch. IV.

communication both with his subordinates in Illinois and with the home authorities and was in a position to know the general state of affairs in the West as well as to keep in touch with ministerial opinion. Sir William Johnson, by virtue of his office as superintendent of Indian affairs for the northern district, was in a peculiarly strategic position for acquiring information. His Indian agents were stationed at all the western posts and he was in constant correspondence with the Board of Trade relative to the Indian and trade conditions. In the ministry itself the correspondence of Lord Hillsborough perhaps best reflects the prevailing opinion of the government. He was one of the few ministerial authorities who took any considerable interest in the western problem and information coming from him must therefore have weight.

That the British commandant of the fort in the Illinois country had no commission to govern the inhabitants, except that power which naturally devolves upon the military officer in the absence of all other authority,[11] appears amply clear from a recommendation transmitted by General Gage to his superior, Secretary Conway, shortly after the occupation of Fort de Chartres: "If I may presume to give my opinion further on this matter, I would humbly propose that a Military Governor should be appointed for the Illinois [sic] as soon as possible. The distance of that country from any of the Provinces being about 1400 Miles, makes its Dependance upon any one of them im-

---

[11] "The Secretary of State having signified to me that as my Commission under the Great Seal as Commander-in-Chief of all His Majesty's Forces in North America includes Florida and the Country ceded by Spain, on this Continent, and likewise the Country ceded by France on the left side of the Mississippi; It is the King's Pleasure I should give the necessary Orders to the Officers commanding the Troops, etc." Amherst to Lieutenant-Colonel Robertson, August 24, 1763, P. R. O., B. T. Papers, no. 19, fol. 49.

STATUS IN THE EMPIRE

practicable, and from its Vicinity to the French Settlements, no other than a Military Government would answer our purpose." [12] In the following year he took a similar view in a communication to Sir William Johnson, his co-laborer in America: "I am quite sensible of the irregular behavior of the Traders and have intimated to his Majesty's Secretary of State what I told the Board of Trade four or five years ago: That they must be restrained by Law, and a Judicial Power invested in the Officer Commanding at the Posts to see such Law put in force. And without this, Regulations may be made, but they will never be observed." [13]

During this period the authorities seemed unable to combat successfully the condition of comparative anarchy in the Illinois country and indeed in all the western posts and throughout the Indian country. Had all the regulations outlined in 1764 in the plan for the management of Indian affairs [14] been put into operation, the Indian department would have been able to cope more successfully with that phase of the situation. But neither military nor Indian departments had legal authority to administer justice in the West. [15] In 1767, speaking of his inability to handle the

[12] Gage to Conway, March 28, 1766, B. T. Papers (Hist. Soc. Pa.), vol. XX.

[13] Gage to Johnson, January 25, 1767, Johnson MSS. (N. Y. State Library), vol. XIV, no. 28.

[14] See below, ch. V.

[15] In the Mutiny Act, passed in 1765, a clause was inserted regulating criminal procedure in the Indian country, whereby persons accused of crimes were directed to be conveyed to the civil magistrate of the next adjoining province, where they should be tried. " . An Act for punishing Mutiny and Desertion, and for the better Payment of the Army and their Quarters." 5 Geo. III, cap. XXXIII. This was evidently too slow a process. I have found but one case in the history of the Illinois colony where the clause was executed. October 7, 1769, Gage wrote to Hillsborough: "Two persons are confined in Fort Chartres for murther, and the Colonel [Wilkins] proposes to send them to Philadelphia, about fifteen hundred miles, to take their Tryall." P. R. O., Am. and W. I., vol. 125.

situation for lack of sufficient powers, Johnson declared that "The authority of Commissaries is nothing, and both the Commanding Officers of Garrisons and they, are liable to a civil prosecution for detaining a Trader on any pretence."[16] Writing of the disturbances which occurred in Illinois a few years later, the commanding general observed still more emphatically: "And I perceive there has been wanting judicial powers to try and determine. There has been no way to bring Controversys and Disputes properly to a determination or delinquents to punishment."[17]

There is probably some justification for the current belief that the government placed the inhabitants under a military rule, inasmuch as the actual government proved in the last analysis to be military. That the British ministry consciously attached the interior settlements to the military department is, however, far from the truth. Such a system of government was probably contemplated by no one between the years 1763 and 1765 when the reorganization of the new acquisitions was under consideration. A large part of the new territory was believed to be within the fur-bearing region and the desire for the development of the fur trade controlled in the main the policy of the ministry relative to the disposition of the "peltry" districts. The interests of the settlements were therefore completely ignored.

Secretary Hillsborough, who helped formulate the western

[16] "Review of the Trade and Affairs of the Indians in the Northern District of America", *N. Y. Col. Docs.*, VII, 964.

[17] Gage to Hillsborough, August 6, 1771, P. R. O., Am. and W. I., vol. 128. See also Gage to Hillsborough, October 7, 1769, *ibid.*, vol. 125. Lieutenant George Phyn, who went with a detachment of troops from Fort Pitt down the Ohio and Mississippi rivers to Mobile in 1768, making a visit of several weeks at Fort de Chartres, wrote to Sir William Johnson: "There is no settled administration of Justice, but the whole depends upon the mere will and fancy of the Officer commanding the Troops." April 15, 1768, Johnson MSS., vol. XXV, no. 109.

policy in 1763 and 1764, doubtless gave the most adequate explanation when, in 1769, he wrote: "With regard to the Posts in the interior Country considered in another view in which several of your letters have placed them; I mean as to the Settlements formed under their protection, which, not being included within the jurisdiction of any other Colony are exposed to many Difficulties and Disadvantages from the Want of some Form of Government necessary to Civil Society, it is very evident that, if the case of these Settlements had been well known or understood at the time of forming the conquered Lands into Colonies, some provision would have been made for them, and they would have been erected into distinct Governments or made dependent upon those other Colonies of which they were either the offspring, or with which they did by circumstances and situation, stand connected. I shall not fail, therefore, to give this matter the fullest consideration when the Business of the Illinois Country is taken up." [18]

Hillsborough's declaration that no provision for the government of the settlements had ever been made is borne out by other testimony. A writer in the *Annual Register* for 1763,[19] after describing the boundaries of the various governments provided for by the royal proclamation, commented as follows: " The reader will observe and possibly with some surprise, that in this distribution, much the largest, and perhaps, the most valuable part of our conquests, does

---

[18] Hillsborough to Gage, December 9, 1769, P. R. O., Am. and W. I., vol. 124. "If the people are left to shift for themselves entirely without any arrangements made for them, its possible they would no longer consider themselves subjects, join openly with enemy Indians, and British traders going to the Ilinois might be refused admittance and drove out of the Country." Gage to Hillsborough, March 4, 1772, Sparks MSS. (Harvard College Library), XLIII, vol. 3, pp. 164–165.

[19] *Annual Register*, VI, 20.

not fall into any of the governments; that the environs of the great lakes, the fine countries on the whole course of the Ohio and Wabashe, and almost all that tract of Louisiana, which lies on the hither branch of the Mississippi, are none of them comprehended in this distribution . . ."

In 1774 during the course of the debate in the House of Lords on the Quebec Act, which provided for the form of government and the extension of the boundaries of that colony to the Ohio and Mississippi rivers, Lord North observed that " It takes in no countries regularly planted by British settlers, but merely distant military posts, at present without any government but that of the respective commanding officers. Now, the question here is merely this, Will you annex them under the present government? Will you leave them without any government? or will you form Separate governments and colonies of them?"[20] Finally the existence of such a large area of territory without a government was recognized in the preamble of the Quebec Act as ultimately passed : " And whereas, by the Arrangements made by the said Royal Proclamation, a very large Extent of Country, within which there were several Colonies and Settlements of the Subjects of *France*, who claimed to remain therein under the Faith of the said Treaty, was left without any Provision being made for the Administration of Civil Government therein."[21]

[20] *Parl. Hist.*, XVII, 1358. William Knox, the under secretary for the colonies, in a contemporaneous pamphlet makes the following assertion: "As these settlers had been put entirely under the direction of the commanding Officers of the forts [during the French rule], when the *French* garrisons were withdrawn, and military orders ceased to be law, they were altogether without law or government; . . They had been accustomed to obey French military orders, and the English officers, . . of their own authority exercised the same command over them." *Justice and Policy of the Quebec Act*, 39.

[21] *Can. Const. Docs., 1759–1791*, 401. In a paper entitled "Proposed Extension of Provincial Limits", one of the reasons given for the

English troops took formal possession of Fort de Chartres, the military post in the Illinois country, in 1765. It was not intended, however, that the army should continue there indefinitely.[22] Nevertheless as time went on the necessity became evident of being constantly prepared to crush a possible uprising of the savages and to repel the constant invasion of the French and Spanish traders from beyond the Mississippi, whose influence over the Indians, it was feared, would be detrimental to the peace of the empire. In its policy of retrenchment owing to the trouble with the colonies, the government at various times contemplated the withdrawal of the troops,[23] but each time the detachment was allowed to remain; the sole reason given was to guard that portion of the empire against the French and Indians.[24]

Attention has now been called to the entire absence of regulations for the government of the western settlements in any of the official documents relating to that territory prior to 1774. The proclamation of 1763, which had definitely extended the laws of England to the new provinces of Quebec and the Floridas, made no similar provision for the West. This statement also holds for other state papers such

extension of the Quebec boundary was to " extend the benefits of Civil Government to the Settlements of Canadian Subjects that have been formed in the different parts of " the interior country, *ibid.*, 381. In the first two draughts of the Quebec Act no reference is made to the western settlements, *ibid.*, 376–380.

[22] Hillsborough to Gage, February 17, 1770, P. R. O., Am. and W. I., vol. 125.

[23] " The situation and peculiar circumstances of the Ilinois Country, and the use, if that Country is maintained, of guarding the Ohio and Ilinois Rivers at or near their junctions with the Mississippi has been set forth to your Lordship in my letter of the 22d of Feb. last. It is upon that plan the Regiment is posted in the Disposition in the Ilinois Country." Gage to Shelburne, April 3, 1767, *ibid.*, vol. 123.

[24] See for example, Hillsborough to Gage, February 17, 1770, *ibid.*, vol. 125; Gage to Shelburne, April 3, 1767, *ibid.*, vol. 123.

as the plan of 1764 for the management of Indian affairs and General Gage's proclamation to the inhabitants of Illinois in 1765. Nor in any of the correspondence relating to the various documents has any reference to the government of the French been discovered. On the other hand after 1765 we have the positive statements of such officials as Sir William Johnson, General Gage, Lord Hillsborough, and Lord North to the effect that the settlements in question had been left entirely without any arrangement for their government. Similar assertions in the Quebec Act and in contemporary works, books, and pamphlets contribute additional testimony.

In the course of this inquiry relative to the legal status of Illinois and the West no mention has been made of the extension or non-extension of English law and custom to the West after the cession. This is one of the more important general aspects of the western problem and merits attention inasmuch as it may throw further light on the legal position of the settlements. During the seventeenth and eighteenth centuries, the great era of English colonization, the necessity of fixing definitely the legal status of the colonies called forth a series of judicial opinions and legal commentaries. It is to these that we have to look to determine the theory held regarding the application of English law to the colonies and particularly to conquered provinces. In general it may be said that Blackstone represents the usual view taken by jurists during these two centuries. In his *Commentaries* published in 1765 he declared that " In conquered or ceded countries, that have already laws of their own, the king may indeed alter and change those laws, but until he actually does change them, the ancient laws of the country remain."[25] This opinion is supported by the

---

[25] Blackstone, *Commentaries* (3d ed., Cooley), Intro., sec. 4, 107.

authority of Lord Mansfield in his decision in the case of Campbell *v.* Hall,[26] rendered in 1774, which involved the status of the island of Grenada, a conquered province. He laid down in this decision the general principle that the "laws of a conquered country continue in force until they are altered by the conquerer. The justice and antiquity of this maxim are incontrovertible . . ."[27]

As has already been suggested the proclamation of 1763 failed to extend English law to the West, nor did the crown ever take such action. We may therefore lay down the general principle that although with the change of sovereignty the public law of England was substituted for that of France, the private law of the province remained unchanged. The British government then was obliged to govern its new subjects in this region according to the laws and customs hitherto prevailing among them; any other course would manifestly be illegal. The commanding general of the army in America and his subordinates, who were embarrassed by the presence of this French settlement for which no provision had been made by the ministry, and who found it necessary to assume the obligation of enforcing some sort of order in that country, had no power to displace any of the laws and customs of the French inhabitants. It will be pointed out in succeeding chapters that this general principle, although adhered to in many respects, was not uniformly carried out.

---

[26] Text of decision in *Can. Const. Docs.*, *1759–1791*, 366–372.

[27] Other important leading cases, such as Calvin's case, involving the status of Jamaica, are of the same effect. See also Sioussat, *English Statutes in Maryland* (J. H. U. Studies, XXI), 481–487, and especially Walton, *The Scope and Interpretation of the Civil Code of Lower Canada*, 6–7, 26–27. The same opinion is expressed by Attorney-General Thurlow in a speech in Parliament in 1774 on the subject of the Quebec Act. This speech is found in Egerton and Grant, *Canadian Const. Development*, 33–41.

It is apparent from the foregoing considerations that the government of the Illinois people was *de facto* in its nature. It had no legal foundations. Every act of the military department was based on expediency. Although in general this course was accepted by the home authorities, all officials concerned were aware that such a status could not continue indefinitely. Nevertheless it did continue for about a decade, during which time the inhabitants were at the mercy of some six or seven different military commandants. In 1774, however, Parliament passed the Quebec Act, which provided, among other things, for the union of all the western country north of the Ohio River, which but for the cataclysm of the American Revolution would have secured civil government for the whole region.

CHAPTER III.

OCCUPATION OF THE ILLINOIS COUNTRY

By the treaty of Paris the title to the Illinois region passed to Great Britain, but Fort de Chartres was not immediately occupied. Detachments of British troops had taken possession of practically every other post in the newly ceded territory as early as 1760. The occupation of the forest posts of Green Bay, Mackinac, St. Joseph, Ouiatanon, Detroit, Fort Miami, Sandusky, Niagara, and others seemed to indicate almost complete British dominion in the West. The transfer of the Illinois posts, however, remained to be effected, and although in the summer of 1763 orders were forwarded from France to the officers commanding in the ceded territory to evacuate as soon as the English forces appeared,[1] almost three years elapsed before the occupation was accomplished; for soon after the announcement of the treaty of cession, the chain of Indian tribes stretching from the fringe of the eastern settlements to the Mississippi River rose in rebellion.[2] This unexpected movement had to be reckoned with before any thought of the occupation of the Illinois country could be seriously entertained.

Of the two great northern Indian families, the Iroquois had generally espoused the English cause during the recent

[1] Parkman, *Conspiracy of Pontiac*, II, 272–273.

[2] For the Indian rebellion the best secondary accounts are: Parkman, *Conspiracy of Pontiac*; Kingsford, *Hist. of Can.*, V, 1–112; Poole, "The West", in Winsor, *Narr. and Crit. Hist. of Am.*, VI, 684–700; Winsor, *Miss. Basin*, 432–446; Bancroft, *Hist. of U. S.* (ed. of 1852, containing references), IV, 110–133.

war, while the Algonquin nations, living in Canada and the lake and Ohio regions, had supported the French. At the close of the war the greater portion of the French had sworn fealty to the English crown, although the allegiance of their allies, the Algonquins, was at best only temporary. It was thought that, since the power of France had been crushed, there would be no further motive for the Indian tribes to continue hostilities. From 1761, however, there had been a growing feeling of discontent among the western Indians. So long as France and Great Britain were able to hold each other in check in America the Indian nations formed a balance of power, so to speak, between them. England and France vied with each other to conciliate the savages and to win their good-will. As soon, however, as English dominion was assured, this attitude was somewhat changed. The fur trade under the French had been well regulated, but its condition under the English from 1760 to 1763 was deplorable.[3] The English traders were rash and unprincipled men[4] who did not scruple to cheat and insult their Indian clients at every opportunity. The more intelligent of the western and northern Indians perceived that their hunting grounds would soon be overrun by white settlers with a fixed purpose of permanent settlement.[5] This was probably the chief cause of the Indian uprising. There remained in the forests many French and renegade traders and hunters who constantly concocted

---

[3] Parkman, *Conspiracy of Pontiac*, I, 182; Pownall, *Admin. of the Cols.*, I, 187-188. Although Pownall discusses the situation somewhat earlier, he appears to hold the same view which Johnson and other contemporaries express later.

[4] Johnson to Lords of Trade, *N. Y. Col. Docs.*, VII, 929, 955, 960, 964, 987; Pownall, *Admin. of the Cols.*, I, 188; Kingsford, *Hist. of Can.*, V, 121ff.

[5] Johnson to Amherst, July 11, 1763, *N. Y. Col. Docs.*, VII, 532; Pownall, *Admin. of the Cols.*, I, 187-190.

insidious reports as to English designs and filled the savage minds with hope of succor from the king of France. Many of the French inhabitants had since 1760 emigrated beyond the Mississippi, because, as the Indians thought, they feared to live under English rule.[7] This doubtless contributed something towards the rising discontent of the savages. Finally the policy of economy in expenses, which General Amherst inaugurated, cut off a large part of the Indian presents, always so indispensable in dealing with that race, and augured poorly for the future welfare of the Indians.

The mass of the Indians rose chiefly from resentment, but Pontiac, the great chief of the Ottawas, acted from a deeper motive. He determined to rehabilitate French power in the West and to reunite all the Indian nations into one great confederacy in order to ward off approaching dangers. During the years 1761–1762 he developed the plot and in 1762 he despatched his emissaries to all the Indian nations. The ramifications of the conspiracy extended to all the Algonquin tribes, to some of the nations on the lower Mississippi, and even to a portion of the Six Nations. The original aim of the plot was the destruction of the garrisons on the frontier, after which the settlements were to be attacked. The assault on the outposts, beginning in May, 1763, was sudden and overwhelming; Detroit, Fort Pitt, and Niagara alone held out, the remainder of the posts falling without an attempt at defense. Had the proclamation of 1763, which aimed at the pacification of the Indians by reserving to them the western lands, been

[6] Johnson to Amherst, July 11, 1763, *N. Y. Col. Docs.*, VII, 532; Pownall, *Admin. of the Cols.*, I, 187–190.

[7] Parkman, *Conspiracy of Pontiac*, I, 181, quoting from a letter of Sir William Johnson to Governor Colden, December 24, 1763; Winsor, *Miss. Basin*, 433.

issued earlier in the year, this devastating war might have been avoided. Peaceful pacification was now, however, out of the question. During the summers of 1763 and 1764 Colonel Bouquet raised the siege of Fort Pitt, penetrated the enemy's country in the upper Ohio Valley, and completely subdued the Shawnee and Delaware tribes upon whom Pontiac had depended. Previous to Bouquet's second campaign, Colonel Bradstreet had advanced with a detachment along the southern shore of Lake Erie, penetrating as far west as Detroit, whence companies were sent to occupy the posts in the upper lake region. In the campaign as a whole the Bouquet expedition was the most effective. After the ratification of a series of treaties, in which the Indians promised allegiance to the English crown, the eastern portion of the rebellion was broken.

It now remained to reach the Illinois country in order to relieve the French garrison at Fort de Chartres. Pontiac had retired thither in 1764, after his unsuccessful attempt upon Detroit. There he had hoped to rally the western tribes and sue for the support of the French. But as we shall see, his schemes received a powerful blow by the refusal of the commandants to countenance his plans.

To what extent Pontiac was assisted by French intriguers in the development of his plans may never be positively known. As has already been pointed out, French traders were constantly among the Indians, filling their minds with hopes and fears. That the plot included French officials may be doubted, although Sir William Johnson and General Gage seemed convinced that such was the case.[8] Their

[8] Johnson to Lords of Trade, July 1, 1763, *N. Y. Col. Docs.*, VII, 525; Johnson to Amherst, July 8, 1763, *ibid.*, 531; Johnson to Lords of Trade, December 26, 1764, *ibid.*, 688-689; Gage to Bouquet, June 5, 1764, Can. Arch. (Ottawa), series A, vol. 8, p. 409; Gage to Bouquet, October 21, 1764, *ibid.*, p. 479; Johnson to Governor Colden, January 22, 1765, Johnson MSS., vol. X, no. 99.

belief, however, was based almost wholly upon reports from Indian runners, whose credibility as witnesses may well be questioned. A perusal of the correspondence of the French officials [9] residing in Illinois and Louisiana, and of their official communications with the Indians during this period goes far to clear them of complicity in the affair. [10]

General Gage, who succeeded Amherst as commander-in-chief of the British army in America in November, 1763, was convinced that the early occupation of the western posts was essential, [11] since it would in a measure cut off communication between the French and the Indian nations dwelling in that vicinity. The Indians, finding themselves thus inclosed, would be more easily pacified. The participation in the rebellion of the Shawnee and Delaware tribes of the upper Ohio River region precluded for a time, however, the possibility of reaching the Mississippi posts by way of Fort Pitt without a much larger force than Gage had at his command in the East, and the colonies were already avoiding the call for additional troops. [12] The only other available route was by way of New Orleans and the Mississippi River, whose navigation had been declared open to

[9] *Can. Arch. Report*, 1905, I, 470; Neyon to Kerlerec, December 1, 1763, Bancroft Coll. (Lenox Library); extracts from letters of d'Abbadie, January, 1764, *Can. Arch. Report*, 1905, I, 471; d'Abbadie to the French minister, 1764, *ibid.*, 472.

[10] This is the view taken by Parkman, *Conspiracy of Pontiac*, II, 279, and by Bancroft, *Hist. of U. S.*, V, 133, 136. But Kingsford, *Hist. of Can.*, V, 25, takes an opposite view. He says that the "high character claimed for Pontiac cannot be established . . He can be looked upon in no higher light, than the instrument of the French officials and Traders." On page 6 he declares that "there is no evidence to establish him as the central figure organizing this hostile feeling."

[11] Gage to Halifax, July 13, 1764, Bancroft Coll., Eng. and Am., 1764–1765; Winsor, *Miss. Basin*, 444, 456; Winsor, *Narr. and Crit. Hist. of Am.*, VI, 702.

[12] Beer, *British Colonial Policy*, 263; Kingsford, *Hist. of Can.*, V, 68.

the French and English alike by the treaty of Paris. Little opposition might be expected from the southern Indians toward whom a liberal policy had been pursued. Presents to the value of four or five thousand pounds had been sent to Charleston in 1763 for distribution among the southern nations which counteracted in a large measure the machinations of the French traders from New Orleans.[13] The Florida posts, Mobile and Pensacola, were already occupied by English troops, and Gage and his associates believed that with the cooperation of the French governor of Louisiana a successful ascent could be made.[14]

Accordingly in January, 1764, Major Arthur Loftus, with a detachment of three hundred and fifty-one men from the Twenty-second Regiment embarked at Mobile for New Orleans, where preparations were to be made for the voyage.[15] A company of sixty men from this regiment were to be left at Fort Massac on the Ohio River, and the remainder were to occupy Kaskaskia and Fort de Chartres.[16] At New Orleans boats had to be built, supplies and provisions procured, and guides and interpreters provided.[17] The expedition set out from New Orleans February 27. Three weeks later the flotilla was attacked by a band of Tonica Indians near Davion's Bluff, or Fort Adams,[18] about two hun-

---

[13] Winsor, *Miss. Basin*, 433; Ogg, *Opening of the Miss.*, 301.

[14] Bouquet to Amherst, December 1, 1763, Can. Arch., series A, vol. 4, p. 443; Gage to Bouquet, December 22, 1763, *ibid.*, vol. 8, p. 341. Early in February, 1764, Captain George Johnston arrived at Pensacola with a detachment of troops. On February 24th he despatched Loftus to take possession of Fort de Chartres, Albach, *Annals of the West*, 88.

[15] Lieutenant-Colonel Robertson to Gage, March 8, 1764, Bancroft Coll., Eng. and Am., 1764–1765: de Villiers du Terrage, *Les dernières Années de la Louisiane française*, 180.

[16] Robertson to Gage, March 8, 1764, Bancroft Coll., Eng. and Am., 1764–1765. [17] *Ibid.*

[18] Loftus to Gage, April 9, 1764, *ibid.*; Gage to Halifax, May 21, 1764, *ibid.*; Parkman, *Conspiracy of Pontiac*, II, 283, 285; Kings-

OCCUPATION

dred and forty miles above New Orleans. After the loss of several men in the boats composing the vanguard Loftus ordered a retreat and the expedition was abandoned. Depleted by sickness, death, and desertion the regiment made its way from New Orleans back to Mobile.[19]

Major Loftus placed the blame for the failure of his expedition upon Governor d'Abbadie and other French officials at New Orleans.[20] There is probably sufficient evidence, however, to warrant the conclusion that his accusations against the governor were without foundation. The correspondence of d'Abbadie, Gage, and others indicates that official aid was given the English in making their preparations for the journey,[21] and letters were issued to the commandants of the French posts on the Mississippi to render the English convoys all the assistance in their power.[22]

---

ford, *Hist. of Can.*, V, 69–74; Winsor, *Narr. and Crit. Hist. of Am.*, VI, 701, 702; Gayarré, *Louisiana*, II, 102–103. See map, "Course of the Mississippi River", by Lieutenant Ross, London, 1772, showing where Loftus' force was driven back. A section of this map is reproduced in Winsor, *Miss. Basin*, 450.

[19] Loftus to Gage, April 9, 1764, Bancroft Coll., Eng. and Am., 1764–1765; de Villiers du Terrage, *Les dernières Années de la Louisiane française*, 182–184; Claiborne, *Hist. of Miss.*, I, 104–105.

[20] Loftus to Gage, April 9, 1764, Bancroft Coll., Eng. and Am., 1764–1765.

[21] Robertson to Gage, March 8, 1764, Bancroft Coll., Eng. and Am., 1764-1765; "Account of what happened in Illinois when the English attempted to take possession of it by way of the Mississippi", in Archives of the Ministry of the Colonies, summarized in *Can. Arch. Report*, 1905, I, 470-471; Parkman, *Conspiracy of Pontiac*, II, 284, n. 1, containing a letter from Gage thanking d'Abbadie for his efforts in behalf of the English.

[22] Summary of the correspondence of d'Abbadie with the French commandants, January, 1764, *Can. Arch. Report*, 1905, I, 471. Parkman, who made a careful study of the correspondence in the French archives, came to the conclusion that the French officials may be exonerated. Winsor holds a similar view, *Miss. Basin*, 452. See also Gayarré, *Louisiana*, II, 101. Kingsford, *Hist. of Can.*, V, 69–74, places no dependence, however, in d'Abbadie's statements. On the other hand he bases most of his argument upon a letter of Loftus which

There may have been some justification for the suspicion of Loftus that intrigues were at work, for the French as a whole were not in sympathy with the attempt, and the success of the English would mean the cessation of the lucrative trade between New Orleans and Illinois. They were no doubt delighted at the discomfiture of the English officer, for when some of the chiefs engaged in the ambuscade entered New Orleans they are said to have been publicly received.[23]

Granting, however, the machinations of the French, the chief reason for the failure of Loftus may be found in the absence of precautions before undertaking the journey. Governor d'Abbadie had given the English officer warning of the bad disposition of a number of tribes along the Mississippi River, among whom Pontiac had considerable influence, and had assured him that unless he carried presents to the Indians, he would be unable to proceed far up the river.[24] The policy of sending advance agents with convoys of presents for the Indians was successful the following year when the Illinois posts were finally reached from the east, but no such policy was adopted at this time.[25] No action was taken to counteract any possible intrigues on the part of the French; d'Abbadie's advice was not heeded, and his prophecy was fulfilled. General Gage, in his official correspondence relative to a second attempt, implied that he did not think sufficient care had been exer-

---

he quotes at length, but gives no hint as to its location, date, etc. It is evidently not the letter written to Gage, which is quoted above.

[23] Loftus to Gage, April 9, 1764, Bancroft Coll., Eng. and Am., 1764-1765.

[24] Gage to Halifax, April 14, 1764, *N. Y. Col. Docs.*, VII, 619.

[25] This has reference to those tribes along the Mississippi River who were in direct communication with Pontiac and the French. The great Cherokee and Chickasaw nations were favorable to the English.

OCCUPATION

cised to insure success, and expressed his belief that if Loftus would make use of the "necessary precautions" he might reach the mouth of the Ohio with little interruption.[26] This want of judgment, therefore, accounts in a large degree for the unfortunate termination of the plans for an approach from the south.

The news of the defeat of Loftus had two results. First, it gave Pontiac renewed hope that he might be able to rally again the western and northern Indians, and, with French assistance, block the advance of the English. In the second place it led General Gage to determine upon an advance from the east, down the Ohio River, which was made practicable by the recent submission of the Shawnee and Delaware Indians.

Meanwhile the Illinois country in 1764 presented an anomalous situation. St. Ange was governing, in the name of Louis XV, a country belonging to another king. Although he was under orders to surrender the place as soon as possible to its rightful owner, the prospect of such surrender seemed remote. He was not only surrounded by crowds of begging, thieving savages, but was also being constantly petitioned by the emissaries of Pontiac for his active support against the approaching English. A considerable portion of the French traders of the villages were secretly, and sometimes openly, supporting the Indian cause, which added greatly to the increasing embarrassment of the commandant. So distressing was the situation in 1764 that Neyon de Villiers, St. Ange's predecessor, had called the latter from Vincennes on the Wabash to Fort de Chartres

[26] Gage to Bouquet, May 21, 1764, Can. Arch., series A, vol. 8, p. 393; Gage to Halifax, May 21, 1764, Bancroft Coll., Eng. and Am., 1764-1765; Gage to Haldimand, May 27, 1764, Brit. Mus., Add. MSS., 21, 662; Gage to Halifax, July 13, 1764, Bancroft Coll., Eng. and Am., 1764-1765.

and left the country in disgust, taking with him to New Orleans sixty soldiers and eighty of the French inhabitants.[27] He had shortly before indignantly refused to countenance the proposals of Pontiac, and had begged the Indians to lay down their arms and make peace with the English.[28]

The news of Loftus' defeat aroused in Pontiac the thought of meeting and repelling the advance from the east as it had been met and repelled in the south. In spite of the news of the defeat of his allies by Bouquet and the report that preparations were being made by his victorious enemy to advance against him, Pontiac determined to make a supreme effort. By a series of visits among the tribes dwelling in the Illinois country, on the Wabash, and in the Miami country, he succeeded in arousing in them the instinct of self-preservation, in firing the hearts of all the faltering Indians, and in winning the promise of their cooperation in his plan of defense. It was under these circumstances that he met and turned back Captain Thomas Morris in the Miami country early in the autumn of 1764. Morris had been sent by Bradstreet, who was at this time engaged in his campaign against the northern Indians, from the neighborhood of Detroit with messages to St. Ange in the Illinois country, whence he was to proceed to New Orleans.[29] After

[27] Parkman, *Conspiracy of Pontiac*, II, 275; Winsor, *Miss. Basin*, 454.

[28] St. Ange to d'Abbadie, August 16, 1764, *Can. Arch. Report*, 1905, I, 471; Parkman, *Conspiracy of Pontiac*, II, 279-280.

[29] The original journal kept by Morris during this journey is reprinted in Thwaites, *Early Western Travels*, I, 298-328. There is also a biographical sketch in the same volume. See account by Henry C. Van Schaack, "Captain Thomas Morris in the Illinois Country", *Mag. of Am. Hist.*, VIII, Pt. 2, pp. 470-479. Correspondence relating to the Morris mission is to be found in the Bouquet Collection, Can. Arch., series A, vol. 8, pp. 475-491. For good accounts of the incident, see Parkman, *Conspiracy of Pontiac*, II, 198-208, and Kingsford, *Hist. of Can.*, V, 8.

OCCUPATION

being maltreated and threatened with the stake Morris effected an escape and made his way to Detroit.[30] It was during his interview with Pontiac that the latter informed him of the repulse of Loftus, of the journey of his own emissaries to New Orleans to seek French support, and of the determination of the Indians to resist the English to the last.[31]

A few months later, in February, 1765, there arrived at Fort de Chartres an English officer, John Ross, accompanied by a trader named Crawford. They were probably the first Englishmen to penetrate thus far into the former French territory since the beginning of the war.[32] They had been sent from Mobile by Major Farmer, the commandant at that place, to bring about the conciliation of the Indians in the Illinois country.[33] Instead of following the Mississippi they worked their way northward through the great Choctaw and Chickasaw nations to the Ohio, descended the latter to the Mississippi and proceeded thence to the Illinois villages.[34] Although St. Ange received them cordially[35] and did all in his power to influence the savages to receive the English,[36] the mission of Ross was a failure. The western Indians had nothing but expressions of hatred

---

[30] This incident illustrates the practical failure of Bradstreet's campaign against the Indians in the lake region. While he retook the posts, his terms were so easy that the Indians were not in the least awed by the proximity of his army.

[31] Thwaites, *Early Western Travels*, I, 305.

[32] Ross to Farmer, February 21, 1765, Bancroft Coll., Eng. and Am., 1764-1765; Gage to Halifax, August 10, 1765, *ibid.*

[33] Ross to Farmer, May 25, 1765, Bancroft Coll., Eng. and Am., 1764-1765; H. Gordon to Johnson, August 10, 1765, Johnson MSS., vol. XI, no. 73.

[34] Ross to Farmer, May 25, 1765, Bancroft Coll., Eng. and Am., 1764-1765.

[35] Ross to Farmer, May 25, 1765, Bancroft Coll., Eng. and Am., 1764-1765. [36] *Ibid.*

and defiance for the English; even the Missouri and Osages from beyond the Mississippi had fallen under the influence of Pontiac.[37] Ross and his companion remained with St. Ange nearly two months, but about the middle of April were obliged to go down the river to New Orleans.[38]

During the winter of 1764–1765 preparations were made to send a detachment of troops down the Ohio from Fort Pitt to relieve Fort de Chartres. To pave the way for the troops two agents were despatched in advance. Sir William Johnson selected his deputy, George Croghan, for the delicate and dangerous task of going among the Indians of that country to assure them of the peaceful attitude of the English, to promise them better facilities for trade, and to accompany the promise with substantial presents.[39] The second agent was Lieutenant Fraser,[40] whose mission was to carry letters from General Gage to the French commandant

---

[37] *Ibid.*; "Copy of Council held at the Illinois in April, 1765", P. R. O., Home Office Papers, Dom., Geo. III, vol. 3, no. 4 (1); copy of minutes of council, April 4, 1765, summarized in *Can. Arch. Report*, 1905, I, 473. See also de Villiers du Terrage, *Les dernières Années de la Louisiane française*, 220.

[38] Ross to Farmer, May 25, 1765, Bancroft Coll., Eng. and Am., 1764–1765.

[39] Johnson to Gage, June 9, 1764, Johnson MSS., vol. XIX, no. 111; Johnson to Lords of Trade, December 26, 1764, *N. Y. Col. Docs.*, VII, 689; Bouquet to Gage, January 5, 1765, Can. Arch., series A, vol. 7, p. 111; Parkman, *Conspiracy of Pontiac*, II, 291–292; Winsor, *Narr. and Crit. Hist. of Am.*, VI, 702. Croghan is one of the most interesting figures of the period. He had charge, as Sir William Johnson's deputy, of the Indians in the Ohio River region, and was thoroughly conversant with western affairs. For biographical sketch, see Thwaites, *Early Western Travels*, I, 47–52, or *N. Y. Col. Docs.*, VII, 690.

[40] Gage to Bouquet, December 24, 1764, Can. Arch., series A, vols 8, p. 499; same to same, December 30, 1764, *ibid.* This distinction is not generally made. Writers have usually inferred that Fraser accompanied Croghan in an unofficial capacity. See however, Winsor, *Miss. Basin*, 456. Ogg, *Opening of the Miss.*, 310, places Fraser's journey a year previous to Croghan's, which is obviously an error.

OCCUPATION

and a proclamation for the inhabitants.[41] January 24, 1765, Fraser and Croghan set out from Carlisle, Pennsylvania,[42] followed a few days later by a large convoy of presents.[43] During the journey the convoy was attacked by a band of Pennsylvania borderers,[44] and a large part of the goods destined for the Indians was destroyed[45] together with some valuable stores which certain Philadelphia merchants were forwarding to Fort Pitt for the purpose of opening up the trade as early as possible.[46] Croghan found it necessary therefore to tarry at Fort Pitt to replenish his stores and to await the opening of spring.[47] Another matter, however, intervened which forced him to postpone his departure for more than two months. A temporary defection had arisen among the Shawnee and Delaware Indians.[48] They had failed to fulfill some of the obligations imposed upon them by Bouquet in the previous summer, and there was some fear lest they might not permit Croghan to pass through their country. His influence was such however, that in an assembly of the tribes at Fort Pitt he not only received their consent to a safe passage, but some of their number volunteered to accompany him.[49]

[41] Gage to Johnson, February 2, 1765, Parkman Coll. (Mass. Hist. Soc.), Pontiac–Miscell., 1765–1778.

[42] Jos. Galloway to B. Franklin, January 23, 1765, Sparks MSS., XVI, 54, 55.

[43] Parkman, *Conspiracy of Pontiac*, II, 292.

[44] The frontiersmen could not understand the significance of the movement and were incensed at the idea of giving valuable presents to the Indians.

[45] Johnson to Lords of Trade, May 24, 1765, *N. Y. Col. Docs.*, VII, 716; Parkman, *Conspiracy of Pontiac*, II, 292–297.

[46] Johnson to Lords of Trade, May 24, 1765, *N. Y. Col. Docs.*, VII, 716.

[47] Parkman, *Conspiracy of Pontiac*, II, 297.

[48] Johnson to Lords of Trade, January 16, 1765, *N. Y. Col. Docs.*, VII, 694.

[49] Croghan's "Journal of transactions", February 28 to May 12,

Meantime Lieutenant Fraser, Croghan's companion, decided to proceed alone, inasmuch as Gage's instructions to him were to be at the Illinois country early in April.[50] On March 23 he departed, accompanied by two or three whites and a couple of Indians,[51] and reached the Illinois posts in the latter part of April, shortly after the departure of Lieutenant Ross and his party. Here Fraser found many of the Indians in destitution and some inclined for peace.[52] Nevertheless, instigated by the traders and encouraged by secret presents, the savages as a whole would not listen to him. He was thrown into prison, his life threatened, and was finally saved only by the intervention of Pontiac himself.[53] Fraser, feeling himself to be in a dangerous situation, unable to hear from Croghan, whom he was daily ex-

---

1765, MS. in Parkman Coll.; Johnson to Burton, June 6, 1765, Johnson MSS., vol. X, no. 263. Johnson had expected Croghan to meet Pontiac at Fort Pitt, but in this he was disappointed. Johnson to Lords of Trade, May 24, 1765, *N. Y. Col. Docs.*, VII, 716.

[50] Croghan's "Journal of transactions", February 28 to May 12, 1765, MS. in Parkman Coll.

[51] Maissonville, a Frenchman, and one Andrew, an interpreter, were among the whites. Shawnee and Seneca Indians also accompanied the party. Note the error in Kingsford, *Hist. of Can.*, V, 116, and in Wallace, *Illinois and Louisiana under French Rule*, 354, wherein Sinnott is said to have accompanied Fraser. Sinnott had been sent about the same time from the south by Indian agent Stuart. On arriving at the Illinois his goods were plundered and he was finally forced to flee to New Orleans. Johnson to Lords of Trade, September 28, 1765, *N. Y. Col. Docs.*, VII, 765; same to same, November 16, 1765, *ibid.*, 776. Apparently Sinnott must have arrived at Illinois after Fraser's departure for New Orleans, since Croghan implies that Sinnott was still at Fort de Chartres during his own captivity at Vincennes. See Croghan's "Journal and transactions", May 15 to September 25, 1765, as printed in *N. Y. Col. Docs.*, VII, 780.

[52] Parkman, *Conspiracy of Pontiac*, II, 300.

[53] Fraser to Gage, May 15, 1765, Bancroft Coll., Eng. and Am., 1764–1765; Fraser to Crawford, May 20, 1765, *Mich. Pioneer and Hist. Colls.*, X, 216–218; Fraser to Gage, May 26, 1765, Bancroft Coll., Eng. and Am., 1764–1765; Gage to Johnson, August 12, 1765, Parkman Coll., Pontiac-Miscell., 1765–1778.

pecting, and frequently insulted and maltreated by the drunken savages, took advantage of his discretionary orders and descended the Mississippi toward New Orleans.[54] Although the French traders continued to supply the Indians with arms and ammunition, and to buoy up their spirits by stories of aid from the king of France, Pontiac himself was being rapidly disillusioned. He had given Fraser the assurance that if the Indians on the Ohio had made a permanent peace he would do likewise.[55] St. Ange continued to refuse the expected help,[56] so that when the news came of the failure of the mission to New Orleans and of the transfer of Louisiana to Spain, the ruin of the Indian cause was complete.

Having adjusted affairs with the Indians at Fort Pitt, Croghan set out from there on May 15th with two boats, accompanied by several white companions and a party of Shawnee Indians.[57] In compliance with messages from Croghan, representatives from numerous tribes along the route met him at the mouth of the Scioto and delivered up a number of French traders who were compelled to take an oath of allegiance to the English crown, or pass to the west

---

[54] Fraser to Gage, June 16, 1765, Bancroft Coll., Eng. and Am., 1764-1765; Parkman, *Conspiracy of Pontiac*, II, 302; de Villiers du Terrage, *Les dernières Années de la Louisiane française*, 220-221. Reports were current in the East that Fraser and his party were killed by Indians. See Gage to Johnson, June 17, 1765, Myers Coll. (Lenox Library); Johnson to Lords of Trade, July, 1765, Johnson MSS., vol. XI, no. 43. One of the party, Maissonville, remained in Illinois, Thwaites, *Early Western Travels*, I, 146. Fraser accompanied Farmer back to Fort de Chartres later in the year, Fraser to Gage, December 16, 1765, B. T. Papers (Hist. Soc. Pa.), vol. XX.

[55] Fraser to Campbell, May 20, 1765, *Mich. Pioneer and Hist. Colls.*, X, 216-218.

[56] St. Ange to d'Abbadie, *Can. Arch. Report*, 1905, I, 471.

[57] A party of traders headed by one Crawford preceded Croghan. They were, however, cut off before reaching the Illinois country. Shuckburgh to Johnson, July 25, 1765, Johnson MSS., vol. XI, no. 56.

of the Mississippi.[58] The only other incident of importance on this voyage was an attack by the Kickapoos and Mascoutin Indians near the mouth of the Wabash on June 8th,[59] which contributed greatly to the success of the mission. After the attack, in which two whites and several Shawnees were killed, the assailants expressed their profound sorrow, declaring that they thought the party to be a band of Cherokees with whom they were at enmity.[60] Nevertheless, they plundered the stores and carried Croghan and the remainder of the party to Vincennes, a small French town on the Wabash. Croghan was now separated temporarily from his companions and carried to Fort Ouiatanon, about two hundred and ten miles north of Vincennes. The political blunder of the Kickapoos in firing upon the convoy now became apparent;[61] they were censured on all sides for having attacked their friends, the Shawnees, since the latter might thus be turned into deadly enemies.[62] During the first week of July deputations from all the surrounding tribes visited Croghan, assuring him of their desire for peace and of their willingness to escort him to the Illinois country

---

[58] Croghan's journal in Thwaites, *Early Western Travels*, I, 131; Parkman, *Conspiracy of Pontiac*, II, 304. The chief sources of information for this journey are Croghan's journals, most of which have been printed in Thwaites, *Early Western Travels*, I, 126–166. For good secondary accounts see Parkman, *Conspiracy of Pontiac*, II, 304–315; Kingsford, *Hist. of Can.*, V, 116–120; Winsor, *Narr. and Crit. Hist. of Am.*, VI, 704; Winsor, *Miss. Basin*, 456–457.

[59] Croghan's journal, in Thwaites, *Early Western Travels*, I, 131; Gage to Conway, September 23, 1765, Bancroft Coll., Eng. and Am., 1764–1765.

[60] Croghan's journal, in Thwaites, *Early Western Travels*, I, 139.

[61] Croghan to Murray, July 12, 1765, Bancroft Coll., Eng. and Am., 1764–1765; Gage to Conway, September 23, 1765, *ibid.*

[62] Croghan to Murray, July 12, 1765, Bancroft Coll., Eng. and Am., 1764–1765; Croghan's journal, in Thwaites, *Early Western Travels*, I, 146.

OCCUPATION

where Pontiac was residing.[63] July 11th, Maissonville, whom Fraser had a few weeks before left at Fort de Chartres, arrived at Ouiatanon with messages from St. Ange requesting Croghan to come to Fort de Chartres to arrange affairs in that region.[64] A few days later Croghan set out for the Illinois country, attended by a large concourse of savages, but had advanced only a short distance when he met Pontiac himself who was on the road to Ouiatanon. They all returned to the fort where, at a great council, Pontiac signified his willingness to make a lasting peace and promised to offer no further resistance to the approach of the English troops.[65] There was now no need to go to Fort de Chartres; instead Croghan turned his steps toward Detroit, where late in the summer of 1765, another important Indian conference was held in which a general peace was made with all the western Indians.[66]

Immediately after effecting an accommodation with Pontiac at Ouiatanon, Croghan sent an account of the success of his negotiations to Fort Pitt,[67] where Captain Sterling

[63] Croghan to Murray, July 12, 1765, Bancroft Coll., Eng. and Am., 1764–1765; Croghan's journal, in Thwaites, *Early Western Travels*, I, 144–145; Johnson to Lords of Trade, July, 1765, Johnson MSS., vol. XI, no. 43.

[64] Croghan's journal, in Thwaites, *Early Western Travels*, I, 145–146.

[65] Croghan's journal, in Thwaites, *Early Western Travels*, I, 145–146; Jas. Macdonald to Johnson, July 24, 1765, Johnson MSS., vol. XI, no. 50; Thos. Hutchins to Johnson, August 31, 1765, *ibid.* no. 97; Gage to Conway, September 23, 1765, Bancroft Coll., Eng. and Am., 1764–1765.

[66] Croghan's journal, in Thwaites, *Early Western Travels*, I, 154–166; Johnson to Wallace, September 18, 1765, Johnson MSS., vol. XI, no. 56; Gage to Conway, September 23, 1765, Bancroft Coll., Eng. and Am., 1764–1765; Johnson to Lords of Trade, September 28, 1765, *N. Y. Col. Docs.*, VII, 766; Gage to Conway, November 9, 1765, Bancroft Coll., Eng. and Am., 1764–1765. The editor of the *N. Y. Col. Docs.*, VII, 982, says that Croghan went to Fort de Chartres, which is erroneous.

[67] Gage to Conway, September 23, 1765, Bancroft Coll., Eng. and

with a detachment of about one hundred men of the Forty-second or Black Watch Regiment, had been holding himself in readiness for some time, waiting for a favorable report before moving to the relief of Fort de Chartres. Although the Thirty-fourth Regiment under Major Farmer was supposed to be making its way up the Mississippi to relieve the French garrison in Illinois, General Gage would not depend upon its slow and uncertain movements.[68] Upon receipt of the news from Croghan, on the 24th of August Sterling left Fort Pitt[69] and began the long and tedious journey. Owing to the season of the year the navigation of the Ohio was very difficult, forty-seven days being required to complete the journey.[70] The voyage on the whole was without incident until about forty miles below the Wabash River. Here Sterling's force encountered two boats loaded with goods, in charge of a French trader, and accompanied by some thirty Indians and a chief of the Shawnees, who had remained in the French interest.[71] On account of the allegations of a certain Indian that his party had planned to fire on the English before they were aware of the latter's strength, Sterling became apprehensive lest the attitude of the Indians had changed since Croghan's visit. He therefore sent Lieutenant Rumsey, with a small party, by land from Fort Massac to Fort de Chartres, in order to ascertain

---

Am., 1764–1765; Johnson to Wallace, September 18, 1765, Johnson MSS., vol. XI, no. 56; Johnson to Lords of Trade, September 28, 1765, *N. Y. Col. Docs.*, VII, 766.

[68] Gage to Conway, September 23, 1765, Bancroft Coll., Eng. and Am., 1764–1765.

[69] *Ibid.*; Letter of Jas. Eidington, October 17, 1765, P. R. O., Chatham Papers, vol. 97.

[70] Sterling to Gage, October 18, 1765, P. R. O., Am. and W. I., vol. 122.

[71] *Ibid.*

OCCUPATION

the exact situation and to apprise St. Ange of his approach.[72] Rumsey and his guides, however, lost their way and did not reach the villages until after the arrival of the troops.[73] Sterling arrived on the 9th of October,[74] and on the following day St. Ange and the French garrison were formally relieved.[75] With this event the last vestige of French authority east of the Mississippi River passed away.

[72] Sterling to Gage, October 18, 1765, P. R. O., Am. and W. I., vol. 122.

[73] *Ibid.*

[74] *Ibid.*; Sterling alleged that the Indians and French were unaware of his approach until he was within a few miles of the villages, and that the Indians upon learning of the weakness of the English forces, assumed a most insolent and threatening attitude. He further asserted that although Croghan claimed to have made a peace with all the Illinois chiefs, he is assured that not one was present at the peace at Ouiatanon, and that his own sudden appearance at the villages was the real cause of his success. Sir William Johnson, in a letter to Croghan, February 21, 1766, casts doubt upon the representations of Sterling. He says that it is easy to account for his motives, and that he has written General Gage fully upon the subject. The letter referred to has probably been destroyed, at any rate it is not in any of the large collections. Johnson MSS., vol. XII, no. 60.

[75] Sterling to Gage, October 18, 1765, P. R. O., Am. and W. I., vol. 122; Eidington to ——, October 17, 1765, P. R. O., Chatham Papers, vol. 97; Gage to Johnson, December 30, 1765, MS. in Hist. Soc. Pa.; Gage to Barrington, January 8, 1766, P. R. O., Am. and W. I., vol. 122; Gage to Conway, January 16, 1766, *ibid.*; Johnson to Lords of Trade, January 31, 1766, *N. Y. Col. Docs.*, VII, 808; Articles of surrender, inventory of goods, etc., P. R. O., Am. and W. I., vol. 122. These documents are printed in *Transactions* of the Ill. State Hist. Soc. for 1907. For secondary account of the surrender, see Stone, *Life of Sir William Johnson*, II, 252. Captain Sterling relates in his letter to Gage that he had considerable difficulty in persuading St. Ange to surrender his ammunition and artillery stores. St. Ange claimed he had positive orders to surrender only the fort and a few pieces of artillery. Parkman, *Conspiracy of Pontiac*, II, 314, says Sterling arrived at Fort de Chartres in the early part of winter, and Nicollet, in his sketch of St. Louis, states that the fort was reached in mid-summer. From the references already quoted, however, there can be no doubt as to the exact date.

CHAPTER IV.

FIVE YEARS OF DISORDER, 1765–1770.

WHAT actual events took place in the Illinois country after the English occupation has long been problematical. Previous writers, almost without exception, have dismissed with a sentence the first two or three years of the period. Indeed, the whole thirteen years of British administration have generally been crowded into two or three paragraphs. Although the available historical material relating to the field in general has been considerably augmented, gaps yet remain which must be bridged before a complete history of the colony under the British can be written.

The first duty of the British commandant after taking formal possession of Fort de Chartres in October, 1765, was to announce to the inhabitants the contents of Gage's proclamation, defining the status of the individual inhabitants of Illinois. One of the leading features of this document was a clause granting to the French the right of the free exercise of the Roman Catholic religion " in the same manner as in Canada ",[1] which was the fulfilment on the part of the British government of the pledge given in the fourth article of the treaty of Paris, which contained the following clause: " His Brittanic Majesty agrees to grant the liberty of the Catholic religion to the inhabitants of Canada; he will consequently give the most precise and

---

[1] *Am. State Papers, Pub. Lands*, II, 209; Dillon, *Hist. of Indiana*, I, 93-94.

effectual orders, that his new Roman Catholic subjects may profess the worship of their religion, according to the rites of the Roman Catholic Church, as far as the laws of Great Britain permit." This provision appertained to the whole western territory as well as to Canada proper. Prior to the treaty of cession the Illinois and Wabash settlements were subject to the jurisdiction of Louisiana, and approximately the country north of the fortieth parallel had been within the limits of Canada. But in the treaty all the territory lying between the Alleghanies and the Mississippi River was described as a dependency of Canada. The government was thus committed to religious toleration within the whole extent of the ceded territory. This meant, however, that only the religious privileges of the church had been secured, for the clause in the treaty, " as far as the laws of Great Britain permit ",[2] meant that the authority of France would not be tolerated within the British empire.

Other clauses provided that all the inhabitants of Illinois who had been subjects of the King of France, might if they desired, sell their estates and retire with their effects to Louisiana. No restraint would be placed on their emigration, except for debt or on account of criminal processes.[3] This was also a fulfilment of the pledges made in the treaty of Paris.[4] All the inhabitants who desired to retain their estates and become subjects of Great Britain were guaranteed security for their persons and effects, and liberty of trade upon taking the oath of allegiance and fidelity to the crown.[5]

When Captain Sterling proceeded to Kaskaskia to post

---

[2] *Can. Const. Docs.*, *1759–1791*, 75.
[3] *Am. State Papers*, *Pub. Lands*, II, 209.
[4] *Can. Const. Docs.*, *1759–1791*, 75.
[5] *Am. State Papers*, *Pub. Lands*, II, 209.

the proclamation and to administer the oath of allegiance as authorized by the commanding general, he was confronted by an unexpected movement on the part of the inhabitants. A petition was presented, signed by representative Frenchmen of the village, asking for a respite of nine months in order that they might settle their affairs and decide whether they wished to remain under the British government or withdraw from the country.[6] According to treaty stipulations the inhabitants of the ceded territory had been given eighteen months in which to retire, the time to be computed from the date of the exchange of ratifications.[7] The limit thus defined had long since expired, and it was therefore beyond the legal competence of Sterling or of his superior, General Gage, to grant an extension of time. Sterling, indeed, refused at first to grant the request,[8] but when he perceived that unless some concessions were made the village would be immediately depopulated, he extended the time to the first of March, 1766,[9] with the stipulations that

[6] Sterling to Gage, October 18, 1765, P. R. O., Am. and W. I., vol. 122. "Nous avons eu l'honneur de faire, à cette Occasion, nos justes Representations à Mr. Sterling, et lui avons demandé un Delai de neuf Mois, pour attendre que les Commerçans Anglais étant arrivés, et la Confiance rétablie avec le Commerce, ceux d'entre nous qui voudront quitter puissent tirer parti de leurs Biens fonds et Maisons." Petition of the inhabitants to Gage, P. R. O., Am. and W. I., vol. 122.

[7] *Can. Const. Docs.*, *1759–1791*, 86.

[8] Sterling to Gage, October 18, 1765, P. R. O., Am. and W. I., vol. 122.

[9] *Ibid.* "Comme il n'à pas cru pouvoir prendre sur lui d'accorder que jusqu'au Mois de Mars prochain, il nous a promis d'appuyer auprès de Votre Excellence, la justice de notre Cause, ainsi que l'Impossibilité de rien vendre dans le Moment présent. L'entière Confiance que nous avons en Sa Parole, nous borne à remettre seulement sous vos yeux, que personne n'a pu prendre des arrangements antérieurs à l'arrivée des Troupes Anglaises dans ce Païs, que nous étions tous les jours prêts l'abandonner, par les Violences des Sauvages enhardis par notre petit nombre." Petition of inhabitants, *ibid.*

YEARS OF DISORDER

a temporary oath of allegiance be taken,[10] and that all desiring to leave the country should give in their names in advance.[11] To this tentative proposal the French in Kaskaskia agreed on condition that Sterling forward to the commanding general a petition in which they asked for a further extension.[12] An officer was then despatched to the villages of Prairie du Rocher, St. Philippe, and Cahokia, where similar arrangements were made.[13]

The machinery of government in operation under the French had become so unsettled during the French and Indian war that when the English troops entered the country affairs were in a chaotic state. The commandant of the English troops had of course no commission to govern the inhabitants, but he found himself confronted with conditions which made immediate action imperative. Practically the only civil officials Sterling found on the English side of the river were Joseph Lefebvre, who acted as judge, attorney-general, and guardian of the royal warehouse, and Joseph Labuxiere, who was clerk and notary public.[14] These men, however, retired to St. Louis with St. Ange and the French soldiers shortly after the arrival of the English.[15] This brought the whole governmental machinery to a standstill,

---

[10] Sterling to Gage, October 18, 1765, P. R. O., Am. and W. I., vol. 122.

[11] *Ibid.*; Farmer to Gage, December 19, 1765, B. T. Papers (Hist. Soc. Pa.), vol. XX.

[12] P. R. O., Am. and W. I., vol. 122. The petition is signed by such prominent Frenchmen as La Grange, who acted as civil judge under the British, Rocheblave, who became the last British commandant in Illinois, Blouin, a wealthy merchant and later a prominent advocate of a civil government, J. B. Beauvais, Charleville, and others. Gage granted the request without waiting for an answer from London, thus indorsing the action of his subordinate. Gage to Conway, January 16, 1766, *ibid*.

[13] Sterling to Gage, October 18, 1765, *ibid*.

[14] Sterling to Gage, December 15, 1765, *ibid*.

[15] *Ibid*.

and the English commander was forced to act. He determined to appoint a judge and after consulting the principal inhabitants of the villages, selected La Grange, who was intrusted " to decide all disputes according to the Law and Customs of the Country ", with liberty of appeal to the commandant in case the litigants were dissatisfied with his decision.[16] The captains of militia seem to have retained their positions under the British, their duties being practically the same as in the French régime. Each village or parish had its captain who saw to the enforcement of decrees and other civil matters as well as to the organization of the local militia.[17] The office of royal commissary was also continued and James Rumsey, a former officer in the English army, was appointed to this position.[18] But who was to continue the duties of the old French commandant with both his civil and military functions? Obviously the most logical person was the commanding officer of the English troops stationed at the fort, with the difference that the French official held a special commission for the performance of these duties, and the English commandant had no such authorization. A further and more fundamental difference lay in the fact that formerly the French had the right to appeal to the Superior Council at New Orleans,[19] while apparently no such corresponding safeguard was given them by the new arrangement.

Sterling did not long retain command of the post[20] for on

[16] Sterling to Gage, December 15, 1765, *ibid.*

[17] Sterling to Gage, December 15, 1765, P. R. O., Am. and W. I., vol. 122; Cahokia Records (Belleville, Ill.), British period.

[18] Sterling to Gage, October 18, 1765, P. R. O., Am. and W. I., vol. 122.   [19] See above, ch. I, p. 11.

[20] Monette, *Hist. of Miss. Valley* (1846), I, 411, says that "Capt. Stirling died in December; St. Ange returned to Fort Chartres, and not long afterward Major Frazer, from Fort Pitt, arrived as commandant." The statement is wholly incorrect. Sterling later served in the

December 2, he was superseded by Major Robert Farmer,[21] his superior in rank, who arrived from Mobile with a detachment of the Thirty-fourth Regiment, after an eight months' voyage.[22] Their arrival was exceedingly welcome to Sterling and his men, who were becoming greatly embarrassed for lack of provisions, ammunition, and presents for the Indians.[23] When they left Fort Pitt in August, it had not been deemed necessary to take more than sixty pounds of ammunition, inasmuch as Fort de Chartres was expected to yield a sufficient supply, and both Gage and Sterling believed that Croghan, with his cargo of supplies,

Revolutionary war, and lived until 1808. The "Major Frazer" referred to was doubtless the Lieutenant Fraser who preceded George Croghan to the Illinois country early in 1765. He never commanded in Illinois at any time, nor is there the slightest evidence that St. Ange, the last French commandant at Fort de Chartres, ever returned. This tradition of Sterling's death and of the succession of Fraser has been perpetuated by Reynolds, *The Pioneer Hist. of Ill.* (1852), 55; Blanchard, *Hist. of Ill.* (1883), 35; Billon, *Annals of St. Louis* (1886), I, 36; Dunn, *Hist. of Indiana* (1905), 76. Blanchard, in his *Discovery and Conquest of the Northwest* (1879), 179, after repeating the story, states that "both Peck and Brown erroneously give this commandant's name as Farmer. It should be Fraser, the same who first advanced to the place from Fort Pitt." For a sketch of Sterling's career see *N. Y. Col. Docs.*, VII, 786, or *Dict. Nat. Biog.*

[21] For sketch of Farmer's life see *N. Y. Col. Docs.*, VII, 816.

[22] Farmer to Gage, December 16 and 19, 1765, B. T. Papers (Hist. Soc. Pa.), vol. XX; Johnson to Lords of Trade, March 22, 1766, *N. Y. Col. Docs.*, VII, 816; Gage to Conway, March 28, 1766, B. T. Papers (Hist. Soc. Pa.), vol. XX; Campbell to Johnson, March 29, 1766, Parkman Coll., Pontiac-Miscell., 1765–1778; Farmer to Gage, March 11, 1765, P. R. O., Home Office Papers, vol. XX, no. 41. In the letter last cited Farmer blames Governor Johnstone of West Florida for the long delay in starting for the Illinois country and for the scant supply of provisions he carried. It appears that Farmer had planned to start early in the spring of 1765, and he alleges that Johnstone questioned his right to take provisions from the store, and insisted upon all the officers and men taking passes from himself, and in many other ways delayed the departure for several weeks.

[23] Sterling to Gage, October 18, 1765, P. R. O., Am. and W. I., vol. 122; letter of Eidington, October 17, 1765, P. R. O., Chatham Papers, vol. 97.

would be awaiting the arrival of the troops at the fort.[24] Neither expectation, however, was realized. Croghan was back in the colonies prior to Sterling's arrival at the post, and when the fort was transferred it yielded neither ammunition nor any other supplies in sufficient quantity to meet the needs of the troops.[25]

An assembly of three or four thousand Indians had been accustomed to gather at the fort each spring to receive annual gifts from the French. But the English had made no provision for such a contingency, which, coupled with the weakness of the garrison and the recent hostility of the Indians, would probably lead to serious complications. A probable defection of the Indians therefore necessitated a large supply of military stores[26] which it was possible to obtain only from the French merchants in the villages. The latter agreed to furnish the soldiers with ammunition on condition that they would also purchase other provisions,[27] for which, the English allege, they were charged an exorbitant price.[28] Sterling was compelled to acquiesce, for the merchants had sent their goods across the river where he could not get at them.[29]

---

[24] Sterling to Gage, October 18, 1765, P. R. O., Am. and W. I., vol. 122; letter of Eidington, October 17, 1765, P. R. O., Chatham Papers, vol. 97. Nevertheless in the Audit Office records are two entries wherein 293 pounds sterling is allowed Sterling for presents to the Indians in the Illinois country. P. R. O., Declared Accounts, Audit Office, bundle 163, roll 446.

[25] Letter of Eidington, October 17, 1765, P. R. O., Chatham Papers, vol. 97.

[26] *Ibid.*; Sterling to Gage, October 18, 1765. P. R. O., Am. and W. I., vol. 122. [27] *Ibid.* [28] *Ibid.*

[29] Sterling to Gage, October 18, 1765, P. R. O., Am. and W. I., vol. 122. The French afterwards declared that their reluctance to sell provisions to the English was occasioned by the pay they received, which was in bills on London or New York. These they were obliged to sell to the merchants of New Orleans from whom they purchased their goods, at a loss of fifty and sixty per cent. They were also averse to any

The large supply of provisions which the colony had produced in former years seems to have decreased; at any rate it fell far short of the expectations of the English officers. One officer writes at this time that "they have but little here, and are doing us a vast favor when they let us have a Gallon of French Brandy at twenty Shillings Sterling and as the price is not as yet regulated the Eatables is in the same proportions."[30] The wealth of the colony had been considerably impaired since the occupation on account of the exodus of a large number of families who disobeyed the order of Sterling that all who desired to withdraw should give in their names in advance. Taking their cattle, grain, and effects across the ferries at Cahokia and Kaskaskia, they found homes at St. Louis and St. Genevieve on the Spanish side.[31] Probably a larger part of the emigrants left in the hope that in Louisiana they might still enjoy their ancient laws and privileges,[32] and others from fear lest the Indians, who were now assuming a threatening attitude, might destroy their crops and homes.[33]

---

kind of paper currency, owing to its bad management by the French government of Louisiana prior to 1763. Croghan to Gage, January 12, 1767, Johnson MSS., vol. XIV, no. 12. For an account of the paper money issued during the French régime, see Pittman, *Present State of the European Settlements on the Miss.*, ed. Hodder, 47–48.

[30] Letter of Eidington, October 17, 1765, P. R. O., Chatham Papers, vol. 97.

[31] Sterling to Gage, December 15, 1765, P. R. O., Am. and W. I., vol. 122.

[32] Fraser to Gage, December 16, 1765, B. T. Papers (Hist. Soc. Pa.), vol. XX; Farmer to Gage, December 19, 1765, *ibid*. Fraser alleged that St. Ange, who acted as commandant at St. Louis after his retirement from Fort de Chartres, instigated many of the French to cross over, and that other residents of the Spanish side endeavored to frighten the inhabitants of Illinois by representing Major Farmer as a rascal who would deprive them of their former privileges. See also Fraser's "Report of an Exploratory Survey", May 4, 1766, Can. Arch., series B, vol. 26, p. 24.

[33] Memorial of the inhabitants to Gage, October, 1765, P. R. O.,

The serious situation of the garrison continued through the winter and spring of 1765 and 1766.[34] Farmer estimated that all the provisions available (barely enough to last the garrison until July),[35] amounted to no more than 50,000 pounds of flour and 1,250 pounds of cornmeal, a portion of which would have to be given to the Indians since representatives of that department had not yet appeared. These circumstances obliged Major Farmer to send Sterling and his troops to New York by way of the Mississippi River and New Orleans.[36] In response to a series of urgent requests for assistance, Gage employed a force of Indians to transport a cargo to Fort de Chartres,[37] which reached there

Am. and W. I., vol. 122; Fraser to Gage, December 16, 1765, B. T. Papers (Hist. Soc. Pa.), vol. XX. The movement across the river was considerable during the early years of the occupation. In the summer of 1765 there were approximately 2,000 whites on the English side. Fraser to Gage, May 15, 1765, P. R. O., Am. and W. I., vol. 122. Three years later in 1768 the approximate number was 1,000, "State of the Settlements in the Illinois Country", P. R. O., Am. and W. I., vol. 125.

[34] Farmer to Gage, December 16 and 19, 1765, B. T. Papers (Hist. Soc. Pa.), vol. XX; same to Barrington, March 19, 1766, P. R. O., Am. and W. I., vol. 122.

[35] Farmer to Gage, December 16 and 19, 1765, B. T. Papers (Hist. Soc. Pa.), vol. XX. Farmer had just received word that Colonel Reed was on his way from Mobile to the Illinois country with about fifty men and just enough provisions for the journey. Reed was expecting to receive further supplies at Fort de Chartres, *ibid*.

[36] Farmer to Gage, December 16 and 19, 1765, B. T. Papers (Hist. Soc. Pa.), vol. XX; Gage to Johnson, June 2, 1766, Gage's Letters (Harvard College Library). This was contrary to Gage's orders, *ibid*.

[37] Gage to Conway, June 24, 1766, P. R. O., Am. and W. I., vol. 122. "Soon after the Regiment's arrival at Illinois, with the concurrence of the Captains present there was small notes Issued out, I believe to the amount of two months' Subsistance in order to provide the men with small Articles and Necessarys, the Paymaster gave the Merchants and others that brought in these Circulating Notes, bills on the Agent in London for the amount of them. And this is all the subsistance the Regiment received during the time I was with them at Illinois." Farmer to Haldimand, July 29, 1768, B. M., Add. MSS., 21, 677, fol. 103. Among the Kaskaskia Records is a proclamation issued by Farmer to the French assurring them that these notes would be redeemed.

early in the summer of 1766, by which time also representatives of the English merchants at Philadelphia had arrived with large stores of supplies.[38] Henceforth we hear nothing of a shortage of provisions in Illinois, for not only did the English merchants import supplies from the East, but cargoes were brought up the river from New Orleans by the French,[39] and for a time the English government itself transported the necessary provisions from Fort Pitt.[40]

Late in the summer of 1766 Farmer was superseded by Lieutenant-Colonel John Reed who came from Mobile with another detachment of the Thirty-fourth Regiment.[41] By this time a growing discontent among the Indians was manifesting itself, and became one of the most important problems confronting the new commandant of Fort de Chartres. Although the majority of the western tribes had professed their allegiance to Great Britain prior to the occupation of Illinois, there were still large numbers who considered themselves as allies of the king of France. Moreover, agents of the French merchants were roaming at will among the various tribes, spreading stories of English greed and duplicity[42] in order to retain control of the lucrative fur trade.[43] With false promises of succor from France in case the

[38] Gage to Conway, July 15, 1766, P. R. O., Am. and W. I., vol. 122; Baynton, Wharton and Morgan to Gage, August 10, 1766, Johnson MSS., vol. XIII, no. 30.

[39] See below, ch. V.

[40] Gage to Shelburne, August 24, 1767, P. R. O., Am. and W. I., vol. 123.

[41] I have been unable to determine the exact date of the change. The first document appearing with Reed's signature as commandant is dated September 8, Johnson MSS., vol. XIII, no. 104. Major Farmer appears to have expected the arrival of his successor in July or August. Farmer to Barrington, March 19, 1766, P. R. O., Am. and W. I., vol. 122.

[42] Johnson to Shelburne, December 16, 1766, *N. Y. Col. Docs.*, VII, 882–883. [43] *Ibid.*

Indians chose to rebel,[44] the French emissaries were rapidly laying the foundation for another outbreak like that of 1763. It was therefore imperative to adopt some immediate and effective measure for the conciliation of the western tribes.

One of the evidences of English neglect to which these agents referred was the apparent absence of any arrangements for regulating and developing the fur trade and for providing presents and other concrete proofs of the goodwill of the English nation. We find Captain Sterling himself complaining of the "disagreeable situation" he was in, "without an Agent or Interpreter for the Indians, or Merchandize for presents to them which they all expect."[45] The English government had indeed been very slow in formulating and executing any definite program for Indian management. In 1764, shortly after the announcement of the proclamation of 1763, guaranteeing the Indians in the possession of their lands, Lord Hillsborough and the Board of Trade draughted a plan providing for the government of the Indian reservation and the regulation of the trade.[46] Among other things it was provided that in the future Indian affairs would be directed by two superintendents, one in the northern and one in the southern district. In the former, which included the territory north of the Ohio River, an interpreter, a gunsmith, and a commissary, who was to represent the government in all political transactions with the Indians and to look after the enforcement of the trade regulations defined in the plan, were to reside at each Indian post,

---

[44] Johnson to Lords of Trade, March 22, 1766, *ibid.*, 817; Johnson to Shelburne, December 16, 1766, *ibid.*, 882–883; Johnson to Lords of Trade, January 15, 1767, Dartmouth Papers, *Fourteenth Report, Royal Hist. MSS. Comm.*, Appendix X.

[45] Sterling to Gage, October 18, 1765, P. R. O., Am. and W. I., vol. 122.

[46] *Can. Arch. Report*, 1904, 242–246.

under the immediate direction of the general superintendent and his deputies. The military officials were expected to give advice and assistance but they could take no independent action except in cases of emergency or where the negotiations were purely military.

This plan of the Board of Trade, however, was proposed at an unfortunate time. The Stamp Act, which had been recently passed with the view of raising money for imperial purposes, met with such vigorous opposition on the part of the colonies, that Parliament hesitated to take formal action on a measure entailing considerable additional expense. Although no definite Parliamentary action was ever taken on the plan, the Board of Trade directed the Indian superintendents to put into execution such parts of it as they found practicable.[47] For some reason, however, Sir William Johnson, who had directed Indian affairs in America since 1756 and who had been appointed superintendent for the northern department, delayed for more than a year the appointment of the Indian officers indicated in the plan.[48] When finally on April 17, 1766, he appointed Edward Cole to be commissary of Indian affairs in the Illinois country,[49]

[47] "Representation of the Lords of Trade on Indian Affairs, March 17, 1768", *N. Y. Col. Docs.*, VIII, 24. See also Johnson to Lords of Trade, March 22, 1766, Johnson MSS., vol. XII, no. 101, and *N. Y. Col. Docs.*, VII, 817. For further notice of the plan see below, ch. V.

[48] In this Johnson apparently acted on the advice of Gage. See Gage to Johnson, February 2, 1765, Parkman Coll., Pontiac–Miscell., 1765–1778. It is probable that they wanted to make sure that such appointments could be supported.

[49] Cole to Johnson, June 23, 1766, Johnson MSS., vol. XII, no. 218. See also the deed for a house purchased at Fort de Chartres by the government through Cole as commissary, which was sworn to by commandant Reed. Johnson MSS., XIII, no. 104. Almost all previous writers on western history have given currency to the idea that Edward Cole was the military commandant at Fort de Chartres from 1766 to 1768 and that he was followed by Colonel Reed who governed but a

it was found necessary to send an additional representative of the Indian department to Fort de Chartres to perfect, if possible, a general pacification of the western Indians.

Early in February General Gage and Sir William Johnson arranged with George Croghan to undertake a second mission in the West.[50] Croghan was probably the best-fitted man in the colonies for such an undertaking. He had been one of the most successful traders in the West and knew personally the chiefs of most of the western tribes. His familiarity with the languages and customs of the various nations gave him a prestige which perhaps few English officials, except Sir William Johnson, could command. Equipped with Indian presents to the value of over three thousand pounds[51] and with instructions as to their distribution and the general purpose of the mission,[52] Croghan set out

---

few months. This is an error, which has been repeated by the following writers: Moses, *Ill., Hist. and Statis.*, I, 137; Moses, "Court of Enquiry at Ft. Chartres", in *Chicago Hist. Soc. Colls.*, IV, 292; Mason, *Chapters from Ill. Hist.*, 278; Parrish, *Historic Ill.*, 184; Wallace, *Ill. and La. under French Rule*, 395; Dunn, *Hist. of Indiana*, 76.

[50] Croghan to Johnson, February 14, 1766, Johnson MSS., vol. XII, no. 42; Johnson to Croghan, February 21, 1766, *ibid.*, no. 60.

[51] Gage to Johnson, April 7, 1766, Gage's Letters.

[52] Instructions to George Croghan, April 16, 1766, Parkman Coll., Pontiac-Miscell., 1765–1778. The instructions to Croghan are signed by General Gage. While, generally speaking, Sir William Johnson was the chief authority in Indian affairs, there seems to have been no very clear line of division between the Indian and military departments. While on the one hand all the correspondence with the subordinate Indian officials and with the home government was carried on by Sir William Johnson, as an examination of the *New York Colonial Documents* and the Johnson MSS. will indicate, on the other hand all the receipts for Indian expenditures had to pass through Gage's hands and receive his approval before becoming valid. On one occasion he refused to sign the bills drawn by Commissary Cole. See Cole to Croghan, December 19, 1767, Johnson MSS., vol. XV, no. 183; Gage to Hillsborough, March 12, 1768, P. R. O., Am. and W. I., vol. 124. For further evidence of this confusion see Johnson to Shelburne, April 1, 1767, *N. Y. Col. Docs.*, VII, 914.

YEARS OF DISORDER

for Fort de Chartres late in April, 1766,[53] arriving there August 20th.[54] The newly appointed commissary, Edward Cole, arrived from Detroit about the same time.[55]

Croghan found several nations of Indians collected at Kaskaskia, and after consulting with Commandant Reed, issued a call for a general meeting to be held on August 25th. The chiefs and principal warriors of eight nations, comprising some twenty-two tribes, obeyed the summons. Deputies from the Six Nations and the Delaware and Shawnee tribes had accompanied Croghan from Fort Pitt,[56] so that the congress became one of considerable importance. Although the presence of so many tribes made the negotiations difficult to carry on, Croghan was able in a few days to finish the business to the satisfaction of nearly every one present. A general peace and alliance was declared between the English and all the western and northern Indians[57] except those tribes with whom the French had sufficient influence to keep them from the conference.[58]

---

[53] Gage to Johnson, April 13, 1766, Gage's Letters. He probably left New York at that time. He left Fort Pitt June 18, accompanied by the merchant, George Morgan, and by Lieutenant Hutchins and Captain Gordon of the army, Morgan to his wife, June 20, 1766, MS. letter in possession of Mrs. E. S. Thacher, Nordhoff, Cal.

[54] Croghan to Johnson, September 10, 1766, Johnson MSS., vol. XIII, no. 80.

[55] Cole to Johnson, June 23, 1766, *ibid.*, vol. XII, no. 218.

[56] Croghan to Johnson, September 10, 1766, *ibid.*, vol. XIII, no. 80; Morgan to his wife, June 29, 1766, MS. letter in possession of Maria P. Woodbridge, Marietta, Ohio. Morgan's letters contain a good description of a portion of this journey down the Ohio.

[57] Croghan to Johnson, September 10, 1766, Johnson MSS., vol. XIII, no. 80; Gage to Shelburne, December 23, 1766, B. T. Papers (Hist. Soc. Pa.), vol. XXVII; Johnson to Shelburne, January 15, 1767, *N. Y. Col. Docs.*, VII, 892; Johnson to Lords of Trade, *Fifth Report, Royal Hist. MSS. Comm.*, p. 319; Croghan to Gage, January 16, 1767, *ibid.*

[58] Croghan to Johnson, September 10, 1766, Johnson MSS., vol. XIII, no. 80.

Nevertheless the chiefs who had attended the congress soon persuaded these tribes to enter the peace and on September 5th they came to Fort de Chartres and publicly announced their friendship for the English.[59]

Reed remained in command of Fort de Chartres until 1766. According to the meagre information we have for these years the relation between commandant and people, both French and English, was very unhappy. If we may trust our informants,[60] Reed's rule was characterized by numerous petty tyrannies. By imposing a high fee for administering the oath of allegiance[61] and for the issuance of marriage licenses,[62] and by inflicting exorbitant fines and even imprisonment for trivial offences,[63] the commandant won the ill-will of nearly every resident in the country.[64] This constant interference with the inhabitants led to a movement early in 1768 for the establishment of a civil

---

[59] *Ibid.*

[60] The chief source of information is a letter book kept by George Morgan, a prominent merchant in Illinois during the British occupation. A copy of this letter book is in the Illinois State Historical Library. It is my opinion, however, that some of his statements should be discounted somewhat. In July, 1768, Morgan established a store at Vincennes on the Wabash River, and in a letter of instructions to his agent, Alexander Williamson, occurs the following passage: "If you write to any of your friends do not let them know but that the trade is excessive Bad at the Post, lest some of the Traders there shou'd be induced to interfere with you . . ." Morgan doubtless followed this method himself. It is possible that his many statements regarding the tyranny of the military government were written for the purpose of deterring other merchants from entering the field. There was some ground, however, for his strictures, since there are some references to the commandant's conduct in the correspondence of the parish priest.

[61] Morgan to Baynton and Wharton, December 10, 1767, Morgan's MS. letter book.

[62] Father Meurin to Bishop Briand, June 11, 1768, *Jesuit Relations*, ed. Thwaites, LXXI, 43. The charge was six piasters.

[63] Morgan to Baynton and Wharton, December 10, 1767, Morgan's MS. letter book. Morgan himself was thrown into prison for a time.

[64] *Ibia.*

government,[65] but the matter was not pushed at the time, for in February Colonel Reed was recalled[66] and the post was left temporarily in charge of Captain Forbes, a subordinate officer.

But the friction between the military commandant and the French inhabitants, although somewhat minimized, did not entirely disappear during the short rule of Captain Forbes. This was illustrated by their attitude on the occasion of another threatened outbreak of the Indians in the spring and summer of 1768. Although the peace of 1766 had been kept in good faith by the few tribes of Illinois Indians who resided in the immediate vicinity of the post,[67] those nations dwelling in the surrounding country began to grow restless in the course of the following year. The French and Spanish traders from Louisiana continued to circulate war belts and messages among the Indians[68] which effectively alienated them from their new masters. Moreover, the character and method of the British traders, whose lawlessness was frequently condemned by contemporary English observers,[69] likewise contributed to turn the savages to their old friends and allies. Not only were the Indians along the Wabash and Mississippi rivers affected, but the

[65] Morgan to Baynton and Wharton, February, 1768. "They have appointed Mr. Rumsey and myself to forward this Petition to Governor Franklin to inclose and recommend it to the Board of Trade." *Ibid.*

[66] Gage to Hillsborough, June 18, 1768, P. R. O., Am. and W. I., vol. 124.

[67] Cole to Johnson, July 3, 1767, Johnson MSS., vol. XV, no. 2; Morgan's MS. letter book, *passim.*

[68] Johnson to Gage, January 15, 1767, Johnson MSS., vol. XIV, no. 15; Johnson to Shelburne, October, 1767, *N. Y. Col. Docs.*, VII, 986; Johnson to Lords of Trade, October 20, 1767, *ibid.*, 987.

[69] See for example, Johnson to Lords of Trade, October 20, 1767, *N. Y. Col. Docs.*, VII, 987, and Gage to Johnson, January 25, 1767, Johnson MSS., vol. XIV, no. 28.

disaffection extended to the powerful Delaware and Shawnee tribes of the upper Ohio River. [70]

It was in preparing to meet a probable attack upon the fort that Commandant Forbes, in April, 1768, ordered all the Englishmen, to the number of fifty or sixty, to organize themselves into a militia, [71] and likewise requested the French to form themselves into companies. [72] To this demand the French at first refused to accede. They took the ground that from the nature of the oath of allegiance they had taken, they were not obliged to take up arms which would only give offence to the Indians with whom they had no quarrel. [73] They were, therefore, determined to remain neutral, [74] and when Forbes insisted upon obedience they threatened to go over to the Spanish side of the river. But as soon as the French found that the commandant was not to be influenced by threats they consented to be enrolled. [75]

[70] Morgan to Baynton and Wharton, April 5, 1768, Morgan's MS. letter book; Gage to Shelburne, March 12, 1768, Dartmouth Papers, *Fourteenth Report, Royal Hist. MSS. Comm.*, Appendix X, p. 61.

[71] Morgan to Baynton and Wharton, April 5, 1768, Morgan's MS. letter book.

[72] Gage to Hillsborough, August 17, 1768, P. R. O., Am. and W. I., vol. 124; same to same, January 6, 1769, Dartmouth Papers, *Fourteenth Report, Royal Hist. MSS. Comm.*, Appendix X, p. 66; Gage to Hillsborough, March 5, 1769, P. R. O., Am. and W. I., vol. 125.

[73] Gage to Hillsborough, August 17, 1768, P. R. O., Am. and W. I., vol. 124. [74] *Ibid*.

[75] *Ibid*. The following passage from a letter of Lord Hillsborough to Gage throws some light on the former's attitude towards the French inhabitants: "I must presume that Capt. Forbes had both good reason and proper authority, tho' they do not appear from your Letter, for forming the Inhabitants of the Illinois into a regular militia; but I must wait for further information before I can with precision form any judgement or opinion upon a measure, which I confess seems in the general view of it, considering the temper and disposition of the people with regard to whom it was to take place, at least of doubtful policy, if not of dangerous tendency." October 12, 1768, P. R. O., Am. and W. I., vol. 124. See answer of Gage to Hillsborough, March 5, 1769, P. R. O., Am. and W. I., vol. 125. Two years later, during a war between

YEARS OF DISORDER 63

Forbes's preparations were well timed, for on May 5, 1768, word reached him that war parties from the Chippewa, Ottawa, Pottawottomi, and Kickapoo tribes were preparing for an attack upon the fort.[76] The defence was immediately organized, and night and day watches were set. A close guard was kept during the following week, but the projected attack was never made.[77] A day or two before news of the contemplated attack came, a band of Pottawottomies had captured a soldier and his wife near Chartres village. Shortly afterward a party of ten Indians belonging to the same nation entered the village and requested from Commissary Cole shelter and provisions for the night. The party was given lodging in the Indian house, but Captain Forbes resolved to retain them as prisoners and therefore summoned them to the fort for a conference. The Indians, however, frightened at the sight of the soldiers under arms, jumped from the windows and fled.[78] It is probable that the knowledge thus gained of the defensive preparations at the fort induced the Indians to give up the assault. Although for a time numerous bands of belligerent savages were frequently seen in the neighborhood of the villages,[79] no further attempt was made against the English garrison.[80]

---

the Missouri and Illinois Indians, the French again objected to being called into service. "Lieut. Col. Wilkins complains greatly of the behavior of the French, who could not be persuaded to speak to the Invaders, tho' the domestic Indians declared any Frenchman might go in safety. He says in those disagreeable circumstances, he summoned the militia, encouraged and threatened, but met with little better than an absolute refusal, and he was shortly after informed, and for a certainty that one of them declared the Inhabitants would rebel." Gage to Hillsborough, January 6, 1770, P. R. O., Am. and W. I., vol. 126.

[76] Jenning's Journal (MS. in Hist. Soc. Pa. Library), May 5, 1768.

[77] *Ibid.*, May 10, 1768.

[78] Jenning's Journal, May 6, 1768.

[79] *Ibid., passim.*

[80] Acts of hostility were frequent during the summer of 1768, espe-

The unhappy relation existing between commandant and people during the administrations of Reed and Forbes continued under Willkins, who took command September 5 1768.[81] There were, moreover, numerous disagreements between the English residents and the French, and among the French themselves there was almost continual strife.[82] Naturally a litigious people, the French were thrown into disorder when the judicial system to which they had been accustomed since the foundation of the colony was transferred to the Spanish side. It is true that the first English commandant had ordered the establishment of a civil court, with the right of appeal to the commandant, but we have no record of any activity on the part of such a court.

---

cially along the Ohio River. Early in July a hunting party of ten or twelve men sent from Fort de Chartres by Baynton, Wharton and Morgan was attacked near the mouth of the Wabash River and all but one were killed. A little later a party of whites from Virginia was fired upon in the same region and only one man escaped. Similar outrages occurred in other localities about the same time. Morgan to Baynton and Wharton, July 20, 1768, Morgan's MS. letter book; Forbes to Gage, July 28, 1768, Johnson MSS., vol. XVI, no. 117; Wilkins to Gage, August 15, 1768, *ibid.*, no. 140; Gage to Johnson, October 10, 1768, Gage's Letters; Gage to Hillsborough, October 14, 1768, P. R. O., Am. and W. I., vol. 124; same to same, November 8, 1768, *ibid.* These isolated instances appear insignificant, but judging from the official correspondence of the time, their importance can scarcely be overestimated by the student of the American Revolution. There was a constant apprehension on the part of the officials that another Indian rebellion would break out. It was well known that the French and Spanish were doing all in their power to bring about such an event. Note the apprehension at this time of Gage, Johnson, and Hillsborough, in Gage to Shelburne, March 12, 1768, Dartmouth Papers, *Fourteenth Report, Royal Hist. MSS. Comm.*, Appendix X, p. 61; Hillsborough to Gage, October 12, 1768, P. R. O., Am. and W. I., vol. 124; Johnson to Hillsborough, October 23, 1768, *N. Y. Col. Docs.*, VIII, 105-106.

[81] Moses, "Court of Enquiry", in *Chicago Hist. Soc. Colls.*, IV, 292. He brought several companies of the Eighteenth or Royal Regiment of Ireland from Philadelphia, leaving there in June. Gage to Hillsborough, June 18, 1768, P. R. O., Am. and W. I., vol. 124.

[82] Ensign Butricke to Geo. Barnsley, February 12, 1769, *Hist. Magazine*, VIII, 262: Moses, "Court of Enquiry", in *Chicago Hist. Soc. Colls.*, IV, 292-293.

YEARS OF DISORDER 65

There is some evidence, however, that in the various villages there were certain local courts [83] and resort was frequently had to courts of arbitration. [84] The fact nevertheless remains that there was no settled judicial power in Illinois, with the result that the peace of the villages was disturbed by the constant bickerings of the inhabitants, both French and English. [85]

In an effort to correct this evil Commandant Wilkins issued a proclamation on November 12, 1768, declaring his resolution to establish a court of judicature for the settlement of all civil disputes. [86] Commissions of the peace were granted to six of the more prominent inhabitants, both French and English, who were authorized " to form a Civil Court of Judicatory, with powers expressed in their Commissions to Hear and Try in a Summary way all Causes of Debt and Property that should be brought before them and

---

[83] " Antoine Cecirre, Captain, judge and commandant accompanied by the notary and sergeant, etc." Cahokia Records, British Period. In another document the same person is called "juge et Commandant du village des Cahokias", *ibid*. He is also called "Captain of militia and commandant", *ibid*. James Rumsey signed himself in 1768 as " Judge Advocate of the Province of Illinois ". His duties, however, were confined to administering the oath of allegiance and examining land titles. He was purely an assistant to Commandant Wilkins. See *Ill. Hist. Colls.*, I, 315–316.

[84] For example, in Cahokia there was a case of arbitration in regard to the estate of a deceased Jacques Compte. Cahokia Records, British Period.

[85] See account of an address of the French to Commandant Wilkins in letter of George Morgan to Baynton and Wharton, October 29, 1768, Division of Pub. Records, Pa. State Library.

[86] MS. Court Record (Chester, Ill.), p. 23; Ensign Butricke to Barnsley, February 12, 1769, *Hist. Magazine*, VIII, 262; Edmund Flagg, *The Far West*, reprinted in Thwaites, *Early Western Travels*, XXVII. Flagg's narrative was written in 1836. In a note (p. 79) he quotes several paragraphs from the court record, including merely the account of the preliminary proceedings of the court. He says, by way of explanation, that " it purports to be transcribed from the state records, and first appeared in a western newspaper."

66   THE ILLINOIS COUNTRY, 1763-1774

to give their Judgement thereon according to the Laws of England to the Best of their Judgement and understanding."[87] We may fairly ask at this point, by what authority the military commandant could authorize a court to give "Judgement according to the laws of England". Attention has been called in another chapter to the fact that until the laws of Great Britain were definitely extended to this territory the French could be judged only by their own laws.[88] It has likewise been pointed out that no act of king or Parliament had ever extended English law to the West. It was therefore beyond the legal competence of Commandant Wilkins or of the commander-in-chief of the army to make such alteration.

Turning to another point of view, did Wilkins create the court on his own responsibility? Historians have generally taken the view that Wilkins's action was in pursuance of explicit orders from the commander-in-chief, General Gage.[89] There is, indeed, some justification for this view, for Wilkins declared in 1770 that he had created the court "by virtue of the power to me given by his Excellencey Major General Thomas Gage, commander-in-chief of his

---

[87] MS. Court Record, p. 23. See also Butricke to Barnsley, February 12, 1769, *Hist. Magazine*, VIII, 262; Flagg, *The Far West*, in Thwaites, *Early Western Travels*, XXVII, 79. There is a slight misconception as to the number of judges appointed. Moses, *Ill., Hist. and Stat.*, I, 137, and the same author, "Court of Enquiry", in *Chicago Hist. Soc. Colls.*, IV, 292; Wallace, *Ill. and La. under French Rule*, 396, and a number of others, including Bancroft, state that there were seven judges appointed. Ensign Butricke, who wrote concerning the court, asserted that there were "several" judges, but according to the record itself there were but six commissions issued and only six judges ever appear.

[88] See above, ch. II.

[89] Moses, *Ill., Hist. and Stat.*, I, 137; Moses, "Court of Enquiry", in *Chicago Hist. Soc. Colls.*, IV, 292; Winsor, *Westward Movement*, 40; Wallace, *Ill. and La. under French Rule*, 396; Davidson and Stuvé, *Complete Hist. of Ill.*, 165; Bancroft, *Hist. of U. S.* (ed. 1854), VI, 224-225.

YEARS OF DISORDER

Majesty's forces in North America."[90] Considered alone, this sounds convincing. But Gage evidently had not the slightest knowledge of the existence of the court. In all of that officer's official correspondence with the home government, with subordinate officials in Illinois, and with Sir William Johnson, there is not the least mention of a court of any character. In fact Gage declared in 1771, when writing of the conditions which had prevailed in Illinois since 1765 : " I perceive there has been wanting judicial power to try and determine. There has been no way to bring Controversys and Disputes properly to a determination or delinquents to punishment."[91] Lord Hillsborough, secretary for the colonies, whose knowledge of occurrences in Illinois was remarkable, and whose comments on conditions are always noteworthy, likewise gives no intimation that he was aware of the existence of the court. Moreover, Wilkins himself is silent on the subject when he writes to Gage, Secretary-at-War Barrington, and others.[92] It is therefore probable that Wilkins received no order from Gage to establish a court, and that he merely used, as a basis for his action, the general instructions of the commander-in-chief to keep order in the country.

The court consisted of six judges throughout its history

---

[90] MS. Court Record, p. 23. He made a similar statement about the same time: " D'autant que par les Pouvois que . . etoient donnés par Son Excellence l'Hon. Thomas Gage . . " Proclamation of Wilkins concerning the justices of the court, March 12, 1770, Kaskaskia Records, British Period.

[91] Gage to Hillsborough, August 6, 1771, P. R. O., Am. and W. I., vol. 128.

[92] A few of the longer and more detailed letters relating especially to Illinois from 1768 to 1770 have been selected for citation: Gage to Hillsborough, February 4, 1769, P. R. O., Am. and W. I., vol. 125; same to same, August 12, 1769, *ibid.*; same to same, September 9, 1769, *ibid.*; Wilkins to Barrington, December 5, 1769, *ibid.*; Hillsborough to Gage, December 9, 1769, *ibid.*; same to same, July 31, 1770, *ibid.*, vol. 126; Gage to Hillsborough, November 10, 1770, *ibid.*

from December, 1768 to June, 1770. In the beginning it was composed of four Englishmen, George Morgan, James Rumsey,[93] James Campbell, and James McMillan, and two Frenchmen, Jean Baptiste Barbau and Pierre Girardot.[94] The commandant designated Morgan as the first president of the court.[95] Morgan was an English trader who played an important role in the affairs of the Illinois country from 1766 to 1771. He was born in Philadelphia in 1741 and was educated in Princeton College. Through the influence of his father-in-law, John Baynton, he was admitted to the firm of Baynton and Wharton of Philadelphia. This company had traded extensively among the Indians on the Pennsylvania border prior to 1765, and during the Indian wars had lost heavily. In an attempt to retrieve their fortunes a branch house was established in the Illinois country in 1766, and Morgan became the firm's personal representative in the West. He first appeared in Illinois in the early part of 1766, remaining there the greater part of the next five years.[96] According to a contemporaneous letter,[97] the appointment of Morgan was considered an offence by the French inhabitants. "The French all hate the Morganians", the writer declares, and Morgan himself is "universally hated by them." Whether Morgan was so "universally hated" does not appear from any other document.

---

[93] Rumsey was private secretary to Wilkins.

[94] MS. Court Record, p. 1; Flagg, *The Far West*, in Thwaites, *Early Western Travels*, XXVII, 79.

[95] Butricke to Barnsley, February 12, 1769, *Hist. Magazine*, VIII, 262; MS. Court Record, p. 1.

[96] After his experience in the Illinois country Morgan served the Revolutionary cause in the capacity of Indian agent. He died in 1810. For further details of Morgan's life see "Biography of Col. George Morgan", by Julia Morgan Harding, in the Washington (Pa.) *Observer*, May 21, 1904.

[97] Butricke to Barnsley, February 12, 1769, *Hist. Magazine*, VIII, 262.

YEARS OF DISORDER 69

It is probable, however, that the appointment was made in order to favor the trading company which Morgan represented in Illinois, for Wilkins and Morgan were at first intimate friends, and we find the former making large grants of land to the English merchants, receiving in return a portion as compensation.[98]

The court retained its original composition until November, 1769, when the name of David Williams appeared as judge.[99] It is impossible to ascertain which judge he superseded, for there were few sittings in which the entire court was present. From this time changes were made rapidly. In February, 1770, Louis Viviat, a prominent Frenchman of Kaskaskia, became a judge,[100] and in May, Charleville and Louviere were given commissions.[101] The court then consisted of Morgan, who still acted as president, Barbau, Girardot, Viviat, Charleville, and Louviere, all the Englishmen except Morgan having been displaced by Frenchmen. This complete transformation was of course the work of Wilkins himself, for the court was in every sense his own creation. March 4, 1770, we find him extending its jurisdiction to criminal as well as civil cases: "And whereas several Disputes and Controversys have from time to time arisen Between the Inhabitants of the Country aforesaid as well as Assaults and Batteries Committed which by the Powers by me Heretofore given to Said Court may not appear to be cognizable by them, . . . And as the present

---

[98] Statement of George Morgan and Jas. Rumsey that Wilkins had granted lands to Joseph Galloway, Jas. Rumsey, John Baynton and Company, and Baynton, Wharton and Morgan on April 12, 1769, and on April 15, certain land to George Morgan and Samuel Wharton. Wilkins was to receive one-seventh part. The statement is sworn to at Fort de Chartres, June 25, 1769. Record of Deeds, p. 131, Kaskaskia Records, British Period.

[99] MS. Court Record, p. 21.

[100] *Ibid.*, p. 22.   [101] *Ibid.*, p. 28.

Establishment of the Country does not admit of Tryals by Juries on account of its Small number of Inhabitants as Well as their Want of Knowledge of the Laws and Customs of England. I do hereby therefore Further Authorize and Impower the Said Court to Hear, Try and Determine in a Summary Way all Disputes, Controversys and Debates Brought before them whether the Same be Assaults, etc., upon the Person or Trespass upon the Property of the Inhabitants of the Country aforesaid, and to impose and bring such Fines and Inflict such Corporate Punishment or commit Offenders to Jayle at the discretion of the said Court . . . "[102] A little later we find him complaining that the people are not sufficiently interested to consent to serve as justices.[103]

In the early period of the history of the court cases between French and English were generally decided in favor of the latter; but with the change in its composition this partiality in favor of Englishmen vanished,[104] and with it

[102] MS. Court Record, p. 23. It will be observed that trial by jury was not introduced into Illinois at this time. The contrary has, however, been generally stated by historians of the period. Justin Winsor writes that the "severest wrench to the feelings of the French . . . came with the establishment, under orders from Gage, of a court and jury according to English usage . . . ", *Westward Movement*, 40. The same statement is made by Wallace, *Ill. and La. under French Rule*, 396, Davidson and Stuvé, *Complete Hist. of Ill.*, 165, and Moses, *Ill., Hist. and Stat.*, I, 140. In a later work Moses takes the other and more correct view, although adducing no proof. See "Court of Enquiry", in *Chicago Hist. Soc. Colls.*, IV, 292. In addition to the testimony of Wilkins and the court record itself, we have the statement of Butricke, an eye-witness, that the court was "to determine on all causes of debt, without a Jury", letter to Barnsley, February 17, 1769, *Hist. Magazine*, VIII, 262.

[103] Proclamation by Wilkins, March 4, 1770, concerning the justices of the peace at Fort de Chartres, Kaskaskia Records, British Period.

[104] Out of twenty-one cases heard between December 6, 1768, and June 6, 1770, of which there is record (pp. 5-10 of the record being gone), eleven were between English and French, the former winning nine decisions. Of the other two, one decision was given in favor of

disappeared in a measure evidences of national antagonism. In place of the latter came the formation of two new parties, one headed by Wilkins and his secretary, Rumsey, and the other by Morgan, which was composed of the greater portion of the discontented French. The genesis of these factions is found in the definite break between court and commandant on June 6, 1770, when the judges acted contrary to the wishes and orders of the commandant. The court in one instance ordered the sale for debt of a house belonging to Captain Philip Pittman,[105] which was contrary to the explicit order of Wilkins.[106] Another cause of friction was the decision of the judges to hold the future sessions of the court at Kaskaskia.[107] Until March, 1770, the sessions had been held alternately at Kaskaskia and Chartres village, but after that date they were held at Chartres village only.[108] The change to Kaskaskia was very inconvenient to the commandant, since his home was at Fort de Chartres.

On the same day, June 6, Joseph L'Esperance, an attorney-at-law, complained to the court of his inability to obtain writs of attachment for which he had applied to the commandant and his secretary.[109] The complainant further alleged that one of the writs prayed for was at the instance of his client, George Morgan, president of the court, and

---

one Daniel Blouïn, a son-in-law of Charleville, and a person always favored by the English. Four cases were between Englishmen, and six involved Frenchmen alone, in which Blouïn was either defendant or plaintiff and won every decision. MS. Court Record, *passim.*

[105] The same Pittman who wrote *Present State of the European Settlements on the Miss.*

[106] MS. Court Record, pp. 38ff.   [107] *Ibid.*, pp. 37ff.

[108] Chartres village, December 6, 1768; Kaskaskia, January 2, 1769; Chartres village, April 4, 1769; Kaskaskia, May 3, 1769; Chartres village, November, 1769; Kaskaskia, December 5, 1769; Chartres village, February 6, March 6, April 3, June 5, 1770; Kaskaskia, June 6, 1770.

[109] MS. Court Record, p. 45.

Morgan then added his testimony to the effect that on several occasions since the 14th of May he had applied in vain to Wilkins for a similar writ.[110] In consequence of these relations the court drew up and unanimously adopted a memorial to the commandant, setting forth that his action was very prejudicial and unfair to creditors and praying that he might not interfere with the course of justice.[111] The court then adjourned to meet the following month,[112] but there is no record of any further meetings after June 6. Presumably Wilkins abolished the institution which no longer supported him. The importance of the details connected with the termination of the court will be seen in a later chapter in connection with the movement inaugurated by the French for the establishment of a civil government in Illinois.

Side by side with the court of judicature there grew up another method of settling civil disputes, by what were termed courts of inquiry, composed of military officers. A court of inquiry was called January 13, 1769, to settle certain disputes between the merchant, George Morgan, and a number of complaining Frenchmen. It continued until January 20, and the result was satisfactory to neither party.[113] Another court was convened September 24, 1770 to adjust difficulties between Baynton, Wharton and Morgan and Richard Bacon.[114] The details of the hearing afford further evidence of the existence of factional strife between the Morgan and Wilkins parties.

---

[110] MS. Court Record, p. 45.   [111] *Ibid.*   [112] *Ibid.*, p. 46.

[113] *Hist. Magazine*, VIII, 270.

[114] The complete record of the proceedings has been printed by Moses, in *Chicago Hist. Soc. Colls.*, IV, 294–356. Moses states that he obtained a manuscript copy from the Wisconsin Historical Society Library, but Dr. Thwaites, the secretary, finds no such papers there now. There is, however, a manuscript copy in somewhat different form, in the Division of Public Records of the Pennsylvania State Library.

Wilkins had his share of trouble with the Indian problem. There were constant rumors of war [115] and of attacks upon the Illinois post,[116] and murders of whites became frequent in the vicinity of Fort de Chartres. [117] It was therefore necessary to be on guard continuously against a possible surprise. Moreover, after the year 1768, the commandant was forced to look after the local management of Indian affairs; for in

[115] Gage to Hillsborough, January 5, 1769, Dartmouth Papers, *Fourteenth Report, Royal Hist. MSS. Com.*, Appendix X; same to same, February 3, 1767, *ibid.*; same to same, February 4, 1769, P. R. O., Am. and W. I., vol. 125; Johnson to Hillsborough, June 26, 1769, *N. Y. Col. Docs.*, VIII, 173; same to same, August 26, 1769, *ibid.*, 184-185; Gage to Hillsborough, August 12, 1769, P. R. O., Am. and W. I., vol. 125; same to same, September 9, 1769, *ibid.* A congress of all the western and southern Indians was held on the Scioto River in the summer of 1768, where the Delaware and Shawnee Indians attempted to form a general union against the English. See Gage to Hillsborough, September 9, 1769, P. R. O., Am. and W. I., vol. 125; Gage to Haldimand, August 28, 1770, B. M., Add. MSS., 21, 664, fol. 178, and Hillsborough to Johnson, November 15, 1770, *N. Y. Col. Docs.*, VIII, 254.

[116] Butricke to Barnsley, June 25, 1769, *Hist. Magazine*, VIII, 270ff.; Gage to Hillsborough, October 7, 1769, P. R. O., Am. and W. I., vol. 125; Johnson to Gage, April 6, 1770, Johnson MSS., vol. XVIII, no. 266; Gage to Johnson, April 16, 1770, Gage's Letters; Hillsborough to Gage, June 12, 1770, P. R. O., Am. and W. I., vol. 126; Gage to Hillsborough, December 4, 1771, P. R. O., Am. and W. I., vol. 128. In addition to the Indian troubles, the English residents and soldiers had to contend with a most distressing sickness during the years 1768-1770. At one time, late in 1768, nearly all the soldiers were ill with fevers peculiar to that locality. See Morgan's MS. letter book, *passim*; Morgan to Baynton and Wharton, October 30, 1768, Division of Pub. Records, Pa. State Library; same to John Baynton, October 30, 1768, *ibid.*; Butricke to Barnsley, February 12, 1769, *Hist. Magazine*, VIII, 262.

[117] Morgan to Baynton and Wharton, April 24, 1769, Division of Pub. Records, Pa. State Library; Gage to Hillsborough, August 18, 1770, P. R. O., Am. and W. I., vol. 126; Gage to Johnson, September 3, 1770, Gage's Letters; Gage to Hillsborough, September 3, 1771, P. R. O., Am. and W. I., vol. 127; *Pa. Packet and General Advertiser*, April 6, 1772, containing letters from Kaskaskia, June 14, 1771; Gage to Johnson, August 14, 1771, Gage's Letters; same to same, September 10, 1771, September 24, 1774, *ibid.*; Gage to Hillsborough, October 1, 1771, P. R. O., Am. and W. I., vol. 128.

that year the home government withdrew all the special Indian agents from the various posts in consequence of the transference of the management of the Indians to the colonies.[118] Edward Cole, Indian commissary in Illinois, left early in 1769,[119] and with him went others employed in the Indian service.[120] Thus was additional work imposed upon the military department. The significance of the change, moreover, was not lost upon the Indians, who looked upon it as another evidence of the negligence of the British government.[121] Wilkins succeeded, however, in keeping the large body of Indians pacified.[122] The murder of Pontiac by an Indian in 1769[123] led to a civil war among themselves,[124] which turned their attention from the white settlers.

Wilkins's relations with the Roman Catholics were apparently amicable, a large part of the regiment stationed at

[118] Hillsborough to Johnson, April 15, 1768, *N. Y. Col. Docs.*, VIII, 57, 58; Johnson to Hillsborough, October 23, 1768, *ibid.*, 105–106; same to same, February 15, 1769, *ibid.*, 151.

[119] Cole to Johnson, June 13, 1769, Johnson MSS., vol. XVII, no. 189. There was considerable dissatisfaction with Cole's management of Indian affairs on the ground of his alleged extravagance. See Maturin (Gage's secretary) to Baynton, Wharton and Morgan, May 7, 1768, Division of Pub. Records, Pa. State Library.

[120] Return of people employed in the Indian Department at the Illinois (1767):

A Commissary	L 200 Sterling
A Gunsmith	L 100 "
An Interpreter	L 80 "
A Doctor	L 80 "
	L 460

[121] Johnson to Hillsborough, October 23, 1768, *N. Y. Col. Docs.*, VIII, 105–106; same to same, *ibid.*, VII, 151.

[122] Gage to Hillsborough, August 12, 1769, P. R. O., Am. and W. I., vol. 125; same to same, August 18, 1770, *ibid.*, vol. 126.

[123] Cole to Johnson, June 13, 1769, Johnson MSS., vol. XVII, no. 189; Gage to Johnson, August 6, 1769, Gage's Letters.

[124] Gage to Hillsborough, August 12, 1769, P. R. O., Am. and W. I., vol. 125; Gage to Johnson, July 15, 1771, Gage's Letters.

Fort de Chartres being members of the Roman Catholic church. The legal position of the church had been well defined by the treaty of Paris and by succeeding documents, and on the whole the course pursued by the English government toward the Catholics of Illinois was an honorable one. In the Illinois country the Jesuits had had charge of the parish at Kaskaskia and of the mission among the Indians of the same name. By a royal decree in 1764 the Jesuit order in France and its dependencies was abolished, and the decree was executed in the Illinois country in the same year,[125] the property being confiscated for the use of the French king.[126] Not only did the Jesuits leave, but the Sulpitians likewise abandoned their parishes,[127] so that at the beginning of the British occupation not a single priest was in the country. Father Meurin, however, one of the expelled priests, obtained leave to return to minister to the abandoned parishes.[128] Illinois had always been attached to the bishopric of Quebec, and in 1768 Bishop Briand of Quebec made Father Meurin his vicar-general in Illinois.[129] But owing to his age and ill-health, and the widely scattered parishes, it was impossible for Meurin to carry on the work

---

[125] The best contemporary account of this incident is in *Bannissement des Jésuites de la Louisiane*, September 3, 1764, in *Jesuit Relations*, ed. Thwaites, LXX, 211–301.

[126] General Gage complained that the sale was illegal, because made after the treaty of cession of 1763, Gage to Conway, June 24, 1766, P. R. O., Am. and W. I., vol. 122.

[127] M. Forget, the only remaining priest of that order in 1764, sold the property at Cahokia and carried the proceeds with him, although his action was opposed by many of the inhabitants, Sterling to Gage, December 15, 1765, P. R. O., Am. and W. I., vol. 122; Meurin to Bishop Briand, June 11, 1768, *Jesuit Relations*, ed. Thwaites, LXXI, 37.

[128] *Bannissement des Jésuites de la Louisiane*, September 3, 1764, *Jesuit Relations*, ed. Thwaites, LXX, 291; Shea, *Life of Archbishop Carroll*, 113.

[129] *Ibid.*, 116.

alone. The English authorities made efforts to secure an additional priest [130] but without success. In 1768, however, Bishop Briand sent Father Pierre Gibault, who took up his residence at Kaskaskia, Meurin retiring to the less populous parish of Cahokia. [131] Throughout the entire British period we find little or no complaint by church officials of the attitude of the English government. Although politically the French had much to complain of during the first five years of British rule, their religious privileges were accorded them at all times.

[130] Gage to Conway, June 24, 1766, P. R. O., Am. and W. I., vol. 122.

[131] Shea, *Life of Archbishop Carroll*, 125. Father Meurin had not had a very happy experience with the Kaskaskians. They refused to pay their tithes, and in numerous other ways showed him disrespect. He tells us that the people had lost their piety almost entirely during the years of chaos incident to the removal of the Jesuits and the arrival of the British, Meurin to Bishop Briand, June 11, 1768, *Jesuit Relations*, ed. Thwaites, LXXI, 41ff.; Shea, *Life of Archbishop Carroll*, 114–129.

CHAPTER V.

Trade Conditions in the Illinois Country, 1765–1775.

The peltry trade had been one of the chief elements in the rivalry between France and England in the Ohio and Mississippi valleys. It was the main support of the French government in Canada and now that the English were in possession of the great peltry districts the management of the trade deserved most serious consideration. It was becoming of increasing importance to the manufacturing monopoly of the mother country, and therefore, in the minds of English statesmen, deserved far more attention than did the few thousand French colonists scattered throughout the West. The desire to increase this branch of commerce dictated in large measure those clauses in the proclamation of 1763, which forbade the formation of settlements or the purchase of lands within the Indian reservation, but which at the same time declared that trade with the Indians should be free and open to all English subjects alike. Again, the plan proposed in 1764 related solely to the management of the Indians and to the regulation of the trade with a view to making the English monopoly of intrinsic value to the empire. Even towards the close of the period under consideration there was little or no change of policy so far as official utterances are concerned. In 1772, in a report to the crown, the Lords of Trade made the following declaration : " ' The great object of colonizing upon the continent of North America has been to improve and extend the commerce, navigation, and manufactures of this kingdom . . . it does appear to us, that the extension of the fur trade depends entirely upon the Indians being undisturbed in the possession of their hunting grounds; that all colonizing does in its nature, and must in its consequences, operate to the prejudice of that branch of commerce.' . . . ' Let the savages enjoy their deserts in quiet... Were they driven from their forests the peltry trade would decrease.' "[1]

Under the French régime the western Indians and their trade had been managed with greater success than had the tribes living under English influence. The success of France was due largely to her policy of centralization, combined with the genial character of the French fur trader and the influence of the missionary. The English, on the contrary, had managed their relations with the Indians through the agency of the different colonies, without a semblance of union or cooperation, each colony competing for the lion's share of the trade, a policy which resulted disastrously to the peace of the empire.

In 1755 the English government, under the influence of

---

[1] Franklin's *Works*, ed. Sparks, IV, 303–323. "I conceive that to procure all the commerce it will afford at as little expense to ourselves as we can is the only object we should have in view in the interior Country for a century to come." Gage to Hillsborough, November 10, 1770, P. R. O., Am. and W. I., vol. 126: "This Traffick was the Principal Benefit in View, in the Extent of Territory in N. America made by the late Peace." Conway to Gage, March 27, 1766, Conway's MS. letter book in Library of Congress. It may be noted, however, that some members of the government had serious doubts as to this policy. Such men as Shelburne favored an early opening of the country to colonization. See below, ch. VI. Shelburne, however, was also convinced that the management of the Indians and their trade should be considered first among American affairs. *Calendar of Home Office Papers*, 1766–1769, no. 348. For a similar view of Shelburne's in 1774 see *Parl. Hist.*, XVIII, 672.

TRADE CONDITIONS

Halifax, president of the Board of Trade, took over the political control of the Indians, and appointed two superintendents to have charge of the different nations.[2] A little later, in 1761, the purchase of Indian lands was taken out of the hands of the colonies and placed under the control of the home government.[3] No further change is to be noted until after the issue of the war was known, when the whole question was again taken under consideration. The most important step yet taken respecting the Indian and his concomitant, the fur trade, appeared in the proclamation of 1763, issued in October following the treaty of cession. Some of its provisions for the West have already been noted. In addition to reserving for the present the unorganized territory between the Alleghany Mountains and the Mississippi River for the use of the Indians, the government guaranteed the Indians in the possession of these lands by announcing in the proclamation that no governor or commander-in-chief would be allowed to make land grants within this territory, and further prohibited all land purchases and the formation of settlements by private individuals without royal consent. Trade within this reservation was, however, made free to all who would obtain a license from the governor or commander-in-chief of the colony in which they resided.[4]

The Indian trade now came to be regarded as British rather than colonial,[5] since its management was now directed by the central government. In the course of the

[2] Alvord, "Genesis of the Proclamation of 1763", in *Mich. Pioneer and Hist. Colls.*, XXXVI, 25.

[3] *Ibid.*

[4] *Can. Const. Docs., 1759–1791*, 122.

[5] Johnson to Lords of Trade, May 17, 1759, *N. Y. Col. Docs.*, VII, 375. Franklin pointed out the same thing in 1766. Franklin's *Works*, ed. Biglow, III, 429.

year following the issuance of the proclamation an elaborate plan was outlined by Hillsborough[6] comprehending the political and commercial relations of all the Indian territory.

According to the proposed scheme[7] British North America was to be divided, for purposes of Indian management, into two districts, a northern and a southern, each under the control of a general superintendent or agent appointed by the crown, the Ohio River being designated as the approximate line of division. In the northern district, with which we are here concerned, the regulation of such Indian affairs as treaties, land purchases, questions of peace and war, and trade relations was to be given into the hands of the superintendent who was to be entirely free from outside interference. Without his consent no civil or military officer could interfere with the trade or other affairs of any of the Indian tribes. Three deputies were to be appointed to assist the superintendent and at each post a commissary, an interpreter, and a smith were to reside, acting under the immediate direction of the superintendent and responsible only to him for their conduct. For the administration of justice between traders and Indians and between traders themselves, the commissary at each post was to be empowered to act as justice of the peace in all civil and criminal cases. In civil cases involving sums not exceeding ten pounds the commissary was to have summary jurisdiction, but an appeal might be taken to the superintendent. The Indian trade was to be under the direct supervision of the general superintendent. Traders who desired to go among the Indians to ply their trade could do so by obtaining a license from the province from which they came.

[6] See above, ch. II, pp. 16–17.
[7] *Can. Arch. Report*, 1904, 242; *N. Y. Col. Docs.*, VII, 637–641.

TRADE CONDITIONS

The region into which the traders intended to go was to be clearly defined in the license and each had to give bond for the observance of the laws regulating the trade. The superintendent, together with the commissary at the post and a representative of the Indians, was to fix the value of all goods, and traders were forbidden to charge more than the price fixed. For the still better regulation of the trade, it was to be centered about the regularly fortified and garrisoned forts. Regulations for the sale of land were also proposed: outside the limits of the colonies no individual or company could legally purchase land from the Indians unless at a general meeting of the tribe presided over by the superintendent.

The plan thus outlined by the ministry was never carried into effect by parliamentary action, although the superindents used the outline as a guide in their dealings with the Indians.[8] The original intention had been to levy a tax on the Indian trade to defray the expense of putting the scheme into operation, but it was found that the budget was already too greatly burdened,[9] and the Stamp Act disturbances which followed illustrated the probable inexpediency of imposing such a duty.[10]

The foregoing considerations serve to indicate the importance which the ministry attached to the Indian trade in general. But what of the trade in the Illinois country? This region had been one of the great centers of the Indian

[8] Practically all the provisions were adopted by the superintendents, "Representation of Lords of Trade on the State of Indian Affairs", March 17, 1768, *N. Y. Col. Docs.*, VIII, 24.

[9] Franklin's *Works*, ed. Bigelow, V, 38; Knox, *Justice and Policy of the Quebec Act*, 39; "Proposed Extension of Provincial Limits", *Can. Const. Docs.*, *1759–1791*, 381; Johnson to Gage, March 9, 1765, Parkman Coll., Pontiac–Miscell., 1765–1778.

[10] Knox, *Justice and Policy of the Quebec Act*, 39.

trade under the French régime ; and in addition the French inhabitants had been one of the main supports of New Orleans since its foundation early in the century. The commercial connection between the Illinois villages and New Orleans had never been broken, and at the time of the occupation of Illinois in 1765, French fur traders and merchants still plied their traffic up and down the Mississippi River. Now that the title to this trade centre had passed to England it was expected that the volume of trade would be turned eastward up the Ohio River. The necessity for this was patent if any material benefits were to accrue to the empire from the cession, for failure to carry out the plan would leave the country a dead weight on the empire.

The home and colonial authorities early saw the importance of turning the course of the trade. They hoped and expected that a trade would be opened with the Indians in and about the Illinois country immediately after the active occupation by the English troops.[11] A large number of individual traders were early aware of this and representatives of some of the large trading companies of the East were also preparing to take advantage of the opening of the West to trade. In 1765 Fort Pitt became the great rendezvous for this element. From this point traders, with their cargoes to exchange for the Indians' furs, followed the army to Fort de Chartres as soon as the season of the year would permit.

Among the more prominent figures was George Morgan, a member of the firm of Baynton, Wharton and Morgan, and the company's personal representative in the Illinois country. Other representatives of the company left Fort Pitt in March of the same year with a large cargo of goods,

[11] Johnson to Governor Penn, April 12, 1765, Johnson MSS., vol. X, no. 190.

TRADE CONDITIONS 83

which reached Fort de Chartres during the summer.[12] Firms such as Franks and Company of Philadelphia and London, and Bentley and Company of Manchac, on the lower Mississippi, also traded extensively in the Illinois region during the following years; all the larger British companies becoming rivals for that portion of the Indian trade which the English were able to command. Other and perhaps greater sources of profit to the English merchants lay in the privilege of furnishing the garrison with provisions [13] and the Indian department with the goods for Indian presents.[14] Although the houses of Baynton, Wharton and Morgan, and of Franks and Company were usually competitors for the former privilege, the latter company generally had the monopoly.[15] On the other hand Baynton, Wharton and Morgan derived their greatest profits from the sale of enormous quantities of goods to the government through the Indian department for distribution among the Indians accustomed to assemble at the Illinois villages.[16] But whether all these houses received profits commensurate with the risks undertaken is problematical.[17]

In the Indian trade, in which all the merchants were in-

[12] Five bateaux loaded with goods under the command of John Jennings, sailed from Fort Pitt, March 9, 1765. Joseph Dobson to Baynton, Wharton and Morgan, March 9, 1765, MS. letter in Hist. Soc. Pa. Library. In 1767 the firm wrote: "Our Speculation has been attended with the most favorable circumstances to his Majesty's Interest, As we are the only English Merchants who have ventured to forward British Merchandize to the Illinois Country; Whereby the King's Agents have been enabled, in some Degree to counteract the French and Spanish on the opposite side of the Mississippi." Baynton, Wharton and Morgan to Macleane, October 9, 1767, B. T. Papers (Hist. Soc. Pa.), vol. XXVI. The best sources of information for the company's methods and operations in the West are Morgan's MS. letter book and the firm's papers in the Division of Pub. Records, Pa. State Library.

[13] Morgan's MS. letter book.   [14] *Ibid.*   [15] *Ibid.*   [16] *Ibid.*

[17] Gage wrote in 1770 that the "Company from Philadelphia [Baynton, Wharton and Morgan] failed in the Illinois trade", Gage to Hillsborough, December 7, 1770, P. R. O., Am. and W. I., vol. 126.

terested, they not only had to compete with each other and with independent English traders, but with the French and Spanish who had not ceased to ply their trade among their old friends the Indians. This continuance of foreign traders in British territory was probably the most serious problem in the trade situation. Not only did it affect English traders but the interests of the empire itself were seriously threatened by the presence within its limits of unlicensed foreign traders. It is therefore evident that the close of hostilities between France and England in 1763 and the formal transfer of Canada and the West to Great Britain by no means closed the intense rivalry between the fur-trading elements of the two nations for predominance in the western trade. It rather accentuated it. As has already been suggested, France, until the cession of the West, had naturally possessed the dominant influence among the savages of the Mississippi Valley and Canada, and consequently the monopoly of the fur trade accrued to her subjects. In the upper Ohio River region and among the tribes bordering on or living within the limits of the English colonies, the British, during the first half of the eighteenth century, were either strong rivals of the French or were completely dominant. It was therefore generally expected that after the cession of the West the British would inherit the influence of the French among the Indians and succeed to the monopoly of the fur trade just as Great Britain had succeeded to the sovereignty of the territory itself. But the conspiracy of Pontiac, due in large part to the machinations of the French traders, postponed for a considerable period the entry of the British traders, during which time the French became more strongly entrenched than ever in the affections of the savages.

The French methods of trade had from the beginning

TRADE CONDITIONS

been different from those pursued by their neighbors and rivals. The government divided the Indian country into districts corresponding to the divisions recognized by the Indians themselves, and licenses were adapted to the several " hunts " with reference to the customs and habits of the natives.[18] Traders were absolutely forbidden under severe penalties to trade or hunt beyond the limits of their respective districts.[19] The traders, moreover, lived among the Indians, affected their manners, treated them kindly and respectfully, and supplied all their wants, and the missionary, the connecting link between the two races, was ever present. This association of religion which was one of the causes of the success of the French in gaining such a permanent foothold in the affections of the Indians, was entirely absent in the British relations with that race. The English traders were in general unscrupulous[20] in their dealings with the savages and deficient in that tact which enabled Frenchmen to overcome the natural prejudice of the Indian and acquire an interest with him which would be difficult to sever. In that section of the Indian country where the influence of Great Britain was such that her traders could go among the Indians, there was always considerable dissatisfaction on account of the methods employed by a large number of independent and irresponsible traders. Many carried large quantities of rum, some dealing in nothing else.[21] English traders frequently attended public

---

[18] Pownall, *Admin. of the Cols.*, 187.   [19] *Ibid.*

[20] Johnson to Hillsborough, October 23, 1768, *N. Y. Col. Docs.*, VIII, 105-106; same to Shelburne, *ibid.*, VII, 929; same, " Review of the Trade and Affairs of the Indians", September, 1767, *ibid.*, 955, 960, 964; same to Lords of Trade, *ibid.*, 987; Johnson to Carleton, January 27, 1767, Can. Arch., series Q., vol. 4, p. 115.

[21] Johnson to Hillsborough, August 14, 1770, *N. Y. Col. Docs.*, VIII, 226. See extract from " Ponteach, or the Savages of North America: A Tragedy ", in Parkman, *Conspiracy of Pontiac*, II, 344ff.

meetings of Indians, gave them liquor during the time for business, and defrauded them of their furs.[22] This abuse was one of the great causes of complaint against British traders.[23] Indeed wherever they participated in the trade, its condition was deplorable. Many of the independent traders had little or no credit so that the legitimate merchants suffered as well as the Indians.[24] The unlicensed traders adopted various expedients to draw trade from each other, such as selling articles below first cost, thus ruining a large number of merchants.[25] Fabrications dangerous to the public were frequently created to explain the prices and condition of goods.[26] But probably more injurious still to imperial interests, was the fact that whole cargoes of goods were sometimes sold by English firms to French traders, thus enabling the latter to engross a great part of the trade, and depriving the empire of the benefit of the revenue accruing from the importation of furs into England. This practice was probably followed to a greater degree in the farther West,[27] where the French continued to have a monopoly in the trade long after the English occupation.

It had been expected that the Illinois villages would be the center of trade for the English side of the upper Mississippi Valley[28] just as it had been one of the centers dur-

[22] Johnson to Hillsborough, August 14, 1770, *N. Y. Col. Docs.*, VIII, 226.

[23] Johnson to Hillsborough, April 4, 1772, *ibid.*, 292.

[24] Johnson, "Review of the Trade and Affairs of the Indians", September, 1767, *ibid.*, VII, 964–965.   [25] *Ibid.*   [26] *Ibid.*

[27] Gage to Shelburne, January 17, 1767, B. T. Papers (Hist. Soc. Pa.), vol. XXVII; Johnson to Lords of Trade, November 16, 1767, *N. Y. Col. Docs.*, VII, 776; Croghan to B. Franklin, January 27, 1767, Sparks MSS., V, vol. I, p. 46. Croghan, writing from New York, says that "persons here of no inconsiderable Consequence supply the French at New Orleans with Goods to carry on their Contraband Trade in the Illinois Country." *Ibid.*

[28] Lords of Trade to Johnson, *N. Y. Col. Docs.*, VII, 635.

TRADE CONDITIONS

ing the French regime. But the British were not so well situated to command the trade as the French had been. Previous to this time the trade of the Missouri River region had centered at the Illinois posts, but after the cession of the West to England and the foundation of St. Louis by Laclede in 1764, the latter place drew all the trade west of the Mississippi. Moreover, except for the few tribes of Illinois Indians in the immediate vicinity very few savages found their way to Fort de Chartres for trading purposes. English traders, on the other hand, did not trust themselves far beyond this narrow circle,[29] but their French and Spanish rivals from Louisiana, many of whom formerly lived in the Illinois country, carried on a trade in all directions both by land and by water.[30] They ascended the Ohio, Wabash, and Illinois rivers[31] and crossed the Mis-

---

[29] "Information of the State of Commerce given by Capt. Forbes, 1768", P. R. O., Am. and W. I., vol. 125. General Gage declared in 1770 that the posts had failed as centers of trade. Gage to Hillsborough, November 10, 1770, *ibid.*, vol. 126.

[30] Gordon's "Journal down the Ohio", 1766, MS. in Hist. Soc. Pa. Library; Lieutenant Geo. Phyn to Johnson, April 15, 1768, Johnson MSS., vol. XXV, no. 109. Morgan complained in 1767 that the great number of French hunters who went up the Ohio from New Orleans had almost exterminated the buffalo. Morgan to Baynton and Wharton, December 10, 1767, Morgan's MS. letter book.

[31] Morgan to Baynton and Wharton, December 10, 1767, Morgan's MS. letter book; Gage to Shelburne, April 24, 1768, P. R. O., Am. and W. I., vol. 124; Gage to Hillsborough, April 24, 1768, *ibid.* Early in 1768 the Indians attacked a party of Frenchmen crossing the country from Vincennes with eight horses loaded with peltry, Morgan to Baynton and Wharton, April 10, 1768, Morgan's MS. letter book. On April 23, 1768, Morgan again writes: "A single boat has just arrived at Misere (St. Genevieve) loaded with Wine, Taffia and Brandy, four other Boats were to leave New Orleans Eight Days after. What their Cargoes consist of I cannot exactly learn but I fear chiefly Liquors. On their Arrival and their Cargoes Will greatly depend the Sales we shall make this Spring." MS. letter book. "They are even so impudent as to wear English Colours up the Ohio on Acct. of the Cherokees", Morgan to Baynton and Wharton, December 10, 1767, *ibid.*

sissippi River above the Illinois, plying their traffic among the tribes in the region of the Wisconsin and Fox rivers.[32] This was probably the most productive area in the Mississippi Valley in the supply of fur-bearing animals. The Mississippi River northward from its junction with the Illinois was also considered especially good for the peltry business, the otter, beaver, wolf, cervine, and martin being found in abundance,[33] but the British traders dared not venture into that quarter.[34] The loss of this trade, however, cannot be attributed altogether to their misconduct, for the French had never allowed it to pass from their own hands. The latter continued to intrigue with the Indians throughout the greater part of this period just as they had done prior to 1765. As we have seen they pointed out to the savages how they would suffer from the policy of economy practised by the British government.[35] Thus by giving presents and by circulating stories and misrepresentations the French subjects of Spain attempted to checkmate every move of

---

[32] Gage to Hillsborough, November 10, 1770, P. R. O., Am. and W. I., vol. 125; Hutchins, "Remarks upon the Country of the Illinois, 1771", MS. in Hist. Soc. Pa. Library. It may be noted that during the French régime the French-Canadians traded extensively in this region. See Gage's "Report on the State of the Government of Montreal", *Can. Const. Docs., 1759-1791*, 69-72.

[33] Wilkins to Barrington, December 5, 1769, P. R. O., Am. and W. I., vol. 125; Gage to Hillsborough, November 10, 1770, *ibid.*, vol. 126.

[34] "To ascend the Mississippi or Illinois Rivers with Goods would be certain Death, so great is the Influence of the French there." Morgan to Baynton and Wharton, December 10, 1767, MS. letter book. Lieutenant Hutchins, an English engineer, who spent a year in the Illinois country, stated that the "Pelties in general that are sent from the British Side are obtained from the French Traders on the Spanish Shore, as no Englishman can with safety venture among the Savages." Hutchins, "Remarks upon the Country of the Illinois", MS. in Hist. Soc. Pa. Library.

[35] Johnson to Carleton, January 27, 1767, Can. Arch., series Q, vol. 4, p. 115.

TRADE CONDITIONS

the English.[36] The Indians were constantly reminded of bad designs on the part of England, and were encouraged with unauthorized promises of aid in case they should take up the hatchet in defense of their hunting grounds.[37]

This state of affairs continued throughout the greater part of the period, although it was probably modified to some extent after 1770. In answer to a number of vigorous protests from General Gage,[38] O'Reilly, the Spanish governor of Louisiana, issued an order to all the commandants in that colony to prohibit the inhabitants crossing the river in the pursuit of trade and whenever any excesses were committed to give satisfaction to the English commandant according to the laws of nations.[39]

During the first years of the British occupation there was considerable friction in the contact of the two alien peoples in the Illinois villages. In spite of the fact that the French who remained became subjects of Great Britain sharp competition existed for several years between the English and French residents in the vicinity of the villages.[40] The latter were on terms of friendship with the savages and could go

---

[36] Johnson to Hillsborough, February 18, 1771, *N. Y. Col. Docs.*, VIII, 263; same to same, October 23, 1768, *ibid.*, 105-106.

[37] Gage to Hillsborough, April 24, 1768, P. R. O., Am. and W. I., vol. 124. There was considerable apprehension among English officials throughout this period lest the Indians should be stirred up for an attack upon Canada. See Hillsborough to Carleton, November 4, 1769, Can. Arch., series Q, vol. 6, p. 121.

[38] Gage to Hillsborough, April 24, 1768, P. R. O., Am. and W. I., vol. 124; Gage to Shelburne, April 24, 1768, Dartmouth Papers, *Fourteenth Report, Royal Hist. MSS. Com.*, Appendix X.

[39] Order of O'Reilly, January 27, 1770, P. R. O., Am. and W. I., vol. 126.

[40] " Information of the State of Commerce in the Illinois Country, given by Captain Forbes, 1768 ", P. R. O., Am. and W. I., vol. 125. Morgan informed his partners that " a Number of French Merchants have combined against us and made Application to Captain Forbes and offered to supply the Crown at a much lower rate than we do." April 5, 1768, Morgan's MS. letter book.

into any part of the country without difficulty and those Indians who came to Fort de Chartres to trade generally preferred to deal with their trusted friends. The French often carried the packs of furs thus obtained across the river to St. Louis or transported them directly to the New Orleans market. Although the British merchants were occasionally able to pool their interests with the French residents, such cases were exceptional prior to 1770. In that year, however, General Gage informed the home government that " the competition between his Majesty's old and new Subjects is greatly abated and must by degrees subside, for if carried to extremes it would be very prejudicial to both." [41]

Naturally the large quantities of furs and skins obtained by such contraband trade as well as by the French residents of Illinois were taken directly to New Orleans and there embarked for the ports of France and Spain.[42] These foreign interlopers, however, only followed the route to which they had long been accustomed. On the other hand it was expected by the government that the traders who carried English manufactured goods down the Ohio River would return by the same route with their cargoes of peltry for the purpose of transporting them to England. But in this the government was disappointed. English traders and merchants followed the line of least resistance, the route down the Mississippi to New Orleans.[43] Moreover, the

[41] Gage to Hillsborough, November 10, 1770, P. R. O., Am. and W. I., vol. 126.

[42] Morgan to Baynton and Wharton, December 10, 1767, Morgan's MS. letter book. "The French in open Day and without the least Ceremony send their Peltries from hence to New Orleans or to the West Side of the Mississippi", *ibid.*

[43] Gage to Shelburne, January 17, 1767, B. T. Papers (Hist. Soc. Pa.), vol. XXVII.

TRADE CONDITIONS

New Orleans market was attractive, for peltries sold at a higher price there than in the British markets.[44] The tendency of the English traders and merchants to follow this course was discovered soon after the occupation.[45] In a communication to Secretary Shelburne in 1766 Gage informed the government that "It is reported that the Traders in West Florida carry most of their Skins to New Orleans, where they sell them at as good a price as is given in London. As I had before some Intelligence of this, the Officer commanding at Fort Pitt had orders to watch the Traders from Pensilvania who went down the Ohio in the Spring to Fort Chartres; and to report the quantity of Peltry they should bring up the Ohio in the Autumn. He has just acquainted me that the traders do not return to his Post, that they are gone down the Mississippi with all their Furrs and Skinns under the pretense of embarking them at New Orleans for England."[46] A few weeks later he wrote again in a similar strain: "That Trade will go with the Stream is a maxim found to be true from all Accounts that have been received of the Indian trade carried on in that vast Tract of Country which lies on the Back of the British Colonies; and that the Peltry acquired there is carried to the Sea

[44] Gage to Shelburne, December 23, 1766, *ibid.*; Johnson to Gage, January 29, 1767, Johnson MSS., vol. XIV, no. 35; Gage to Shelburne, February 22, 1767, B. T. Papers (Hist. Soc. Pa.), vol. XXII; Gage to Johnson, January 25, 1767, Johnson MSS., vol. XIV, no. 28; George Phyn to Johnson, April 15, 1768, *ibid.*, vol. XXV, no. 109; Gage to Dartmouth, May 5, 1773, P. R. O., Am. and W. I., vol. 128. Gage wrote in 1766 that skins and furs bore a price ten pence per pound higher at New Orleans than at any British market. Gage to Conway, July 15, 1766, *ibid.*, vol. 122.

[45] Gage to Conway, July 15, 1766, *ibid.* Remarks of Gage on Barrington's plan, May 10, 1766, Lansdowne MSS., vol. L, pp. 45–61.

[46] Gage to Shelburne, December 23, 1766, B. T. Papers (Hist. Soc. Pa.), vol. XXVII. In 1767, George Morgan informs his partners, Baynton and Wharton, that he will "send a Boat with a few Packs of Peltry to New Orleans". Morgan's MS. letter book.

either by the River St. Lawrence or River Mississippi."[47] Gage seemed to believe that the part which went down the St. Lawrence would be transported to England; but that the peltry passing through New Orleans would never enter a British port.[48] "Nothing but prospect of a superior profit or force will turn the Channel of Trade contrary to the above maxim."[49] "The Traders from these Colonies say that it will answer to carry Goods down the Ohio, but that it will not answer to return with their Peltry by the same Route, as they can get to the Sea at so much less expense, and greater expedition by means of the Rapidity of the Mississippi, and pretend that they have Ships at New Orleans to transport their Peltry to England."[50] ". . . the British Traders at the Illinois who carry their goods above three hundred miles by land before they have the convenience of Water Carriage cannot afford to return the same way with the produce of their Trade."[51] In this opinion Sir William Johnson likewise concurred.[52] Lieutenant John Phyn, of the British army, who spent some time at Fort de Chartres in 1768, also declared that " as long as New Orleans is in the hands of another power, the whole produce of that country must centre there. For our merchants will

---

[47] Gage to Shelburne, February 22, 1767, B. T. Papers (Hist. Soc. Pa.), vol. XXVII. Lieutenant-Governor Carleton of Canada complained that owing to the restraints on the fur trade in that colony, all the trade was going down the Mississippi, Carleton to Johnson, March 27, 1767, *Mich. Pioneer and Hist. Colls.*, X, 222-224.

[48] Gage to Shelburne, February 22, 1767, B. T. Papers (Hist. Soc. Pa.), vol. XXVII. [49] *Ibid.*

[50] Gage to Shelburne, January 17, 1767, B. T. Papers (Hist. Soc. Pa.), vol. XXVII, For a similar view see Gage to Johnson, January 19, 1767, Johnson MSS., vol. XIV, no. 23, and Gage to Johnson, January 25, 1767, *ibid.*, no. 28.

[51] Gage to Hillsborough, November 10, 1770, P. R. O., Am. and W. I., vol. 126.

[52] Johnson to Gage, January 29, 1767, Johnson MSS., vol. XIV, no. 35; same to same, February 24, 1767, *ibid.*, p. 67.

TRADE CONDITIONS 93

always dispose of their peltry or whatever the country produces, at New Orleans where they get as good a price as if they were to ship them off." [53]

In 1768 some steps were taken toward the better regulation of the trade. In that year Captain Forbes, the commandant at Fort de Chartres, issued a placard forbidding the traders to send any peltry down the river without informing the commandant of the number of packs, and at the same time giving a bond of two hundred pounds sterling that they would land them in a British port.[54] At the same time General Gage served notice on Governor Ulloa of Louisiana to prohibit the inhabitants of that province from going up the Illinois, Ohio, and Wabash rivers. The commandant at Fort de Chartres was then given directions to scour the river with armed boats, and to make prisoners of all persons acting contrary to the order of Don Ulloa and to carry them to Fort Pitt.[55]

Conditions, however, grew no better as time went on. In 1773 we find Gage complaining that "the Trade of the Mississippi, except that of the upper parts from whence a portion may go to Quebec, goes down that River; and has, as well as everything we have done on the Mississippi . . . tended more to the Benefit of New Orleans than of ourselves." [56]

An examination of the customs returns for the period

[53] Phyn to Johnson, April 15, 1768, Johnson MSS., vol. XXV, no. 109.

[54] Forbes to Gage, April 15, 1768, P. R. O., Am. and W. I., vol. 124. This had been advised before by the trader and Indian agent, George Croghan. Croghan to Franklin, January 27, 1767, Lansdowne MSS., vol. XLVIII.

[55] Gage to Hillsborough, April 24, 1768, P. R. O., Am. and W. I., vol. 124; Gage to Johnson, August 14, 1768, Gage's Letters.

[56] Gage to Dartmouth, May 5, 1773, P. R. O., Am. and W. I., vol. 128.

from 1763 to 1775 indicates that the statements of English officials relative to the productivity of the West were not groundless. Instead of an increase in the number and value of furs and skins imported into England as a result of the French cession of the great fur-bearing regions of Canada and the Northwest, there is a decided decrease each year.[57] A diminution is likewise to be noted in the value of the exports from Canada during the same period.[58]

It is difficult to figure exactly what the loss to imperial interests was under these conditions. Furs and skins, however, being among the enumerated commodities [59] some loss certainly accrued to British shipping and to the government through loss of the duty, as well as to English manufactures. Although practically no peltries reached the Atlantic ports from the Illinois region, large quantities were carried to New Orleans. The few who have left any estimate of the amount of peltries exported to New Orleans agree in general that from five hundred to one thousand packs were shipped annually from the Illinois country.[60] According to the usual estimate five hundred

[57] The value, as given in P. R. O., Customs Accounts, vols. 64–68, of beaver skins exported from America from Christmas, 1763, to Christmas, 1768, was as follows:

    1764, £28,067 S18   1767, £20,262 S 2
    1765, £27,801 S11   1768, £18,923 S18
    1766, £24,657 S 0

[58] The total value of beaver skins exported from Canada in 1764 was 17,259 pounds sterling, and in 1768 it was 13,166 pounds sterling. P. R. O., Customs Accounts, vols. 64–68.

[59] *Parl. Hist.*, VII, 913–916.

[60] "An account of the exports from the Illinois from Sept., 1769 to Sept., 1770", in Hutchins's "Remarks upon the Country of the Illinois, 1771", MS. in Hist. Soc. Pa. Library:

From the British Territory:

Flour to New Orleans, 120,000 weight which may yield 4 Dollars pr Cwt. Sterling L 1120.

Peltries 550 Packs which on an average if no damage happen

TRADE CONDITIONS

packs were worth in New Orleans about five thousand five hundred pounds sterling.[61] At the same time the expense of maintaining the various posts and the Indian department was heavy. The Indian expenses at Fort de Chartres alone between September, 1766, and September, 1767, were more than six thousand pounds sterling.[62] In the following year the expenses for nine months in Indian affairs, fitting out an armed galley to prevent illicit trade, and in repairs on Fort de Chartres and new works of defense in expectation of an Indian rupture exceeded two thousand pounds sterling.[63]

> to them may yield at London, Ten Pounds each Pack. 5,500 Pounds.
> Total: Sterling L 6,620.
> From the Spanish Territory:
> Flour 15,000 Weight L 150
> Peltries 835 Packs   L 8350
>
> L 8,500
>
> Total value of the Exports in the year 1768: L 15,120.

The merchant Geo. Morgan declared that if proper regulations were adopted and enforced, 3000 packs per annum could be procured on the British side. Morgan to Baynton and Wharton, December 10, 1767, Morgan's MS. letter book. In 1763, 8000 packs of beaver peltry had been exported from New Orleans, Marsh to Haldimand, November 20, 1767, B. M., Add. MSS., 21,728.

[61] Hutchins, "Remarks upon the Country of the Illinois, 1771." From New Orleans, where all the western trade finally centered, it was estimated that peltries worth between 75,000 and 100,000 pounds sterling were sent annually to foreign ports. Gage estimated it at 80,000 pounds sterling, Gage to Shelburne, January 17, 1767, B. T. Papers (Hist. Soc. Pa.), vol. XXVII. "New Orleans remits one hundred thousand pounds Sterling worth of Peltry annually to France", Baynton, Wharton and Morgan to McLeane, October 9, 1767, *ibid.*, vol. XXVI.

[62] P. R. O., Audit Office, Declared Accounts, bundle 1530, roll 2, Indian Affairs. Gage estimated Commissary Cole's expense for the same period at ten thousand pounds sterling, Gage to Johnson, April 4, 1768, Gage's Letters.

[63] Gage to Hillsborough, October 7, 1769, P. R. O., Am. and W. I., vol. 125. In a speech in the House of Lords in 1783, in which he defended the cession of the Northwest to the United States, Lord Shelburne declared: "The exports of this country to Canada, then, were

There seems to have been unanimity of opinion respecting the commercial inutility of the Illinois and surrounding country under existing conditions. Effective though expensive measures would have to be taken to change the course of trade and to expel foreign traders. But General Gage was very doubtful about the probable efficiency of any further regulations. Early in 1767 he declared that it would " not answer to England to be at much expense about the Mississippi " so long as better prices prevailed at New Orleans.[64] Secretary Hillsborough took the same view a few years later, in an argument against the planting of western colonies: " This Commerce cannot . . . be useful to Great Britain otherwise than as it furnishes a material for her Manufactures, but it will on the contrary be prejudicial to her in proportion as other Countries obtain that

only 140,000 pounds and the imports were no more than 50,000 pounds. Suppose the entire fur trade sunk into the sea, where is the detriment to this country? Is 50,000 pounds a year imported in that article any object for Great Britain to continue a war of which the people of England, by their representatives, have declared their abhorence? . . . But much less must this appear in our sight, when I tell Parliament, and the whole kingdom, that for many years past, one year with another, the preservation of this annual import of 50,000 pounds has cost this country, on an average, 800,000 pounds. I have the vouchers in my pocket, should your lordships be inclined to examine the fact." *Parl. Hist.*, XXIII, 409.

[64] Gage to Johnson, January 19, 1767, Johnson MSS., vol. XIV, no. 23. Captain Forbes, commandant at Fort de Chartres during part of 1768, wrote to Gage: "As I am very sensible of the immense expense this Country is to the Crown and the little advantage the public has hitherto reaped by the trade with savages, and the reason is that the Inhabitants have continued to send their Peltry to New Orleans which is shipped from thence for Old France and all the money that is laid out for the Troops and Savages is immediately sent to New Orleans, for which our Subjects get French Manufactures. I hope, Sir, you will excuse me when I observe to Your Excellency, that the Crown of Great Britain is at all the expence and that France reaps the advantages." Forbes to Gage, April 15, 1768, P. R. O., Am. and W. I., vol. 124. Commandant Wilkins wrote the same year that "the French of New Orleans are the sole gainers in this Trade and the public suffer greatly thereby." Wilkins to Gage, September 13, 1768, *ibid*.

TRADE CONDITIONS

material from us without its coming here first; and whilst New Orleans is the only Port for Exportation of what goes down the Mississippi, no one will believe that that town will not be the market for Peltry or that those Restrictions, which are intended to secure the exportation of that Commodity directly to G. Britain, can have any effect under such circumstances."[65]

The original intention of the British government had been to use Fort de Chartres, on the east bank of the Mississippi between the Illinois and Kaskaskia rivers, to guard the rivers in order to prevent contraband trading.[66] But its inefficiency was soon apparent.[67] Although well constructed, its location was not strategic; it commanded nothing but an island in the river.[68] An indication to the Indians of British dominion[69] and a place of deposit for English merchants[70] constituted about the sum total of its efficiency. In order to make the Illinois country effective as a barrier against foreign aggression and to keep the trade in

[65] Hillsborough to Gage, July 31, 1770, *ibid.*, vol. 126.

[66] Gage to Shelburne, April 3, 1767, *ibid.*, vol. 123.

[67] Gage to Johnson, February 8, 1767, Johnson MSS., vol. XIV, no. 44; Remarks by Gage on Barrington's plan, May 10, 1766, Lansdowne MSS., vol. L, p. 53.

[68] "It has not the least command of the River, owing to an Island which lies exactly opposite to it, and the Channel is entirely on the other side for a great part of the year. This is impassible from a sand bar which runs across even for small boats, and the French and Spaniards on the other side pass and repass at pleasure with contraband goods, forcing an illicit Trade, to our great disadvantage and a certain and very considerable loss to His Majesty's Revenue." Commandant Wilkins to Secretary-at-War Barrington, December 5, 1769, P. R. O., Am. and W. I., vol. 123. See also Morgan to Baynton and Wharton, April 24, 1769, Division of Pub. Records, Pa. State Library.

[69] Gordon's "Journal down the Ohio, 1766," MS. in Hist. Soc. Pa. Library; Gage to Johnson, February 8, 1767, Johnson MSS., vol. XIV, no. 44; Hillsborough to Gage, July 31, 1770, P. R. O., Am. and W. I., vol. 126.

[70] Gage to Hillsborough, June 16, 1768, *ibid.*, vol. 124.

English hands, it was necessary to adopt measures looking toward the closing of those natural entrances into the country, the mouths of the Illinois and the Ohio rivers.[71] Almost all the correspondence of the time relating to Illinois, contains references to the practicability of erecting forts at the junctions of the Illinois and Ohio rivers with the Mississippi. In most cases this was insisted upon as the only practicable measure to make the country of value.[72] Suggestions were also offered relative to the erec-

[71] Gage to Shelburne, April 3, 1767, *ibid.*, vol. 123; Johnson, "Review of the Trade and Affairs of the Indians," *loc. cit.*; Morgan to Baynton and Wharton, December 10, 1767, Morgan's MS. letter book. "A Post up the Mississippi at or near the Ilinois River might leave to us the greater part of the Trade that is now carried to the Settlements on the other side." Hutchins, "Remarks upon the Country of the Ilinois, 1771", MS. in Hist. Soc. Pa. Library. George Croghan wrote: "With respect to the building some new Forts there—I conceive they are indispensably necessary, One at the Mouth of the Illinois and one on the Wabashe; as they would effectually prevent the French and Spaniards from entering into the Indian Country and thereby seducing the trade from us, to France and Spain. Croghan to Franklin, January 27, 1767, Lansdowne MSS., vol. XLVIII, fol. 135.

[72] Gage to Halifax, August 10, 1765, Dartmouth Papers, *Fourteenth Report, Royal Hist. MSS. Com.*, Appendix X, p. 17; Gage to Conway, July 15, 1766, P. R. O., Am. and W. I., vol. 122. "As for the Post at, or near the conflux of the Ohio and Mississippi, I have now that affair under consideration, and sent the Chief Engineer about six weeks ago to survey all that Country." Gage to Brigadier Taylor of Pensacola, June 26, 1766, B. M., Add. MSS., 21,662, fol. 220. See also Gordon's "Journal down the Ohio, 1766", MS. in Hist. Soc. Pa. Library; Gage to Johnson, January 25, 1767, Johnson MSS., vol. XIV, no. 28; same to same, February 8, 1767, *ibid.*, no. 44; Gage to Shelburne, January 17, 1767, B. T. Papers (Hist. Soc. Pa.), vol. XXVII; same to same, April 3, 1767, P. R. O., Am. and W. I., vol. 123; Johnson, "Review of the Trade and Affairs of the Indians," *loc. cit.*; Morgan to Baynton and Wharton, December 10, 1767, Morgan's MS. letter book; Phyn to Johnson, April 15, 1768, Johnson MSS. vol. XXV, no. 109; Wilkins to Gage, September 13, 1768, P. R. O., Am. and W. I., vol. 124; Wilkins to Barrington, December 5, 1769, *ibia.*, vol. 125; Gage to Hillsborough, November 10, 1772, *ibid.*, vol. 126. The merchant Morgan wrote from Fort de Chartres in 1768 that "nothing is wanting but proper Posts at the Illinois River, St. Vincents and Manchac, a Civil Government and encouragement to Settlers from the Frontiers of Pennsylvania, Maryland and Virginia to make this a most

tion of a fort on the Mississippi river above its junction with the Illinois for the protection of that section of the peltry district.[73] Moreover, projects were likewise proposed for the establishment of proprietary colonies on the Ohio and Illinois rivers.[74] Gage himself suggested that all the French villages along the Mississippi be amalgamated into one settlement, which would also be the center of the military establishment, and from which detachments could be sent out to guard the rivers and prevent British traders from descending the stream to New Orleans and likewise watch for foreign interlopers.[75]

At one time it was the hope of such men as Gage, Johnson, Haldimand, and Hillsborough that the opening of the Iberville River would prove feasible, thus enabling English vessels to reach the British ports of West Florida through lakes Maurepas and Pontchartrain without going by way of New Orleans. This would necessitate the maintenance of a post at the junction of the Iberville and Mississippi rivers in order to turn English boats into the proposed channel. Numerous surveys were made and at one time the work of clearing the channel was actually begun.[76]

flourishing Colony. Without these means taken 'tis not worth keeping possession of as to any immediate Advantage resulting therefrom, As the English Nation is now at the whole expence of maintaining the Country and France reaps all the benefits from the Trade . . . " Morgan's MS. letter book.

[73] Gordon's "Journal down the Ohio, 1766", MS. in Hist. Soc. Pa. Library; Morgan to Baynton and Wharton, December 10, 1767, Morgan's MS. letter book. "It is acknowledged by the French themselves, that should a Settlement be made at Cape au Gres on the Mississippi, about 250 miles above the Illinois river, those on the French side would be ruined as it would draw and intercept the Trade of the upper Mississippi." Hutchins, "Remarks upon the Ilinois Country, 1771", MS. in Hist. Soc. Pa. Library.

[74] See below, ch. VI.

[75] Gage to Hillsborough, June 16, 1768, P. R. O., Am. and W. I., vol. 124.

[76] Gage to Taylor, June 10, 1766, B. M., Add. MSS., 21,662, fol.

None of these projects, however, were ever adopted. One of the principal reasons for this apparent neglect may well be summed up in a statement by Hillsborough, who appeared by 1770 to have given up the hope of any immediate advantages from the West. He declared in that year that under existing conditions "Forts and Military Establishments at the Mouths of the Ohio and Illinois Rivers, admitting that they would be effectual to the attainment of the objects in view, would yet, I fear, be attended with an expence to this Kingdom greatly disproportionate to the advantage proposed to be gained. . ."[77]

The matter of expense was not the only reason why the government refused to adopt any of the schemes suggested for the betterment of western conditions. The ministry had in mind a different plan, which if carried out would have completely changed the situation. The idea of the conquest of Louisiana from Spain was kept in mind during the greater part of the period under consideration and received more serious thought than perhaps any other western plan. Much of the correspondence between Gage and Brigadier Haldimand, the English commander in West Florida, related to the best method of attacking New Orleans, and many official and private letters also contained expressions

214; same to same, June 26, 1766, *ibid.*; Taylor to Gage, January 23, 1767, *ibid.*, 21,671; Gage to Haldimand, March 20, 1767, *ibid.*, 21,663, fol. 14; same to same, April 16, 1767, Can. Arch., series B, vol. 3, p. 24; same to same, April 30, 1767, B. M., Add. MSS., 21,663, fol. 33; Captain Home to Haldimand, May 6, 1767, Can. Arch., series B, vol. 68, p. 173; Hillsborough to Gage, July 31, 1770, P. R. O., Am. and W. I., vol. 126; Gage to Hillsborough, November 10, 1770, *ibid.*; Gordon's "Notes on the Country along the Mississippi from Kaskaskia in the Illinois to New Orleans", MS. copy in Champaign, Ill., Pub. Library; Hutchins to Haldimand, April 8, 1773, B. M., Add. MSS., 21,730, fol. 25; Pittman, *European Settlements on the Miss.*, ed. Hodder, 62–63.

[77] Hillsborough to Gage, July 31, 1770, P. R. O., Am. and W. I., vol. 126.

TRADE CONDITIONS

favorable to such a move.[78] In 1770–1771, when the Falkland Islands dispute was about to drag England and Spain into war, the opportunity had apparently come for the proposed conquest. Early in 1771 Secretary Hillsborough issued orders to Gage in New York to mobilize an army and prepare for an immediate descent upon New Orleans by way of the Ohio and Mississippi rivers.[79] Gage's preparations, however, were never completed, for the question at issue was settled peacefully.[80]

In the beginning Great Britain had hoped to realize in the development of the fur trade one of her chief returns for taking over the western country. But her traders found the French hard to dislodge. The character and methods of the French fur traders appealed to the Indians, and England's failure to realize more from the trade may be traced in part to this cause. Moreover, that portion of the western trade which went to the English centered in a large degree in a foreign port. With the means at hand attempts were made to check this tendency, and numerous plans were projected to induce a change of conditions, but no expensive measures were undertaken. The problem of the western trade confronted the ministry at a most unfortunate time, for during the decade following the treaty of Paris questions of graver importance were arising and demanding immediate attention. The necessity became apparent of increasing the revenue for purposes of imperial defence and of colonial administration, and the question of the readjustment of all the relations between the mother country

---

[78] See, for example, George Phyn to Johnson, April 15, 1768, Johnson MSS., vol. XXV, no. 109; Gage to Hillsborough, November 10, 1770, P. R. O., Am. and W. I., vol. 126; Hillsborough to Gage, July 31, 1770, *ibid.*; Reasons for the Establishment of a Colony in Illinois, 1766, B. T. Papers (Hist. Soc. Pa.), vols. XXVII, XXVIII.

[79] January 2, 1771, P. R. O., Am. and W. I., vol. 127.

[80] For a fuller account of the movement see below, ch. VII.

and the colonies was thereby introduced. When the colonial opposition to Parliamentary taxation manifested itself in the outcry against the Stamp Act and other revenue measures, the expenditure of large sums of money on new projects was out of the question. Instead of seeking new schemes upon which to expend money, every opportunity was seized upon to curtail expenses.[81] We find that not only was the plan for the management of Indians outlined in 1764 never put into full operation because of the added financial burden which it would entail, but also that in 1768 the management of the trade was transferred from the crown to the colonies [82] in order that the budget might be further reduced. The western question had become subordinated to that of the empire. Furs were important to the manufacturing monopoly of Great Britain, but at this time of rising discontent in the colonies any new projects entailing further expense were out of the question.

[81] The following extract from a letter of General Gage to Brigadier Taylor of Pensacola, illustrates something of the situation: "I have no doubt of the Exactitude or Necessity of the Expenses incurred, and would beg you to believe so, but the strictest Oeconomy is become the general Topick, and is recommended in every letter I receive from Home; in Compliance therewith, It's my part to notify the several Military Commanders what's hoped for, and expected by His Majesty's Ministers . . .; Estimates of the probable Expences of every Department have been expected in almost every Letter, and imply no more, than that a Calculation may be made therefrom, of the necessary Expences of North America, which being laid before Parliament, a Fund may be appropriated for the same. . ." March 20, 1767, B. M., Add. MSS., 21,663, fol. 12.

[82] Hillsborough to Johnson, April 15, 1768, *N. Y. Col. Docs.*, VIII, 57-58. In this letter the secretary announced the new plan, and declared that it was due largely to the necessity of curtailing expenses. Alvord, *Ill. Hist. Colls.*, II, xxix, misinterprets this measure. He says it was done for the purpose of turning the channel of trade up the Ohio. Within a year it was evident that this change made conditions worse. The Indians were aggrieved because of the removal of the commissaries and interpreters, and the trade conditions in the interior country became worse through lack of supervision. See Johnson to Hillsborough, August 26, 1769, *N. Y. Col. Docs.*, VIII, 184.

CHAPTER VI.

SCHEMES FOR THE COLONIZATION OF THE ILLINOIS COUNTRY,
1763-1768.

THE first step in the establishment of British colonies west of the Alleghany Mountains was in 1738, when the assembly of the colony of Virginia established Augusta County, with the Blue Ridge Mountains as the eastern boundary and the "utmost limits of Virginia" as the western and northwestern.[1] In spite of French claims to this region, the old sea-to-sea charters still possessed a potential value in the minds of the colonists, and from this time on there was a steady move westward. Gradually, toward the middle of the century, the more enterprising and farsighted of the colonists who appreciated the future value of the region began to lay plans for its systematic exploitation. In 1748, shortly after the peace of Aix-la-Chapelle, the Ohio Company, composed of London merchants and Virginia land speculators, obtained from the crown a grant of land south of the Ohio River. This was the precursor of several companies formed for similar purposes. In 1754 the question of western expansion had become of sufficient importance to engage the attention of the Albany Congress and plans for the creation of western colonies were discussed by that body.[2] The following year Samuel Hazard of

[1] Alden, *New Governments West of the Alleghanies before 1780* (University of Wisconsin Bulletin, vol. II, no. 1), 1.

[2] *Ibid.*, 1-3. No attempt is made in this study to add any new con-

Philadelphia outlined a proposition looking toward the formation of a western colony,[3] probably the first which comprehended the Illinois country.

The treaty of cession in 1763 gave a new impetus to the colonizing spirit which had lain dormant during the early years of the war. The English now believed that they were free to occupy at will the unsettled lands as far westward as the Mississippi River. Pamphlet literature was printed and disseminated throughout England and America from 1763 on, advocating the feasibility and necessity of settling the new lands. Soon after the conclusion of peace there appeared in Edinburgh a pamphlet entitled *The Expediency of securing our American Colonies by settling the country adjoining the River Mississippi*, which pointed out the expediency of locating a colony between the Ohio and Mississippi rivers and the fresh-water lakes to the northward. Such a colony, the author set forth, would give Great Britain command of the continent, would serve as a protection against the incursions of French and Indians, and secure the fur trade of the Northwest.[4] The government was urged to encourage settlers by giving lands on easy tenure, and by furnishing cattle, tools, and other necessaries. The colonists should also be given "a set of well contrived good rules with respect to their constitution, policy, economy and order, wise prudent Governors, and a sufficient number of able approven Clergymen and teachers."[5] There were doubtless many other pamphlets issued

tribution to the period preceding 1763. Mr. Alden's monograph includes an account of all the projects during that period, such as Hazard's, Pownall's, and Franklin's earlier plan.

[3] Alden, *New Governments West of the Alleghanies before 1780*, 7-11.   [4] *Ibid.*, 16.

[5] *Expeaiency of Securing our American Colonies*, 43. For a summary of other details see Alden, *New Governments West of the Alleghanies*, 14.

during the period of land fever, descriptive of the new country and its possibilities, of which we have no record.[6]

Throughout the colonies and in England many of the leading men as well as the more venturesome pioneers on the borders of New York, Pennsylvania, and Virginia were ready to take an active hand in the exploitation of the rich lands lying to the westward. Early in the summer of 1763, before the British ministry had had time to consider and determine upon its policy toward the new acquisitions, there was formed an organization known as the Mississippi Land Company,[7] for the purpose of planting a colony in the Illinois and Wabash regions. In this project some of the most prominent residents of Virginia and Maryland were directly interested; indeed, membership in the organization was drawn almost entirely from those two colonies and from England. Some of the original members of the company were George, Samuel, and John Washington; the Lees—William, Thomas, Francis Lightfoot, Richard Henry, and Arthur; Henry and William Fitzhugh, Presly Thornton, and Benedict Calvert.[8] There were thirty-eight sub-

[6] In this connection the following is of interest: "As the happy possession of the Illinois Country is the Subject of much conversation, both in England and America, we beg leave to inclose,—a small pamphlet, wrote lately, on a very interesting point—to wit, The Establishment of a Civil Government there. The Author has borrowed some of his Sentiments from De. Pratz." Baynton, Wharton and Morgan to Sir William Johnson, March 30, 1766, Johnson MSS., vol. XII, no. 128.

[7] Original Articles of Agreement of the Mississippi Company, P. R. O., Chatham Papers, vol. 97. Another copy, in the handwriting of George Washington, is in the Library of Congress. This has recently been printed by A. B. Hulbert in *Ohio Arch. and Hist. Publications*, XVII, 436–439. Most of the information concerning the proposition comes from a collection of papers relating to the company and its transactions, all in the handwriting of William Lee, which was found in a miscellaneous collection of the Earl of Chatham's papers, in the Public Record Office.

[8] Original Articles of Agreement of the Mississippi Company, P. R. O., Chatham Papers, vol. 97.

scribers to the agreement, but the company was eventually to be composed of fifty members who were to contribute equally towards the maintenance of an agent in England.[9] To this agent was intrusted the duty of soliciting from the crown a grant of two million five hundred thousand acres of land on the Mississippi [10] and its tributaries, the Wabash and Ohio rivers, including not only the so-called Illinois country of that time, but the western portion of the present States of Kentucky and Tennessee.[11]

In their petitions the memorialists enumerated the advantages which would accrue to the empire in case the land were granted, especial emphasis being laid on two points of view, commerce and defense. "The Increase of the people, the extension of trade and the enlargement of the revenue are with certainty to be expected, where the fertility of the soil, and mildness of the Climate invite emigrants (provided they can obtain Lands on easy terms)

[9] *Ibid.* The first agent in London was Thomas Cumming, who was also a stockholder in the company, Memorial to the Crown, September 9, 1763, *ibid.* Cumming's successor was Arthur Lee, Petition to the Crown, December 12, 1768, *ibid.*, printed in Butler, *Hist. of Ky.*, 381-383; see also petition of company in Privy Council Office, Unbound Papers, 1768.

[10] Memorial to the Crown, prepared at a meeting of the company at Belleview, Va., September 9, 1763, P. R. O., Chatham Papers, vol. 97, printed below in the Documentary Appendix, no. 1.

[11] For the boundaries of the proposed grant, see below, Documentary Appendix, no. 1. The original articles of agreement do not give the exact location of the proposed grant. The subscribers were to be free to retain their lands twelve years, or more at the pleasure of the crown, without the payment of taxes or quit rents. Within the same period also the company was to be obliged to settle two hundred families in the colony, unless prevented by Indians or a foreign enemy. In order to insure against any such interruption it was hinted that the government might establish and garrison two forts, one at the confluence of the Cherokee and Ohio rivers, and the other at the mouth of the Ohio. Memorial to the Crown, Documentary Appendix, no. 1. The last suggestion was withdrawn four years later at the suggestion of their London agent, Thomas Cumming. Letter of the company to Cumming, March 1, 1767, P. R. O., Chatham Papers, vol. 97.

SCHEMES FOR COLONIZATION

to settle and cultivate commodities most wanted by Great Britain and which will bear the charges of a tedious navigation, by the high prices usually given for them,—such as Hemp, Flax, Silk, Wine, Potash, Cochineal, Indigo, Iron, etc., by which means the Mother Country will be supplied with many necessary materials, that are now purchased of foreigners at a very great expense." [12]

From the point of view of both trade and defense, the company proposed "that by conducting a trade useful to the Indians on the borders of the Mississippi they will effectually prevent the success of that cruel policy, which has ever directed the French even in time of peace, to prevail with the Indians their Neighbors to lay waste the frontiers of Your Majestie's Colonies thereby to prevent their increase." [13]

Lastly the establishment of a buffer colony would effectually prevent the probable encroachment of the French from the west side of the Mississippi and cut off their political and commercial relations with the Indians. They would "thereby be prevented from instigating them to War, and the harrassing the frontier Counties as they have constantly done of all the Colonies." [14]

---

[12] Memorial to the Crown, Documentary Appendix, no. 1. Some of the members declared their intention of becoming early settlers in the new colony. The richness of the soil and mildness of the climate beyond the mountains, coupled with the "dearness and preoccupancy of the lands, within their respective colonies" which rendered it "impracticable to make a proper landed provision for their numerous families; a circumstance which begins already to restrain early marriage, and therefore speedy population", were set forth as reasons for their determination, Petition to the Crown, December 16, 1768, printed in Butler. *Hist. of Ky.*, 381–383. It may be noted that no suggestion is made with reference to the form of government for the proposed colony.

[13] Memorial to the Crown, Documentary Appendix, no. 1.

[14] Letter of the company to Thomas Cumming, September 26, 1763, P. R. O., Chatham Papers, vol. 97.

The plan received its first official check in the year of its inception, when in October, 1763, the British ministry announced its western policy in a proclamation according to which all the territory lying north of the Floridas and west of the Alleghanies was reserved for the use of the Indians.[15] Thereafter the colonial governors were forbidden to issue patents for land within this reservation without the consent of the crown.[16] However, the enunciation of this policy did not deter the Mississippi Land Company and similar organizations from pressing their claims upon the Board of Trade. The more farsighted of the Americans had probably correctly interpreted the proclamation as temporary in character and as promulgated to allay the minds of the savages.[17] The Mississippi Company therefore continued to solicit the grant until 1769, when it was decided that on account of the temper of the ministry towards America, it would be advisable to drop the affair for a time in the hope that a change of ministry would bring a cor-

---

[15] *Can. Const. Docs., 1759–1791*, 122. See also above, ch. II, pp. 13–14.

[16] *Ibid.*

[17] " I can never look upon that proclamation in any other light (but this I say between ourselves), than as a temporary expedient to quiet the minds of the Indians, and must fall, of course, in a few years, especially when those Indians are consenting to our occupying the lands." Washington to Crawford, September 21, 1767, *Writings of Washington*, ed. Ford, II, 220–221. The report of the Board of Trade on Indian affairs in 1769 admitted these claims to be "mere provisional arrangements, adopted to the exigence of the time." *Pa. Archives*, IV, 315. The same opinion is expressed in "Remarks on Lord Barrington's Plan, no. 2 " (1766), Lansdowne MSS., vol. L, p. 78. For an extreme example of the notion held by some members of the government that the proclamation of 1763 should be strictly adhered to and that all western military posts should be abandoned and à general restrictive policy toward the West adopted, see Lord Barrington's Plan relative to the Out Posts, Indian Trade, etc., 10 May, 1766, Lansdowne MSS., vol. L, pp. 49–61. Barrington, who was Secretary at War, reveals a remarkable ignorance of western affairs.

SCHEMES FOR COLONIZATION 109

responding change of policy.[18] But at no time does it appear that the promoters of the colony received the slightest encouragement from those in authority.[19]

About the time of the organization of the Mississippi Company in 1763, General Charles Lee [20] outlined a scheme

---

[18] Letter to William Lee, London, May 30, 1769, P. R. O., Chatham Papers, vol. 97.

[19] No account of any further activity on the part of the company has been found. In 1774 a copy of the correspondence was sent to the Earl of Chatham, which may have been done in the hope that his interest might be aroused in the undertaking. The bundle of papers contains the following indorsement: "Mississippi Co^s. Papers, sent to the Right Honble William Earl of Chatham, on Saturday the 20th of April 1774." Charles Lee, in speaking of this undertaking, said: "Another society solicited for lands on the lower part of the Illinois, Ohio and on the Mississippi: this was likewise rejected; but from what motives it is impossible to define, unless they suppose that soldiers invested with a little landed property, would not be so readily induced to act as the instruments of the oppression of their fellow subjects, as those whose views are solely turned, if not reduced, to farther promotion; and if reduced, to full pay." *Lee Papers*, IV (*N. Y. Hist. Soc. Colls.*, Fund series, VII), 98. Benjamin Franklin apparently knew nothing of the existence of the company until 1768. He states in his famous reply to Hillsborough, *Works*, ed. Bigelow, V, 44: "Consistent, however, with our knowledge, no more than one proposition for the settlement of a part of the lands in question has been presented to government and that was from Dr. Lee, thirty-two other Americans, and two Londoners, in the year of 1768, praying that his Majesty would grant to them without any purchase-money, two million five hundred thousand acres of land, in one or more surveys, to be located between the thirty-eighth and forty-second degree of latitude and over the Alleghany Mountains . . ." The company is mentioned in *Considerations on the Agreement . . . with the Honourable Thomas Walpole . . .*, 25-26, as being comprised of "thirty-three gentlemen of character and fortune in Virginia and Maryland, several of whom were of his Majesty's council in Virginia, and many of them, members of the house of assembly, both of that colony and of the province of Maryland." Perkins, *Annals of the West*, 130; Sato, *Hist. of the Land Question in the U. S.*, 25; H. B. Adams, *Maryland's Influence upon the Land Cessions to the U. S.*, 14; De Hass, *History of the Early Settlement and Indian Wars of Western Virginia*, 139, and the author of *Plain Facts*, 69, all note the existence of the company, but place the date of its organization in 1767. The first three quote from *Plain Facts*.

[20] The Charles Lee of Revolutionary fame.

for the establishment of two colonies, one on the Ohio River below its junction with the Wabash, and the other on the Illinois River.[21] It was his plan to organize a company and petition the crown for the necessary grants of land.[22] A portion of the settlers were to be procured in New England, and the remainder from among the Protestants of Germany and Switzerland.[23] In narrating the probable advantages to be derived from such settlements, Lee takes practically the same point of view as the promoters of the Mississippi Company, adding the suggestion that a new channel of commerce would be opened up through the Mississippi River and the Gulf of Mexico.[24] This proposal suffered the same fate as its contemporary in being rejected by the ministry, whose policy of allowing no settlements in the country beyond the mountains had been too recently adopted.[25] Apparently the authors of these projects did not have the ear of such members of the ministry as Lord Shelburne, whose general attitude gave some ground for the belief that in the end plans for western settlements would be adopted.[26]

The next definite schemes of which we have knowledge appeared in 1766, although it is probable that there were many others,[27] for during those years half of England was

[21] *Lee Papers*, IV, 214; Draper, Life of Boone (MS.), III, 266; Sparks, *Life of Charles Lee*, 19.

[22] *Lee Papers*, IV, 214.

[23] *Ibid.* [24] *Ibid.* [25] *Ibid.*

[26] B. Franklin to W. Franklin, September 27 and October 11, 1766, and June 13, August 28, and November 25, 1767, in Franklin's *Works*, ed. Bigelow, IV, 138–144; Shelburne to Gage, November 14, 1767, P. R. O., Am. and W. I., vol. 123.

[27] See for example references to Colonel Bouquet's proposition in Bouquet to Franklin, August 22, 1764, Franklin Papers (Am. Phil. Soc.), vol. I, no. 94, summarized in *Calendar of the Franklin Papers*, ed. Hays, I, 31. Among the papers in the Lansdowne collection are a number which discuss the matter in general terms.

said to have been "New Land mad and every body there has their eye fixt on this Country."[28] It is hardly probable, therefore, that the few definite proposals of which we have record were the only plans projected during those years. Indeed the colonial plan of 1766, promoted by prominent merchants and land speculators of New York, Pennsylvania, and New Jersey, had its origin, we may safely say, as early as January, 1764. At that time the Board of Trade received a communication from one of the promoters, George Croghan, who was then in England,[29] asking their Lordships "whether it would not be good policy at this time while we certainly have it in our power to secure all the advantages we have got there by making a purchase of the Indians inhabiting the Country along the Mississippi from the mouth of the Ohio up to the sources of the River Illinois, and there plant a respectable colony, in order to secure our frontiers, and prevent the French from any attempt to rival us in the Fur trade with the Natives, by drawing the Ohio and Lake Indians over the Mississippi, which they have already attempted by the last accounts we have from Detroit."[30] In spite of the recent announcement in the proclamation of 1763 of the land policy of the government, which interdicted all settlements beyond the line of the Alleghanies, without royal consent, the ministry at this time must have been favorably im-

[28] Croghan to Johnson, March 30, 1766, Johnson MSS., vol. XII, no. 127.

[29] Sir William Johnson sent his agent Croghan to England to sound the ministry on the question of the boundary between the frontier and the Indian territory. Winsor, *Westward Movement*, 9; *cf.* also *N. Y. Col. Docs.*, VII, 603. Croghan was also instructed to petition the government for a grant of land south of the Ohio to satisfy the claims of the Ohio company, and of those soldiers whom Dinwiddie had enlisted in 1754 with promises of land, Winsor, *Westward Movement*, 8.

[30] *N. Y. Col. Docs.*, VII, 605.

pressed by Croghan's advice, for the latter informs us a few months later that "there is a talk of setleing a Colony from the mouth of the Ohio to the Illinois, which I am tould Lord Halifax will Desier my opinion of in a few Days. Mr. pownal tould me yesterday that I would be soon sent for to attend the board of Trade. what Meshures they will Take the Lord knows, but nothing is talkt of except Oconomy."[31]

No further action, however, was taken at this time. But the tentative proposition thus suggested to the Board was in essence the same plan that Croghan and his associates developed two years later. In the general outline of Croghan's earlier plan there is no suggestion that he intended to include the cultivated lands of the French inhabitants of the Illinois villages who might leave that country after the occupation by the British.[32] Two years subsequently, however, Sir William Johnson, Croghan's superior in the Indian department in America and his constant associate in colonizing enterprises, in a communication to the Board of Trade, gave as his opinion that " some of the present Inhabitants may possibly incline to go home, and our Traders will, I dare say, chuse to purchase their rights, this may be the foundation for a Valuable Colony in that Country, . . . this may be effected in time, and large concessions obtained of the Natives."[33] The idea of basing a colony in

---

[31] Croghan to Johnson, March 10, 1764, Johnson MSS., vol. VIII, no. 202. The style of the letter is characteristic of Croghan. His official letters, however, were usually put into form by some one else.

[32] Later, however, he adopted that idea, Croghan to Johnson, March 30, 1766, Johnson MSS., vol. XII, no. 127,

[33] Johnson to Lords of Trade, January 31, 1766, *N. Y. Col. Docs.*, VII, 809. When Croghan was preparing to go to the Illinois villages in 1766 to bring about a general pacification of the Indians, Johnson wrote him: " So soon as I hear farther from the General [Gage] I shall write you and send the Instructions in which I shall insert an Article directing you to enquire into the French Bounds and Property at the Illinois. I have no objection to what you propose on that sub-

part upon lands vacated by the French was also taken up and emphasized a few weeks later by General Gage.

Very early in the period of the British occupation of the West the chief representatives of the military department, upon whom devolved the responsibility of governing the territory, became exceedingly embarrassed on account of the immense expense which the department was called upon to meet in providing for the maintenance of garrisons among the French inhabitants scattered throughout the Indian country. In 1766, the year of the repeal of the Stamp Act, the imperial government was conscious not only of the necessity of maintaining in America a force sufficient to put down a probable uprising of the Indians and to guard the country against French encroachments, but also of the obligation to curtail expenses. General Gage, therefore, became keenly alive to the necessity of resorting to some expedient to reduce the enormous cost of transporting provisions and other necessities from the seacoast to such distant parts as Fort de Chartres. With reference to the Illinois country in particular, he reported to the home government [34] that he was "a good deal disappointed that any Demand should be made for Provisions, as the country used to abound with it, and none can be supplied from our Provisions, but with great difficulty, and at enormous Expense." "This want," he continued, "must arise from the Inhabitants abandoning their Farms to go over to the new French Settlements, and the only method which appears to me the most proper to obviate

ject there, and as the French are now said to be retiring fast, you will have the better opportunity of making a good Choice on which the value will chiefly depend." Johnson to Croghan, March 28, 1766, Johnson MSS., vol. XII, no. 121.

[34] Gage to Conway, March 28, 1766, B. T. Papers (Hist. Soc. Pa.), vol. XX.

Difficulties on account of Food, as well as to strengthen those parts at the least Expense, is to grant the Lands deserted by the French, which I presume forfeited, as well as other Lands unsettled, using necessary Precautions to avoid Disputes with the Indians, to the British Settlers. All Endeavours must be used to procure a Supply of Provisions upon the Spot, and I have directed the Officer commanding to get seed, and try to make his men cultivate the Ground near the Fort." Gage next proposed, as we have already noted in another connection,[35] that a military governor be appointed immediately for the Illinois country, on account of the distance of the villages from any of the English provinces and because of their proximity to the French settlements on the Spanish side of the river, which would make any other form of government impracticable. Amplifying his idea further he declared that "Lands should be granted without Delay, by any Person authorized properly to do it; but no fees to be taken by the person who grants, or by Secretarys, Clerks, Surveyors, or other Persons whatever: That no large Tracts should be given, but the Lands granted in Farms, consisting of an Hundred and Fifty or Two Hundred Acres of good Land, unless perhaps to Half Pay Officers, who might have Four or Five Hundred Acres. People may be tempted on these Advantages to transport themselves with a Year's Provisions, Seed Corn and Tools for Husbandry, down the Ohio. The Lands shall be held of the King on condition of Military Service, and such other Obligations as shall be convenient."

It has seemed necessary to go into Gage's plan in some detail because in the first place it represents an attitude toward western colonization quite contrary to the position he assumed a few years later, when he strongly opposed

[35] See above, ch. II, pp. 18–19.

SCHEMES FOR COLONIZATION

such movements.[36] In addition these details give us some perception of the purposes which Gage had in mind in the establishment of a colony, the saving of the heavy expense incurred in transporting provisions into the interior, and to protect the empire, by a buffer colony, from possible incursions of French and Spanish.

Although not connected with any other projects of the time this proposal of General Gage undoubtedly gave some encouragement to the promoters of a larger colony, who now began to develop the ideas of Croghan and Johnson into something tangible. About the same time Governor William Franklin of New Jersey, together with the Philadelphia firm of Baynton, Wharton and Morgan, and Joseph Galloway and John Hughes, also of the colony of Pennsylvania, conceived the idea of forming a land company for the definite purpose of purchasing such lands at the Illinois villages as the French might desire to sell, as well as to obtain a grant for other lands in the adjoining country. Accordingly, in March, 1766, they drew up some articles of agreement [37] for the proposed company, which provided among other things that application was to be made to the crown for a grant of 1,200,000 acres of land in the Illinois country or "more if to be procured".[38] Provision was also made for ten equal shareholders, the stipulation to be subject to change in case others desired to enter the company.[39] Apparently Sir William Johnson and his deputy, Croghan, were not directly concerned in the formation of this company, but they were immediately invited to enter,

---

[36] See below.

[37] Articles of Agreement, dated March 29, 1766, MS. in Hist. Soc. Pa. Library.

[38] Articles of Agreement, March 29, 1766.   [39] *Ibid.*

and Croghan, who was then in Philadelphia, signed the contract on behalf of himself and Johnson.[40]

The land company thus organized was intended to be the foundation of a permanent colony in the northwest country. Governor Franklin, in a letter to his father, Dr. Franklin, who was at the time in London as agent for the colony of Pennsylvania, explained the proposition to him as follows: "A few of us, from his [Croghan's] Encouragement, have form'd a Company to Purchase of the French Settled at the Illinois, such Lands as they have a good Title to, and are inclined to dispose of. But as I thought it would be of little Avail to buy Lands in that Country, unless a Colony were established there, I have drawn up some Proposals for that Purpose, which are much approved of by Col. Croghan and the other Gent^m. concerned in Philad^l. and are sent by them to S^r. W. for his Sentiments which when we receive, the whole will be forwarded to

[40] Writing to Johnson, March 30, Croghan explained: "Soon after my Return here [Philadelphia] from your Honour's I wrote you about the Scheme of purchasing whatever Grants the french was possess'd of in the Illinois Country and imform'd your Honour that Governor franklin with some other Gentlemen hear had form'd the same scheme and offered me to be concerned with them and your Honour, since w'h I have agreed with them in behalf of your Honour and myself . . . itt is likewise preposed to apply for a grant of 1200,000 acres to the crown in that Country and to take into this Grant two or three Gentlemen of Fortune and Influence in England and Governor franklin and those other Gentlemen Desire to know whome your Honour wold chouse to be concerned, and that you wold write to them if you should nott name ye whole you would chouse they Designe to Save y Nomination of such as you dont to Dr. franklin who they prepose to send the proposals to . . ." Johnson MSS., vol. XII, no. 127. According to the Articles of Agreement, as we have them, there were to be ten equal shareholders, but Croghan informs Johnson that the persons and shares were as follows: Sir William Johnson, 2/16, Governor Franklin, 2/16, John Baynton, 2/16, George Croghan, 2/16, Samuel Wharton, 2/16, George Morgan, 2/16, Joseph Wharton, Jr., 1/16, Joseph Wharton, Sr., 1/16, John Hughes, 1/16, and Joseph Galloway, 1/16, *ibid*. It may be suggested that possibly a different arrangement was made after the signing of the original contract.

SCHEMES FOR COLONIZATION

you. It is proposed that the Comp^y. shall consist of 12 now in America, and if you like the Proposals, you will be at Liberty to add yourself, and such other gentlemen of Character and Fortune in England as you may think will be likely to promote the Undertaking." [41]

The proposals mentioned in Governor Franklin's letter were outlined by him along with the Articles of Agreement; indeed the substance of the latter was included in the proposals for a colony.[42] Franklin enumerates a number of reasons why the establishment of a colony on the Mississippi River and its environs was desirable. The attention of the ministry was called to some of the natural products of the Illinois and the Mississippi valley countries and to the many advantages of soil and climate over other regions of North America. He declared that if the lands on the Mississippi were settled " we should be enabled to supply all Europe with those commodities, and at a far cheaper Rate than they could be afforded from any other Country." The adaptability of the western country to the cultivation of tobacco, hemp, flax, indigo, and silk was positively affirmed. " Great Britain might also ", he continued, " be furnished from thence with Cotton, Copper, Iron, Pot Ash, Wine, Salt Petre, a great variety of valuable Medicinal Drugs, and

---

[41] April 30, 1766, Franklin Papers (Am. Phil. Soc.), II, no. 17. He observes further that "Mr. Galloway has met with a Pamphlet at Mr. Hill's on the Subject, which I wish I had seen before I had drawn up the Proposals, as it might have afforded some Hints. However, as I believe you have not seen it, it being printed, and I believe wrote in Scotland, I send it enclosed. You will find your Name ment. in it, page 52." The reference to the pamphlet is doubtless to *Expediency of Securing our American Colonies by Settling the Country adjoining the River Mississippi.*

[42] "Reasons for establishing a British Colony at the Illinois with some proposals for carrying the same into immediate Execution ", B. T. Papers (Hist. Soc. Pa.), vols. XXVII–XXVIII; Franklin Papers (Am. Phil. Soc.), vol. LVIII, no. 4. See Documentary Appendix, no. 2.

other Articles, which, with those mentioned before, make the great Ballance of Trade against the Nation, and drain it of its Treasure."

Speaking more specifically of the district of Illinois, he asserted confidently that Great Britain would "carry on a more extensive and advantageous Fur-Trade, with the numerous Indian Nations which reside near the Lakes and the different Branches of the Mississippi, than was ever known since the first settlement of America—Supplying them with British Manufactures to a vast Amount." It is pointed out that the French could not rival the English in that branch of commerce because the latter could transport goods through Pennsylvania and Virginia to the West much more cheaply than could be done from New Orleans up the Mississippi. "For want of this Opening thro' the middle Provinces of North America to the Mississippi, the French never had it in their Power to reap so much advantage from that Country as the English now may."

Governor Franklin then raised the question of the most efficacious method of supporting the posts which had so recently been taken from the French. The solution offered was the establishment of a colony with a civil government. This, it will be noticed, differed from the plan of Gage, in that he believed a military government best suited to the circumstances. "If We have not a Colony on the Spot to support the Posts We are now possessed of in that Country, the French who have a Fort and an increasing Settlement on the opposite Shore of the Mississippi, will have it in their Power, by means of their influence with the Indians, to intercept our Supplies, interrupt our Trade, and ultimately cutt off all Communication between the Illinois and the present English Colonies." The suggestion was made that a well-established colony would not only prevent the French

SCHEMES FOR COLONIZATION

and Indians from interfering, but the English would be enabled to dispossess the French of the remainder of Louisiana, "should a future War make it expedient".

The more important proposals submitted for the consideration of the ministry were:[43] (1) To purchase from the Indians all their rights to the territory in the Illinois country, not already occupied by the French. (2) To establish a civil government.[44] (3) To lay out the proposed land grant in townships.[45] (4) To give grants to provincial officers

---

[43] To each proposal was appended a paragraph of remarks, which may have been added by Sir William Johnson, to whom the proposals had been sent for such amendments or alterations as he thought necessary. Croghan to Johnson, March 30, 1766, Johnson MSS., vol. XII, no. 127; Governor Franklin to his father, April 30, 1766, Franklin Papers (Am. Phil. Soc.), II, 17.

[44] The promoters of the colony evidently thought that the government intended to establish a civil government in the West. In the Articles of Agreement of the land company, we find the statement that, "it is expected that a Civil Government will be established by his Majesty in the Illinois country at or near Fort Chartres." Croghan about the same time wrote: "By Leters from England there is the greatest reason to believe that a government will soon take place there, if so a thing of this Kind must be very valuable provided we succeed." Croghan to Johnson, March 30, 1766, Johnson MSS., vol. XII, no. 127. John Baynton, one of the original subscribers, and a prominent merchant of Philadelphia, wrote to James Rumsey that a civil government was soon to be formed in the Illinois country, March 1, 1766, Ohio Company Papers (Hist. Soc. Pa.), I, 52. Note also the reference in note 6, above. The following extract is of interest in this connection: "In case of laying aside the superintendents [of Indian affairs], a provision is thought of for Sir William Johnson. He will be made governor of the new colony." B. Franklin to his son, August 28, 1767, *Works*, ed. Bigelow, IV, 141.

[45] Evidently the authors of the proposals made use of the suggestions in Smith's *Historical Account of the Expedition against the Ohio Indians*. " Let all the Lands which may be granted within the first twenty years be laid out in Townships, after the manner practised in some of the New England Colonies, or according to the Plan laid down in the Historical Account of the Expedition under Colonel Bouquet, lately published (quod vide)." In this work the township system as we know it to-day was outlined. The work is most available now in the Ohio Valley Historical Series, see below in Bibliography. Sir William Johnson was doubtless familiar with the work, for in January, 1766,

and soldiers who served in the French war. (5) To concede mines and minerals to the owners of the land in which they may be found, except royal mines, from which the crown might reserve one fifth.[46] (6) To reserve five hundred acres in every township for the maintenance of a clergyman of the Established Church of England.[47] (7) To bound the colony as follows : " From the mouth of the Ouisconsin (or Wisconsing) River down the Mississippi agreeable to Treaty, to the Fork or Mouth of the Ohio. Then up the same River Ohio to the River Wabash, thence up the same River Wabash to the Portage at the head thereof, Then by the said Portage to the River Miamis and down the said River Miamis to Lake Erie. Thence along the several Courses of the said Lake to Riviere al Ours (or Bear River) and up the said River thereof, and from thence in a Straight Line, or by the Portage of St. Joseph's River and down the same River to Lake Michigan, then along the several Courses of said Lake on the South and West Side thereof to the point of Bay Puans, and along the several courses on the East Side of the said Bay to the Mouth of Foxes River, thence up to the Head thereof and from thence by a Portage to the Head of Ouisconsin River, and down the same to the

Dr. William Smith, of Philadelphia, sent him a copy. See article by Charles Whittlesey, in *Journal of the Association of Engineering Societies*, vol. III, no. 11, p. 278.

[46] Lead-mining was an important industry in the Illinois country in the eighteenth century, but at this time it was largely in the hands of the French and Spanish west of the Mississippi River, see Thwaites, " Early Lead-mining in Illinois and Wisconsin," in *Annual Report, Amer. Hist. Assoc.*, 1893, pp. 191-196.

[47] This clause throws an interesting side-light. In the " Remark," presumably by Johnson (see above, note 43), appended to the clause he says the church " ought to be well supported there, otherwise Presbyterianism will become the Established Religion in that Country. It is interesting to note that the Bayntons, the Whartons, Morgan, and the other participants in this movement were Quakers.

1768 he stated definitely that no objection could be had to such colonies,[102] and at the first suggestion of the Vandalia grant south of the Ohio, warmly supported it.[103]

It is necessary to bear in mind that the imperial government during the decade under consideration was becoming more and more embarrassed by the many problems of imperial administration. The great war just closed had resulted in bringing upon the government many new responsibilities, not the least of which was the administration of the newly-ceded territories and the defence of the empire. It is not surprising, therefore, that the members of the ministry should hesitate to sanction the establishment of new colonial governments when questions of administration and finance were already causing serious difficulties between the mother country and the established colonies. The factor of expense entered into the consideration of every new project and the colonial schemes were no exception to this rule, especially since the government was asked to bear a certain part of the expense.

The correspondence of Shelburne and Franklin shows that at the first suggestion of the proposed settlements this factor was uppermost in the mind of the former.[104] Shelburne became convinced that ultimately this objection would be

---

[102] "Representation of the Lords of Trade on the State of Indian Affairs, March 7, 1768", *N. Y. Col. Docs.*, VIII, 28–31.

[103] Franklin to his son, July 14, 1773, *Works*, ed. Bigelow, V, 197. With the reason for Hillsborough's later opposition the present study is not concerned.

[104] Franklin to his son, October 11, 1766, *Works*, ed. Bigelow, IV, 139, quoted above in note 63. "In case your Lordships should think it right to advise his Majesty to establish these New Governments, you will consider whether it will not be practicable to fall upon such a Plan as will avoid great part of the Expense incurred by the Estimates of the New Governments established after the Peace." Shelburne to Lords of Trade, October 5, 1767, B. T. Papers (Hist. Soc. Pa.), vol. XXVII; and *N. Y. Col. Docs.*, VII, 981.

overcome, but Hillsborough was not of that opinion. Writing to Gage shortly after the issuance of the report he dwelt at considerable length upon the necessity of avoiding an increased expense on any account: [105] " It appears to his Majesty that in the present state of the Kingdom its future Safety and Welfare do in great measure depend upon the relieving it from every Expence that is not an absolute necessity, and therefore though his Majesty applauds the Motives which induced the first Institution of the present plan of Indian Superintendency, which was evidently calculated to regain the Confidence, and combine the Force of the Savages against a then powerful Enemy, yet, as in the present State of America, the main object of that Plan, if not entirely removed are at least greatly diminished . . . His Majesty concurs in opinion with his Board of Trade, that the laying aside that part of it [the Plan of Superintendency] which relates to the Indian Trade and entrusting the entire management of that Trade to the colonies themselves will be of Publick Utility and Advantage, as a means of avoiding much Difficulty and saving much Expense to this Country both in present and in future . . . The Propriety therefore of entrusting the Management of the Trade with the Indians to the Colonies, does . . . appear to His Majesty to depend in great measure upon a reduction of such Posts in the Indian Country, as are by their situation, exposed to the Resentment of the Savages, it being evident that in Proportion as the number of such Posts is diminished, the Necessity of carrying on an Indian War at the Expense of this Kingdom will be less. . . . His Majesty has not failed in this great and extensive Consideration to give due attention to Propositions, which have

[105] April 15, 1768, P. R. O., Am. and W. I., vol. 124.

been made with regard to the Establishments on the Rivers Mississippi, Ohio and Illinois. But as his Majesty has doubts concerning the Utility of Establishments in such remote situations, which consequently cannot be kept up, but at an immense Expence, it is the King's pleasure that you should report your Opinion with regard to the continuance of any of the Forts in those situations. . . ."[106]

It should be noted that in the report of the Board of Trade in 1768 great emphasis is placed upon the general commercial and political inutility of the proposed colonies, but there is no suggestion that the matter of expense stood in the way. On the other hand there is an intimation that the clause in the proclamation of 1763, reserving the interior country for the use of the Indians, was inserted there on the principle that all settlements should be confined to the sea-coast. Again in a similar report in 1772 against

[106] A few weeks later Gage replied to Hillsborough: "From what has been represented your Lordship will perceive that I am not of opinion that a Post at the Illinois will be productive of advantages equal to the expence of supporting it." June 16, 1768, P. R. O., Am. and W. I., vol. 124. Two years later he again wrote to Hillsborough: "I conceive that to procure all the commerce it will afford and at as little expence to ourselves as we can, is the only object we should have in view in the interior Country for a century to come . . . I am of opinion the advantages we might propose to gain from Civil and Military Establishments at the mouths of those Rivers [Ohio and Illinois] would be greatly disproportionate to the Expences, they would be attended with." November 10, 1770, *ibid.*, vol. 126. Hillsborough writes in the same year: "Forts and Military Establishments at the mouths of the Ohio and Illinois Rivers, admitting that they would be effectual to the attainment of the objects in view would yet, I fear, be attended with an Expence to this Kingdom greatly disproportionate to the advantages to be gained and those objections to Civil Establishments which I have above stated, do weigh so strongly against that measure in the scale both of general and local policy, as greatly to discourage that idea." The latter part refers to his argument against the commercial utility of a regular settlement in the West, which he declared, "cannot be of that commercial benefit to the state which it would be of in other places". Hillsborough to Gage, July 31, 1770, *ibid.*

the proposed Vandalia or Walpole grant,[107] emphasis is placed upon that clause; indeed it is advanced as the chief argument for the rejection of the proposition.[108] But nowhere in the Hillsborough-Gage correspondence is there the slightest intimation that Hillsborough had the proclamation of 1763 in mind. It would seem reasonable to assume that if he believed that the clause in that document

---

[107] After 1768 the attention of land and colony promoters was turned to the region of the upper Ohio River valley. In 1768 the long-proposed Indian boundary line was determined at the treaty of Fort Stanwix and there was opened up for colonization a wide strip of territory in that region. A company was formed in the same year for the establishment of a colony, some of the members being Benjamin Franklin, Thomas Pownall, Thomas Walpole, and the firm of Baynton, Wharton and Morgan. In 1770, the crown was petitioned for a grant, but in 1772 the Board of Trade, still under the leadership of Hillsborough, reported adversely. This report called forth a vigorous answer from Dr. Franklin, which completely demolished the arguments of Hillsborough. His successor, Lord Dartmouth, began at once to make arrangements for the establishment of a colony, but the whole matter was dropped on the outbreak of the American Revolution. For a full account see Alden, *New Governments West of the Alleghanies before 1780*, 19–35. The following writers have confused the Walpole grant with the plan of 1766: Hinsdale, *Old Northwest*, 133; Peyton, *Hist. of Augusta Co., Va.*, 144 ff; Fitzmaurice, *Life of Shelburne*, II, 31; Bigelow, in Franklin's *Works*, IV, 136; Perkins, *Annals of the West*, 127; Adams, *Maryland's Influence upon the Land Cessions to the U. S.*, 13.

[108] This interpretation by Hillsborough may be entirely disregarded. He was not responsible for that particular clause in the proclamation. It was conceived and written by Lord Shelburne himself, as has been pointed out by Alvord, "Genesis of the Proclamation of 1763", in *Mich. Pioneer and Hist. Colls.*, XXXVI, 31 ff. He has shown that Shelburne did not have in mind the principle of confining the colonies to the sea-coast. Coffin, in *Province of Quebec and the Am. Rev.*, 428, and Alden, in *New Governments West of the Alleghanies before 1780*, 43–44, have also rejected Hillsborough's interpretation. For the old view that the proclamation was intended to confine the colonies to the sea-coast, see for example Hinsdale, *Old Northwest*, ch. VIII, and the same author, "The Western Land Policy of the British Government from 1763 to 1775", in *Ohio Archaeological and Historical Quarterly*, December, 1887. There is positive proof of Shelburne's position in a minute submitted by him to the cabinet in 1767, Lansdowne MSS., vol. L, p. 185.

SCHEMES FOR COLONIZATION

stood in the way, some mention of it would have been made in his many communications to General Gage and Sir William Johnson. Nor does Franklin intimate it in any of his private correspondence on the subject. In order to justify his position with some appearance of legality, it is probable that Hillsborough brought forward that clause in the proclamation, which had been interpreted by nearly every one else as merely temporary in character.

There was still another important reason for the rejection of interior settlements, which comes to light in contemporary correspondence, but which is not contained in the report of the Board of Trade. During this period Louisiana, with New Orleans commanding the mouth of the Mississippi River, was in the hands of Spain. New Orleans was practically the only outlet for the western country, and it was the settled conviction of many that so long as it remained in the possession of a foreign power, it was useless to expect much from the West. In 1768 Lieutenant George Phyn of the regular army was sent from Fort Pitt down the Ohio and Mississippi rivers to Mobile, and in writing to Sir William Johnson he declared that the country in and about the Illinois region would never be settled " with any advantage to England " unless New Orleans were procured.[109]

In a communication to Secretary Hillsborough in 1770, in which he argued at length against the establishment of settlements or of any additional military posts in the West, General Gage declared that no further time or money should

---

[109] April 15, 1768, Johnson MSS., vol. XXV, no. 109. He affirmed that a settlement "will never happen with any advantage to England until we can procure the Ideal Island of Orleans: . . could we find passage for even small craft to go to the Sea, the Country of the Illinois would be worthy of attention, but had we the Island of Orleans, that country would in a very short time I believe be equal to any of our Colonies." *Ibid.*

be expended on that country, and particularly the Illinois country, because it would be of no conceivable " advantage to the King's subjects, unless New Orleans was added to His Majesty's Possessions ".[110]

In the same year Lord Hillsborough himself mentioned one of the chief objections which he considered to "lie against Colonies in the Illinois with a view to the Peltry Trade, which is the peculiar Commerce of that Country." "This Commerce", he affirmed, "cannot (I apprehend) be useful to Great Britain otherwise than as it furnishes a material for her Manufactures, but it will on the contrary be prejudicial to her in proportion as other Countries obtain that material from us without its coming here first; and whilst New Orleans is the only Port for Exportation of what goes down the Mississippi, no one will believe that that town will not be the market for Peltry or that those Restrictions, which are intended to secure the Exportation of that Commodity directly to G. Britain, can have any effect under such circumstances."[111]

In this connection it should be noted that throughout this decade there were serious thoughts of an attack upon Louisiana and New Orleans should a war with Spain afford the opportunity. One of the reasons offered by Governor Franklin in 1766 for the establishment of a colony in the Illinois country was that such a colony would enable the English to get possession of the whole of Louisiana " should a future war make it expedient".[112] We find Gage himself discussing with General Haldimand, who was stationed in

---

[110] November 10, 1770, P. R. O., Am. and W. I., vol. 126.

[111] Hillsborough to Gage, July 31, 1770, *ibid*.

[112] Reasons for the Establishment of a Colony, Franklin Papers (Am. Phil. Soc.), vols. XXVII, XXVIII; same idea expressed in Remarks on Lord Barrington's Plan, no. 2, Lansdowne MSS., vol. L, p. 80.

SCHEMES FOR COLONIZATION

West Florida during the latter half of this period, possible plans for an attack in case war should be declared.[11]

In 1770 the cherished opportunity seemed to have arrived. In that year the dispute between England and Spain over the possession of certain of the Falkland Islands, lying near the Strait of Magellan, brought the two nations to the verge of war.[114] Hillsborough evidently expected war, for in January, 1771, he communicated secret instructions to Gage in New York[115] to mobilize an army and to prepare for the invasion of Louisiana. He commissioned Gage as commander of the invading forces and instructed him to use his own judgment as to the time and method of attack. Gage replied[116] that he would at once assemble a body of troops and prepare for the invasion. He further

---

[113] Hamilton, *Colonial Mobile*, 2–29. The English officers in West Florida were instructed to inform Gage as to the number of troops and inhabitants the Spaniards might bring to Louisiana, and whether any of the old French colonial troops entered the Spanish service, Gage to Brigadier Taylor, June 10, 1766; B. M. Add. MSS., 21, 662, fol. 214. In 1767, General Haldimand sent Captain Marsh from Pensacola to New Orleans to make a special inquiry relative to the British trade, the disposition of the French and Acadians towards the Spanish, and the treatment of the Indians and French by the Spaniards, J. Marsh to Haldimand, November 20, 1767, *ibid.*, 21, 728. The keenest interest was always taken in the movements of the Spanish, especially with reference to how many troops were to be sent up the Mississippi and how many and what ports on that river were to be garrisoned. See for example, Captain Innis to Haldimand, October 11, 1769, Can. Arch., series B, vol. 69, p. 60. Haldimand wrote to Gage, June 12, 1770, that "although on the one hand the military Force, which you are informed General O'Reilly intends to leave in the Colony, is too small to create much alarm, yet on the other the appointment of a Company of French under the Command of an Active French Officer for the upper Posts of the Mississippi is a circumstance that wears a suspicious appearance." P. R. O., Am. and W. I., vol. 126.

[114] Hunt, *Pol. Hist. of Eng.*, X, 112–114.

[115] January 2, 1771, P. R. O., Am. and W. I., vol. 127. See Documentary Appendix, no. 3.

[116] Gage to Hillsborough, April 2, 1771, P. R. O., Am. and W. I., vol. 127. See Documentary Appendix, no. 4.

declared his intention of approaching Louisiana and New Orleans by way of the Ohio and Mississippi rivers, and actually sent reinforcements to Fort de Chartres.[117] Soon after the despatch of Hillsborough, however, Spain acceded to the demands of England, and the attack upon New Orleans was given up.[118]

In conclusion it may be observed that after 1768 the attention of those most interested in the colonizing of Illinois was turned in another direction. In that year, at the treaty of Fort Stanwix, the boundary line between the Indians and the whites was determined, thus opening for settlement a large tract of land in the region south of the Ohio River. There was formed in the same year a company, called the Walpole or Vandalia Company, for the purpose of establishing a colony there. Although Hillsborough again opposed the scheme, he was overruled, and the grant was made. But the Revolution put an end to further progress in the scheme. In the Illinois country there was another revival of land speculation in 1773, which, however, was simply an attempt of individuals and companies to purchase large tracts of land from the Indians without applying to the crown, a proceeding manifestly contrary to the proclamation of 1763.[119]

[117] "I have advices that the Artillery and Stores sent down the Ohio for Fort Chartres, have got into the Mississippi, and were going up to the Fort. The prospect of a war with Spain could not be concealed, for the news had been conveyed by many hands." Gage to Hillsborough, August 6, 1771, P. R. O., Am. and W. I., vol. 127.

[118] Gage to Hillsborough, March 7, 1771, *ibid.*

[119] It is of interest to note that in 1770, Dr. Connolly, a nephew of George Croghan, and a prominent land speculator in the West, proposed to George Washington that a colony ought to be erected south of the Ohio River, "to be bounded . . . by the Ohio northward, and westward, the ridge that divides the waters of the Tennessee or Cherokee River southward and westward, and a line to be run from the falls of Ohio, or above, so as to cross the Shawna River above the fork of it". "Washington's Tour on the Ohio", *Writings*, ed. Ford, II, 315.

CHAPTER VII.

THE STRUGGLE FOR A CIVIL GOVERNMENT, 1770-1774.

THE action of Commandant Wilkins in abolishing the court of judicatory and in assuming again all judicial powers,[1] aroused the French people in Illinois to take a decided stand for their rights. From this time they ceased to depend on their English associates, whose actions were often inspired by selfish motives, and who were frequently connected with the speculative schemes of the eastern merchants for exploiting the country by means of American settlers. The French people perceived that their interests would not be subserved by such measures, and that they might fulfill by themselves along different lines what had been in the minds of the English speculators. Under the administration of Lord Hillsborough, the great opponent of western expansion, restriction seemed to have become a permanent policy, and by 1770 many of the English traders, who had been interested in the promoters' schemes, had become disheartened and were leaving Illinois. The plan of a French colony appeared to be justified, however, by the actual settlements in existence, and the French leaders might reasonably hope that, proper representations being made to the ministry, no opposition to the creation

[1] See above, ch. IV, p. 72. Regular sessions of a court were held from July, 1770, to January 30, 1773, but there were no regular judges, and the judgments were those of the military commandants, see MS. Court Record (Chester, Illinois).

of a French colonial government on the Mississippi would be met.

It was with this idea in mind that the leaders of the French inhabitants called an assembly on August 24, 1770, shortly after the downfall of the court.[2] Daniel Bloüin, a citizen of Kaskaskia, was chosen to go to New York and explain the situation to General Gage.[3] He took with him a document enumerating some of the grievances of the people against the military commandant and certain of the English merchants,[4] and instructions to use all possible efforts to obtain the promise of a civil government for the country.[5] The French people had thus advanced beyond their position of 1768,[6] and, without the assistance of the resident English,[7] had assumed the initiative in a new movement for the extension of civil rights to the colony.

The French agent, Daniel Bloüin, chose as an associate in this mission William Clazon, a Frenchman with some understanding of English usages.[8] Arriving in New York

[2] MS. Court Record, p. 108.

[3] *Ibid.*, p. 107; Hamilton to Gage, August 8, 1772, P. R. O., Am. and W. I., vol. 128; Gage to Dartmouth, January 6, 1773, *ibid.*

[4] Gage to Hillsborough, August 6, 1771, *ibid.*, vol. 127; Gage to Dartmouth, January 6, 1773, *ibid.*, vol. 128; Bloüin to Dartmouth, October 6, 1773, B. T. Papers (Hist. Soc. Pa.), vol. XXXI.

[5] He was authorized "à faire toutes les Démarches légitimes qui 'l conviendera de faire en notre nom pour tâcher d'obtenir de son Excellence Monsieur le Major Général Thomas Gage . . . le redressement de nos Griefs, et Prier sa ditte Excellence . . . d' entercéder Pour nous auprès de sa Majesté afin d'en obtenir l'Establissement du Gouvernement Civil . . . " MS. Court Record, p. 107.

[6] See above, ch. IV, p. 60.

[7] There is no trace of Morgan in Illinois after 1770. Many others left about the same time, see Gage to Dartmouth, May 5, 1773, P. R. O., Am. and W. I., vol. 128.

[8] Gage to Hillsborough, August 6, 1771, *ibid.*, vol. 127. Clazon's name does not appear as a resident of the Illinois villages, nor has his name been located in the Canadian genealogical registers. For Gage's estimate of Clazon see below, p. 151.

STRUGGLE FOR CIVIL GOVERNMENT

in 1771, they presented their credentials and memorial to General Gage on July 9th,[9] and prayed that a civil government be established in the Illinois country. Although their reception was not very favorable, Gage finally did demand an outline of their plan.[10] The agents set to work to produce a draft of government [11]—Gage speaks of it as a rough

---

[9] Bloüin to Dartmouth, October 6, 1773, B. T. Papers (Hist. Soc. Pa.), vol. XXXI. The exact date of their departure from Illinois and arrival in New York does not appear. September 3, 1770, Bloüin gave power of attorney to continue during his absence to Joseph Charleville, his father-in-law, Louis Viviat, and Piérre Girardot, Kaskaskia Record Book, British Period. He was still in Illinois in November, 1770, for in that month he acted as attorney for Viviat, *ibid.*, p. 171. It is probable that they arrived in New York in the early summer of 1771.

[10] Gage to Dartmouth, January 6, 1773, P, R. O., Am. and W. I., vol. 128.

[11] This episode has been discussed by several writers. In *Hist. of U. S.*, IV, 741, Bancroft states that the people of Illinois met together and prepared a plan of government, providing for institutions like those of Connecticut, which was forwarded by them to General Gage through their agent Daniel Bloüin. This, however, is an error. In detailing the account of his negotiations with the agents, Gage declared that "he [Bloüin] presented me memorials that related solely to complaints of which he desired redress, but delivered no memorials containing propositions for the forming of a Civil Constitution which from the contents of my Dispatch, Your Lordship was led to conclude I had received from him. The people's wishes or desires of a Civil Government being however, mentioned, gave occasion to my sending afterwards to Mr. Bloüin and his associate Mr. Clazon to know what kind of Government the people expected and w'd be satisfied with . . . ; and received for answer that it would require a great deal of time to form a plan of the kind." He then asked for a brief outline of their plan, and they drew up a "rough sketch", Gage to Dartmouth, January 6, 1773, P. R. O., Am. and W. I., vol. 128. This letter was in answer to that of John Pownall, one of the under secretaries, who wrote on October 7, 1772: "I think it necessary in the absence of Lord Dartmouth who is at present in the Country, to acquaint you that your Dispatch No. 76, has been received and laid before the King, but the regulations for a Civil Government proposed by the Inhabitants of the Illinois . . . were not included in your Packet." *Ibid.*, and Dartmouth Papers, *Fourteenth Report, Royal Hist. MSS. Comm.*, Appendix X, 98. Gage answered Pownall as follows: "You had good

outline—which was probably the work of Clazon, for the model of the proposed government was the constitution of Connecticut,[12] the most liberal of the eastern colonies, of which the average Illinois Frenchman could have known nothing.

Such a proposition was naturally rejected by the general,[13] who, in order to gain more information concerning their actual sentiments, and to discredit, if possible, the two representatives,[14] directed Major Hamilton, the acting commandant in Illinois, to sound the people as to their

Reasons from my Letter and the Extract inclosed, to suppose that there had been an Omission in not transmitting the said Proposals of the Inhabitants, but I never received them from Monsieur Bloüin and I explain that matter by this Opportunity to the Earl of Dartmouth." January 6, 1773, P. R. O., Am. and W. I., vol. 128. Bancroft's error has been repeated by Mason, *Chapters from Ill. Hist.*, 282, and by Parrish, *Historic Ill.*, 158.

[12] Gage to Dartmouth, January 6, 1773, P. R. O., Am. and W. I., vol. 128.

[13] "It cannot be suggested that a regular Constitutional Government can be established amongst a people who are settled and scattered in a far distant desert . . . They don't deserve so much attention or expence . . ." Gage to Hillsborough, March 4, 1772, Sparks MSS., XLIII, vol. 3, p. 164. "They were told propositions of that sort would not be received, and that I would not confer with them on the Subject of a Government to be so constituted." Gage to Dartmouth, January 6, 1773, P. R. O., Am. and W. I., vol. 128. The proposal would have met the same fate had it been carried to the ministry, for upon hearing of the movement, Secretary Hillsborough, just before his retirement, wrote to Gage: "Some arrangements for the Inhabitants of the Illinois Country may be necessary, but as I agree with you in opinion that a regular Constitutional Government for that District would be highly improper, I am not without apprehension that any Plan, however limited, may be wrested [*sic*] to bad purposes, and will in a greater or less degree operate to fix what we both think it would be better to remove." July 1, 1772, Sparks MSS., LXIII, vol. 3, p. 165.

[14] "These two people have been a long time here, and are not to be relied on", Gage to Haldimand, June 3, 1773, Can. Arch., series B, vol. 5, p. 142. See also Gage to Hillsborough, September 2, 1772, P. R. O., Am. and W. I., vol. 127, and Gage to Haldimand, January 5, 1774, B. M., Haldimand Papers, Corr. with Gage, 1758-1777, vol. IV.

STRUGGLE FOR CIVIL GOVERNMENT

wishes.[15] The commandant was likewise requested to circulate among the French a plan of government draughted by Gage himself,[16] which if endorsed by them, might be

[15] Gage to Hillsborough, April 13, 1772, P. R. O., Am. and W. I., vol. 127.

[16] The current opinion has been that Lord Dartmouth, who succeeded Hillsborough as secretary for the colonies in August, 1772, drew up the sketch and forwarded it through Gage to Illinois. Bancroft, *Hist. of U. S.*, IV, 472, says that Dartmouth "censured the ideas of the inhabitants of the Illinois District with regard to a Civil Constitution . . . and rejected their proposition to take some part in the election of their rulers . . . A plan of Government was therefore prepared of great simplicity, leaving all power with the executive officers of the crown, . . ." "Dartmouth prepared and forwarded to Illinois what he called a 'Sketch of Government for Illinois'", Mason, *Chapters from Ill. Hist.*, 283. "His [Hillsborough's] successor, Lord Dartmouth, took a similar view, and immediately drew up what he termed 'A Sketch of Government for Illinois', and returned it with his compliments, into the western wilderness . . ." Parrish, *Historic Ill.*, 159. The statements quoted are quite inaccurate. Gage wrote to Hillsborough April 13, 1772, as follows: "The Officer commanding at the Illinois . . . is directed to sound the sentiments of the people on the subject of a Civil Government . . . I sent him a Sketch of what I proposed which I have now the honour to transmit Your Lordship, with a list of the Officers of Government and their respective Salarys." P. R. O., Am. and W. I., vol. 128. There is an abstract (in English) of the sketch in the Public Record Office, endorsed as having been inclosed in Gage's letter of the 13 of April. On July 1 Gage reported to the secretary that he "had not yet received an answer concerning the Government proposed to the Inhabitants of Illinois", *ibid.* In the summer of 1773 Gage was summoned to England to give the government information on colonial affairs and General Haldimand was left in charge of the American army and of the West. October 6, 1773, Bloüin wrote to Dartmouth from New York: "That worthy general had scarcely departed from America, when a secret Enemy to his Glory . . . found means to cause the Inhabitants of the Illinois to be assembled by the Commanding Officer there, and presented with an anonymous Writing, which, they were told, came from the General, and a Plan of the Form of Government, which they were requested to solicit through his Intercession." B. T. Papers (Hist. Soc. Pa.), vol. XXXI. A few weeks later he again wrote to Dartmouth: "I have delivered to Gen'l Haldimand a literal Copy of the Sketch I mentioned to your Lordship in the letter of which I now enclose the duplicate with another Copy and translation of that Sketch." November 4, 1773, P. R. O., Am. and W. I., vol. 128. It is curious that Bancroft should have made the mistake, since he refers to other portions of this letter in his text, and there is among his manuscripts a copy of the letter. Note

granted by the ministry. The plan [17] contained some popular elements, but provided also for certain appointive officers—a governor of the district, and a magistrate for each of the villages of Kaskaskia and Cahokia, and one for the three remaining villages. A grand council was to be formed, consisting of the governor, and five or six councilors elected by the inhabitants. In minor civil and criminal cases the individual magistrates were to have jurisdiction. The "Chamber of Kaskaskia" was the next higher court, consisting of three magistrates sitting together. From this court an appeal might be taken to the grand council, whose decision was to be final. The governor and council were also to legislate for the better government of

---

also the following extract of a letter from Gage to Haldimand, written from London, January 5, 1774: "The Paper given you by Bloüin and Clajon, is an exact Copy of that I sent to the Illinois, for the Commandant to show the Inhabitants, and endeavour to persuade them to petition for a Government of that Nature." B. M., Haldimand Papers, Corr. with Gage, 1758–1777, vol. IV. For another declaration from Gage as to his part, see Gage to Haldimand, June 3, 1773, Can. Arch., series B, vol. 5, p. 142. It may be observed further that when the sketch of government was drawn up and sent to Illinois, Lord Dartmouth had nothing to do with American affairs. He did not take charge of the colonial office until August, 1772. See Appendix to Hunt's *Pol. Hist. of Eng.*, X, 473.

[17] The original sketch, in French, unsigned and undated, is among the Kaskaskia Papers. There is also a copy in the British Museum, Add. MSS., 21,687, subscribed to by a notary public in Kaskaskia, June 13, 1773, and by William Clazon in New York, November 2, 1773. It is endorsed, however, as being a "Memoire des Habitants des Illinois, qui fut presenté par Mess. Bloüin et Clargeon." This copy had been sent by the inhabitants of Illinois to their representatives in New York, according to the letter of Bloüin to Dartmouth cited above in note 9, and was placed by them in Haldimand's hands. The endorsement is evidently the work of a clerk, who did not understand the situation, and has caused one or two errors to be made. In the calendar of Haldimand Papers, *Can. Arch. Rept.*, 1885, 203, the document is described as a "Memorial of the inhabitants of the Illinois for a Civil Government, presented by Messrs. Bloüin and Clargeon, on the 3rd of November, 1773 (in French)." Coffin, *The Province of Quebec and the Early Am. Rev.*, 417, n. 2, takes the statement in the *Can. Arch. Rept.* in good faith.

STRUGGLE FOR CIVIL GOVERNMENT 151

the country, regulate fees for the support of the courts, and fines for certain crimes, which, with confiscations, were to be applied to the extra expenses of the government. The estimated expense of the proposed government was three hundred and nine pounds, seven shillings sterling per annum.[18]

In pursuance of Gage's orders Commandant Hamilton convened the principal inhabitants of the village in the summer of 1772, and addressed them on the subject of a civil government.[19] " They were very high on the Occasion", however, and " expected to appoint their Governor and all other Civil Magistrates."[20] Upon being requested to draw up their plan in writing and sign it, the French informed Hamilton that they had deputed Daniel Blouïn to represent them before General Gage, and that until they could learn what success he had met with, they would give no definite answer.[21]

A few weeks later Gage transmitted to Secretary Hillsborough the following account of the negotiations up to that time: "An answer has been returned to the Proposals sent to the Illinois for the arrangements for that Country with an Account of the motives the people of those Settlements have formed of a Civil Government; which I transmit your Lordship in the inclosed Extract of a Letter from Major Hamilton. Those ideas were given them by the Mons. Blouïn mentioned in the Major's Letter, or rather an associate of his named Clajon, a Frenchman by birth, an ad-

---

[18] "Civil Officers for the Illinois", in General Gage's of April 13, 1772, P. R. O., Am. and W. I., vol. 127. In this memorandum Gage suggested that the governor receive 182 pounds sterling per annum, each of the magistrates 800 French livres, and a secretary to the governor and council and keeper of the records 500 livres.

[19] Hamilton to Gage, August 8, 1772, P. R. O., Am. and W. I., vol. 127.

[20] *Ibid.*   [21] *Ibid.*

venturer, artful and intelligent, who, after passing some years in these Colonies went to the Spanish side of the Mississippi and during his residence in the Colonies, he learnt the English language and got a shallow knowledge of our Laws. Those two People came to me from the Illinois about twelve Months ago; but from their character, the disturbance they had occasioned in the Country, and the extravagant proposals they brought, I refused to enter into any Conference with them on subjects that had relation to Civil Government."[22]

Although Gage apparently gave the French leaders little encouragement, they had hope that in time some sort of civil government would be established. During the visit of the French representatives in New York there was published in Philadelphia, in 1772, a pamphlet entitled "Invitation Sérieuse aux Habitants des Illinois", which emanated from some member of the French party seeking a new government.[23] The writer of this French tract urged his neighbors in Illinois to shake off the lethargy which had so long enveloped them, and win economic independence for the colony. They were urged to follow the example of their enterprizing friends who lived among them. He argued that if the British government had fully understood the situation of the Illinois French who had not as yet enjoyed any ben-

[22] September 2, 1772, P. R. O., Am. and W. I., vol. 127. Gage further declares that "Clazon is the chief mover, and puts all into the mouth of Bloüin, and since his residence in our Provinces is become a mere Republican." Gage to Haldimand, January 5, 1774, B. M., Haldimand Papers, Add. MSS., 21,655. In a letter to Haldimand, June 3, 1773, Gage wrote: "They [Bloüin and Clazon] shewed me a Sketch of a Republican Government two years ago, which they were told would not be received." Can. Arch., series B, vol. 5, p. 142.

[23] See reprint of this pamphlet in *Publications of Club for Colonial Reprints*, IV, with introduction and notes by C. W. Alvord and C. E. Carter, wherein an attempt is made to trace its authorship to Bloüin and Clazon.

SCHEMES FOR COLONIZATION

1768 he stated definitely that no objection could be had to such colonies,[102] and at the first suggestion of the Vandalia grant south of the Ohio, warmly supported it.[103]

It is necessary to bear in mind that the imperial government during the decade under consideration was becoming more and more embarrassed by the many problems of imperial administration. The great war just closed had resulted in bringing upon the government many new responsibilities, not the least of which was the administration of the newly-ceded territories and the defence of the empire. It is not surprising, therefore, that the members of the ministry should hesitate to sanction the establishment of new colonial governments when questions of administration and finance were already causing serious difficulties between the mother country and the established colonies. The factor of expense entered into the consideration of every new project and the colonial schemes were no exception to this rule, especially since the government was asked to bear a certain part of the expense.

The correspondence of Shelburne and Franklin shows that at the first suggestion of the proposed settlements this factor was uppermost in the mind of the former.[104] Shelburne became convinced that ultimately this objection would be

---

[102] "Representation of the Lords of Trade on the State of Indian Affairs, March 7, 1768", *N. Y. Col. Docs.*, VIII, 28–31.

[103] Franklin to his son, July 14, 1773, *Works*, ed. Bigelow, V, 197. With the reason for Hillsborough's later opposition the present study is not concerned.

[104] Franklin to his son, October 11, 1766, *Works*, ed. Bigelow, IV, 139, quoted above in note 63. "In case your Lordships should think it right to advise his Majesty to establish these New Governments, you will consider whether it will not be practicable to fall upon such a Plan as will avoid great part of the Expense incurred by the Estimates of the New Governments established after the Peace." Shelburne to Lords of Trade, October 5, 1767, B. T. Papers (Hist. Soc. Pa.), vol. XXVII; and *N. Y. Col. Docs.*, VII, 981.

overcome, but Hillsborough was not of that opinion. Writing to Gage shortly after the issuance of the report he dwelt at considerable length upon the necessity of avoiding an increased expense on any account: [105] "It appears to his Majesty that in the present state of the Kingdom its future Safety and Welfare do in great measure depend upon the relieving it from every Expence that is not an absolute necessity, and therefore though his Majesty applauds the Motives which induced the first Institution of the present plan of Indian Superintendency, which was evidently calculated to regain the Confidence, and combine the Force of the Savages against a then powerful Enemy, yet, as in the present State of America, the main object of that Plan, if not entirely removed are at least greatly diminished . . . His Majesty concurs in opinion with his Board of Trade, that the laying aside that part of it [the Plan of Superintendency] which relates to the Indian Trade and entrusting the entire management of that Trade to the colonies themselves will be of Publick Utility and Advantage, as a means of avoiding much Difficulty and saving much Expense to this Country both in present and in future . . . The Propriety therefore of entrusting the Management of the Trade with the Indians to the Colonies, does . . . appear to His Majesty to depend in great measure upon a reduction of such Posts in the Indian Country, as are by their situation, exposed to the Resentment of the Savages, it being evident that in Proportion as the number of such Posts is diminished, the Necessity of carrying on an Indian War at the Expense of this Kingdom will be less. . . . His Majesty has not failed in this great and extensive Consideration to give due attention to Propositions, which have

[105] April 15, 1768, P. R. O., Am. and W. I., vol. 124.

SCHEMES FOR COLONIZATION 139

been made with regard to the Establishments on the Rivers Mississippi, Ohio and Illinois. But as his Majesty has doubts concerning the Utility of Establishments in such remote situations, which consequently cannot be kept up, but at an immense Expence, it is the King's pleasure that you should report your Opinion with regard to the continuance of any of the Forts in those situations. . . ."[106]

It should be noted that in the report of the Board of Trade in 1768 great emphasis is placed upon the general commercial and political inutility of the proposed colonies, but there is no suggestion that the matter of expense stood in the way. On the other hand there is an intimation that the clause in the proclamation of 1763, reserving the interior country for the use of the Indians, was inserted there on the principle that all settlements should be confined to the sea-coast. Again in a similar report in 1772 against

---

[106] A few weeks later Gage replied to Hillsborough: "From what has been represented your Lordship will perceive that I am not of opinion that a Post at the Illinois will be productive of advantages equal to the expence of supporting it." June 16, 1768, P. R. O., Am. and W. I., vol. 124. Two years later he again wrote to Hillsborough: "I conceive that to procure all the commerce it will afford and at as little expence to ourselves as we can, is the only object we should have in view in the interior Country for a century to come . . . I am of opinion that the advantages we might propose to gain from Civil and Military Establishments at the mouths of those Rivers [Ohio and Illinois] would be greatly disproportionate to the Expences, they would be attended with." November 10, 1770, *ibid.*, vol. 126. Hillsborough writes in the same year: "Forts and Military Establishments at the mouths of the Ohio and Illinois Rivers, admitting that they would be effectual to the attainment of the objects in view would yet, I fear, be attended with an Expence to this Kingdom greatly disproportionate to the advantages to be gained and those objections to Civil Establishments which I have above stated, do weigh so strongly against that measure in the scale both of general and local policy, as greatly to discourage that idea." The latter part refers to his argument against the commercial utility of a regular settlement in the West, which he declared, "cannot be of that commercial benefit to the state which it would be of in other places". Hillsborough to Gage, July 31, 1770, *ibid.*

the proposed Vandalia or Walpole grant,[107] emphasis is placed upon that clause; indeed it is advanced as the chief argument for the rejection of the proposition.[108] But nowhere in the Hillsborough-Gage correspondence is there the slightest intimation that Hillsborough had the proclamation of 1763 in mind. It would seem reasonable to assume that if he believed that the clause in that document

---

[107] After 1768 the attention of land and colony promoters was turned to the region of the upper Ohio River valley. In 1768 the long-proposed Indian boundary line was determined at the treaty of Fort Stanwix and there was opened up for colonization a wide strip of territory in that region. A company was formed in the same year for the establishment of a colony, some of the members being Benjamin Franklin, Thomas Pownall, Thomas Walpole, and the firm of Baynton, Wharton and Morgan. In 1770, the crown was petitioned for a grant, but in 1772 the Board of Trade, still under the leadership of Hillsborough, reported adversely. This report called forth a vigorous answer from Dr. Franklin, which completely demolished the arguments of Hillsborough. His successor, Lord Dartmouth, began at once to make arrangements for the establishment of a colony, but the whole matter was dropped on the outbreak of the American Revolution. For a full account see Alden, *New Governments West of the Alleghanies before 1780*, 19–35. The following writers have confused the Walpole grant with the plan of 1766: Hinsdale, *Old Northwest*, 133; Peyton, *Hist. of Augusta Co., Va.*, 144 ff; Fitzmaurice, *Life of Shelburne*, II, 31; Bigelow, in Franklin's *Works*, IV, 136; Perkins, *Annals of the West*, 127; Adams, *Maryland's Influence upon the Land Cessions to the U. S.*, 13.

[108] This interpretation by Hillsborough may be entirely disregarded. He was not responsible for that particular clause in the proclamation. It was conceived and written by Lord Shelburne himself, as has been pointed out by Alvord, "Genesis of the Proclamation of 1763", in *Mich. Pioneer and Hist. Colls.*, XXXVI, 31 ff. He has shown that Shelburne did not have in mind the principle of confining the colonies to the sea-coast. Coffin, in *Province of Quebec and the Am. Rev.*, 428, and Alden, in *New Governments West of the Alleghanies before 1780*, 43–44, have also rejected Hillsborough's interpretation. For the old view that the proclamation was intended to confine the colonies to the sea-coast, see for example Hinsdale, *Old Northwest*, ch. VIII, and the same author, "The Western Land Policy of the British Government from 1763 to 1775", in *Ohio Archaeological and Historical Quarterly*, December, 1887. There is positive proof of Shelburne's position in a minute submitted by him to the cabinet in 1767, Lansdowne MSS., vol. L, p. 185.

stood in the way, some mention of it would have been made in his many communications to General Gage and Sir William Johnson. Nor does Franklin intimate it in any of his private correspondence on the subject. In order to justify his position with some appearance of legality, it is probable that Hillsborough brought forward that clause in the proclamation, which had been interpreted by nearly every one else as merely temporary in character.

There was still another important reason for the rejection of interior settlements, which comes to light in contemporary correspondence, but which is not contained in the report of the Board of Trade. During this period Louisiana, with New Orleans commanding the mouth of the Mississippi River, was in the hands of Spain. New Orleans was practically the only outlet for the western country, and it was the settled conviction of many that so long as it remained in the possession of a foreign power, it was useless to expect much from the West. In 1768 Lieutenant George Phyn of the regular army was sent from Fort Pitt down the Ohio and Mississippi rivers to Mobile, and in writing to Sir William Johnson he declared that the country in and about the Illinois region would never be settled " with any advantage to England " unless New Orleans were procured.[109]

In a communication to Secretary Hillsborough in 1770, in which he argued at length against the establishment of settlements or of any additional military posts in the West, General Gage declared that no further time or money should

---

[109] April 15, 1768, Johnson MSS., vol. XXV, no. 109. He affirmed that a settlement "will never happen with any advantage to England until we can procure the Ideal Island of Orleans: . . could we find passage for even small craft to go to the Sea, the Country of the Illinois would be worthy of attention, but had we the Island of Orleans, that country would in a very short time I believe be equal to any of our Colonies." *Ibid.*

be expended on that country, and particularly the Illinois country, because it would be of no conceivable "advantage to the King's subjects, unless New Orleans was added to His Majesty's Possessions". [110]

In the same year Lord Hillsborough himself mentioned one of the chief objections which he considered to "lie against Colonies in the Illinois with a view to the Peltry Trade, which is the peculiar Commerce of that Country." "This Commerce", he affirmed, "cannot (I apprehend) be useful to Great Britain otherwise than as it furnishes a material for her Manufactures, but it will on the contrary be prejudicial to her in proportion as other Countries obtain that material from us without its coming here first; and whilst New Orleans is the only Port for Exportation of what goes down the Mississippi, no one will believe that that town will not be the market for Peltry or that those Restrictions, which are intended to secure the Exportation of that Commodity directly to G. Britain, can have any effect under such circumstances." [111]

In this connection it should be noted that throughout this decade there were serious thoughts of an attack upon Louisiana and New Orleans should a war with Spain afford the opportunity. One of the reasons offered by Governor Franklin in 1766 for the establishment of a colony in the Illinois country was that such a colony would enable the English to get possession of the whole of Louisiana "should a future war make it expedient". [112] We find Gage himself discussing with General Haldimand, who was stationed in

---

[110] November 10, 1770, P. R. O., Am. and W. I., vol. 126.

[111] Hillsborough to Gage, July 31, 1770, *ibid*.

[112] Reasons for the Establishment of a Colony, Franklin Papers (Am. Phil. Soc.), vols. XXVII, XXVIII; same idea expressed in Remarks on Lord Barrington's Plan, no. 2, Lansdowne MSS., vol. L, p. 80.

SCHEMES FOR COLONIZATION

West Florida during the latter half of this period, possible plans for an attack in case war should be declared.[11]

In 1770 the cherished opportunity seemed to have arrived. In that year the dispute between England and Spain over the possession of certain of the Falkland Islands, lying near the Strait of Magellan, brought the two nations to the verge of war.[114] Hillsborough evidently expected war, for in January, 1771, he communicated secret instructions to Gage in New York[115] to mobilize an army and to prepare for the invasion of Louisiana. He commissioned Gage as commander of the invading forces and instructed him to use his own judgment as to the time and method of attack. Gage replied[116] that he would at once assemble a body of troops and prepare for the invasion. He further

---

[113] Hamilton, *Colonial Mobile*, 2-29. The English officers in West Florida were instructed to inform Gage as to the number of troops and inhabitants the Spaniards might bring to Louisiana, and whether any of the old French colonial troops entered the Spanish service, Gage to Brigadier Taylor, June 10, 1766; B. M. Add. MSS., 21, 662, fol. 214. In 1767, General Haldimand sent Captain Marsh from Pensacola to New Orleans to make a special inquiry relative to the British trade, the disposition of the French and Acadians towards the Spanish, and the treatment of the Indians and French by the Spaniards, J. Marsh to Haldimand, November 20, 1767, *ibid.*, 21, 728. The keenest interest was always taken in the movements of the Spanish, especially with reference to how many troops were to be sent up the Mississippi and how many and what ports on that river were to be garrisoned. See for example, Captain Innis to Haldimand, October 11, 1769, Can. Arch., series B, vol. 69, p. 60. Haldimand wrote to Gage, June 12, 1770, that "although on the one hand the military Force, which you are informed General O'Reilly intends to leave in the Colony, is too small to create much alarm, yet on the other the appointment of a Company of French under the Command of an Active French Officer for the upper Posts of the Mississippi is a circumstance that wears a suspicious appearance." P. R. O., Am. and W. I., vol. 126.

[114] Hunt, *Pol. Hist. of Eng.*, X, 112-114.

[115] January 2, 1771, P. R. O., Am. and W. I., vol. 127. See Documentary Appendix, no. 3.

[116] Gage to Hillsborough, April 2, 1771, P. R. O., Am. and W. I., vol. 127. See Documentary Appendix, no. 4.

declared his intention of approaching Louisiana and New Orleans by way of the Ohio and Mississippi rivers, and actually sent reinforcements to Fort de Chartres.[117] Soon after the despatch of Hillsborough, however, Spain acceded to the demands of England, and the attack upon New Orleans was given up.[118]

In conclusion it may be observed that after 1768 the attention of those most interested in the colonizing of Illinois was turned in another direction. In that year, at the treaty of Fort Stanwix, the boundary line between the Indians and the whites was determined, thus opening for settlement a large tract of land in the region south of the Ohio River. There was formed in the same year a company, called the Walpole or Vandalia Company, for the purpose of establishing a colony there. Although Hillsborough again opposed the scheme, he was overruled, and the grant was made. But the Revolution put an end to further progress in the scheme. In the Illinois country there was another revival of land speculation in 1773, which, however, was simply an attempt of individuals and companies to purchase large tracts of land from the Indians without applying to the crown, a proceeding manifestly contrary to the proclamation of 1763.[119]

[117] "I have advices that the Artillery and Stores sent down the Ohio for Fort Chartres, have got into the Mississippi, and were going up to the Fort. The prospect of a war with Spain could not be concealed, for the news had been conveyed by many hands." Gage to Hillsborough, August 6, 1771, P. R. O., Am. and W. I., vol. 127.

[118] Gage to Hillsborough, March 7, 1771, *ibid.*

[119] It is of interest to note that in 1770, Dr. Connolly, a nephew of George Croghan, and a prominent land speculator in the West, proposed to George Washington that a colony ought to be erected south of the Ohio River, "to be bounded . . . by the Ohio northward, and westward, the ridge that divides the waters of the Tennessee or Cherokee River southward and westward, and a line to be run from the falls of Ohio, or above, so as to cross the Shawna River above the fork of it". "Washington's Tour on the Ohio", *Writings*, ed. Ford, II, 315.

CHAPTER VII.

THE STRUGGLE FOR A CIVIL GOVERNMENT, 1770-1774.

THE action of Commandant Wilkins in abolishing the court of judicatory and in assuming again all judicial powers,[1] aroused the French people in Illinois to take a decided stand for their rights. From this time they ceased to depend on their English associates, whose actions were often inspired by selfish motives, and who were frequently connected with the speculative schemes of the eastern merchants for exploiting the country by means of American settlers. The French people perceived that their interests would not be subserved by such measures, and that they might fulfill by themselves along different lines what had been in the minds of the English speculators. Under the administration of Lord Hillsborough, the great opponent of western expansion, restriction seemed to have become a permanent policy, and by 1770 many of the English traders, who had been interested in the promoters' schemes, had become disheartened and were leaving Illinois. The plan of a French colony appeared to be justified, however, by the actual settlements in existence, and the French leaders might reasonably hope that, proper representations being made to the ministry, no opposition to the creation

[1] See above, ch. IV, p. 72. Regular sessions of a court were held from July, 1770, to January 30, 1773, but there were no regular judges, and the judgments were those of the military commandants, see MS. Court Record (Chester, Illinois).

of a French colonial government on the Mississippi would be met.

It was with this idea in mind that the leaders of the French inhabitants called an assembly on August 24, 1770, shortly after the downfall of the court.[2] Daniel Blouin, a citizen of Kaskaskia, was chosen to go to New York and explain the situation to General Gage.[3] He took with him a document enumerating some of the grievances of the people against the military commandant and certain of the English merchants,[4] and instructions to use all possible efforts to obtain the promise of a civil government for the country.[5] The French people had thus advanced beyond their position of 1768,[6] and, without the assistance of the resident English,[7] had assumed the initiative in a new movement for the extension of civil rights to the colony.

The French agent, Daniel Blouin, chose as an associate in this mission William Clazon, a Frenchman with some understanding of English usages.[8] Arriving in New York

[2] MS. Court Record, p. 108.

[3] *Ibid.*, p. 107; Hamilton to Gage, August 8, 1772, P. R. O., Am. and W. I., vol. 128; Gage to Dartmouth, January 6, 1773, *ibid.*

[4] Gage to Hillsborough, August 6, 1771, *ibid.*, vol. 127; Gage to Dartmouth, January 6, 1773, *ibid.*, vol. 128; Blouin to Dartmouth, October 6, 1773, B. T. Papers (Hist. Soc. Pa.), vol. XXXI.

[5] He was authorized "à faire toutes les Démarches légitimes qui 'l conviendera de faire en notre nom pour tâcher d'obtenir de son Excellence Monsieur le Major Général Thomas Gage . . . le redressement de nos Griefs, et Prier sa ditte Excellence . . . d' entercéder Pour nous auprès de sa Majesté afin d'en obtenir l'Establissement du Gouvernement Civil . . ." MS. Court Record, p. 107.

[6] See above, ch. IV, p. 60.

[7] There is no trace of Morgan in Illinois after 1770. Many others left about the same time, see Gage to Dartmouth, May 5, 1773, P. R. O., Am. and W. I., vol. 128.

[8] Gage to Hillsborough, August 6, 1771, *ibid.*, vol. 127. Clazon's name does not appear as a resident of the Illinois villages, nor has his name been located in the Canadian genealogical registers. For Gage's estimate of Clazon see below, p. 151.

in 1771, they presented their credentials and memorial to General Gage on July 9th,[9] and prayed that a civil government be established in the Illinois country. Although their reception was not very favorable, Gage finally did demand an outline of their plan.[10] The agents set to work to produce a draft of government [11]—Gage speaks of it as a rough

[9] Blouin to Dartmouth, October 6, 1773, B. T. Papers (Hist. Soc. Pa.), vol. XXXI. The exact date of their departure from Illinois and arrival in New York does not appear. September 3, 1770, Blouin gave power of attorney to continue during his absence to Joseph Charleville, his father-in-law, Louis Viviat, and Piérre Girardot, Kaskaskia Record Book, British Period. He was still in Illinois in November, 1770, for in that month he acted as attorney for Viviat, *ibid.*, p. 171. It is probable that they arrived in New York in the early summer of 1771.

[10] Gage to Dartmouth, January 6, 1773, P, R. O., Am. and W. I., vol. 128.

[11] This episode has been discussed by several writers. In *Hist. of U. S.*, IV, 741, Bancroft states that the people of Illinois met together and prepared a plan of government, providing for institutions like those of Connecticut, which was forwarded by them to General Gage through their agent Daniel Blouin. This, however, is an error. In detailing the account of his negotiations with the agents, Gage declared that " he [Blouin] presented me memorials that related solely to complaints of which he desired redress, but delivered no memorials containing propositions for the forming of a Civil Constitution which from the contents of my Dispatch, Your Lordship was led to conclude I had received from him. The people's wishes or desires of a Civil Government being however, mentioned, gave occasion to my sending afterwards to Mr. Blouin and his associate Mr. Clazon to know what kind of Government the people expected and w'd be satisfied with . . . ; and received for answer that it would require a great deal of time to form a plan of the kind.'' He then asked for a brief outline of their plan, and they drew up a " rough sketch '', Gage to Dartmouth, January 6, 1773, P. R. O., Am. and W. I., vol. 128. This letter was in answer to that of John Pownall, one of the under secretaries, who wrote on October 7, 1772: " I think it necessary in the absence of Lord Dartmouth who is at present in the Country, to acquaint you that your Dispatch No. 76, has been received and laid before the King, but the regulations for a Civil Government proposed by the Inhabitants of the Illinois . . . were not included in your Packet." *Ibid.*, and Dartmouth Papers, *Fourteenth Report, Royal Hist. MSS. Comm.*, Appendix X, 98. Gage answered Pownall as follows: " You had good

outline—which was probably the work of Clazon, for the model of the proposed government was the constitution of Connecticut,[12] the most liberal of the eastern colonies, of which the average Illinois Frenchman could have known nothing.

Such a proposition was naturally rejected by the general,[13] who, in order to gain more information concerning their actual sentiments, and to discredit, if possible, the two representatives,[14] directed Major Hamilton, the acting commandant in Illinois, to sound the people as to their

Reasons from my Letter and the Extract inclosed, to suppose that there had been an Omission in not transmitting the said Proposals of the Inhabitants, but I never received them from Monsieur Bloüin and I explain that matter by this Opportunity to the Earl of Dartmouth." January 6, 1773, P. R. O., Am. and W. I., vol. 128. Bancroft's error has been repeated by Mason, *Chapters from Ill. Hist.*, 282, and by Parrish, *Historic Ill.*, 158.

[12] Gage to Dartmouth, January 6, 1773, P. R. O., Am. and W. I., vol. 128.

[13] "It cannot be suggested that a regular Constitutional Government can be established amongst a people who are settled and scattered in a far distant desert . . . They don't deserve so much attention or expence . . ." Gage to Hillsborough, March 4, 1772, Sparks MSS., XLIII, vol. 3, p. 164. "They were told propositions of that sort would not be received, and that I would not confer with them on the Subject of a Government to be so constituted." Gage to Dartmouth, January 6, 1773, P. R. O., Am. and W. I., vol. 128. The proposal would have met the same fate had it been carried to the ministry, for upon hearing of the movement, Secretary Hillsborough, just before his retirement, wrote to Gage: "Some arrangements for the Inhabitants of the Illinois Country may be necessary, but as I agree with you in opinion that a regular Constitutional Government for that District would be highly improper, I am not without apprehension that any Plan, however limited, may be wrested [*sic*] to bad purposes, and will in a greater or less degree operate to fix what we both think it would be better to remove." July 1, 1772, Sparks MSS., LXIII, vol. 3, p. 165.

[14] "These two people have been a long time here, and are not to be relied on", Gage to Haldimand, June 3, 1773, Can. Arch., series B, vol. 5, p. 142. See also Gage to Hillsborough, September 2, 1772, P. R. O., Am. and W. I., vol. 127, and Gage to Haldimand, January 5, 1774, B. M., Haldimand Papers, Corr. with Gage, 1758–1777, vol. IV.

wishes.[15] The commandant was likewise requested to circulate among the French a plan of government draughted by Gage himself,[16] which if endorsed by them, might be

[15] Gage to Hillsborough, April 13, 1772, P. R. O., Am. and W. I., vol. 127.

[16] The current opinion has been that Lord Dartmouth, who succeeded Hillsborough as secretary for the colonies in August, 1772, drew up the sketch and forwarded it through Gage to Illinois. Bancroft, *Hist. of U. S.*, IV, 472, says that Dartmouth "censured the ideas of the inhabitants of the Illinois District with regard to a Civil Constitution . . . and rejected their proposition to take some part in the election of their rulers . . . A plan of Government was therefore prepared of great simplicity, leaving all power with the executive officers of the crown, . . ." "Dartmouth prepared and forwarded to Illinois what he called a 'Sketch of Government for Illinois'", Mason, *Chapters from Ill. Hist.*, 283. "His [Hillsborough's] successor, Lord Dartmouth, took a similar view, and immediately drew up what he termed 'A Sketch of Government for Illinois', and returned it with his compliments, into the western wilderness . . ." Parrish, *Historic Ill.*, 159. The statements quoted are quite inaccurate. Gage wrote to Hillsborough April 13, 1772, as follows: "The Officer commanding at the Illinois . . . is directed to sound the sentiments of the people on the subject of a Civil Government . . . I sent him a Sketch of what I proposed which I have now the honour to transmit Your Lordship, with a list of the Officers of Government and their respective Salaries." P. R. O., Am. and W. I., vol. 128. There is an abstract (in English) of the sketch in the Public Record Office, endorsed as having been inclosed in Gage's letter of the 13 of April. On July 1 Gage reported to the secretary that he "had not yet received an answer concerning the Government proposed to the Inhabitants of Illinois", *ibid*. In the summer of 1773 Gage was summoned to England to give the government information on colonial affairs and General Haldimand was left in charge of the American army and of the West. October 6, 1773, Blouïn wrote to Dartmouth from New York: "That worthy general had scarcely departed from America, when a secret Enemy to his Glory . . . found means to cause the Inhabitants of the Illinois to be assembled by the Commanding Officer there, and presented with an anonymous Writing, which, they were told, came from the General, and a Plan of the Form of Government, which they were requested to solicit through his Intercession." B. T. Papers (Hist. Soc. Pa.), vol. XXXI. A few weeks later he again wrote to Dartmouth: "I have delivered to Gen'l Haldimand a literal Copy of the Sketch I mentioned to your Lordship in the letter of which I now enclose the duplicate with another Copy and translation of that Sketch." November 4, 1773, P. R. O., Am. and W. I., vol. 128. It is curious that Bancroft should have made the mistake, since he refers to other portions of this letter in his text, and there is among his manuscripts a copy of the letter. Note

granted by the ministry. The plan [17] contained some popular elements, but provided also for certain appointive officers—a governor of the district, and a magistrate for each of the villages of Kaskaskia and Cahokia, and one for the three remaining villages. A grand council was to be formed, consisting of the governor, and five or six councilors elected by the inhabitants. In minor civil and criminal cases the individual magistrates were to have jurisdiction. The "Chamber of Kaskaskia" was the next higher court, consisting of three magistrates sitting together. From this court an appeal might be taken to the grand council, whose decision was to be final. The governor and council were also to legislate for the better government of

---

also the following extract of a letter from Gage to Haldimand, written from London, January 5, 1774: "The Paper given you by Bloüin and Clajon, is an exact Copy of that I sent to the Illinois, for the Commandant to show the Inhabitants, and endeavour to persuade them to petition for a Government of that Nature." B. M., Haldimand Papers, Corr. with Gage, 1758–1777, vol. IV. For another declaration from Gage as to his part, see Gage to Haldimand, June 3, 1773, Can. Arch., series B, vol. 5, p. 142. It may be observed further that when the sketch of government was drawn up and sent to Illinois, Lord Dartmouth had nothing to do with American affairs. He did not take charge of the colonial office until August, 1772. See Appendix to Hunt's *Pol. Hist. of Eng.*, X, 473.

[17] The original sketch, in French, unsigned and undated, is among the Kaskaskia Papers. There is also a copy in the British Museum, Add. MSS., 21,687, subscribed to by a notary public in Kaskaskia, June 13, 1773, and by William Clazon in New York, November 2, 1773. It is endorsed, however, as being a "Memoire des Habitants des Illinois, qui fut presenté par Mess. Bloüin et Clargeon." This copy had been sent by the inhabitants of Illinois to their representatives in New York, according to the letter of Bloüin to Dartmouth cited above in note 9, and was placed by them in Haldimand's hands. The endorsement is evidently the work of a clerk, who did not understand the situation, and has caused one or two errors to be made. In the calendar of Haldimand Papers, *Can. Arch. Rept.*, 1885, 203, the document is described as a "Memorial of the inhabitants of the Illinois for a Civil Government, presented by Messrs. Bloüin and Clargeon, on the 3rd of November, 1773 (in French)." Coffin, *The Province of Quebec and the Early Am. Rev.*, 417, n. 2, takes the statement in the *Can. Arch. Rept.* in good faith.

the country, regulate fees for the support of the courts, and fines for certain crimes, which, with confiscations, were to be applied to the extra expenses of the government. The estimated expense of the proposed government was three hundred and nine pounds, seven shillings sterling per annum.[18]

In pursuance of Gage's orders Commandant Hamilton convened the principal inhabitants of the village in the summer of 1772, and addressed them on the subject of a civil government.[19] " They were very high on the Occasion", however, and " expected to appoint their Governor and all other Civil Magistrates." [20] Upon being requested to draw up their plan in writing and sign it, the French informed Hamilton that they had deputed Daniel Blouin to represent them before General Gage, and that until they could learn what success he had met with, they would give no definite answer.[21]

A few weeks later Gage transmitted to Secretary Hillsborough the following account of the negotiations up to that time: "An answer has been returned to the Proposals sent to the Illinois for the arrangements for that Country with an Account of the motives the people of those Settlements have formed of a Civil Government; which I transmit your Lordship in the inclosed Extract of a Letter from Major Hamilton. Those ideas were given them by the Mons. Blouin mentioned in the Major's Letter, or rather an associate of his named Clajon, a Frenchman by birth, an ad-

---

[18] " Civil Officers for the Illinois ", in General Gage's of April 13, 1772, P. R. O., Am. and W. I., vol. 127. In this memorandum Gage suggested that the governor receive 182 pounds sterling per annum, each of the magistrates 800 French livres, and a secretary to the governor and council and keeper of the records 500 livres.

[19] Hamilton to Gage, August 8, 1772, P. R. O., Am. and W. I., vol. 127.

[20] *Ibid.*   [21] *Ibid.*

venturer, artful and intelligent, who, after passing some years in these Colonies went to the Spanish side of the Mississippi and during his residence in the Colonies, he learnt the English language and got a shallow knowledge of our Laws. Those two People came to me from the Illinois about twelve Months ago; but from their character, the disturbance they had occasioned in the Country, and the extravagant proposals they brought, I refused to enter into any Conference with them on subjects that had relation to Civil Government."[22]

Although Gage apparently gave the French leaders little encouragement, they had hope that in time some sort of civil government would be established. During the visit of the French representatives in New York there was published in Philadelphia, in 1772, a pamphlet entitled "Invitation Sérieuse aux Habitants des Illinois", which emanated from some member of the French party seeking a new government.[23] The writer of this French tract urged his neighbors in Illinois to shake off the lethargy which had so long enveloped them, and win economic independence for the colony. They were urged to follow the example of their enterprizing friends who lived among them. He argued that if the British government had fully understood the situation of the Illinois French who had not as yet enjoyed any ben-

[22] September 2, 1772, P. R. O., Am. and W. I., vol. 127. Gage further declares that "Clazon is the chief mover, and puts all into the mouth of Bloüin, and since his residence in our Provinces is become a mere Republican." Gage to Haldimand, January 5, 1774, B. M., Haldimand Papers, Add. MSS., 21,655. In a letter to Haldimand, June 3, 1773, Gage wrote: "They [Bloüin and Clazon] shewed me a Sketch of a Republican Government two years ago, which they were told would not be received." Can. Arch., series B, vol. 5, p. 142.

[23] See reprint of this pamphlet in *Publications of Club for Colonial Reprints*, IV, with introduction and notes by C. W. Alvord and C. E. Carter, wherein an attempt is made to trace its authorship to Bloüin and Clazon.

efits from becoming English subjects, it would long since have granted them a civil government. He also prophesied that in a short time the right to enjoy their religion would be confirmed and a civil government established.

The French party failed, however, to obtain a government along the lines applied for.[24] Not only was Lord Hillsborough opposed to it, but his successer Lord Dartmouth declared himself against such a popular form of government. Writing to Gage March 3, 1772, he explained his position: "The Propositions toward forming a Government for the Illinois Country, suggested to you long ago by the Inhabitants of that District were certainly in the outline of them too absurd and extravagant to afford the least ground for consideration."[25]

The attention of the authorities had been called, however, to the needs of the Illinois villages: indeed for a number of years considerable thought had been given to their disposition. The idea was at times advanced of removing

[24] Compare this movement with the proposals of Major Robert Rogers to erect a civil government at Michilimakinac in 1767. In a long report on Indian and trade conditions at the northern post Major Rogers declares that the only remedy for existing evils is to establish a government there. He proposes that "Michillimackinac and its dependencies, should be erected into a Civil Government; with a Governer, Lieutenant Governer, and a Council, of Twelve; chose out of the Principal Merchants, that carry on this valuable branch of Trade [furtrade] with Power to enact, such Laws as may be necessary and these be transmitted to the king, etc., for Approbation: That the Governer, should be Agent for the Indians, and Commandant of the Troops, that may be ordered to Garrison the Fort . . . " In a closing paragraph he says: "Whereas by the propos'd Plan, all are under a Civil Power and ye Gov. Commandant of the Troops, and Agent to the Indians— Which wou'd cause every Branch to be countenanc'd for the mutual safety of each other." "Journal of Major Rogers' Proceedings with the Indians at the Garrison of Michilimakinac from May the 24th to July 23d, 1767", MS. in Am. Antiq. Soc. Lib.

[25] Dartmouth to Gage, March 3, 1773, B. M., Haldimand Papers, Add. MSS., 21,697. For the same opinion, see same to same, November 4, 1772, P. R. O., Am. and W. I., vol. 128.

all the inhabitants from Illinois to Canada.[26] Although this was deemed impracticable,[27] it may nevertheless be said that the government was thoroughly anxious to reach a satisfactory solution of the problem. Secretary Hillsborough was fully aware of the situation and was awakened to the necessity of taking some steps, for in 1769 he declared that "if the case of these settlements had been well known or understood at the time of forming the conquered Lands into Colonies, some provision would have been made for them, and they would have been erected into distinct Governments or made dependent upon those Colonies of which they were either the offspring, or with which they did by circumstances and situation, stand connected. I shall not fail, therefore, to give this matter the fullest consideration when the business of the Illinois Country is taken up."[28] We find his successor, Lord Dartmouth, expressing the opinion in 1772 that the "state of the Illinois District appears to me in every light in which it is viewed to require a very serious consideration, and I will not fail to collect as soon as possible those informations which may enable me to form a judgment, as well of the arrangements which have been already made respecting that Country, as of those which may be further necessary, considering it in a light of a Colony of the King's subjects."[29] And more emphatically still a little later he wrote: "It has always appeared,

---

[26] Hillsborough to Gage, December 4, 1771, P. R. O., Am. and W. I., vol. 127; Gage to Hillsborough, March 4, 1772, Sparks MSS., XLIII, vol. 3, p. 165.

[27] "I fear there are but too many obstacles to such a measure, and therefore it will be the more necessary to consider whether any permanent plan ought to be adopted." Hillsborough to Gage, December 4, 1771, P. R. O., Am. and W. I., vol. 126.

[28] Letter to Gage, December 9, 1769, *ibid.*, vol. 124.

[29] Letter to Gage, November 4, *ibia.*, vol. 128.

and does still appear to me, that if those Inhabitants have (as I conceive they have) a Right, under the Treaty of Paris to continue in their possessions, it is both dangerous and disgraceful to leave that District without such Regulations as may on the one hand insure to the Inhabitants that Protection in their Civil Rights which they are entitled to expect, as on the other hand to secure their Allegiance as Subjects. I shall, therefore, think it my Duty to make this an Object of my attention."[30]

In the meantime events were taking place in Illinois which changed somewhat the attitude of the people. Under the administration of Wilkins the people had evidently suffered a good many indignities. Moreover, at the beginning of his régime we have seen that he did not look with disfavor upon the questionable operations of one of the great trading companies in Illinois, inasmuch as his private interests were being subserved at the same time. But eventually his connection with Baynton, Wharton and Morgan was broken, and party factions began to form. From 1770 to 1772 the whole country was apparently torn by party strife.[31] Wilkins also attempted to enrich himself at the expense of the government by falsifying his accounts and by misappropriating large sums of money.[32] Finally the officers of his regiment preferred

---

[30] Letter to Gage, March 3, 1773, B. M., Add. MSS., 21,697.

[31] "There has been a strange work at Illinois, very bad Proceedings carried on—indeed most shameful ones. A Quarrel amongst them has laid open scandalous Scenes, and able is Faction." Gage to Haldimand, September 13, 1771, *ibid.*, 21,655.

[32] Engineer Hutchins to Captain Sowers, April 8, 1771, *ibid.*; Gage to Haldimand, September 13, 1771, *ibid.*; Gage to Wilkins, September 16, 1771, Can. Arch., series B, vol. 5, p. 50; Captain Sowers to Gage, September 17, 1771, *ibid.*; Gage to Haldimand, June 9, 1772, *ibid.*, p. 103. For a denial by Wilkins see Wilkins to Gage, April 7, 1772, *ibid.*, p. 76.

serious charges against him,[33] and he was dismissed from the service in September, 1772.[34] His successor, however, did not arrive until the following spring, after which Wilkins sailed for England.[35] Major Isaac Hamilton took charge of the fort temporarily,[36] but was relieved in a few weeks by Captain Hugh Lord,[37] who took up his post at Fort Gage, near Kaskaskia, because Commandant Hamilton,[38] acting under orders from Gage,[39] had destroyed Fort de Chartres on account of the ravages of the Mississippi River.[40] During the next two years the relation between

[33] Gage to Haldimand, September 1, 1773, B. M., Add. MSS., 21,655.

[34] Gage to Haldimand, September 13, 1771, *ibid.*

[35] Haldimand to Gage, July 14, 1772, Can. Arch., series B, vol. 5, p. 109.

[36] Gage to Hillsborough, July 1, 1772, P. R. O., Am. and W. I., vol. 128. There is but one document, aside from a letter, in which Hamilton signs himself as commandant in Illinois. June 6, 1772, he approves the decision of an arbitration court, Kaskaskia Record Book, p. 180.

[37] Gage to Hillsborough, September 2, 1772, P. R. O., Am. and W. I., vol. 128.

[38] Thomas Willing to Haldimand, July 6, 1772, B. M., Add. MSS., 21,721; Gage to Hillsborough, September 2, 1772, P. R. O., Am. and W. I., vol. 128; Gage to Johnson, September 4, 1772, General Gage's Letters, Harvard College Library; Gage to Haldimand, June 3, 1773, Can. Arch., series B, vol. 5, p. 142.

[39] Cabinet Minute, December 1, 1771, Dartmouth Papers, *Fourteenth Report, Royal Hist. MSS. Commission*, Appendix X, 81; Hillsborough to Gage, December 4, 1771, P. R. O., Am. and W. I., vol. 127; Gage to Hillsborough, March 4, 1772, Sparks MSS., XLIII, vol. 3, p. 165; Gage to Haldimand, March 16, 1772, Can. Arch., series B, vol. 5, p. 73; Gage to Hillsborough, April 13, 1772, P. R. O., Am. and W. I., vol. 128. The current opinion has heretofore been that the Mississippi floods destroyed the fort. See any State history for statement to that effect.

[40] For an account of the anxiety felt for the security of the fort, and of the various attempts to secure it, see Wilkins to Gage, September 13, 1768, P. R. O., Am. and W. I., vol. 124; Gage to Hillsborough, January 6, 1770, *ibid.*, vol. 126; same to same, December 7, 1770, *ibid.*; Hillsborough to Gage, February 11, 1771, *ibid.*, vol. 127; same to same, July 3, 1771, *ibid.*

commandant and people was greatly altered. Captain Lord entered upon a policy of conciliation, and in a short time won the confidence and respect of the inhabitants,[41] with the result that their clamor for a change of government was considerably minimized. The tact which he displayed in his relations with the French, and his boldness in dealing with the Indian nations [42] likewise elicited the commendation both of the commanding general and of the home authorities.[43] The abuses and disorders of previous years had been largely a matter of controversy and mutual accusation, but with the removal of Wilkins, and the ejec-

[41] See for example, letter of Daniel Blouïn to Dartmouth, October 6, 1773, wherein he speaks of Captain Lord as acting "so fairly", B. T. Papers (Hist. Soc. Pa.), vol. XXXI. The Kaskaskia Records show no evidence of the least hostility to Lord, and the official correspondence likewise reveals no proof of friction.

[42] The period from 1772 to 1774 was a critical one in Indian affairs throughout the West. In 1774 occurred the Dunmore War, involving the borders of Pennsylvania and Virginia, and at the same time all the western Indians were extremely uneasy. Murders and raids were especially frequent in Illinois. For illustrations of this and of Commandant Lord's conduct, see Lord to Gage, April 20, 1772, Can. Arch., series B, vol. 27, p. 204; Letter of Charles Stuart, May 1, 1772, *ibid.*, vol. 12, p. 118; Gage to Hillsborough, May 6, 1772, P. R. O., Am. and W. I., vol. 128; Gage to Johnson, May 12, 1772, General Gage's Letters, Harvard College Library; Hamilton to Stuart, May 29, 1772, Can. Arch., series B, vol. 12, p. 75; Lord to Stuart, May 30, 1772, *ibid.*, p. 77; Gage to Johnson, September 4, 1772, General Gage's Letters; Dartmouth to Gage, November 4, 1772, P. R. O., Am. and W. I., vol. 128; Gage to Johnson, December 15, 1772, General Gage's Letters; Gage to Johnson, March 31, 1773, *ibid.*; same to same, April 25, 1773, *ibid.*; Lord to Gage, April 20, 1773, B. M., Add. MSS., 21,687; Gage to Dartmouth, June 2, 1773, P. R. O., Am. and W. I., vol. 128; Haldimand to Gage, August 31, 1773, Can. Arch., series B, vol. 5, p. 182; Haldimand to Dartmouth, August 31, 1773, B. M., Add. MSS., 21,695; Dartmouth to Johnson, December 1, 1773, *N. Y. Col. Docs.*, VIII, 404; letter to Gage, July 3, 1774, Can. Arch., series B, vol. 5, p. 280; letter to Charles Stuart, July 22, 1774, *ibid.*, vol. 12, p. 388.

[43] Gage to Dartmouth, February 8, 1773, P. R. O., Am. and W. I., vol. 128; same to same, May 5, 1773, *ibid.*; same to same, June 2, 1773, *ibid.*; Dartmouth to Haldimand, December 1, 1773, Johnson MSS., vol. XXV, no. 221.

tion from the country of the English and French concerned in the disputes,[44] complaints became less frequent.[45]

The government was anxious, nevertheless, to displace the military government by one more suited to the needs of the people. Although the constitution proposed by the French representatives was not acceptable, the authorities were willing to establish one along the lines suggested by Gage in 1772,[46] which was certainly an improvement over the military government and over the system under which they had lived during the French régime. Gage ordered the commandant, therefore, to give the people another trial and to intimate to them that their request for a government of such a character would be favorably received, provided their petition be forwarded from Illinois through the regular military channels.[47] But the changed condition of things in Illinois had brought about a feeling of

[44] Gage to Haldimand, May 5, 1773, P. R. O., Am. and W. I., vol. 128.

[45] *Ibid.*

[46] "A Civil Establishment at the Ilinois has been very long an object of consideration; and as I have comprehended the matter, the only obstacle towards the completion of it, has been the Difficulty of forming a Government of small Expence, and suitable to their Situation and Circumstances." Gage to Dartmouth, May 5, 1773, *ibid.* "There have been Thoughts of a Civil Government at the Ilinois, if the people should desire one in such a Form as His Majesty could grant and suitable to their situation." Gage to Haldimand, June 3, 1773, Can. Arch., series B, vol. 5, p. 142.

[47] "I have . . . wrote to the Commanding Officer at Kaskaskies to desire he would confer again with the people of the Ilinois on the subject of a Civil Government, and endeavour to prevail on them to send, thro' him, some reasonable proposals on that head . . ." Gage to Dartmouth, April 7, 1773, P. R. O., Am. and W. I., vol. 128. "Captain Lord has again Orders to try the people on the Subject and to prevail on them to apply properly through their Commanding Officer." Gage to Haldimand, June 3, 1773, Can. Arch., series B, vol. 5, p. 142. Gage further says that he "gave the Inhabitants of that Country to Understand I should receive no Proposals but through their Commander". Gage to Haldimand, January 5, 1774, B. M., Add. MSS., 21,665.

indifference towards the whole question. In a report to General Haldimand, the acting commander-in-chief in 1773, Commandant Lord wrote that "The Inhabitants have given me no answer on the subject of a Civil Establishment." "I believe", he continued, "the apprehension they have of losing all the Troops should the Civil Government be fixed makes them so inactive in the matter. The little money that circulates now comes first from the Troops. Should they be recalled, the inhabitants having no market for their Property, would soon be reduced to the most miserable situation in life."[48] There is no evidence that any further interest was taken in the subject by the inhabitants themselves.[49]

[48] September 3, 1773, Can. Arch., series B, vol. 31, p. 7.

[49] This is somewhat contrary to the current view. Bancroft says on this point: "It was on the fourth of November that the fathers of the Commonwealth of Illinois, through their agent Daniel Bloüin, forwarded their indignant protest against the proposed form, which they rejected as oppressive and absurd; much worse than any of the French or even the Spanish Colonies; . . . 'Should a Government so evidently tyranical be established', such was their language to the British minister, 'it could be of no long duration; there would exist the necessity of its being abolished'." *Hist. of U. S.*, ed. 1854, VI, 472. Mason, *Chapters from Ill. Hist.*, 283, and, quite recently, Parrish, *Historic Ill.*, have enlarged upon the story. They declare that, in a public meeting, and under the leadership of Daniel Bloüin, a protest was drawn up by the inhabitants against the plan proposed by the government, and forwarded to Lord Dartmouth. This is a myth, pure and simple. Bancroft's original statement is based upon a letter written to Dartmouth by Bloüin, dated at New York, November 4, 1773. From this letter Bancroft extracted the detached phrases regarding the oppression, etc., of the plan quoted in his statement. A careful reading of the whole letter indicates, however, that the sentiments expressed are those of Bloüin and Clazon, and not of the people of Illinois. For this letter see P. R. O., Am. and W. I., vol. 128. There is absolutely no record to indicate that any public meeting was held in 1773 to consider a government. Proof of the apathy of the people has just been cited. Nor is there any evidence that Bloüin was in Illinois between 1771 and 1774. For evidence that he was in New York or the East during this time, see Bloüin to Dartmouth, October 6, 1773, B. T. Papers (Hist. Soc. Pa.), vol. XXXI, and Haldimand to Lord, October 13, 1773, B. M., Add. MSS., 21,693.

Another wave of land speculation[50] similar to that of 1766 occurred in 1773, when we find the organization of the Illinois Land Company, composed chiefly of Philadelphians, and in 1775, upon the formation of the Wabash Land Company. William Murray, representing the Illinois Company, purchased from the Indians in 1773 one large tract of land on the Illinois River, and another south of Kaskaskia on the Ohio, both of which the company purposed to colonize. Later the Wabash Company, through its agent Viviat, an Illinois Frenchman, purchased tracts on the Wabash River. These purchases were in direct contravention of the proclamation of 1763, and, although the purchasers exhibited the opinions of Lord Camden and Chancellor York to the effect that such transactions were valid,[51] the government through General Gage annulled the

---

[50] The following extract from a letter of Gage is of interest in this connection: "There have many reports spread through America concerning New Governments on the Ohio and the Mississippi, and a Book called *Political Essays* has been lately published in London, wherein the Author treats largely of the Colonies. He finds great fault with England for Colonizing in the Manner she has done in the Northern Provinces, and blames the Ministers for not endeavouring to remedy past Errors, by opening new Tracts of fertile Lands to the Westward, to tempt the Northern People to move thither; and talks of the great advantage to be obtained by establishing new Governments . . . He advances many things as Facts, which we all know to be absolute Falsehoods." Letter to Haldimand, May 18, 1772, B. M., Add. MSS., 21,693. Gage refers doubtless to *Political Essays concerning the Present State of the British Empire*, etc. Under section IV, "Defects in the Establishment of the Colonies and the means of Remedying them", he treats of the desirability of settlements on the Mississippi and Ohio. He criticises severely the proclamation of 1763 restricting settlements east of the Alleghany Mountains. James Adair, another contemporary writer, in an elaborate argument, censures the policy of the English Government in refusing to found colonies and governments in the West, on the Ohio and Mississippi rivers, where the surplus population of England and the colonies might go, *History of the American Indian*, 454–460.

[51] Gage to Haldimand, February 2, 1774, Can. Arch., series B, vol. 5, p. 214; Lord to Gage, July 3, 1773, B. M., Add. MSS., 21,687. For the opinion of York see B. M., Add. MSS., 21,687.

STRUGGLE FOR CIVIL GOVERNMENT 161

grants.[52] This ended the successive attempts to create an independent colony in the Illinois country.

In 1774 came the opportunity to make a final disposition of the Illinois French. During the period under consideration events had so shaped themselves in the neighboring colony of Canada that the ministry was under the necessity of reorganizing the government of that province. The proclamation of 1763 had extended English law to Canada with the result that the French inhabitants were subjected to many hardships. Their grievances were now to be taken into consideration by the government, and as the solution of the western and Canadian problems seemed to be closely connected, the two questions were taken up at the same time. General Gage was summoned home in 1773, and was directed to bring with him every paper relating to the West which might tend to "explain as well the causes as the effects" of the abuses and disorders in Illinois.[53]

---

[52] For an account of the Illinois and Wabash land companies, see a pamphlet published in Philadelphia in 1796 entitled *Account of the Proceedings of the Illinois and Ouabache Land Companies*. See also memorials in *American State Papers, Public Lands*, vols. I and II. The history of their operations may be traced in the following letters: Lord to Haldimand, July 3, 1773, Can. Arch., series B, vol. 70, p. 132; Lord to Gage, July 3, 1773, Johnson MSS., vol. XXV, no. 211; Johnson to Haldimand, September 30, 1773, B. M., Haldimand Papers, Corr. with Sir William Johnson, 1759-1774; Haldimand to Dartmouth, October 6, 1773, Can. Arch., series B, vol. 35; Haldimand to Lord, October 10, 1773, *ibid.*, p. 110; Haldimand to Johnson, October 20, 1773, B.M., Haldimand Papers, Corr. with Sir William Johnson, 1759-1774; Dartmouth to Haldimand, November 1, 1773, Can. Arch., series B, vol. 35, p. 52; Haldimand to Dartmouth, November 13, 1773, B. M., Haldimand Papers, Corr. with Lord Dartmouth, 1773-1775; Dartmouth to Haldimand, December 1, 1773, Johnson MSS., vol. XXV, no. 221; Haldimand to Dartmouth, January 5, 1774, Can. Arch., series B, vol. 35, p. 62; Dartmouth to Haldimand, January 8, 1774, P. R. O., Am. and W. I., vol. 128; Haldimand to Lord, March 9, 1774, Can. Arch., series B, vol. 33, p. 233; Haldimand to Gage, March 4, 1774, B. M., Add. MSS., 21,655.

[53] Dartmouth to Gage, March 3, 1773, B. M., Add. MSS., 21,697. It was also decided to send an agent into the Illinois country for the

As a result of his recommendations and of the investigations of the ministry the Quebec Act of 1774 was enacted,[54] according to the provisions of which the entire Northwest was included within the limits of the province of Quebec.[55] In the instructions issued to the governor of Canada in January, 1775,[56] we find provisions for the government of Illinois. It was to be governed from Quebec, and a lieutenant-governor or superintendent was to reside at Kaskaskia,[57] at which place also a lower court of King's Bench was to be established to coöperate with the superior courts of the province in general.[58]

These arrangements were not put into execution, however, because of the outbreak of the American Revolution, which absorbed the whole attention of both the home government and Canada. As early as January, 1774, the detachment of troops had been ordered to leave Fort Gage, and the allowance to the commanding officer discontinued.[59]

---

purpose of making an exact report of every phase of the western problem, including Indian affairs and the temper of the French inhabitants. A Major Hay was selected for the mission. Dartmouth to Haldimand, October 14, 1773, P. R. O., Am. and W. I., vol. 128; Haldimand to Dartmouth, March 2, 1774, B. M., Add. MSS., 21,695; Haldimand to Johnson, April 7, 1774, *ibid.*, 21,670; same to same, April 29, 1774, *ibid.*; letter to Robert Basset, April 30, 1774, *Mich. Pioneer and Hist. Colls.*, X, 260; Johnson to Haldimand, May 5, 1774, Can. Arch., series B, vol. X, p. 165; Guy Johnson to Haldimand, August 20, 1774, Can. Arch., series B, vol. X, p. 178. The results of the mission, however, do not appear.

[54] Text of the Act in *Can. Const. Docs.*, *1759-1791*, 401-405. This volume also contains the various draughts of the bill. For the best discussion of the act, see Coffin, *Province of Quebec and the Early Am. Rev.*, 275-562.

[55] *Can. Const. Docs.*, *1759-1791*, 402.

[56] *Can. Arch. Report*, 1904, 229-242.

[57] *Ibid.*, 233.   [58] *Ibia.*, 242.

[59] Barrington to Haldimand, February 2, 1774, B. M., Add. MSS., 21,695. See also "List of Officers who have commanded at the Outposts from 25th December 1772 to 24th December 1773 inclusive", *ibid.*, 21,696. Lord and a few of the soldiers did not, however, leave

From this time on little or no attention was paid to western affairs. Illinois was left in the hands of a Frenchman named Rocheblave, who acted as agent for the government from 1776 to 1778.[60] His best efforts to save the country to Great Britain were, however, in vain. As the government had ignored his call for troops, an American army under George Rogers Clark easily effected the conquest of Illinois, and the whole Northwest in 1778.

until the spring of 1776. There is evidence of this in *A Narrative of the Transactions, Imprisonment and Sufferings of John Connolly, an American Loyalist*, 19–29, and in Carleton to Lord, July 19, 1776, B. M., Add. MSS., 21,699.

[60] Alvord, *Ill. Hist. Colls.*, II, xxxi–xliii.

DOCUMENTARY APPENDIX.

I. Memorial of the Mississippi Company to the King and Resolutions for the Government of the Company.[1]

At a meeting of the Mississippi Company at Belleview Sept. 9th, 1763.

Present,

Thomas Ludwell Lee	Presly Thornton
George Washington	James Douglas
Francis Lightfoot Lee	William Fitzhugh, Sen.
Thomas Bullitt	Henry Fitzhugh
Richard Henry Lee	Francis Thornton
Anthony Stewart	George Stimson
William Lee	William Booth
John Aug. Washington	William Brent
Charles Diggs	Robert Brent

A Memorial to his Majesty being read, some amendments made thereto, the same was agreed to and is as followeth:

To the King's most Excellent Majesty.

The Humble Memorial of Inhabitants of Great Britain, Virginia, Maryland, etc.

May it please Your Majesty,

The Memorialists considering it the duty of all good subjects to improve to the utmost of their power the blessings of peace and reflecting how this improvement may be best obtained by the exertions of their abilities and the applications of their fortunes; have proposed with the approbation and under the pro-

[1] Chatham MSS., vol. 97, Public Record Office, London.

tection of Your Majesty to settle as speedily and as effectually as possible, some part of that vast country on the Mississippi and its waters; now unquestionably your Majesty's territory by the late Treaty of Peace.

The Increase of the people, the extension of trade and the enlargement of the revenue are with certainty to be expected, where the fertility of the soil, and mildness of the Climate invite emigrants (provided they can obtain Lands on easy terms) to settle and cultivate commodities most wanted by Great Britain and which will bear the charges of a tedious navigation, by the high prices usually given for them,—such as Hemp, Flax, Silk, Wine, Potash, Cochineal, Indigo, Iron, etc., by which means the Mother Country will be supplied with many necessary materials, that are now purchased of foreigners at a very great expense. Especially naval stores so essential to the very being of a commercial state, that it must index great restraints, in all transactions with those powers by whom they are furnished. Whilst the inhabitants of the infant settlements, finding their labor most profitably bestowed upon Agriculture will not think of interfering with the Mother Country in Manufactures but afford a never failing demand for them.

To effect these good purposes the memorialists have formed themselves into a Company by the name of the Mississippi Company, that by a Union of their Councils and fortunes they may in the most prudent and proper manner explore and as quickly as possible settle that part of the Country hereafter mentioned, if your Majesty shall be graciously pleased to indulge them with these conditions.

1st That Your Majesty grant unto your memorialists, being fifty in number by name of the Mississippi Company two million five hundred thousand acres of Land on the Mississippi and its waters, to be laid off within the following bounds beginning upon the East side of the River Mississippi one hundred and twenty miles above or to the northward of the confluence of the River Ohio therewith. Thence by a line to strike the River Wabash or St. Ireon eighty miles above its junction with the River Ohio. Thence southerly crossing the River Ohio one hundred and twenty miles above the union of the Ohio and Wabash, and abutting on the main branch of the River Cherokee or Tennessee one hundred and fifty miles above the junction of Cherokee River with Ohio and proceeding thence Westerly in a line to strike the River Mississippi ninety miles below the union of Ohio with that River ; thence upon the said River to the beginning.

2ly That your memorialists shall have liberty of holding their lands twelve or any other larger number of years that your Majesty shall approve (after a survey thereof shall have been made and returned) clear of all composition money quit rent or taxes. And that your memorialists within twelve years shall be obliged to seat the said lands with two hundred families, at the least, if not interrupted by the Savages, or any Foreign Enemy, and to return the Survey thereof to such office as your Majesty shall be pleased to direct, otherwise to forfeit the grant, so to be made by your Majesty, and the said lands liable to the entries of any other Adventurers.

The Memorialists humbly hope that Your Majesty may be graciously moved to grant these favorable terms in consideration of the heavy charges and great expences they must necessarily incur, in the exploring, surveying and settling this distant Country and the great risk they will run of losing their property, from their contiguity to the French and their proximity to the Indian Nations. And because it has been proved by experience, that large tracts of land taken up by Companies may be retailed by them to Individuals, much cheaper than they can obtain them immediately from the Crown, occasioned by the charges arising from the solicitation of patents, making surveys and other contingent expences. Besides the difficulty the poorer sort are under from their ignorance of the proper methods to be taken in solliciting patents as well as their inability to advance ready money for such purposes. Whereas from Companies they have only to receive their Conveyances, without any previous Expence, credit given them to make their payments, when by their industry they become enabled to do so.

And though attempts to settle in this way have sometimes miscarried, in the hands of Gentlemen possessed of afluent fortunes, because of that indolence and inattention frequently attending persons in such circumstances especially when not excited by the near prospect of immediate and considerable profit. The greater part of the present Adventurers being of good families and considerable influence in the Counties where they live, though possessed of but moderate fortunes, are induced from the goodness of the Soil and Climate of the Country upon the Mississippi to believe that by a proper application of their money and industry, they will acquire as well a present advantage as a provision for their prosperity; which being joined by the pleasing prospect of public utility; all their affairs will be conducted with that spirited assiduity, which in matters of danger and difficulty, can only insure success. The truth of this is evident from a determined resolution in several of the members to be themselves among the first settlers.

The Memorialists most humbly submit it to Your Majestie's great Wisdom whether the remote situation of this Country from the Colonies already settled may not render it expedient to protect the Infant Settlement from the insults of the Savages. Which protection might effectually be obtained, if Your Majesty were graciously pleased to order a small Fort to be garrisoned at the confluence of Cherokee River with Ohio; as it would interpose between the first Settlers, and the Chicazaw and Chattaes Indians, the only powerful Nations in that quarter. Which is probable, might by a small garrison, be influenced to continue in their ancient amity with British Subjects. Especially the former of these Nations, whose faith and friendship have ever remained firm and unaltered. At the same time a garrison placed at the junction of Ohio and Mississippi Rivers, if they should be disposed to encroach on the Dominions of Your Majesty, in that part where they appear to have been inclinable to take footing on account of its communication with the northwestern lakes ; and the conveniences wherewith in time of War they can harass and disturb Your Majestie's Colonies already settled.

It is humbly conceived from the mild and friendly disposition of the Southern Indians that the Settlement of the Country proposed, may be obtained more safely and speedily by beginning such settlem$^{t.}$ in their Neighborhood than further North, where the fierce and warlike Irocois, with their six Nations ever accustomed to War and shedding of blood, would certainly obstruct, if not absolutely prevent the Settlement for many years to come, while the southern Settlem$^{t.}$ begun in safety and advancing in security will soon become much too powerful to be prevented in their progress, by the enmity of the Northern or any other Indians. At the same time that by conducting a trade useful to the Indians on the borders of Mississippi they will effectually prevent the success of that cruel policy, which has ever directed the French even in time of peace, to prevail with the Indians their Neighbors to lay waste the frontiers of Your Majestie's Colonies thereby to prevent their increase.

In consideration of the reasons here afforded, the Memorialists most humbly submit this their Memorial to Your Majesty's Wisdom.

Resolved that Wm Lee, Esq., be appointed Treasurer to the Company and that he give Bond with Security, in the Penalty of One thousand pounds current money to the Company for the just and faithful performance of his Office of Treasurer.

Resolved that the annual general meeting of the Company shall be held at Stafford Court House in Virginia on the first day of October if the same should not happen on Sunday ; if it should then the meeting to be on the day following.

Resolved that the following members to wit, Honble Presly Thornton, Thomas Ludwell Lee, Richard Henry Lee, Francis Lightfoot Lee, Henry Fitzhugh, John Augustine Washington, William Booth, William Brodenbrough, Richard Parker Esquire, and Doctor William Flood be appointed a Committee of the Company who are to meet at Westmoreland Court House in Virginia twice a year (that is to say) on the 10th day of May and the 10th day of November, if not on Sunday; if it sho^{d.} happen to be on Sunday, then the meeting to be on the next day and likewise they are to meet as much oftener as the affairs of the Company require ; and the said Committee to have such power as they, by the general Articles of Agreement, are vested with.

Resolved that the said Committee do with all possible diligence transmit the Memorial after the same shall be fairly transcribed, to Thos. Cumming Esqr. of London to be by him laid before the King; that they invite Mr. Cumming to be one of the Company, and desire him to procure subscribers to the Scheme, not exceeding nine of such influence and fortune as may be likely to promote its success. That the Committee request Mr. Cumming, that if he sho'd not choose to be one of the Company or to sollicit their Grant, to put all their affairs into the hands of an Agent or Sollicitor as in his opinion may be most likely by his Interest and Diligence to Succeed; That Mr. Cumming on finding the Ministry disposed to comply with the Company's Memorial give the most early intelligence thereof to the Committee, in order that a meeting of the Company may be had to raise such a Sum of money as may be sufficient to obtain Letters Patent from the Crown, that in the meantime he proceed as far as the nature of the thing will admit in issuing out the said Letters Patent ; That he inform the Committee, the expence that will accrue on the said issuing of such Letters Patent.

Resolved that the Sum of One Hundred and Twenty-two pounds Sterling be forthwith paid by the Company into the hands of the Treasurer to be by him disposed of according to the direction of the Committee. Each member being allowed to pay his proportion in so much current money of Virginia as will amount to his Sterling proportion.

Resolved that the Committee inform Mr. Cumming that if he chooses to undertake the Sollicitation of their affairs they present him with an hundred Guineas as an earnest of their present and future good-will.

DOCUMENTARY APPENDIX 171

Resolved that altho' the Original Articles of Agreement, do declare that a general meeting of the Company shall be had at one particular time and place annually ; yet if it shall happen that the circumstances of affairs render it necessary that a general meeting should be more frequently held, the Committee shall have power to summon the said general meeting (by advertising it twice in the Virginia and Maryland Gazette) as often as shall be requisite, and a majority of such general meeting as meet shall have full and ample power to determine all matters relative to the Company and their determinations to be binding on the whole Company and that it shall be a never failing rule of the Company, whenever a contrariety of opinion shall arise concerning the Sum of money to be raised and different Sums shall be proposed, that the least Sum mentioned shall first be put to question, and rise from thence to the next greatest Sum, untill the highest Sum proposed has been put, and that which has the largest number of votes shall be the Sum to be raised by the Company.

Resolved that if the Company shall be so fortunate as to succeed in their Sollicitations, and a grant be obtained for the Lands they request in that Case when it shall be determined by a general meeting that a division of the Lands shall be made, such a division, shall for the sake of fairness and impartiality, be effected in the following manner: The whole Quantity of Land shall be divided into as many equal lots or parcels, as there shall be members or shares in the Company, and the lots so divided shall be numbered, and as many correspondent numbers being prepared, each member or a substitute by him appointed (provided he make such appointment in twelve months after the Division shall be agreed on, and notice thereof conveyed to him, by the Treasurer for the time being, but if he fail to make such appointment then the majority of the general meeting shall appoint a person to act for such absentee) shall draw from among such corresponding numbers, and whatever number is drawn by each shall take such lot of Land, the number of which agrees with the numbers drawn.

II. "Reasons for establishing a British Colony at the Illinois with some Proposals for carrying the same into immediate Execution."[1]

The Country of the Illinois on the Mississippi, is generally allowed to be the most fertile and pleasant Part of all the Western Territory now in the Possession of the English in North America.

The French Canadians have long called it, *The Terrestrial Paradice*.

It appears from the best Intelligence, that about Four Hundred French Families are now settled in that Country; and that, in all Probability it would have been the most considerable French Settlement in North America, had not the Inhabitants throughout Canada, and Louisiana, particularly those living among, or near Indians, been Subjected to Military Command, liable to be taken from their Farms even in the Time of Harvest, to go upon distant Expeditions, and to have the Product of their Labour seized for the Use of the Army.

It has been the mistaken Policy of the French to aim at establishing Military instead of Commercial, Colonies in North America. Their Views were to expel the English from all their Settlements on the Sea Coast, and thereby to engross the whole of the Continent.

In this, however, they have, thro' Providence, been happily disappointed.

But had the French contented themselves with settling and improving the Country they actually possessed, they would have rivalled the English in their most valuable American Commodities, and have increased the Commerce of France, and consequently the French Power, to a very great Degree. For instance,

---

[1] In Sir William Johnson's letter of July 10, 1766, Board of Trade Papers (Hist. Soc. Pa.), Plantations General, vols. 27 and 28, 1765-1767; Franklin Papers (Am. Phil. Soc.), LVIII, 4.

The Lands in Louisiana produce Tobacco of a much superior Quality to any raised in either Maryland or Virginia, and Rice and Indigo equal to the best of Carolina.

Those Articles, with Skins and Furs, are the principal Commodities which North America has hitherto produced to any great Extent, for European Consumption.

But were the Lands on the Mississippi well settled, we should be enabled to supply all Europe with those Commodities, and at a far cheaper Rate than they could be afforded from any other Country.

But what is of the utmost Consequence to Great Britain, no Country in the known World is better adapted than this for the Raising Hemp, Flax and Silk.

Of the Former, indeed, there are immense Quantities growing Spontaneously on the large extensive Plains of Louisiana, And this wild sort appears from some late Experiments, to have a firmer Texture than that commonly cultivated. The Country likewise abounds with Mulberry Trees and both native and foreign Silk Worms thrive extremely well there.

Great Britain might also be furnished from thence with Cotton, Copper, Iron, Pot Ash, Wine, Salt petre, a great variety of valuable Medicinal Drugs and other Articles, which, with those mentioned before, make the great Ballance of Trade against the Nation, and drain it of its Treasure.

From the Illinois we might likewise carry on a more extensive and advantageous Fur-Trade, with the numerous Indian Nations which reside near the Lakes and the different Branches of the Mississippi, than was ever known since the first Settlement of America;—Supplying them with British Manufactures to a vast Amount.

Nor will the French be able to rival us in this Trade, as we can transport our Goods through Pennsylvania and Virginia to that Country much cheaper than can be done from New Orleans up the Mississippi. This is the only passage the French have now left, and being all the Way, *against the Stream* is extremely difficult and tedious. Whereas the English have now a ready

Communication from Virginia and Pennsylvania to Fort Pitt on the Ohio, and from thence have Water Carriage *with the Stream* to the Mississippi, and when they have disposed of their Goods to the Indians in that Country, they may easily transport the Commodities they receive in Return down the Mississippi to Mobile, and from thence ship them to England.

For want of this Opening thro' the middle Province of North America to the Mississippi, the French never had it in their Power to reap so much advantage from that Country as the English now may.

After several Disappointments, and much Expence and Trouble, the English have at length got possession of all the French posts on the East Side of the Missippi [sic]:

A Question arises. What will be the most efficacious Means of supporting these Posts, so distant from every British Settlement, and yet so necessary to maintain the British Interest amongst the numerous Indians which inhabit that, and the adjacent Country?

It is answered, That there is no Way so effectual as to settle a Colony at the *Illinois* under a good civil Government.

This Colony being in one of the finest Corn Countries in the World, would have it in its Power, not only to supply the different Posts in the Indian Country, but the two *Floridas* with provisions. Several of the French Writers term it the *Granary* of Louisiana, and mention that at a Time when there happened to be a Scarcity at New Orleans, the French Settlement at the Illinois, small as it then was, Sent them upwards of 800,000 Weight of Flour.

If we have not a Colony on the Spot, to support the Posts We are now possessed of in that Country, the French who have a Fort and an encreasing Settlement on the opposite Shore of the Mississippi, will have it in their Power, by means of their Influence with the Indians, to intercept our Supplies, interrupt our Trade, and ultimately cut off all Communication between the Illinois and the present English Colonies.

It is said, that many of the French in Canada, and numbers

of those settled on the East Side of the Mississippi, near our Posts, intend to remove to the Settlement belonging to the French on the opposite Shore.

Should the French succeed in establishing a Colony there (which they probably will as it is in so fine a Country) and we have not another to Balance it, in that part of the World, the Consequences may be very Prejudicial to the British Interest.

It may not be amiss to quote here the Sentiments of a late Writer very conversant with this Subject. In speaking of the Fineness of the Soil and climate of the Country on each Side the Mississippi, near the Illinois, he says "It is this that has made the French undergo so many long and perilous Voyages in North America, upwards of Two Thousand Miles, against Currents, Cataracts, and boisterous Winds on the Lakes, in order to get this Settlement of the *Illinois*; which is nigh to the *Forks of the Mississippi*, the *most important place* in all the inland Parts of North America, to which the French will sooner or later remove from *Canada*; and there erect another Montreal, that will be much more dangerous and prejudicial to us, than ever the other in Canada was. They will here be in the Midst of all their old Friends and Allies, and much more convenient to carry on a Trade with them, to spirit them up against the English etc. than ever they were at Montreal. To this Settlement, where they likewise are not without good Hopes of finding Mines, the French will forever be removing, as long as any of them are left in *Canada*."

The most likely Way to prevent these Mischiefs, and to enable the English to dispossess the French of the remaining Part of Louisiana, should a future War make it expedient, will be, it is thought, to establish a Colony there, agreeable to the following Proposals, Viz^t.

1. Let the Crown purchase of the Indians all their Rights to that Tract of Country lying on the East Side of the River Mississippi, between the Illinois River and the River Ohio, and Fifty Miles back from the said River Mississippi.

Remarks

This Tract includes *Fort Chartres, Cahoke, and Kaskasquias* (three considerable French Settlements) and it is said from good Authority, that the Indians have expressed an Inclination to part with it to the English on very moderate Terms, and that they might easily be persuaded to sell all the Lands as far back as the Heads of the several small Rivers which empty themselves into the Mississippi between the Illinois and the Ohio. They having a greater Quantity of fine Hunting Country than they can ever have any use for. This would be a sufficient Tract to begin a Colony upon, and having a natural Boundary, would be most preferable.

2. Let a Civil Government be established there, agreeable to the Principles of an English Constitution.

3. Let the first Governor be a person experienced in the Management of Indian Affairs, and who has given Proofs of his Influence with the Savages.

Remark

This is a Matter of the utmost Consequence in the first Settlement of a Colony surrounded by Indians: And for want of a due Attention to it, many Undertakings of the like kind have either entirely failed, or been greatly impeded.

4. Let all the Lands which may be granted within the first Twenty Years be laid out in Town Ships, after the Manner practiced in some of the New England Colonies, or according to the Plan laid down in the *Historical Account of the Expedition under Colonel Bouquet*[1], lately published (quod vide).

Remark

The Advantage of this Mode of Settling in a Country surrounded by Savages, who may One Day become Enemies, are too obvious to need mentioning.

5. Let Grants of Land in this Country be offered to the *Pro-*

---

[1] See p. 119. n. 45, and bibliography for account of pamphlet.

vincial Officers and soldiers who served in the late War in America, in the following Terms,-Viz^t

100 Acres to every common Soldier.
150 Acres to every Corporal and Serjeant.
250 Acres to every Ensign.
350 Acres to every Lieutenant.
350 Acres to every Surgeon.
350 Acres to every Chaplain.
500 Acres to every Captain.
750 Acres to every Major.
1,000 Acres to every Lieut. Collonel.
1,200 Acres to every Collonel.

The Soldiers, Corporals and Serjeants who have served more Campaigns than one to have *Ten* Acres besides for each Campaign after the first. The Ensigns, Lieutenants, Surgeons, Chaplains and Captains *Thirty*, and the Majors, Lieut. Colonels, *Fifty* Acres, in like manner Each General Officer (of which there were two or Three) to have a Grant of 5,000 Acres. The whole to be granted in Fee, and to be exempt from Quit Rent for a certain Term of Years, or for, and during the natural Lives of the said Officers and Soldiers; and then to be liable to the same only as is reserved in Virginia. No Grant to be made to any Officer or Soldier under Fifty Years of Age, who does not appear *in person* at the *Illinois* (with a Certificate from the Government, or Commander in Chief of the Province in whose Employ he was, specifying his Station, and the Number of Campaigns he was in the Service) and actually make a Settlement on the Lands for which he shall receive a Warrant of Survey.—But such Officers and Soldiers as are fifty Years of Age and upwards, and who may not incline, or be able to remove to the Illinois, should be allowed either to dispose of their Rights to Grants of Lands to such Persons as will settle them, or place Tenants thereon, as may be most convenient to themselves. Provided; That every Officer and Soldier who does not make, or cause to be made a Settlement and Improvement on the Lands he may be entituled to, within Six Years after the

Arrival of an English Governor at the Illinois in order to establish a Colony there, shall forfeit all Right and Title Thereto. Provided also that every Officer of the Rank of a Captain, and upwards shall at his own proper Cost and Expence settle upon his Grant at least One white Protestant Person for every Hundred Acres thereof within Six Years following the Date of his said Grant—Subject to the Forfeiture of such Proportion of the said Grant, as there shall be a Deficiency of that Number of Settlers.—It would be proper for the Crown to furnish the Soldiery with a few Implements of Husbandry at their first Arrival at the Illinois, and to allow all Settlers the Use of the King's Boats at Fort Pitt, and other Assistance, to transport themselves as far as the Mississippi.

Remark

The giving Encouragement to these Men, who are Soldiers as well as Farmers, etc[a] to engage themselves in the first Settlement of this Country, will be not only, Right in point of Policy, but be an Act of Justice. The Provincial Officers and Soldiers who have served in the several Campaigns during the War in America, and who have undergone equal Fatigues, and run equal Hazards with the King's Troops, think it extremely hard, that they should not be allowed, as well as the disbanded Regulars, a Grant of some of the Lands in that immense Tract of Country, which they have assisted in obtaining from the Enemy, especially as they had not equal Advantages when in Service; The Officers not being entituled to half Pay, nor the Men to Chelsea Hospital. They were generally paid off and discharged, as soon as the Campaign was over. The giving these persons Lands in Proportion to their Rank, and the Number of Campaigns they have served will be likewise a great Encouragement to the Colonists to enter into the Military Service on any future Occasion. And, besides, it is said, that at the Beginning of the late War, the Americans were promised, or given to understand, that such of them as engaged in the Provincial Service, should, when the War was at an End, have some such Gratification in Land as is here proposed.

6. Let all Mines and Minerals belong to the Owners of the Land in which they may be found, except those denominated *Royal Mines*, and of these let the Crown reserve a Fifth, clear of all Charges.

Remark

This will encourage People to be at the Trouble and Expence of searching for and working of Mines, but if the whole or too great a Part is reserved to the Crown, they will want the necessary Inducement to make Discoveries, whereby both the Crown and Nation may be prevented from receiving many Advantages.

7. Let there be 500 Acres reserved in every Township for the maintenance of a Clergyman of the Established Church of England.

Remark

As it is the Interest of every Nation, that the Religion, it has thought proper to establish, should be the Religion most generally prevalent throughout its Dominions, this Matter ought to be particularly attended to in America, and the Church be well supported there, otherwise Presbyterianism will become the Established Religion in that Country. It is much to be regretted, that the Crown did not reserve in each of the Colonies, Lands for this purpose, at the Time of granting their respective Charters. It is however not yet too late for the Crown to cause such Reservations to be made in many of the old settled Colonies, particularly Nova-Scotia, New York, Virginia, North and South Carolina and Georgia. Care should likewise be taken, in Time, to make the like Provision in our new Acquisitions, Canada, and the Two Floridas.

8. Let the Bounds of the Colony be as follows, Viz. From the Mouth of the Ouisconsin (or Wisconsing) River down the Mississippi agreeable to Treaty, to the Forks, or Mouth of the Ohio. Then up the same River Ohio to the River Wabash, thence up the same River Wabash to the Portage at the Head thereof, Then up the said Portage to the River Miamis and

down the said River Miamis to Lake Erie. Thence along the several Courses of the said Lake to Riviere al Ours (or Bear River) and up the said River to the Head thereof, and from thence in a straight Line, or by the Portage of St. Joseph's River and down the same River to Lake Michigan, then along the several Courses of the said Lake on the South and West Side thereof to the point of Bay Puans, and along the several Courses on the East Side of the said Bay to the Mouth of Foxes River, thence up to the Head thereof and from thence by a Portage to the Head of Ouisconsin River, and down the same to the Place of Beginning.

Remark

These being natural Boundaries may be easily ascertained. Altho' no Person should be allowed to settle on any Lands, but what are within the Bounds purchased by the Crown of the Indians, yet it will be highly proper, that the Civil Jurisdiction of the Colony should extend much farther than will be probably purchased for many years to come; otherwise loose, evil disposed Persons may straggle into those Parts, and commit Disorders that may involve the Colony in Disputes with the Indians, and be attended with fatal Consequences. And it might have good Effects if a Civil Authority was likewise established at D'Etroit, to take Cognizance of all Misdemeanors committed by British Subjects upon the Lakes and Country adjacent.

9. But that a Colony may be *speedily* settled at the *Illinois*, and the Crown and Nation receive the Advantages to be derived from it, without Delay, A Company of Gentlemen of Character and Fortune are ready and willing to engage, That if the Crown will make them a Grant, in Fee of [ ] Hundred Thousand Acres of Land free of Quit Rent for [ ] Years to be located in one or more Places as they shall chuse, within the Bounds above mentioned, They will at their own proper Cost and Expence, Settle thereon at least One white Protestant Person for every Hundred Acres within [ ] Years next following the Date of their Grant; Subject to the Forfeiture of such

DOCUMENTARY APPENDIX 181

Proportion of the unsettled part of the said Grant as shall be equal to a Deficiency of that number of Settlers—And the said Company will likewise engage to settle at least 2,000 of the said Persons on the Lands aforesaid within [ ] Years next after the Date of the said Grant, or the Arrival of a Governor in the said Colony: unless an Indian War should happen to put it out of their Power.

The Crown need not be put to much Expence to procure the Settlement of this advantageous Colony. The Principal Charges will be a Salary to the Governor, and some other Officers of Government for a few Years, when the Colonists will be enabled to support their own Civil Establishment.

And if there were two or three Companies of light Infantry, and of light Horse were raised and disciplined in the manner, and on the Terms, recommended by Coll. Bouquet in the Publication before mentioned, They would not only be an effectual Security for the Colony in its Infancy, but also contribute greatly to the Protection of the Frontiers of the Old settled Colonies from the Incursions of the Indians, and they would likewise be of infinite Service in case of a future War with the French. This Corps might be raised and disciplined within a Year, or two at farthest, when the Regiment now posted there might be employed upon other Service more suitable to such Troops, unless indeed it should be thought necessary to keep a few of them to do Garrison Duty for some Time longer. The Officers who served during the War in America in the Corps of light Infantry and Rangers would be the most proper to raise and discipline the Foot Companies; but for the light Horse it will be necessary that Officers should be sent from England, who have been accustomed to that Service. Horses of a good Sort are to be had in great plenty at the Illinois. If a Company, or two of this kind of Soldiery were also kept at each of our principal Posts in the Indian Country, it would be the most likely Means of deterring the Indians from going to War with us in future.

3. LORD HILLSBOROUGH TO GENERAL GAGE.[1]

Most Secret.

WHITEHALL, Jan. 2d, 1771.

Nothing has happened since my last Letter to You to strengthen our hopes that the Public Peace might be preserved; on the contrary, there is but too much reason to apprehend that the matter in Negotiation with the Court of Spain will have its Issue in a speedy war, the Success of which will depend upon the most vigorous Exertions of every Strength this Kingdom is able to put forth.

In this situation it has become necessary to give full Scope to the Consideration not only of those measures which it may be proper to pursue for the Defence and Security of His Majesty's Possessions, but also in what places the Enemy may be annoyed and attacked with the greatest Advantage and best hope of Success, and also what Steps may be advisable, preparatory to any Enterprize that may be undertaken.

The Result of this Deliberation, so far as it regards offensive Operations in America, has been the adopting a Proposition to begin those operations by an attack upon New Orleans.

The Advantage that would attend the entire Possession of the Mississippi, both in point of Commerce and of Security to the rest of the King's Possessions in North America, have been fully expiated upon and explained in the Course of Our Correspondence and those Advantages combined with the general Intelligence of the small Number of Troops left in Louisiana by General O'Reilly, the Indisposition or rather aversion of the French Inhabitants to the Spanish Government, the great Extent and Weakness of the Defenses of the town of New Orleans, and the supposed Practicability of approaching it either on the side of West Florida or By the Rivers Ohio and Mississippi, have been the grounds on which this Proposition has been adopted. The Practicability, however, of such an undertaking,

[1] P. R. O., Am. and W. I., vol. 127.

as well as the Quantum of Force to be employed, and the manner in which the attack is to be made, must entirely depend upon your own Judgement, forming that Judgement on a variety of Facts and Circumstances that cannot be known here; and therefore it is the King's Pleasure that you do give the fullest Consideration to this Proposition, and if you see no reasonable Objections to it that you do take such preparatory Steps as shall be necessary for carrying it into immediate Execution, so soon as you shall receive the King's Orders to commence Hostilities, in Case His Majesty should be driven to that necessity;—An Event that will probably be decided upon in a few days.

It is the King's present intention, from the reliance His Majesty has upon your Ability and Zeal for the Honor of His Arms, that you should command upon this Expedition in Person: and as the Assistance of a Naval Force may be necessary on the side of the Gulph of Mexico to prevent any Succours being thrown in, either before or after the Operations are commenced, the Commander-in-Chief of the Squadron at Jamacia will be ordered to co-operate with you in this important Service, and to afford every aid the nature of his command will admit of.

The King's Servants having submitted to His Majesty their Opinion, that, as well for carrying into Execution the proposed Attack upon New Orleans, as for answering any other purposes which Government may have in view in the Prosecution of a War, it may be advisable that a large body of Troops should be collected together in one convenient Spot; I am therefore commanded to recommend this Measure for your Consideration; but at the same time I must not omit to mention to you that the force in the Province of Quebec should not be diminished, nor any reduction made of that in Newfoundland or in West Florida, nor that the Posts upon the Lakes should be left in a State of Insecurity.

4. GENERAL GAGE TO LORD HILLSBOROUGH.[1]

NEW YORK, April 2d, 1771.

Your Lordship's *Most Secret* of the 2d of January has been received. . . .

From all accounts that have been received hitherto, of the State and Condition of Louisiana, an Attack upon that Province is very practicable, and of the different means of approaching New Orleans the River Mississippi is judged the most advantageous; tho' feigned attacks might at the same time be of service, on the side of the Ohio, and West Florida.

Your Lordships Letter was not received till the 25th ult. the Packet having been about ten weeks from Falmouth, a Passage unfortunately long at this Juncture; but the greatest Diligence will be used to assemble a Body of Troops. And in due Consideration of every circumstance requisite in the fitting out an Expedition, I know no place in North America so proper as the Port of New York. I therefore propose, till camp Equipage is provided, or that the weather permits to encamp the Troops, to post them as near to New York as I shall be able.

Orders have been transmitted for the 64th and 65th Regiments to embark at Halifax for Boston; from whence they will March into some of the Colonys the most contiguous to this, till further Orders; . . .

[1] P. R. O., Am. and W. I., vol. 127.

BIBLIOGRAPHY.

In the descriptive notes which follow comment has been confined to the value of the sources and other works for the special field of the essay.

GUIDES AND BIBLIOGRAPHIES.

Alvord, C. W., "Eighteenth Century French Records in the Archives of Illinois", printed in *Annual Report of the American Historical Association* for 1905, vol. I. Washington, 1906.—Valuable.

Alvord, C. W., *Illinois in the Eighteenth Century*, printed as Bulletin of the Illinois State Historical Library, vol. I, no. 1. Springfield, Ill., 1905.—This is a report on the documents in the St. Clair County Court House at Belleville, Ill.—An illuminating study.

Andrews, Charles M., "Materials in British Archives for American Colonial History", printed in *American Historical Review*, vol. X, pp. 325-349.

Andrews, Charles M., and Frances G. Davenport, *Guide to the Manuscript Materials for the History of the United States to 1783, in the British Museum, in Minor London Archives, and in the Libraries of Oxford and Cambridge*. Carnegie Institution of Washington, Publication No. 90. Washington, 1908.—A work of first importance which appeared too late for use in the present investigation.

Canadian Archive Reports.—This well-known series is especially valuable on account of the extended inventories and calendars it contains of documents in English and French archives. Because of the careless editing of the earlier volumes they must be used with caution. Of most value for this study have been the volumes for 1884-1889, containing lists of the Bouquet and Haldimand papers, and for 1905, I, containing abstracts of documents in the Ministry of Colonies in Paris.

Channing, Edward, and Albert Bushnell Hart, *Guide to the Study of American History*. Boston, 1896.

Day, R. E., comp., *Calendar of the Sir William Johnson Manuscripts in the New York State Library*. Albany, 1909.—Valuable.

Hays, I. Minis, comp., *Calendar of the Papers of Benjamin Franklin in the Library of the American Philosophical Society*, 5 vols. Philadelphia, 1908.

Larned, J. N., ed., *The Literature of American History: a Bibliography*, published for the American Library Association. Boston, 1902.

Lincoln, Charles H., *Calendar of Johnson MSS. in the American Antiquarian Society Library*. Worcester, Mass., 1906.

New York Public Library, *Manuscript Collections in the New York Public Library (Deposited in the Lenox Building)*, printed in the Bulletin of the New York Public Library for July, 1901.—A valuable descriptive list. Of much service in consulting the Bancroft Collection.

New York State Library, *Calendar of Council Minutes, 1668–1783*, printed as Bulletin 58, History 6, March, 1902.

Reports of the Royal Historical Manuscripts Commission.—Especially the Fifth Report, Appendix I, on the Shelburne papers, and the Fourteenth Report, Appendix X, on the Dartmouth papers.

Sabin, Joseph, *A Dictionary of Books relating to America*, 19 vols. New York, 1868–1892.

Thwaites, Reuben G., ed., *Descriptive List of Manuscript Collections of the State Historical Society of Wisconsin. Together with Reports on Other Collections of Manuscript Material for American History in Adjacent States.* Madison, 1906.

Thwaites, Reuben G., Benjamin F. Shambaugh, and Franklin L. Riley, "Report of Committee on Methods of Organization and Work on the Part of the State and Local Historical Societies", printed in *Annual Report of the American Historical Association* for 1905, vol. I. —Contains notes on the collections of source material in the libraries of the various historical societies.

Van Tyne, C. H., and W. G. Leland, *Guide to the Archives of the Government of the United States in Washington*, second edition, Carnegie Institution of Washington, Publication No. 92. Washington, 1907.

Winsor, Justin, *Narrative and Critical History of America*, 8 vols. Boston, 1889.—Of great value for accounts of sources, especially those in vol. V.

MANUSCRIPT SOURCES.

Public Record Office, London.—A large part of the present essay has been based upon documents found in the Colonial Office records, under the title of "Military Correspondence, Series America and West Indies." The greater portion of the correspondence between the ministry and the British agents in America having charge of the West is found in this collection. It cannot be said, however, that the original document is always to be found here; very often a copy or a mere extract is all we have. In the Colonial Office records are also found the "Board of Trade Papers", which contain a few valuable letters. The Home Office records and the War Office records likewise contain a few documents of importance. In a miscellaneous collection of the Earl of Chatham's papers, on deposit in the Public Record Office, is a bundle of papers having an important bearing on the West. The references in the foot-notes are to the old classification. The re-classification of the Public Record Office was commenced in 1908, and is not yet (1910) complete. The Guide to the Manuscript Materials for the History of the United States to 1783 in the Public Record Office, which is being prepared by Professor C. M. Andrews for the Carnegie Institution of Washington, will contain a key enabling references to the former classification to be found in the new classification.

British Museum, London.—The Bouquet Papers, in 17 volumes (Add. MSS., 21,631-21,600), and the Haldimand Papers, in 4231 volumes (Add. MSS., 21,661-21,692), are the important sources in this depository. The Bouquet Papers contain a few documents relating to the early history of the period, with especial reference to early Indian troubles. The Haldimand Papers are indispensable for the latter half of the period. The collection is composed of letters which passed between Haldimand and the home officials, his correspondence with Gage and the officers in the West, besides many other letters which came into his possession. The correspondence throws considerable light upon the political status of the Illinois French. Transcripts of the Bouquet and Haldimand collections are in the Canadian Archives at Ottawa, and have been calendared by Douglas Brymner in the *Reports on Canadian Archives*, for 1884-1889.

Privy Council Office, London.—This collection contains a few important documents bearing on western colonization.

Lansdowne House Manuscripts, London.—The papers of the Earl of Shelburne, found here, are of great value in the study of western trade conditions.

New York State Library, Albany.—Here are found 26 volumes of Sir William Johnson's papers, a very valuable collection, dealing largely with Indian affairs, which came under Johnson's supervision.

There are also important documents relating to western trade and colonization.

Lenox Library, New York City.—This contains the manuscript collection of George Bancroft, which includes a large number of transcripts from the "America and West Indies" series in the Public Record Office. His copies are generally accurate: capitalization and punctuation, however, cannot always be depended upon. There are also in this collection transcripts from the Earl of Shelburne's papers from the Lansdowne House manuscripts. In the selections made to illustrate western history, however, Bancroft evidently omitted some of the more important papers.

Library of the Historical Society of Pennsylvania, Philadelphia.—Considerable use was made of a number of volumes of transcripts of the Board of Trade papers, Plantations General, of which the library contains 180 volumes. A comparison of a few papers with the originals in the Public Record Office indicates that the transcripts were accurately made. There are also a number of minor collections of original manuscripts which are indispensable to students of western history. Among these are the Gratz-Croghan Papers, vol. I, the Ohio Company Papers, vols. I and II, and the Etting Papers, vol. III. These collections deal largely with western trade conditions and land speculation. There are also a number of miscellaneous manuscripts, *e. g.*, the original "Journal" written by Captain Harry Gordon on his trip down the Ohio River in 1766, and a diary kept by John Jennings in Illinois during the years 1766–1768.

American Philosophical Society, Philadelphia.—Here are many valuable letters to Benjamin Franklin on the West, which are not found elsewhere.

Pennsylvania State Library, Harrisburg, Pa.—In the Division of Public Records are most of the account books of the firm of Baynton, Wharton and Morgan, and an important collection of George Morgan's papers.

Library of Congress.—One volume of the correspondence of Secretary Henry S. Conway, which yielded a few scattering letters on western trade conditions and Indian affairs.

Library of the American Antiquarian Society, Worcester, Mass.—Here were found a few original letters of Sir William Johnson having an important bearing on western colonization.

Library of the Massachusetts Historical Society, Boston.—Use was made of the Francis Parkman Collection of transcripts, which relate to the early part of the period. Lack of proper references to the location of the originals, as well as evidence that the copies were not always made with absolute accuracy, render the use of this collection rather difficult.

Harvard College Library.—The chief sources found here were a volume of General Gage's letters, which shed considerable light on Indian affairs in the West, and the Sparks Collection of transcripts from the Public Record Office and the British Museum. Little use was made of the Sparks Collection, however, the originals being consulted in preference, although in a few cases where the latter could not be found the transcripts had to be relied upon.

Canadian Archives, Ottawa, Canada.—Transcripts of the Bouquet and Haldimand Papers are to be found here, as well as of a large number of Colonial Office records.

Kaskaskia Records, British Period.—These papers contain a few important sources bearing on the political events in Illinois. The most important document is the court record, which consists of 256 pages. The collection is at present in the library of the University of Illinois, but belongs to the county of St. Clair, Illinois.

Cahokia Records, Court House, Belleville, Ill.—This collection contains a few papers throwing light on the local government in Illinois during the British period.

Miscellaneous.—Among the documents belonging to private individuals the most important is the letter-book kept by Colonel George Morgan, 1766-1768, which is in the possession of Mr. A. S. M. Morgan, of Pittsburg. There are also important Morgan letters in the possession of Mrs. Maria P. Woodbridge, of Marietta, Ohio, Mrs. E. S. Thacher, of Nordhoff, Cal., Mrs. H. C. More, of Gaviota, Cal., and Mrs. T. C. Smith, of Santa Barbara, Cal.

PRINTED SOURCES.

American State Papers, Public Lands, vols. I–III. Washington, 1832.—Necessary for study of western land schemes.

Canadian Constitutional Development shown by Selected Speeches and Despatches, edited by H. E. Egerton and W. L. Grant. London, 1907. —Important contribution.

Chalmers, George, *A Collection of Treaties between Great Britain and other Powers*. London, 1790.

Chicago Historical Society Collections, vol. IV. Chicago, 1890.— Important miscellaneous documents, the originals of which cannot be traced.

Documents illustrative of the Canadian Constitution, edited by William Houston. Toronto, 1891.

Documents relating to the Colonial History of the State of New York, edited by E. B. O'Callaghan, 15 vols. Albany, 1856.—Important for study of Indian affairs and western colonization. Volumes entitled "Paris Documents" must be used with care.

Documents relating to the Constitutional History of Canada, 1757–1791, selected and edited by Adam Shortt and Arthur G. Doughty. Ottawa, 1907.—Indispensable to the student of the proclamation of 1763 and the Quebec Act.

"Documents relating to the Occupation of the Illinois Country by the British Army", edited by Clarence E. Carter. Printed in *Transactions of the Illinois State Historical Society* for 1907. Springfield, 1908.

Franklin, Benjamin, *Complete Works*, edited by John Bigelow, 10 vols. New York, 1887–1889.—Necessary for study of western colonization.

Franklin, Benjamin, *Life and Writings*, edited by A. H. Smythe, 10 vols. New York, 1905–1907.—Contains some documents on the West not printed in the Bigelow edition.

Franklin, Benjamin, *Works*, edited by Jared Sparks, 10 vols. Boston, 1837–1844.

Grenville Papers, being the correspondence of Richard and George Grenville, their friends and contemporaries, edited with notes by William James Smith, 4 vols. London, 1852.

Illinois Historical Collections, vol. I. Springfield, 1903.—Documents chosen arbitrarily. Not complete.

Michigan Pioneer and Historical Collections, vols. 19, 20. Lansing, 1891, 1892.—Contain selections from the Haldimand Papers. Arrangement and editing poor. Uncritical copies taken from uncritical copies.

New York Historical Society Collections, 9 vols. New York, 1811–1859; Publication Fund series, 18 vols. New York, 1868–1881.—Important for study of western colonies.

Parliamentary History of England, from the Earliest Period to the Year 1813, edited by T. C. Hansard, vol. XVII. London, 1813.—Very useful.

Report on Canadian Archives, 1904, edited by Arthur Doughty, Ottawa. — Contains important documents. See also above under *Guides and Bibliographies*.

Rockingham, Memoirs of the Marquis of, and his contemporaries; with original documents, 2 vols. London, 1852.

BIBLIOGRAPHY

Stiles, Henry R., *Affairs at Fort Chartres, 1768-1781.* Albany, 1864.—Includes a few important letters. The same are also found in the *Historical Magazine*, vol. VIII, no. 8.

Thwaites, Reuben Gold, ed., *The Jesuit Relations and Allied Documents*, vols. LXX and LXXI. Cleveland, 1900-1901.—Contain a few documents of importance for present study. Notes not all trustworthy.

Thwaites, Reuben Gold, ed., *Early Western Travels, 1748-1846*, vols. I and XXVII. Cleveland, 1904 and 1906.—Croghan's "Journals" and Flagg's "The Far West" are the most important documents. Notes to be used with care.

Washington, George, *Writings*, edited by W. C. Ford, 14 vols. New York and London, 1889-1893.

Wisconsin Historical Collections, vol. XVIII. Madison, 1908.—This volume contains documents of considerable value for the British period.

CONTEMPORARY BOOKS AND PAMPHLETS.

Account of the Proceedings of the Illinois and Ouabache Land Companies. Philadelphia, 1796.—Invaluable.

Adair, James, *The History of the American Indians; Particularly those Nations adjoining to the Mississippi, East and West Florida, Georgia, South and North Carolina, and Virginia.* London, 1775. —Valuable for contemporary criticism of western policy of Great Britain.

Annual Register, or a View of the History, Politics, and Literature for the Year 1763, also for 1774. London, 1776.—Supposed to have been written by Edmund Burke. Important source.

Blackstone, William, *Commentaries on the Laws of England* (Cooley edition). Chicago, 1899.

Bossu, M., *Travels throughout that Part of North America called Louisiana.* Translated from the French by J. R. Forster. London, 1771.—Excellent view of the French in the Mississippi Valley prior to 1763.

Considerations on the Agreement of the Lords Commissioners of His Majesty's Treasury, with the Honourable Thomas Walpole and the Associates for Lands upon the River Ohio in North America, in a Letter to a Member of Parliament. London, 1774.—Supposed by W. C. Ford (Bibliography of Franklin), to have been written by Franklin. Contains important statements on western colonization.

Expediency of securing our American Colonies by Settling the Country adjoining the River Mississippi, Considered. Edinburgh, 1763. —Of great importance.

BIBLIOGRAPHY

Historical Account of the Expedition against the Ohio Indians 1764.—Attributed by Charles Whittelsey to Thomas Hutchins, and by Justin Winsor to Dr. William Smith of Philadelphia. In the Library of Congress is a letter by Smith asserting his own authorship of the book. The work is now available in the Ohio Valley Historical Series.

Hunt, William, *The Justice and Policy of the late Act of Parliament for making more Effectual Provision for the Government of the Province of Quebec, Asserted and Proved.* London, 1774.—Invaluable for view on the legal position of the West.

Hutchins, Thomas, *A Topographical Description of Virginia, Pennsylvania, Maryland, and North Carolina.* Reprinted from the original edition of 1778. Edited by F. C. Hicks. Cleveland, 1904.—An excellent account of conditions in British Illinois.

Invitation Sérieuse des Habitants des Illinois, by "Un Habitant des Kaskaskias." Philadelphia, 1772. Reprinted by Club for Colonial Reprints, vol. IV, with introduction and notes by C. W. Alvord and C. E. Carter. Providence, 1908.

Narrative of the Transactions, Imprisonment and Sufferings of John Connolly, an American Loyalist. London, 1783. Reprinted by C. L. Woodward. New York, 1889.

Pittman, Philip, *The Present State of the European Settlements on the Mississippi.* London, 1770.—Written by an English officer who did not thoroughly understand conditions in Illinois either in the French or British periods. Has been trusted too much. Most available in edition of F. H. Hodder. Cleveland, 1906.

Plain Facts. Philadelphia, 1787.—According to Sabin, this pamphlet was written by Benjamin Franklin or A. Benezet. According to W. C. Ford, it was written by neither of these, but by Samuel Wharton. Many later writers have copied from this work.

Political Essays concerning the Present State of the British Empire; Particularly respecting: (I) Natural Advantages and Disadvantages. (II) Constitutions. (III) Agriculture. (IV) Manufactures. (V) Colonies, and (VI) Commerce. London, 1772.—Attributed by Sabin to Dr. John Campbell. This is probably a wrong inference. Contains a contemporary criticism of the western policy of Great Britain.

Pownall, Thomas, *The Administration of the Colonies.* London, 1768.—Valuable for view of an English official relative to the merits of the French and English claims in the West prior to 1763 and to the relations of the two nations with the Indians.

Pownall, Thomas, *A Topographical Description of the English Col-*

onies. London, 1776.—Contains the earliest printed copy of Gordon's Journal down the Ohio in 1766.

Pratz, Le Page du, *Histoire de la Louisiane*, 3 vols. Paris, 1758.— Good treatment of French conditions in Illinois prior to 1763 by a French traveler.

Volney, C. F., *View of the Climate and Soil of the United States.* Translated from the French. London, 1814.—Excellent account of the character of the French in the Mississippi Valley towards the close of the eighteenth century.

CONTEMPORARY NEWSPAPERS.

There is in general little to be found in the newspapers relating to the West during the British period. Some stray bits of information, however, are gleaned from the following newspapers, found in the libraries of the Pennsylvania Historical Society and the American Antiquarian Society:

Pennsylvania Chronicle and Universal Advertiser, 3 vols. 1768–1774.

Pennsylvania Gazette, 34 vols. Philadelphia, 1728–1789.

Pennsylvania Journal, 13 vols. Philadelphia, 1751–1788.

Pennsylvania Packet and General Advertiser, 9 vols. Philadelphia, 1772–1784.

GENERAL HISTORIES AND BIOGRAPHIES.

Bancroft, George, *History of the United States from the Discovery of the American Continent*, 10 vols. Boston, 1834–1874.—For this essay, the early edition, containing references to sources, was used. The portions of the author's last revision which relate to the West, differ in no particular from those of the first edition. Bancroft had access to more material than any other writer, but his interpretations cannot be depended upon. Serious errors which have found their way into most of the western histories are traceable directly to this work.

Draper, L. C., "Life of Boone", 5 vols. MS. in Draper Collection, State Historical Society of Wisconsin.

Fitzmaurice, Lord Edmund, *Life of William, Earl of Shelburne*, 3 vols. London, 1875.—Necessary for understanding of Shelburne's position in England. Perspective very poor.

Franklin, Benjamin, *The Life of Benjamin Franklin, written by himself.* Edited by John Bigelow, 3 vols. Philadelphia, 1899.—Contains one valuable document. Otherwise of little use for present study.

Howard, George E., *An Introduction to the Local Constitutional History of the United States.* J. H. U. Studies. Baltmore, 1889.— No understanding of local institutions in British Illinois.

Hunt, William, and Reginald L. Poole, ed., *Political History of England,* 12 vols. New York, 1906.—Vol. X is of use on account of tables giving ministerial changes.

Kingsford, William, *History of Canada,* 10 vols. Toronto, 1887–1890.—In general a very sane piece of work, although the author is prejudiced against the French.

Parkman, Francis, *Conspiracy of Pontiac and the Indian War after the Conquest of Canada.* New library edition, 2 vols. Boston, 1903.— Invaluable but lacks sympathy for the French.

Parkman, Francis, *La Salle and the Discovery of the Great West.* Boston, 1903.

Parkman, Francis, *Montcalm and Wolfe,* 2 vols. Boston, 1903.

Perkins, James B., *France under Louis XV,* 2 vols. Boston, 1897.

Sabine, Lorenzo, *Loyalists of the American Revolution,* 2 vols. Boston, 1864.

Shea, John Gilmary, *Life of the Most Rev. John Carroll, embracing the History of the Catholic Church in the United States. 1763–1875.* New York, 1888.—Sound, but carelessly constructed. Practically the only trustworthy account of the Catholic Church in the West.

Sparks, Jared, *Life of Charles Lee.* In Library of American Biography, vol. XVIII. Boston, 1846.

Stone, William L., *The Life and Times of Sir William Johnson,* 2 vols. Albany, 1865.—Disappointing with respect to the West in which Johnson was greatly interested. The author had a large amount of material, but failed to master it.

Winsor, Justin, ed., *Narrative and Critical History of America,* 8 vols. Boston and New York, 1889.—Chapter on "The West" by Poole in vol. VI covers the British period, but is practically worthless so far as interpretation is concerned. The editorial notes are, however, very valuable. The chapter on "The Mississippi Valley" in vol. V, by A. McF. Davis, covering the period prior to 1763, is of more value. The bibliographical notes scattered throughout the volumes are indispensable.

SPECIAL AND SECTIONAL TREATISES.

Adams, Herbert B., *Maryland's Influence upon the Land Cessions to the United States.* J. H. U. Studies. Baltimore, 1885.—An uncritical study.

BIBLIOGRAPHY

Alden, George H., *New Governments West of the Alleghany Mountains before 1780*. Bulletin of University of Wisconsin, II, Madison, 1899.—Good. He has confined himself almost entirely to printed sources, but has used them carefully. Interpretations sound.

Alvord, Clarence W., "Genesis of the Proclamation of 1763", in *Michigan Pioneer and Historical Collections*, vol. 37. Lansing, 1908. —Completely refutes old views of the proclamation. Indispensable to students of western history.

Alvord, Clarence W., "Introduction" to *Illinois Historical Collections*, vol. II. Springfield, 1907.—Contains excellent résumé of conditions in British Illinois. Based on original sources.

Alvord, Clarence W., "The British Ministry and the Treaty of Fort Stanwix", in *Proceedings of Wisconsin State Historical Society*. Madison, 1909.—Excellent for analysis of British ministry. Authoritative.

Annals of the West. Embracing a Concise Account of the Principal Events which have occurred in the Western States and Territories from the Discovery of the Mississippi Valley to the Year 1850. Edited by James H. Perkins, Cincinnati, 1846. Revised by John M. Peck, St. Louis, 1850, also by James R. Albach. Pittsburg, 1858.—Antiquated. Must be used with great care.

Babeau, H., *Les Assemblées Génerales des Communautés d'Habitants en France*. Paris, 1893.

Babeau, H., *Le Village sous l'Ancien Régime*. Paris, 1879.—Necessary for an understanding of the French village community life.

Beer, George L., *British Colonial Policy, 1754–1765*.—An excellent, critical study of the colonial problems of Great Britain. He does not seem to appreciate fully, however, the magnitude of the western problem.

Benton, Elbert J., *The Wabash Trade Route in the Development of the Old Northwest*. J. H. U. Studies. Baltimore, 1903.—Confined altogether to printed sources, which have not been used critically. Has failed to grasp the larger aspects of the western trade.

Chalmers, George, *Opinions of Eminent Lawyers on Various Points of English Jurisprudence*. London, 1858.—Valuable for gaining point of view of certain English officials.

Coffin, Victor, *The Province of Quebec and the Early American Revolution: A Study in English-American Colonial History*. University of Wisconsin Bulletin, vol. I, no. 3. Madison, 1896.—Based on manuscript as well as printed sources. Useful for discussion of western land policy of Great Britain. Some of the conclusions reached, however, need revision.

DeHass, Willis, *History of the Early Settlement and Indian Wars of Western Virginia.* Wheeling, 1851.—Of some use in study of western colonization.

Douglas, W. B., "Jean Gabriel Cerré, a Sketch", in *Transactions of the Illinois State Historical Society* for 1903. Springfield, 1904.

Dunn, J. P., "Father Gibault", in *Transactions of the Illinois State Historical Society* for 1905. Springfield, 1906.—Neither of the last-named articles contribute anything new.

Farrand, Max, "The Indian Boundary Line", in *American Historical Review*, vol. X, pp. 782-791.—Has missed many important sources. Will have to be rewritten.

Fernow, Berthold, *The Ohio Valley in Colonial Days.* Albany, 1890.—No contribution.

Franz, Alexander, *Die Kolonization des Mississippitales zum Ausgange der französischen Heershaft.* Leipzig, 1902.—Of value for economic treatment.

Gale, Henry, *The Upper Mississippi or Historical Sketches of the Mound Builders, the Indian Tribes and the Progress of Civilization in the Northwest.* Chicago and New York, 1861.—Valueless.

Hamilton, Peter J., *Colonial Mobile.* Boston and New York, 1897.—The author has had access to important material relating to the occupation of the West. He has also followed Winsor pretty closely.

Harding, Julia Morgan, "Col. George Morgan: His Family and Times". Washington (Pa.) *Observer*, May 21, 1904.—Most complete account of the life of Morgan available.

Hildreth, Samuel R., *Pioneer History: being an Account of the First Examinations of the Ohio Valley, and the Early Settlement of the Northwest Territory.* Cincinnati, 1848.—Uncritical.

Hinsdale, B. A., *The Old Northwest.* New York, 1888.—Not based on original research. Very uncritical.

Hinsdale, B. A., "The Western Land Policy of the British Government from 1763 to 1775", in *Ohio Archæological and Historical Quarterly.* Columbus, Dec., 1887.—Uncritical and unreliable.

Hosmer, James K., *A Short History of the Mississippi Valley.* Boston and New York, 1901.—The author has generalized from secondary authorities. Untrustworthy.

Margry, P., *Decouvertes et etablissements des français dans L'Amerique septentrionale, 1614-1754,* 6 vols. Paris, 1887.

Monette, John W., *History of the Discovery and Settlement of the Valley of the Mississippi*, 2 vols. New York, 1848.—Antiquated and unreliable.

Moore, Charles, *The Northwest under Three Flags, 1635-1796*. New York and London, 1900.—Has used a few good sources in an uncritical manner.

Munro, William B., *The Seigniorial System in Canada: A Study in French Colonial Policy*. New York, 1907.—An excellent, scientific account of institutions in the contemporaneous colony.

Ogg, Frederic A., *The Opening of the Mississippi*. New York, 1904. —A popular treatment, based on secondary authorities. Of little value.

Roosevelt, Theodore, *The Winning of the West*, 4 vols. New York, 1896.—The author has seen many important sources, but has used them uncritically in some instances.

Rozier, Firmis A., *A History of the Early Settlement of the Mississippi Valley*. St. Louis, 1890.—Of little value.

Sato, Shosuke, *A History of the Land Question in the United States*. J. H. U. Studies. Baltimore, 1886.—Superficial.

Schuyler, Robert L., *The Transition in Illinois from British to American Government*. New York, 1909.—Has made excellent use of the printed sources.

Sioussat, St. George L., *The English Statutes in Maryland*. J. H. U. Studies. Baltimore, 1903.—Very useful.

Thwaites, Reuben G., " Early Lead-mining in Illinois and Wisconsin ", in *Annual Report of American Historical Association*, 1893.— Good.

Turner, Frederick J., *Character and Influence of the Indian Trade in Wisconsin*. J. H. U. Studies.—Suggestive treatment.

Viollet, P., *Histoire du Droit Civil Français* (third edition). Paris, 1905.

Walker, Charles J., "The Northwest during the Revolution ", in *Michigan Pioneer and Historical Collections*, vol. III.—Of little value.

Walton, Frederick Parker, *The Scope and Interpretation of the Civil Code of Lower Canada*. Montreal, 1907.—A sound work.

Whittelsey, Charles, "The Origin of Land Surveys", in *Journal of the Association of Engineering Societies*, vol. III, no. 11.—Controversial. Relates to authorship of the *Historical Account of the Expedition of Colonel Bouquet against the Ohio Indians*.

Winsor, Justin, *The Mississippi Basin*. Boston, 1895.—Covers early part of the period. Chief objection is the absence of reference to sources. Seems generally accurate.

Winsor, Justin, *The Westward Movement of the Colonies and the Republic west of the Alleghanies, 1763-1798.* Boston, 1897.—No foot-notes. Based on vast amount of material, but interpretations of events in the West during the British period not altogether reliable.

STATE AND LOCAL HISTORIES.

A single criticism will be sufficient for the greater part of the following works. With a few exceptions, to which attention will be called, they are almost worthless. Sufficient citations have already been made in the foot-notes to indicate the uncritical and unreliable character of most of the writings on western and Illinois history.

Alerding, H., *A History of the Catholic Church in the Diocese of Vincennes.* Indianapolis, 1883.

Billon, Frederick L., *Annals of St. Louis in its Early Days under French and Spanish Dominations*, 2 vols. St. Louis, 1886.—Necessary for the early history of St. Louis. The work of an antiquarian.

Blanchard, Rufus, *History of Illinois to accompany an Historical Map of the State.* Chicago, 1883.

Boggess, Arthur Clinton, *The Settlement of Illinois, 1778-1830.* Chicago, 1908.—Contains important references for study of land question.

Breese, Sidney, *Early History of Illinois.* Chicago, 1884.—Entirely untrustworthy.

Brown, Henry, *The History of Illinois, from its first Discovery and Settlement, to the Present.* New York, 1884.

Butler, Mann, *History of Kentucky.* Louisville, 1834.—Contains important documentary appendix.

Claiborne, J. F. H., *Mississippi as a Province, Territory and State.* Jackson, 1880.

Craig, O. J., "Ouiatanon", in *Indiana Historical Society Publications*, II. Indianapolis, 1895.

Davidson, A., and B. Stuvé, *A Complete History of Illinois from 1763-1884.* Springfield, 1884.

Dillon, John B., *The History of Indiana*, 2 vols. Indianapolis, 1843.—Most original of all the series of state histories.

Dunn, J. P., jr., *Indiana: A Redemption from Slavery.* Boston and New York, 1888.—Fair. Has not used all the available material.

Gayarré, C. E., *A History of Louisiana*, 3 vols. New Orleans, 1906. —The best that is available.

Gerhard, Fred., *Illinois as it is.* Chicago and Philadelphia, 1857.

History of Monroe, Randolph and Parry Counties, Illinois. Philadelphia, 1883.

History of St. Clair County, Illinois. Philadelphia, 1881.

Houck, Louis, *A History of Missouri*, 3 vols. Chicago, 1908.—An accurate, scientific work. Of little value, however, for the present study.

Mason, Edward G., *Chapters from Illinois History.* Chicago, 1901.

Mason, Edward G., *Illinois in the Eighteenth Century; Kaskaskia and its Parish Records.* Chicago, 1889.—Fair.

Mason, Edward G., "Philippe de Rocheblave and Rocheblave Papers", with historical sketch and notes, in *Chicago Historical Society Collections*, vol. IV. Chicago, 1890.—Generally accurate.

Moses, John, *Illinois: Historical and Statistical*, 2 vols. Chicago, 1889.—The best of the popular histories of Illinois.

Moses, John, "Court of Inquiry at Fort Chartres", in *Chicago Historical Society Collections*, vol. IV. Chicago, 1890.—A brief, but good sketch.

Parrish, Randall, *Historic Illinois: The Romance of the Earlier Days.* Chicago, 1906.

Peyton, J. Lewis, *History of Augusta County, Virginia.* Staunton, Va., 1882.

Phelps, Albert, *History of Louisiana.* New York, 1905.—A readable work, but no contribution.

Reynolds, John, *The Pioneer History of Illinois.* Belleville, Ill., 1852.

Smith, George, *A Student's History of Illinois.* Bloomington, 1906.

Terrage, Marc de Villiers du, *Les dernières Années de la Louisiane française.* Paris, 1903.—Good. The author has made better use of the colonial archives in Paris than any other writer. The work contains important quotations from the original sources. Considerable partiality is shown to Governor Kerlerec.

Wallace, Joseph, *History of Illinois and Louisiana under French Rule.* Cincinnati, 1893.—Decidedly uncritical.

ERRATA AND ADDENDA.

Page 51, line 9. "Pounds of ammunition" should be "rounds of ammunition."

Page 60, line 6 from the top. "1766" should be "1768".

Page 63, notes 76 and 78. "Jenning's" should be "Jennings'."

Page 74, note 120. The source is P. R. O., Am. and W. I., vol. 123.

Page 80, line 6 from the bottom. In civil and criminal actions the commissaries were to have all the powers of justices of the peace in any colony. In addition they were to have summary jurisdiction—as justices of the peace had not—of civil cases under 10 pounds sterling, but in such cases an appeal lay to the superintendent, whose decision was final.

Page 101, note 80. "Chapter VII" should be "chapter VI."

Page 124, note 62. For the best discussion of the attitude of the British ministry towards western expansion, see Alvord, "The British Ministry and the Treaty of Fort Stanwix", in Wis. Hist. Soc. *Proceedings*, 1908, pp. 165 ff.

Page 133, line 9 from the bottom. "Shelbourne" should be "Shelburne."

Page 137, note 102. Hillsborough's attitude at this time is best described by Alvord, in "British Ministry and the Treaty of Fort Stanwix", in Wis. Hist. Soc. *Proceedings*, 1908, p. 179.

Page 149, note 16, line 9 from the top. Dartmouth prepared and forwarded to Illinois what he called a "Sketch .of Government for Illinois" should be "Dartmouth prepared and forwarded to Illinois what he called a 'Sketch of Government for Illinois'."

INDEX.

Abbadie, Eugene d', letters from, to French minister, 31 n.; to French commandants, 33 n.; blamed for failure of Loftus' expedition, 33; Kingsford's opinion of, 33 n.; Gage disbelieves in complicity of, 33, 34; gives Loftus advice concerning Indians, 34; letters to, from St. Ange, 36 n., 41 n.

Account of the Proceedings of the Illinois and Wabash Land Companies, cited, 161 n. See also Bibliography

Adair, James, *History of the American Indian*, cited, 160 n. See also Bibliography

Adams, H. B., *Maryland's Influence upon the Land Cessions in the United States*, cited, 109 n., 140 n. See also Bibliography

Aix-la-Chapelle, treaty of, 2, 103

Albany Congress, 123; considers creation of western colonies, 103

Alden, George H., *New Governments West of the Alleghanies before 1780*, cited, 103 n., 104 n., 140 n. See also Bibliography

Algonquin Indians. See Indians, Algonquin

Alleghany Mountains, 3, 47, 79, 108, 109 n., 111, 136, 160 n.

Alvord, C. W., *Illinois Historical Collections*, vol. II, cited, 7 n., 8 n., 9 n., 10 n., 163 n.; *Illinois in the Eighteenth Century*, cited, 9 n.; "Genesis of the Proclamation of 1763", cited, 14 n., 79 n., 140 n.; "The British Ministry and the Treaty of Fort Stanwix", cited, 200. See also Bibliography

America, 1, 2, 5, 13, 25, 28, 31, 57, 67, 78, 102 n., 105, 108, 112, 113, 117, 118, 124 n., 125 n., 126 n., 127 n., 131, 149 n., 160 n.; relations of France and England in, 2, 4; plan for the management of Indians in, 16; agitation in, for the establishment of western colonies, 104

American Revolution, 140; prevents Quebec Act from becoming effective in West, 26; relation of western problem to, 63 n.; checks colonizing schemes, 144, 162

American State Papers, Public Lands, cited, 17 n., 45 n., 47 n., 161 n. See also Bibliography

Amherst, Gen. [Jeffrey], 127; letters from, to Lieut.-Col. Robertson, 18 n.; letters to, from Johnson, 28 n., 29 n., 30 n.; from Bouquet, 31 n.; effect of policy of economy of, on Indians, 29; succeeded by Gage as commander-in-chief of British army in America, 31; proposes creation of western settlements, 127 n., 129 n.

Andrew, Indian interpreter, accompanies Lieut. Fraser to Illinois, 40 n.

Annals of the West, cited, 34 n., 109 n., 140 n. *See also* Bibliography

Annual Register, cited, 14 n., 21. *See also* Bibliography

Annual Report, American Historical Association, 1893, 120 n., 124 n. *See also* Bibliography

Archives of the Ministry of the Colonies, cited, 6 n., 33 n.

Arkansas River, forms southern boundary of Illinois district, 6

Articles of Agreement for the land company of 1766, cited, 115 n., 116 n.; formation and terms of, 115; purpose of, 115, 116; extent of territory in proposed grant, 115, 121 n.; provision for shareholders in, 116 n.; incorporated in Gov. Franklin's proposals for a colony, 117; anticipates establishment of civil government in Illinois country, 119 n.; Franklin recommends change of, to admit increased membership, 130 n.

Assembly, village, 10

Atlantic Ocean, 3

Audit Office records, cited, 52 n.

Augusta County, Va., 103

Austria, 1

Austrian Succession, War of the, 2

Babeau, H., *Le village sous l'ancien régime*, cited, 10 n.; *Les assemblées générales des communautés d'habitants*, cited, 10 n. *See also* Bibliography

Bacon, Richard, 72

Bancroft, George, *History of the United States*, cited, 27 n., 31 n., 66 n., 127 n., 147 n., 149 n., 159 n.; criticism of statements of, concerning struggle for civil government in the Illinois country, 147 n., 149 n., 159 n. *See also* Bibliography

Bancroft Collection (New York Public Library), cited, 31 n., 32 n., 33 n., 34 n., 35 n., 37 n., 38 n., 40 n., 41 n., 42 n., 43 n., 45 n. *See also* Bibliography

Barbau, Jean Baptiste, resident of Prairie du Rocher, 9; appointed member of court of judicature, 68

Barnsley, ———, letters to, from Butricke, 64 n., 65 n., 66 n., 68 n., 70 n., 73 n.

Barrington, Secretary of War, 67; letters to, from Gage, 45 n.; from Farmer, 55 n.; from Wilkins, 67 n., 88 n., 97 n., 98 n.; advocates restrictive policy towards West, 108 n., 136; "Plan relative to the Out Posts, Indian Trade", etc., cited, 108 n., 136 n.; letter from, to Haldimand, 162 n.

Bauvais, ———, 49 n.; family of, residents of Kaskaskia, 9

Baynton, John, letter to, from Morgan, 73 n.; amount of share of, in land company, 116 n.; believes a civil government will be established in Illinois, 119 n.

Baynton and Company, land grant in Illinois to, 69 n.

Baynton and Wharton, letters to, from Morgan, 60 n., 61 n., 62 n., 64 n., 65 n., 73 n., 87 n., 88 n., 89 n., 90 n., 95 n., 97 n., 98 n., 99 n.; from Maturin, 74 n.

Baynton, Wharton and Morgan, 130 n.; letters from, to Gage, 55 n.; to Macleane, 83 n., 95 n.; to Johnson, 105 n., 121 n., 123 n.; hunting party sent out by, attacked by Indians, 63 n.; land grant in Illinois to, 69 n.; court of inquiry called to settle disputes between Richard Bacon and, 72; competition and success of, 83; letters to, from Joseph Dobson, 83 n.; from Johnson, 121 n., 122 n.; enter into articles of agreement for

INDEX

purchase of lands in Illinois, 115; enter Vandalia company, 140 n.; Wilkins' connection with, broken, 155

Beauvais. *See* Bauvais

Bedford party, 134

Beer, G. L., *British Colonial Policy*, cited, 31 n. *See also* Bibliography

Benefice, seigniory compared with, 10

Bentley and Company, trade extensively in Illinois country, 83

Bienville, Le Moine de, plan of, with reference to Mississippi Valley, 3

Billon, H. L., *Annals of St. Louis*, cited, 51 n. *See also* Bibliography

Blackstone, William, *Commentaries*, cited, 24. *See also* Bibliography

Blanchard, R., *History of Illinois*, cited, 51 n.; *Discovery and Conquest of the Northwest*, cited, 51 n. *See also* Bibliography

Blouïn, Daniel, favored by court of judicature, 70; appointed by Illinois French as agent to Gage, 146; letters from, to Dartmouth, 146 n., 147 n., 149 n., 157 n., 159 n.; gives power of attorney during absence from Illinois, 147 n.; outlines draft of government at request of Gage, 147–148; Gage's opinion of, 148 n., 151, 152 n.; returns Gage's draft of government to Haldimand, 149 n., 150 n.; Bancroft's statements concerning part taken by, in struggle for civil government, 159 n.

Blue Ridge Mountains, 103

Board of Trade, 61 n., 79, 112, 124, 125, 127 n., 128, 132, 136, 138, 141; Shelburne president of, 15; Hillsborough president of, 15, 16; plan of, for regulation of the trade and management of the Indians, 16; relations of Sir William Johnson with, 18; Johnson writes to, concerning irregular behavior of traders, 19; devises plan of 1764 for management of Indian affairs, 56; gives directions to Indian superintendents, 57; expresses opinion as to policy to be pursued towards West, 78; is solicited by land companies, 108; interprets proclamation of 1763, 108 n.; receives communication from Croghan relative to establishing a colony in Illinois, 111; Johnson recommends colonial project to, 122; attitude of, towards proposed Illinois colony, 125 n., 126, 127; Shelburne's communication to, 130–131; Shelburne's method of presenting colonial plan to, 132; calls for opinions of merchants, 132; power of, in 1766, 133, 134; makes adverse report on Shelburne's recommendation for western colonies, 134–135; discussion of report of, 139–140; report of, on Vandalia grant, 140

Board of Trade Papers (Historical Society of Pennsylvania), cited, 19 n., 41 n., 49 n., 51 n., 53 n., 59 n., 83 n., 86 n., 90 n., 91 n., 92 n., 95 n., 101 n., 113 n., 117 n., 127 n., 129 n., 137 n., 146 n., 147 n., 149 n., 157 n., 159 n.

Boisbriant, Pierre, commissioned to govern Illinois country, 6; lands of Prairie du Rocher owned by, 11

Bossu, M., *Travels*, cited, 8 n. *See also* Bibliography

Bouquet, Col. Henry, 30, 39, 110 n.; expedition of, and its results, 30; letters to, from Gage, 30 n., 32 n., 35 n., 38 n.; letters from, to Amherst, 32 n.; to Gage, 38 n.; to Franklin,

INDEX

110 n.; effect of victory of, upon Pontiac, 36
Bradstreet, Col. John, leads force along Lake Erie, 30; sends Thomas Morris into Indian country, 36; campaign of, a failure, 37 n.
Breese, Sidney, *Early History of Illinois*, cited, 9 n., 10 n. *See also* Bibliography
Briand, Bishop of Quebec, letters to, from Father Meurin, 60 n., 75 n.; creates Father Meurin vicar-general of Illinois, 75; sends additional priest to Illinois country, 76
British army, 15, 92; occupies most of western posts, 27; Gage succeeds Amherst as commander-in-chief of, 31; occupies Mobile and Pensacola, 32; official aid given, in expedition of Maj. Loftus, 33; Pontiac agrees to offer no further resistance to, 43; takes formal possession of Fort de Chartres, 45; detachment of, in Illinois stricken with sickness, 73 n.
British commandant, immediate duty of, after occupation of Fort de Chartres, 46; problems confronting, 49-50
British government, 48, 88; guarantees by, of the rights of the inhabitants of Illinois under the treaty of Paris, 17; transports provisions from Fort Pitt to Illinois country, 55; is slow in forming definite program for management of Indian affairs, 56; officials of, fear Indian outbreak in 1768, 63 n.; expects to inherit influence of French among Indians of West, 84; loss of customs duty to, 94; expects to use Fort de Chartres to protect trade, 97; adopts policy of economy, 113; anxious to displace military government of Illinois, 158; annuls land grants in Illinois country, 160-161

British ministry, 105, 123 n., 133; discuss policy to be pursued towards West, 13-15; opposing views in, 14; purpose of, 21; announces western policy in proclamation of 1763, 108; attitude of, towards western colonization in 1764, 111
British Museum, Additional Manuscripts, cited, 35 n., 54 n., 73 n., 94 n., 98 n., 99 n., 102 n., 143 n., 150 n., 155 n., 156 n., 157 n., 158 n., 159 n., 160 n., 161 n., 162 n. *See also* Bibliography
Brown, H., *History of Illinois*, cited, 7 n., 51 n. *See also* Bibliography
Bute, Lord, 4
Butler, M., *History of Kentucky*, cited, 106 n., 107 n., 128 n. *See also* Bibliography.
Butricke, Ensign, letters from, to Barnsley, 64 n., 65 n., 66 n., 68 n., 70 n., 73 n.; assertion of, concerning number of judges in court of judicature, 66

Cabinent, 128, 133; plan for western colony approved by, 127; Shelburne presents arguments to, in favor of western colonies, 131. *See also* British ministry
Cahokia, 7, 9, 49; mission established at, 5; foundation of, 5 n.; population of, 7; character of land holdings at, 10; parish at, 11; French cross river at, 53; case of arbitration at, 65 n.; Sulpitian property at, sold, 75 n.; Father Meurin resides at, 76
Cahokia Records, cited, 50 n. *See also* Bibliography
Calendar of Home Office Papers, 1766-1769, cited, 78 n. *See also* Bibliography
Calvert, Benedict, 105
Calvin's case, 25 n.
Camden, Lord, 160
Campbell, Lieut., letter to, from

INDEX

Fraser, 41 n.; letter from, to Johnson, 51 n.
Campbell, James, 68
Campbell *v.* Hall, case of, cited, 25
Canada, 15, 27, 45, 84, 94; population of, 2; separated from English colonies by line of forts, 3; immigrants from, in Illinois, 5, 7, 8; cession of, to England, 8; portion of, reserved for Indians, 15; proposal to place West within jurisdiction of, 15; liberty of Catholic religion given to, by treaty of Paris, 45; Illinois country described as part of, by treaty of Paris, 47; furtrade of, 77, 92 n., 94; statement of Shelburne concerning exports and imports of, 95 n.; proposed removal of Illinois French to, 154; state of affairs in, 1763-1773, 161; instructions to governor of, respecting the Illinois country, 162
Canadian Archives, series A, cited, 30 n., 32 n., 35 n., 36 n., 38 n.; series B, cited, 53 n., 99 n., 143 n., 148 n., 149 n., 152 n., 155 n., 156 n., 157 n., 158 n., 159 n., 160 n., 161 n.; series Q, cited, 85 n., 88 n., 89 n.
Canadian Archives Report, for 1885, cited, 150 n.; for 1904, cited, 56 n., 80 n.; for 1905, cited, 31 n., 33 n., 36 n., 38 n., 41 n. *See also* Bibliography
Canadian Constitutional Development (ed. Egerton and Grant), cited, 25 n. *See also* Bibliography
Cape au Gres, suggestion for settlement at, 99 n.
Captain of militia. *See* French officials
Carleton, Gov. Guy, letters to, from Johnson, 85 n., 88 n.; from Hillsborough, 89 n; letters from, to Johnson, 92 n.

Carlisle, Pa., 39
Catholic missionaries, establish missions at Cahokia and Kaskaskia, 5
Cecirre, Antoine, 65
Céloron, M., 4
Cerré, family of, 9
Chalmers, George, *Collection of Treaties*, cited, 5 n.; *Opinions of Eminent Lawyers*, cited, 127 n. *See also* Bibliography
Charleston, S. C., 32
Charleville, Joseph, 49 n., 70 n.; family of, residents of Kaskaskia, 9; appointed member of court of judicature in 1770, 69; holds power of attorney from Blouin, 147 n.
Chartres village, Indian depredations near, 63; meetings of court of judicature at, 71 n.; controversy over holding court at, 71
Chatham, Earl of, papers of, referred to, 105 n.; papers of Mississippi Land Company sent to, 109 n.; becomes prime minister, 123; attitude of ministry of, towards America, 133
Chatham Papers, cited, 44 n., 45 n., 51 n., 52 n., 53 n., 105 n., 106 n., 107 n., 109 n., 128 n.
Cherokee Indians. *See* Indians, Cherokee
Cherokee River, 106 n., 144 n.
Chicago Historical Society Collections, cited, 58 n., 64 n., 66 n., 70 n., 72 n. *See also* Bibliography
Chickasaw Indians. *See* Indians, Chickasaw
China, Company of, 6 n.
Chippewa Indians. *See* Indians, Chippewa
Choctaw Indians. *See* Indians, Choctaw
Choiseul, Gabriel de, 4
Church, assembly at, 10; description of, in Illinois, 11
Church of England. *See* England

INDEX

Civil government in the Illinois country, 79, 105 n.; movement for establishment of, in 1768, 60-61, 98 n.; promoters of western colony in 1766 expect establishment of, 119 n.; proposed in Gov. Franklin's plan for colony, 119; struggle for, 1770-1774, 145-163; Blouin and Clazon draw up rough draft for, 147; proposal for, rejected by government, 148, 152 n.; Gage and Hillsborough write in opposition to, 148 n.; Gage outlines plan for, 149, 150-151; Hamilton addresses Illinois French on subject of, 151; Gage writes concerning ideas of Illinois French on subject of, 151-152; Lord's report concerning attitude of inhabitants towards, 159

Claiborne, J., *History of Mississippi*, 33 n. See also Bibliography

Clare, Lord, 125, 134

Clark, George Rogers, effects conquest of Illinois, 163

Clazon, William, 147 n., 149 n., 152 n., 159 n.; chosen by Blouin as associate on mission to Gage, 146; sketch of government presented to Gage probably the work of, 148; Gage's opinion of, 148 n., 151, 152 n.; signs Gage's draft of government, 150 n.

Clive, [Robert], 4

Coffin, Victor, *The Province of Quebec and the Early American Revolution*, cited, 140 n., 150 n., 162 n. See also Bibliography

Colden, Gov. C., letters to, from Johnson, 29 n., 30 n.

Cole, Edward, appointed commissary of Indian affairs in the Illinois country, 57; letters from, to Johnson, 57 n., 59 n., 61 n., 74 n.; to Croghan, 58 n.; Gage refuses bills drawn by, 58 n.; arrival of, at Fort de Chartres, 59; provides shelter for Indians, 63; recalled from Illinois, 74; Gage's estimate of expenses incurred in the Illinois country by, 95 n.

Colony, attempts at establishment of, in Illinois prior to 1763, 103-105; plan of Mississippi Land Company for establishment of, 105-108; effect of proclamation of 1763 on projects for, 108; attitude of Charles Lee toward establishment of, in Illinois, 109-110; of Shelburne, 110, 124, 125, 126-127, 129, 130, 131, 132, 136, 137; of Gage, 114, 115, 127 n.; of Gov. Franklin, 116, 117-121, 125 n.; of Johnson, 119 n., 122 n., 123; of Lyman, 124; plan of 1766 for, 111-112, 115-127; description of plan for, submitted to Board of Trade, 128-130; opposition to establishment of, 134-144

Commandant. See French officials

Commissary. See French officials

Commons, laws of, extended to Illinois by French, 10

Company of China. See China, Company of

Company of the East Indies. See East Indies, Company of

Company of the Indies. See Indies, Company of the

Company of the West. See West, Company of the

Compte, Jacques, 65 n.

Connecticut, 124, 147 n., 148

Connolly, John, 144 n.

Considerations on the Agreement with the Honourable Thomas Walpole, cited, 109 n., 129 n., 130 n.

Conway, Sir Henry, 125, 133; letters to, from Gage, 19 n., 42 n., 43 n., 44 n., 45 n., 49 n.,

INDEX

54 n., 55 n., 75 n., 76 n., 91
n., 98 n., 113 n.; from Johnson, 122 n.; opinion of, respecting inclusion of West in cession of 1763, 78 n.; letter from, to Gage, 78 n.; leaves ministry, 123; Franklin's opinion concerning, 123 n.

"Council, Copy of, held at the Illinois in April, 1765", cited, 38 n.

Court, clerk of. *See* French officials

Court of arbitration, 65, 156 n.

Court of inquiry, 72; proceedings of, cited, 72 n.

Court of judicature, establishment and purpose of, 65; authority for establishment of, discussed, 66–67; history of, 68–72; changes in composition of, 69; power of, extended, 69–70; attitude of, towards French, 70; breaks with Wilkins, 71; controversy over place of meeting of, 71; petitions Wilkins not to interfere with its proceedings, 72; abolished, 72; effect of abolition of, on inhabitants, 145; later cessions of, 145 n.

Court of King's Bench, designed for Illinois, 162

Court Record, MS. (Chester, Ill.), cited, 65 n., 66 n., 67 n., 68 n., 69 n., 70 n., 71 n., 72 n., 145 n., 146 n.

Courts, local village, 65

Crawford, a trader, 41 n.; accompanies John Ross to Fort de Chartres, 37

Crawford, Hugh, letters to, from Fraser, 40 n.

Croghan, Col. George, 38 n., 39, 40, 43, 49, 112, 144 n.; sent by Johnson as deputy to Indians, 38; account of journey of, from Carlisle to Fort Pitt, 39; "Journal of Transactions" (Parkman Coll.), cited, 39 n., 40 n.; statement of, relative to Sinnott, 40 n.; experiences of, on journey down the Ohio, 41–42; "Journal of" (Thwaites), cited, 42 n., 43 n.; begins negotiations with western Indians, 42–43; Sterling's doubts concerning peace made by, 45 n.; letters to, from Johnson, 45 n., 58 n., 112 n.; letters from, to Gage, 53 n., 59 n.; to Johnson, 58 n., 59 n., 60 n., 111 n., 112 n., 116 n., 119 n., 121 n., 122 n.; to B. Franklin, 86 n., 93 n., 98 n.; undertakes second mission to western Indians, 58; instructions to, 1766, cited, 58 n.; negotiates general peace with Indians, 59; statement of, respecting contraband trade, 86 n.; plans of, for establishment of colony in the Illinois country, 111; sent to England by Johnson, 111 n.; instructed by Johnson to investigate property of French in Illinois, 112 n.; enters land company for settlement of Illinois, 115; transmits Gov. Franklin's proposals for colony to Johnson, 121 n.; letters and journals of, 123

Cuba, 126

Cumming, Thomas, 106 n., 128; letters to, from Mississippi Land Company, 106 n., 107 n., 128 n.

Customs accounts, cited, 94 n.

Dartmouth, Lord, 140 n., 147, 159 n.; letters from, to Cramahé, 16 n.; to Gage, 153 n., 154 n., 155 n., 157 n., 161 n.; to Haldimand, 157 n., 161 n.; to Johnson, 157 n.; succeeds Hillsborough as secretary of state, 140 n., 149 n.; letters to, from Blouin, 146 n., 147 n., 157 n., 159 n.; from Gage, 91 n., 93 n., 146 n., 147 n., 148 n., 149 n., 158 n.; from

INDEX

Haldimand, 157 n., 161 n.; attitude of, towards civil government for Illinois, 149 n., 153; expresses concern over status of the Illinois country, 154–155

Davidson, A., and B. Stuvé. *A Complete History of Illinois*, cited, 66 n., 70 n. See also Bibliography

Davion's Bluff, 32

De Hars, W.. *History of the Early Settlement and Indian Wars of Western Virginia*, 109 n. See also Bibliography

Delaware Indians. See Indians, Delaware

Detroit, 3, 59, 111; occupation of, 27; holds out against Pontiac, 29; advance of Bradstreet to, 30; Pontiac's attempt to capture, 30; Bradstreet's campaign in vicinity of, 36; escape of Capt. Morris to, 37; Croghan concludes peace with Indians at, 43; Shelburne proposes establishment of colony near, 129; proposed colony at, 131 n., 132

Dictionary of National Biography, cited, 50 n.

Dillon, J., *History of Indiana*, cited, 17 n., 46 n. See also Bibliography

Dinwiddie, Gov. [Robert], 111 n., 128

Dobson, Joseph, letter from, to Baynton, Wharton and Morgan, 83 n.

Documents relating to the Colonial History of the State of New York, cited, 28 n., 30 n., 34 n., 38 n., 39 n., 40 n., 43 n., 45 n., 51 n., 55 n., 56 n., 57 n., 58 n., 59 n., 61 n., 64 n., 73 n., 74 n., 79 n., 80 n., 81 n., 85 n., 86 n., 89 n., 98 n., 102 n., 111 n., 112 n., 127 n., 129 n., 132 n., 134 n., 137 n. See also Bibliography

Documents relating to the Constitutional History of Canada, 1759–1791 (ed. Shortt and Doughty), cited, 5 n., 7 n., 14 n., 15 n., 16 n., 17 n., 22 n., 25 n., 47 n., 48 n., 79 n., 81 n., 88 n., 108 n., 162 n. See also Bibliography

Dunmore War, 157 n.

Dunn, J. P., *History of Indiana*, cited, 51 n., 58 n. See also Bibliography

East Florida. See Florida
East Indies, Company of, 6 n.
Edinburgh, 104
Egremont, Lord, 14, 15; letter from, to Lords of Trade, 14 n.
Eidington, Lieut., letters of, 44 n., 45 n., 51 n., 52 n., 53 n., 69 n.
England, 28, 77, 84, 90, 91, 92, 95 n., 96, 101, 105, 111, 116 n., 117, 119, 122, 125, 128, 130 n., 131, 141 n., 149, 156, 160 n.; relation of, to France in America, 1; cession of Illinois country to, 7; influence of, in Upper Ohio Valley, 84; importation of furs into, 86, 87, 94; promise of aid to Indians against, 89; dispute between, and Spain over Falkland Islands, 101, 143; agitation in, for establishment of western colonies, 104, 105; Mississippi Land Company maintains agent in, 106; Croghan's statement regarding attitude of, towards western colonization, 110–111; established church of, provision for, in plan for colony in the Illinois country, 120 n.; political situation in, in 1767, 133; Spain yields to demands of, 144

England, Political History of (ed. Hunt and Poole), cited, 4 n., 123 n., 134 n., 143 n., 149 n.

English army. See British army
English government. See British government

INDEX

English law, application of, to West, 24–25

English merchants. *See* Traders

English settlers, warning of Céleron to, 4

English troops. *See* British army

Erie, Lake, 30, 129

Europe, 8, 117; situation in, leading to Seven Years' War, 1–2

Evans, Lewis, 124

Expediency of securing our American Colonies by settling the Country adjoining the River Mississippi, contents of, described, 104, 117 n. *See also* Bibliography

Falkland Islands, 101, 143

Farmer, Maj. Robert, 44, 51 n., 54, 55 n.; sends Lieut. Ross to Illinois on mission to Indians, 37; letters to, from Ross, 37 n., 38 n.; letters from, to Gage, 49 n., 51 n., 53 n., 54 n.; to Haldimand, 54 n.; to Barrington, 55 n.; takes command of Fort de Chartres, 51; misrepresented to French in Illinois, 53 n.; superseded in command of Fort de Chartres by Col. Reed, 55

Fitzhugh, Henry, 105

Fitzmaurice, Edmund, *Life of Shelburne*, cited, 133 n., 140 n. *See also* Bibliography

Flagg, Edmund, 65 n.; *The Far West*, cited, 65 n., 66 n., 68 n. *See also* Bibliography

Florida, 18 n., 51 n., 99, 100, 135, 143, 188; cession of, to England, 6; civil government extended to, by proclamation of 1763, 14, 23; posts in, occupied by English troops, 32

Forbes, Capt. Hugh, 62 n., 64, 89 n.; takes command of Fort de Chartres, 61; orders of, to English and French, 62; preparations of, to meet Indian attack, 63; letters from, to Gage, 64 n., 93 n., 96 n.; attempts to regulate trade, 93, 96 n.

"Forbes, Capt., Information of the State of Commerce given by, 1768", 87 n., 89 n.

Forget, Father M., 75 n.

Fort Adams. *See* Davion's Bluff

Fort de Chartres, 18, 19 n., 30, 40, 43, 46, 50 n., 53 n., 55, 57, 60, 69 n., 70 n., 71, 75, 83, 90, 93, 96 n., 97 n., 98 n., 113, 119 n., 144, 156 n.; order for erection of, 6; statement by George Phyn concerning government of, 20 n.; English possession of, 23; troops designed for, 32; St. Ange transferred to, 35; de Villiers leaves, 36; preparations to send troops from, 37; Croghan invited to, 43; preparations for relief of, 44; final occupation of, 45; articles of surrender of, cited, 45 n.; lack of sufficient supplies at, 51–52; supplies sent to, 54; Indian representatives sent to, 58; Col. Reed in command of, 60; preparations to meet Indian attack on, 63; Indian depredations in vicinity of, 73; trade carried on at, 82, 87; estimate of Indian expenses at, 95; intention of British regarding use of, 97; plan for maintenance of, 118; destruction of, 156

Fort Gage, 156, 162

Fort Massac, 32, 44

Fort Miami, 27

Fort Pitt, 20 n., 31, 39, 40 n., 43, 44, 51 n., 59 n., 141; holds out against Pontiac, 29; Bouquet raises siege of, 30; preparations to send troops to Illinois from, 38; goods sent to, 39; Croghan at, 39, 41; provisions sent to Illinois from, 55; rendezvous for English traders, 82; instructions to commander of, regarding English traders, 91; orders to send French traders as prisoners to, 93

Fort Stanwix, 140 n., 144

Fox River, 88

France, 18 n., 29, 47, 53, 77, 84, 98 n.; aggressions of, 1, 2; relations of, with England in America, 2-5, 28, 84; cession of Louisiana and New Orleans to Spain by, 5; immigrants from, in Illinois, 7-8; organization of village community and system of land tenure in, 10; orders sent from, to evacuate Illinois, 27; Jesuits expelled from Illinois by order of, 75; methods employed by, in dealing with Indians, 84-85; furs sent to, from Illinois, 90, 95 n., 96

Franklin, Benjamin, 79 n., 116, 121 n., 123 n., 128, 134, 136, 137, 141; *Works of* (ed. Sparks), cited, 78 n.; *Works of* (ed. Bigelow), cited, 79 n., 81 n., 109 n., 110 n., 119 n., 121 n., 123 n., 124 n., 125 n., 126 n., 127 n., 129 n., 132 n., 137 n., 140 n.; letters to, from Croghan, 86 n., 93 n., 98 n.; from Bouquet, 110 n.; from Johnson, 122 n.; from W. Franklin, 123 n.; from T. Wharton, 130 n.; statement of, relative to Mississippi Land Company, 109 n.; letters from, to W. Franklin, 110 n., 119 n., 122 n., 123 n., 124 n., 125 n., 126 n., 127 n., 129 n., 132 n., 137 n.; to Johnson, 122 n., 123 n.; part taken by, in establishment of Illinois colony, 122, 123, 124, 125, 126, 130 n., 132, 140 n.; *Works of* (ed. Smythe), cited, 123 n. *See also* Bibliography

Franklin Papers (American Philosophical Society), cited, 110 n., 117 n., 119 n., 123 n., 144 n. *See also* Bibliography

Franklin Papers, Calendar of the (ed. Hays), cited, 110 n. *See also* Bibliography

Franklin, Gov. William, 61 n., 119 n., 121 n., 130 n.; letters to, from B. Franklin, 110 n., 119 n., 122 n., 123 n., 124 n., 125 n., 126 n., 127 n., 129 n., 132 n., 137 n.; from Johnson, 121 n., 122 n., 127 n.; part taken by, for establishment of Illinois colony, 115, 116, 117, 119-121, 122 n., 142; letters from, to B. Franklin, 117 n., 123 n.

Franks and Company, 83

Franz, A., *Die Kolonization des Mississippitales*, cited, 10 n. *See also* Bibliography

Fraser, Lieut., 40 n., 43, 50 n.; goes to Illinois, 38-39, 40; experiences of, with Indians, 40-41; letters from, to Crawford, 40 n.; to Gage, 40 n., 41 n., 53 n.; to Campbell, 41 n.; report of death of, 41 n.; accusations of, against St. Ange, 53 n.; "Report on an Exploratory Survey", cited, 53 n.

Frederick the Great, 2, 4

French, of the Illinois country, 29, 31, 36, 59, 72, 112 n., 121 n.; original purpose of colony of, 5; origin of, 7; character of, 8-9; description of government of, 9-10; character of land holdings of, 10-11; characterization of church of, 11; provisions for government of, 14, 15-18, 21, 24-25, 49, 64-66, 70 n., 145, 149-150, 153-155, 158, 161-162; charge English high prices for goods, 52; extent of migration of, in 1765, 53 n.; Farmer issues proclamation to, 54 n.; attempts of, to stir up Indians, 55-56, 64 n.;

INDEX

relations of, with British commandants, 60, 61, 62, 64, 71, 157; friction among, 64, 65; attitude of, towards Morgan, 68; religious privileges accorded, 76; trade carried on by, 28, 86–87, 89–90; Gage recommends establishment of colony on lands vacated by, 113–114; company formed to purchase land from, 115–116; actions of, relative to civil government, 146, 147 n., 151, 152, 159. *See also* Traders, French

French and Indian War, 4, 49, 124

French officials, 9, 10, 31, 33, 34, 49, 50, 65 n.

French traders. *See* Traders

Fur-trade. *See* Trade

Gage, Gen. Thomas, 30, 32, 35, 38, 44, 45 n., 48, 49 n., 51, 54 n., 57 n., 67, 70 n., 95 n., 96 n., 99, 127, 138, 151, 153, 156; proclamation of, to inhabitants of Illinois, 17, 24, 46–47; proposes military government for Illinois, 18, 114; letters from, to Hillsborough, 19 n., 20 n., 21 n., 58 n., 61 n., 62 n., 64 n., 67 n., 73 n., 74 n., 78 n., 83 n., 87 n., 88 n., 89 n., 90 n., 92 n., 93 n., 95 n., 97 n., 98 n., 99 n., 101 n., 127 n., 139 n., 143 n., 144 n., 146 n., 148 n., 149 n., 156 n., 157 n.; to Shelburne, 23 n., 55 n., 59 n., 62 n., 64 n., 86 n., 87 n., 89 n., 90 n., 91 n.; to Bouquet, 30 n., 32 n., 35 n., 38 n.; to Halifax, 31 n., 32 n., 34 n., 35 n., 37 n., 98 n.; to Haldimand, 35 n., 73 n., 99 n., 148 n., 149 n., 152 n., 155 n., 156 n., 158 n., 160 n.; to Johnson, 40 n., 41 n., 45 n., 54 n., 57 n., 59 n., 61 n., 64 n., 73 n., 74 n., 91 n., 92 n., 93 n., 95 n., 96 n., 97 n., 98 n., 156 n., 157 n.; to Conway, 42 n., 43 n., 44 n., 45 n., 49 n., 51 n., 55 n., 75 n., 76 n., 91 n., 98 n., 113 n.; to Barrington, 45 n.; to Dartmouth, 91 n., 93 n., 146 n., 147 n., 148 n., 158 n.; to Pownall, 147 n.; to Hamilton, 151 n.; letters to, from Hillsborough, 21 n., 23 n., 64 n., 67 n., 73 n., 97 n., 99 n., 100 n., 101 n., 134 n., 135 n., 139 n., 142 n., 148 n., 154 n., 156 n.; from Robertson, 32 n., 33 n.; from Loftus, 32 n., 33 n., 34 n.; from Bouquet, 38 n ; from Johnson, 38 n., 61 n., 91 n., 92 n.; from Fraser, 40 n., 41 n., 53 n.; from Sterling, 44 n., 45 n., 48 n., 49 n., 50 n., 51 n., 52 n., 53 n., 56 n., 75 n.; from Farmer, 49 n., 51 n., 53 n., 54 n.; from Croghan, 52 n., 59 n.; from Baynton, Wharton and Morgan, 55 n.; from Forbes, 64 n., 93 n., 96 n.; from Wilkins, 64 n., 96 n., 98 n., 155 n., 156 n.; from Conway, 78 n.; from Taylor, 99 n.; from Shelburne, 110 n., 126 n., 127 n., 131 n.; from Haldimand, 143 n., 156 n., 157 n.; from Pownall, 147 n.; from Dartmouth, 153 n., 154 n., 155 n., 157 n., 161 n.; from Sowers, 155 n.; from Lord, 157 n., 160 n., 161 n.; takes command of British army in America, 31; opinion of, concerning French officials, 33, 34; issues instructions to Fraser, 40; supplies sent to Illinois by, 54; letters of (Harvard College), cited, 54 n., 58 n., 59 n., 64 n., 73 n., 74 n., 93 n., 95 n., 156 n., 157 n.; Croghan sent to Illinois by, 58; extent of authority of, in Indian affairs, 58 n ; fears Indian outbreak, 64 n.; knowledge of, concerning judicial

INDEX

court in Illinois, 66-67; opinion of, concerning sale of church property in Illinois, 75 n.; opinion of, concerning England's object in West, 78 n.; attempts of, to protect trade in Illinois, 87 n., 89, 91, 92, 93, 96, 99; statement of, concerning competition between French and English in Illinois, 90; plans of, for attack upon New Orleans, 100-101, 144; statement of, concerning expenses of military department, 102 n.; part taken by, in efforts to establish Illinois colony, 113-114, 115, 118, 127 n., 129 n., 136, 139 n., 141-142; instructions to, respecting attack upon Louisiana, 143; Blouïn sent to, as representative of Illinois French, 146-147; attitude of, towards civil government for Illinois, 148-153, 158; annuls land grants in Illinois, 160-161

Galloway, Joseph, 69 n., 115, 116 n., 117, 123 n.

Gayarré, C. E., *Louisiana*, cited, 33 n. *See also* Bibliography

Gentry, description of, 8-9

George III, 4

Georgia, colony of, 135

Germany, 110

Gibault, Father Pierre, 76

Girardot, Pierre, 68, 147 n.

Gordon, Capt. Harry, 59 n.; letter from, to Johnson, 34 n.; "Notes on the Country along the Mississippi from Kaskaskia in the Illinois to New Orleans", cited, 99 n.; "Journal down the Ohio, 1766", cited, 87 n., 97 n., 98 n., 99 n.

Government. *See* Civil Government

Grafton, ———, 133

Great Britain, 47, 66, 84, 85, 87, 95 n., 96, 97, 101, 102, 104, 107, 122 n., 126 n., 132, 135, 142, 163; problem confronting, in 1763, 1; Canada ceded to, by France, 5; receives title to Illinois region, 27; inhabitants of Illinois guaranteed rights of subjects of, 47; Indians profess allegiance to, 55; opinions concerning advantages to, by establishment of Illinois colony, 96-97, 118. *See also* England, and items under British army, British government, etc.

Green Bay, 27

Grenada, province of, 14, 25

Grenville ministry, 15

Grenville Papers, cited, 133 n., 134 n.

Haldimand, Gen., 99, 100, 142, 143 n.; letters from, to Gage, 143 n., 156 n., 157 n.; to Dartmouth, 157 n., 161 n.; to Lord, 159 n.; to Johnson, 161 n.; takes command of the American army, 149 n.; plan for civil government for Illinois submitted to, 150 n.; report to, concerning attitude of the Illinois French, 159

Haldimand Papers (British Museum), cited, 148 n., 149 n., 152 n., 153 n., 161 n.

Halifax, Lord, 15, 79, 112; letters to, from Gage, 31 n., 32 n., 34 n., 35 n., 37 n., 98 n.

Hamilton, Maj. Isaac, letters from, to Gage, 146 n., 151 n.; to Stuart, 157 n.; acting commandant in Illinois, 148, 156; circulates among Illinois French a plan of government, 149; addresses inhabitants of Illinois relative to a civil government, 151

Hamilton, P. J., *Colonial Mobile*, cited, 143 n. *See also* Bibliography

Harding, Julia Morgan, "Biography of Col. George Morgan", cited, 68 n. *See also* Bibliography

INDEX 213

Havana, 5

Hay, Maj. John, sent on mission to the Illinois country, 162 n.

Hazard, Samuel, outlines proposal for western colony, 103–104

Hillsborough, Lord, 21, 24, 99, 109 n., 140, 144, 151, 153; president of Board of Trade, 15; author of plan of 1764, 16, 56, 80; interest of, in West, 17; letters from, to Gage, 21 n., 23 n., 64 n., 67 n., 73 n., 97 n., 99 n., 100 n., 101 n., 134 n., 135 n., 139 n., 142 n., 148 n., 154 n., 156 n., 160 n.; to Johnson, 73 n., 74 n., 102 n.; to Carleton, 89 n.; letters to, from Gage, 21 n., 58 n., 61 n., 62 n., 64 n., 67 n., 73 n., 74 n., 78 n., 83 n., 87 n., 88 n., 89 n., 90 n., 92 n., 93 n., 95 n., 97 n., 98 n., 99 n., 101 n., 127 n., 139 n., 143 n., 144 n., 146 n., 148 n., 149 n., 156 n., 157 n.; from Johnson, 64 n., 73 n., 85 n., 86 n., 89 n., 102 n.; attitude of, towards Illinois French, 62 n.; fears Indian outbreak, 63 n ; knowledge of, concerning court of judicature, 67; views of, respecting value of West to England, 96–97, 100; orders of, for conquest of Louisiana, 101, 143; attempt of, to regulate trade, 102 n.; attitude of, on colonial project, 132 n., 133, 134, 135–137, 138, 139 n., 140 n., 142, 144, 148 n.; becomes secretary of state for colonies, 134; interpretation placed on proclamation of 1763 by, 140–141; effect of restrictive policy of, 145; expresses concern over status of western settlements, 154

Hinsdale, B. A., "The Establishment of the First Southern Boundary of the United States", cited, 124 n.; *The Old Northwest*, cited, 140 n.; "The Western Land Policy of the British Government from 1763 to 1775", cited, 140 n. See also Bibliography

Historical Magazine, cited, 64 n., 65 n., 66 n., 68 n., 70 n., 72 n., 73 n. See also Bibliography

Holy Family, parish of, at Cahokia, 11

Home, Capt., letter from, to Haldimand, 99 n.

Hughes, John, 116 n.; enters company for purchase of land in Illinois country, 115

Huron, Lake, 109

Hutchins, Thomas, *A Topographical Description*, cited, 3 n.; letters from, to Johnson, 43 n.; to Haldimand, 100 n.; accompanies Croghan to Illinois, 59 n.; "Remarks upon the Country of the Illinois", cited, 88 n., 94 n., 95 n., 98 n., 99 n. See also Bibliography

Iberville, d' (Lemoine or Lemoyne), 3

Iberville River, 99

Illinois Land Company,160,161 n.

Illinois River, 5, 6, 23 n., 87, 88, 93, 97, 98 n., 99, 100, 109 n., 110, 111, 139, 160

Immaculate Conception, parish of, 11

India, 2, 4

Indian affairs, plan for management of, 16, 19, 77, 80, 81, 102; commissary of, 56 57, 80; superintendents of, 56, 57, 79, 80, 119 n. See also Johnson, Sir William

Indian country, 14, 19. See also West

Indians, 8, 12, 21 n., 31, 39 n., 41, 48 n., 53, 62 n., 82, 85, 87 n., 89 n., 90, 97, 101, 102, 104, 106 n., 107, 108 n., 112 n., 113, 114, 118, 119, 126 n., 131, 132, 135, 139, 153 n.,

157; provisions for regulation of trade with, 15 n., 16, 80–81, 102 n., 138; lands reserved for use of, 16, 79, 108, 139; influence of Spanish over, 23, 61; influence of French over, 23, 30, 41, 61, 78, 84; causes of revolt of, in 1762, 28–29; presents to, 29, 32, 34, 39 n., 51, 52 n., 54, 58, 85; attitude of, towards English, 30, 32, 35, 36, 37, 40, 41–43, 44, 45 n., 52, 55, 60, 61–63, 73–74; attack expedition of Maj. Loftus, 34; Croghan sent to conciliate western, 38; goods designed for, destroyed, 39; employed to carry supplies to Fort de Chartres, 54; incited by French, 55–56, 88–89; plan for government of, 56; Croghan sent on mission to, 58; general peace with, concluded, 59; civil war among, 74; history of English management of, 78–80; expectations concerning trade with, in Illinois country, 82; contrast between English and French methods of dealing with, 85–86; expense of management of, in Illinois country, 95; plans to purchase lands from, in Illinois country, 111, 119, 160; Illinois, 5, 45 n., 61, 62 n., 87; Iroquois, 27; Algonquin, 28, 29; Delaware, 30, 31, 35, 39, 59, 62, 73 n.; Shawnee, 30, 31, 35, 39, 40 n., 41, 42, 44, 59, 62, 73 n.; Tonica, 32; Chickasaw, 34 n., 37; Cherokee, 34 n., 42 n., 87 n.; Choctaw, 37; Osage, 38; Missouri, 38, 62 n.; Seneca, 40 n.; Mascoutin, 42; Kickapoo, 42, 63; Chippewa, 63; Ottawa, 63; Pottawottomi, 63

Indies, Company of, 6, 8

Intendant of Louisiana, civil officials of Illinois responsible to, 10

"Invitation Sérièuse aux Habitants des Illinois", contents of, 152–153; relation of, to struggle for civil government, 152. *See also* Bibliography

Jackson, Richard, recommends establishment of colony in Illinois country, 125 n., 127; counsel to Board of Trade, 127 n.

Jamaica, 25 n.

Jennings, John, Journal of, cited, 63 n. *See also* Bibliography

Jesuit Relations (ed. Thwaites), cited, 60 n., 75 n., 76 n. *See also* Bibliography

Jesuits, 11; property of, in Illinois confiscated, 75

Johnson, Guy, letter from, to Haldimand, 161 n.

Johnson Manuscripts (New York State Library), cited, 19 n., 20 n., 30 n., 37 n., 38 n., 39 n., 41 n., 43 n., 45 n., 52 n., 55 n., 57 n., 58 n., 59 n., 60 n., 61 n., 63 n., 73 n., 74 n., 82 n., 91 n., 92 n., 93 n., 96 n., 97 n., 98 n., 101 n., 105 n., 111 n., 112 n., 116 n., 119 n., 122 n., 123 n., 141 n., 157 n., 161 n. *See also* Bibliography

Johnson, Sir William, 15 n., 19, 24, 30, 38 n., 40 n., 45 n., 48 n., 58, 64 n., 67, 92, 99, 112 n., 116 n., 119 n., 122 n., 123, 124 n., 127 n., 141; letters to, from Gage, 19 n., 40 n., 41 n., 45 n., 54 n., 57 n., 58 n., 59 n., 61 n., 64 n., 73 n., 74 n., 91 n., 92 n., 93 n., 95 n., 96 n., 97 n., 98 n., 156 n., 157 n.; from Phyn, 20 n., 87 n., 91 n., 93 n., 98 n., 101 n.; from Gordon, 37 n.; from Shuckburgh, 41 n.; from Hutchins, 43 n.; from Macdonald, 43 n.; from Campbell, 51 n.; from Cole, 57 n., 59 n., 61 n.,

74 n.; from Croghan, 58 n., 59 n., 60 n., 111 n., 112 n., 116 n., 119 n., 121 n., 122 n.; from Hillsborough, 73 n., 74 n., 102 n.; from Lords of Trade, 86 n.; from Carleton, 92 n.; from Baynton, Wharton and Morgan, 105 n., 121 n., 123 n.; from W. Franklin, 122 n.; from B. Franklin, 122 n., 123 n.; from Dartmouth, 157 n.; from Haldimand, 161 n.; declaration of, concerning government in West, 20; "Review of the Trade and Affairs of the Indians in the Northern District of America", cited, 20 n., 85 n., 86 n., 98 n.; letters from, to Amherst, 28 n., 29 n., 30 n.; to Lords of Trade, 28 n., 30 n., 38 n., 39 n., 41 n., 43 n., 45 n., 51 n., 55 n., 57 n., 59 n., 61 n., 79 n., 85 n., 86 n., 128 n.; to Colden, 30 n.; to Gage, 38 n., 61 n., 73 n., 91 n., 92 n.; to Croghan, 45 n., 58 n., 112 n.; to Shelburne, 55 n., 56 n., 58 n., 59 n., 61 n., 85 n.; to Hillsborough, 64 n., 73 n., 85 n., 86 n., 89 n., 102 n.; to Penn, 82 n.; to Carleton, 85 n., 88 n.; to Baynton, Wharton and Morgan, 121 n., 122 n.; to B. Franklin, 121 n., 122 n.; to W. Franklin, 121 n., 122 n., 127 n.; to Conway, 122 n.; to Haldimand, 161 n.; instructions of, to Croghan, 38, 111 n., 112 n; neglect of Indian affairs by, 57; extent of authority of, in Indian affairs, 58 n.; connection of, with colonial project, 112, 115, 119 n., 121–122; suggested as governor of proposed Illinois colony, 119 n.

Johnstone, Gov., 51 n.

Journal of the Association of Engineering Societies, cited, 119 n. *See also* Bibliography

Judge. *See* French officials
Jury, trial by, 70
Justices of the peace, 16

Kaskaskia, 9, 69, 97, 146, 156, 158 n., 160; mission established at, 5; population of, 7; character of land holdings at, 10; parish at, 11; troops designed for, 32; Capt. Sterling confronted with opposition at, 47–49; French cross river at, 53; meetings of court of judicature at, 71 n.; controversy over holding court at, 71; Jesuits at, 75; Father Gibault takes up residence at, 76; designed as center of government for Illinois, 162

Kaskaskia Records (British Period), cited, 67 n., 69 n., 70 n., 147 n., 150 n., 156 n., 157 n. *See also* Bibliography

Kaunitz, 2
Kentucky, state of, 106
Kerlerec, Gov., letters to, from Neyon, 31 n.
Kickapoo Indians. *See* Indians, Kickapoo
King's attorney. *See* French officials
Kingsford, William, *History of Canada*, cited, 27 n., 28 n., 31 n., 32 n., 33 n., 36 n., 40 n., 42 n. *See also* Bibliography
Knox, William, *Justice and Policy of the Quebec Act*, cited, 22 n., 81 n. *See also* Bibliography

Labuxiere, Joseph, 49
Lachance, family of, 9
Laclede, ———, 87
La Croix, J. B. H., 9
La Grange, M., signs petition of inhabitants of Illinois, 49 n.; appointed judge, 50
Langlois, family of, 11
Lansdowne MSS., cited, 91 n., 93 n., 97 n., 98 n., 108 n., 127 n., 131 n., 136 n., 140 n., 142 n. *See also* Bibliography

La Salle, M. de, 3, 5
Lead-mining, important industry in Illinois country, 120 n.
Lee, Arthur, 105, 109 n., 128
Lee, Charles, 109 n.; outlines plan for colonies in West, 109–110
Lee, Francis Lightfoot, 105
Lee, Richard Henry, 105
Lee, Thomas, 105
Lee, William, 105; letter to, from Mississippi Land Company, 109 n.
Lee Papers (*N. Y. Hist. Soc. Colls.*, Fund series), cited, 109 n., 110 n. *See also* Bibliography
Lefebvre, Joseph, 49
L'Esperance, Joseph, 71
Leuthen, battle of, 4
Lincoln, C. H., *Calendar of MSS. of Sir William Johnson in American Antiquarian Society Library*, cited, 121 n., 122 n. *See also* Bibliography
Loftus, Maj. Arthur, attempts to reach Illinois, 32; attacked by Indians, 32–33; letters from, to Gage, 32 n., 33 n., 34 n.; defeat of, 33, 34, 35, 37
London, 49 n., 52 n., 54 n., 83, 91, 103, 106 n., 116, 124, 128, 132, 149 n., 160 n.
Lord, Capt. Hugh, 162 n.; letters from, to Stuart, 151 n.; to Gage, 157 n., 160 n., 161 n.; to Haldimand, 161 n.; commandant in Illinois, 156; policy of conciliation adopted by, 157; report of, concerning attitude of Illinois French, 159; letters to, from Haldimand, 159 n., 161 n.
Lords, House of, 22, 95 n.
Lords of Trade, letters to, from Johnson, 28 n., 30 n., 38 n., 39 n., 41 n., 42 n., 43 n., 45 n., 51 n., 56 n., 57 n., 59 n., 61 n., 79 n., 85 n., 86 n., 128 n.; from Shelburne, 103 n., 127 n., 129 n.; representation of, on Indian affairs, cited, 57 n., 81 n., 129 n., 132 n., 134 n., 137 n.; letters from, to Johnson, 86 n.
Louis XIV, 1
Louisburg, 3
Louisiana, 22, 32, 93, 142; Illinois country annexed to, 6, 9; becomes a royal province, 7; economic relations of, with Illinois country, 11; effect on Indians of transfer of, to Spain, 41; Illinois and Wabash settlements in jurisdiction of, 47; inhabitants of Illinois migrate to, 47, 53; traders from, 61, 87, 89; plans for conquest of, 100–101, 119, 141–144
Louviere, M., 69
Lyman, Gen. Phineas, 124, 125 n., 128

Macdonald, James, letter from, to Johnson, 43 n.
Mackinac, occupation of, 27
Macleane, L., letters to, from Baynton, Wharton and Morgan, 83 n., 95 n.
McMillan, James, 68
Magazine of American History, VIII, cited, 36 n. *See also* Bibliography
Magellan, strait of, 143
Maissonville, 40 n., 41 n., 43
Manchac, 83, 98 n.
Mansfield, Lord, 25
Margry, P., *Découvertes*, cited, 6 n.
Maria Theresa, 2
Marsh, Capt., letters from, to Haldimand, 95 n., 143 n.
Maryland, 98 n., 105, 109 n.
Mascoutin Indians. *See* Indians, Mascoutin
Mason, Edward G., *Chapters from Illinois History*, cited, 58 n., 147 n., 149 n., 159 n. *See also* Bibliography
Maturin, G., letter from, to

INDEX

Baynton, Wharton and Morgan, 74 n.
Maurepas, Lake, 99
Memorial of the inhabitants of Illinois to Gage, 48, 53 n.
Mercer, Col. George, 128
Meurin, Father, 75. 76 n.; letters from, to Bishop Briand, 60 n., 75 n.
Mexico, 126
Mexico, gulf of, 3, 110, 126
Michigan, Lake, 3
Michigan Pioneer and Historical Collections, cited, 14 n., 40 n., 41 n., 79 n., 92 n., 140 n., 161 n. See also Bibliography
Michilimakinac, 153 n.
Mines, regulations proposed for, 120
Ministry, the. See British ministry
Misere. See St. Genevieve
Mississippi Land Company, 110, 128, 130 n.; organization and history of, 105–109; letters from, to Cumming, 106 n.
Mississippi River, 6, 20 n., 22, 23, 27, 29, 31, 38, 40, 42, 44, 45, 47, 54, 77, 83, 84, 86, 98, 101, 104, 107, 109 n., 110, 111, 118, 120 n., 126, 139, 141, 143 n., 144, 146, 152, 160 n.; Illinois villages situated on, 3; navigation of, declared open, 5, 32; attitude of Indians in region of, 34, 61; attempts to regulate trade on, 82, 87–88, 90, 91, 92, 93, 94, 97, 99, 142; plans to establish a colony on, 106, 117, 124; threatens Fort Chartres, 156
Missouri Indians. See Indians, Missouri
Missouri River, 87
Mobile, 20 n., 33, 37, 51, 54 n., 55, 144; command of Gulf of Mexico given to French by, 3; occupied by English troops, 32
Monette, J. W., *History of the Mississippi Valley*, I, cited, 50 n. See also Bibliography

Montreal, 4
Morgan, George, 69, 82, 87 n., 91 n., 116 n.; goes to Illinois, 59 n.; letters from, to his wife, 59 n.; to Alexander Williamson, 60 n.; to Baynton and Wharton, 60 n., 62 n., 64 n., 65 n., 73 n., 87 n., 88 n., 89 n., 90 n., 95 n., 97 n., 98 n., 99 n.; to John Baynton, 73 n.; statement of, concerning trade in Illinois, 60 n.; letter book of, cited, 60 n., 61 n., 62 n., 64 n., 73 n., 83 n., 87 n., 88 n., 89 n., 90 n., 91 n., 94 n., 98 n., 99 n.; part taken by, towards establishment of a civil government in Illinois, 61 n.; sketch of life of, 68; heads party faction, 71; involved in court of inquiry, 72; suggestions of, concerning regulation of trade, 95, 98 n.; leaves Illinois, 146 n. See also Baynton, Wharton and Morgan; Bibliography
Morris, Capt. Thomas, attempts to reach Illinois, 36; journal of, 36 n.; escapes from Indians, 37
Moses, John, 70 n.; "Court of Enquiry at Ft. Chartres", cited, 58 n., 64 n., 66 n., 70 n.; *Illinois, Historical and Statistical*, cited, 58 n., 66 n., 70 n. See also Bibliography
Munro, W. B., *The Seigniorial System in Canada*, cited, 9 n. See also Bibliography
Murray, ———, letters to, from Croghan, 42 n., 43 n.
Murray, William, 160
Mutiny and desertion, act for punishing, 19 n.
Myers Collection (New York Public Library), 41 n.

Narrative of the Transactions, Imprisonment and Sufferings of John Connolly, an American Loyalist, cited, 163 n.

New England, 110
New Jersey, 111, 115
New Orleans, 2, 3, 12, 31, 33, 36, 38, 40, 54, 87 n., 91 n., 99, 118; ceded to Spain, 5; expedition organized at, to take possession of Illinois, 32; Pontiac seeks aid from, 37, 41; provisions sent to Illinois from, 55; commercial connection of, with Illinois, 82, 86 n., 90, 91, 92, 93, 94-95. 96 n., 97; plans for attack upon, 100-101, 141-144
New York, city of, 17, 52 n., 54, 86 n., 101, 143, 146, 147 n., 149 n., 150 n., 152, 159 n.; colony of, 105, 111
New York Colonial Documents. See Documents relating to the Colonial History of the State of New York
Niagara, 3, 27, 29
North, Lord, 22, 24
North America. *See* America
Notary. *See* French officials
Notes, issuance of, 54 n.
Nouvelle Chartres, 7, 10, 11
Nova Scotia, 135

Observer, Washington (Pa.), cited, 68 n. *See also* Bibliography
Ogg, F. A., *Opening of the Mississippi*, cited, 32 n., 38 n. *See also* Bibliography
Ohio Arch. and Hist. Quarterly, cited, 105 n., 140 n. *See also* Bibliography
Ohio Company, 103, 111 n., 128
Ohio Company Papers, cited, 119 n.
Ohio River, 20 n., 22, 26, 31, 32, 37, 56, 59 n., 62, 77, 80, 84, 87 n., 91, 93, 101, 102 n., 103, 104, 106, 109 n., 111, 112, 114, 130 n., 137, 139, 141, 160 n.; proposal to guard, by maintenance of Illinois posts, 23 n.; preparations made to send troops down, 35, 38; journey of Capt. Sterling down, 44; Indian depredations along, 63; attempts to regulate trade on, 82, 87, 90, 98; plans to plant colony on, 110, 129, 144
O'Reilly, Gov., 89, 143 n.
Osage Indians. *See* Indians, Osage
Ottawa Indians. *See* Indians, Ottawa
Ouiatanon, 6 n., 27, 42, 43, 45 n.

Pacific Ocean, 5
Paris, 127 n.; treaty of, 1, 13, 27, 48 n., 75, 101, 155; terms of, effecting Illinois country, 5, 17, 46-47, 48; Mississippi River declared open by, 31; defines legal position of Roman Catholic church in West, 47; influence of, on colonizing spirit, 104
Parish priest, duties of, 9-10
Parishes of Illinois, 11
Parkman Collection (Mass. Hist. Soc.), cited, 39 n., 40 n., 51 n., 57 n., 58 n. *See also* Bibliography
Parkman, Francis, *La Salle and the Discovery of the Great West*, cited, 5 n.; *Montcalm and Wolfe*, cited, 6 n.; *Conspiracy of Pontiac*, cited, 27 n., 28 n., 29 n., 31 n., 32 n., 33 n., 36 n., 38 n., 39 n., 40 n., 42 n., 45 n., 85 n. *See also* Bibliography
Parliament, 25 n., 26, 57, 66, 95 n., 102, 133
Parliamentary History, cited, 22 n., 78 n., 95 n. *See also* Bibliography
Parrish, Randall, *Historic Illinois*, cited, 58 n., 147 n., 149 n., 159 n.; statements of, relative to struggle for civil government in Illinois, 147 n., 149 n., 159 n. *See also* Bibliography
Party factions, 71, 72
Penn, Gov., letter to, from Johnson, 82 n.
Pennsylvania, 39, 91, 98 n., 105,

115, 116, 118; settlers from, in Ohio valley, 3; residents of, interested in colonial plan of 1766, 111; Indian troubles on frontier of, 157 n.
Pennsylvania Archives, cited, 108 n.
Pennsylvania Packet and General Advertiser, cited, 73 n. *See also* Bibliography
Pennsylvania State Library, Division of Public Records, cited, 65 n., 72 n., 73 n., 74 n., 83 n., 97 n. *See also* Bibliography
Pensacola, 32, 143
Peoria, 5
Perkins, James B., *France under Louis XV*, cited, 2 n. *See also* Bibliography
Peyton, J. L., *History of Augusta Co., Va.*, cited, 140 n. *See also* Bibliography
Philadelphia, 19 n., 39, 64 n., 83, 104, 116, 119 n., 120 n., 152, 161 n.
Phyn, Lieut. George, 92, 141; letters from, to Johnson, 20 n., 87 n., 91 n., 93 n., 98 n., 101 n., 141 n.
Pittman, Capt. Philip, 71; *The Present State of the European Settlements on the Mississippi*, cited, 3 n., 7 n., 9 n., 11 n., 53 n., 71 n., 99 n. *See also* Bibliography
Plain Facts, cited, 109 n. *See also* Bibliography
Political Essays concerning the Present State of the British Empire, cited, 160 n. *See also* Bibliography
Pontchartrain, Lake, 99
Pontiac, 34, 41, 84; motive of, in leading revolt, 29; assistance given to, by French intriguers, 30; effect of Loftus' defeat on, 35–36; influences Missouri and Osage Indians, 38; saves Lieut. Fraser's life, 40; makes peace with English, 43; murder of, 74
Poole, William, "The West", cited, 27 n. *See also* Bibliography
Pottawottomi Indians. *See* Indians, Pottawottomi
Pownall, John, letter to, from Gage, 147 n.; letter from, to Gage, 147 n.
Pownall, Thomas, 140 n.; *Administration of the Colonies*, cited, 6 n., 28 n., 29 n., 83 n. *See also* Bibliography
Prairie du Rocher, 7, 9, 11, 49
Pratz, Le Page du, *Histoire de la Louisiane*, cited, 7 n., 8 n., 15 n. *See also* Bibliography
Privy Council Office, Unbound Papers, cited, 106 n. *See also* Bibliography
Proclamation of 1763, 56, 108, 111, 135, 161; issuance of, 14; purpose of authors of, 16; comment in *Annual Register* on, 21; no provision for West in, 23, 25; trade regulations of, 77, 79; influence of, on Board of Trade, 139–141; violated by land companies, 144, 160
Prussia, 2
Public Record Office, series America and West Indies, cited, 19 n., 20 n., 21 n., 23 n., 44 n., 45 n., 48 n., 49 n., 50 n., 51 n., 52 n., 53 n., 54 n., 55 n., 56 n., 58 n., 61 n., 62 n., 63 n., 64 n., 67 n., 73 n., 74 n., 75 n., 76 n., 78 n., 83 n., 87 n., 88 n., 89 n., 90 n., 91 n., 92 n., 93 n., 95 n., 96 n., 97 n., 98 n., 99 n., 100 n., 101 n., 110 n., 121 n., 125 n., 126 n., 127 n., 134 n., 135 n., 138 n., 139 n., 142 n., 143 n., 144 n., 146 n., 147 n., 148 n., 149 n., 151 n., 152 n., 153 n., 154 n., 156 n., 157 n., 158 n., 159 n., 161 n.; Home Office Papers, cited, 38 n., 51 n.; Declared Accounts, cited, 95 n.; Colonial Office Papers, cited, 128n. *See also* Bibliography; Chatham Papers.

INDEX

Publications of Club for Colonial Reprints, cited, 152 n.

Quebec, 4, 5, 6 n., 11, 14, 23, 75, 93
Quebec Act, 23 n., 24, 25 n.; provisions of, relating to West, 22, 26; passage of, 162

"Reasons for the Establishment of a Colony in Illinois, 1766", cited, 101 n., 117 n. *See also* Documentary Appendix
Recollect fathers, 11
Reed, Lieut.-Col. John, 54 n., 57 n., 59, 64; commands Fort de Chartres, 55, 60; recalled, 61
Regnault, family of, 11
Revenue Act of 1767, 133
Reynolds, John, *The Pioneer History of Illinois*, cited, 51 n. *See also* Bibliography
Robertson, Lieut.-Col., letters from, to Gage, 32 n., 33 n.
Rocheblave, M. de, 49 n.; represents English government in Illinois, 163
Rockingham Memoirs, cited, 134 n. *See also* Bibliography
Rockingham ministry, displacement of, 123
Rogers, Maj. Robert, proposes civil government for Michilimakinac, 153 n.; journal of, cited, 153 n.
Roman Catholic church, rights of, defined in treaty of Paris, 46–47; Wilkins' relations with members of, 74; sketch of, during British period, 75–76
Ross, Lieut. John, letters from, to Farmer, 37 n., 38 n.; attempt of, to conciliate Indians in Illinois, 37–38; departure of, from Illinois, 40
Rossbach, battle of, 4
Royal Historical Manuscripts Commission, Fifth Report, cited, 59 n., 124 n., 127 n., 129 n. *See also* Bibliography

Royal Historical Manuscripts Commission, Fourteenth Report, cited, 56 n., 62 n., 64 n., 73 n., 89 n., 98 n., 147 n., 156 n. *See also* Bibliography
Royal warehouse, keeper of. *See* French officials
Rumsey, Lieut. James, 68, 69 n., 119 n.; sent to Fort de Chartres, 44–45; made royal commissary under British, 50; appointed to forward petition for civil government, 61 n.; duties of, 65 n.; heads party faction, 71

Sabine, L., *Loyalists of the American Revolution*, cited, 124 n. *See also* Bibliography
St. Ange, 36, 38, 50 n.; French commandant at Vincennes, 35; letters from, to d'Abbadie, 36 n., 55 n.; refuses to aid Pontiac, 37, 41; surrenders Fort de Chartres, 45; retires to St. Louis, 49; commandant at St. Louis, 53 n.
St. Anne, parish of, 11
St. Genevieve, 87 n.; French from Illinois found homes at, 33
St. Joseph, 3, 11, 27
St. Lawrence River, 3, 92
St. Louis, 45, 49; French from Illinois found homes at, 53; St. Ange acts as commandant of, 53 n.; foundation of, 87; furs transferred from Illinois to, 90
St. Philippe, 7, 10, 11, 49
St. Vincent. *See* Vincennes
Sandusky, occupation of, 27
Sato, S., *History of the Land Question in the United States*, 109 n. *See also* Bibliography
Saucier, family of, 9
Scioto River, 41, 73 n.
Scrivener of the marine. *See* French officials
Seminary of Foreign Missions, 5 n., 11
Seneca Indians. *See* Indians, Seneca

INDEX

Seven Years' War, 1. 4, 7
Shawnee Indians. *See* Indians, Shawnee
Shea, John G., *Life of Archbishop Carroll*, cited, 11 n., 75 n., 76 n. *See also* Bibliography
Shelburne, Lord, 91, 136, 140 n.; opinions of, concerning disposition of the West, 15–16, 78 n., 95 n.; letters to, from Gage, 23 n., 55 n., 62 n., 64 n., 86 n., 87 n., 89 n., 90 n., 91 n., 92 n., 95 n., 97 n., 98 n., 127 n.; from Johnson, 55 n., 58 n., 59 n., 61 n., 85 n.; letters from, to Gage, 110 n., 125 n., 126 n., 131 n.; to Lords of Trade, 127 n., 129 n., 137 n.; general attitude of, towards western colonies, 110, 123 n., 124, 125, 126–127, 129–131, 132, 137; becomes secretary of state for southern department, 123; retires from ministry, 133–134
Shuckburgh, Richard, letter from, to Johnson, 41 n.
Sinnott, sent to Illinois, 40 n.
Sioussat, St. George L., *English Statutes in Maryland*, cited, 25 n. *See also* Bibliography
Six Nations, 29, 59
Smith, Adam, 136
Smith, William, *Historical Account of the Expedition against the Ohio Indians*, cited, 119 n. *See also* Bibliography
Sowers, Capt., letter from, to Gage, 155 n.
Spain, 18 n., 41, 88, 98 n., 71, 126; brought to terms by England, 4; Louisiana ceded to, 5; furs sent to, 90; proposed conquest of Louisiana from, 100–101, 141–144; disputes with England over Falkland Islands, 143
Spanish traders. *See* Traders
Sparks Manuscripts (Harvard College Library), cited, 21 n., 39 n., 86 n., 130 n., 148 n., 154 n., 156 n. *See also* Bibliography
Stamp Act, 57, 81, 102, 113, 133
Sterling, Capt. Thomas, 50 n., 52 n., 53, 56; takes command of Fort de Chartres, 44–45; letters from, to Gage, 44 n., 45 n., 48 n., 49 n., 50 n., 51 n., 52 n., 53 n., 56 n., 75 n.; announces Gage's proclamation to inhabitants of Illinois, 46–48; petition to, from inhabitants of Illinois, 48; efforts of, to bring about order in Illinois, 49–50, 64; embarrassed by lack of supplies, 51–52; returns to New York, 54
Stone, William L., *Life of Sir William Johnson*, II, cited, 45 n. *See also* Bibliography
Stuart, Charles, 40 n.
Sulpitian fathers, 11, 75
Superintendent of Indian affairs. *See* Indian affairs
Superior Council at New Orleans, 50
Switzerland, 110
Syndic. *See* French officials

Taylor, Brig., letters to, from Gage, 98 n., 99 n., 102 n., 143 n.; letter from, to Gage, 99 n.
Tennessee, state of, 106
Tennessee River, 144 n.
Terrage, Marc de Villiers du. *Les dernières Années de la Louisiane française*, cited, 32 n., 33 n., 38 n., 41 n. *See also* Bibliography
Thornton, Presly, 105
Thurlow, Att.-Gen., 25 n.
Thwaites, R. G., *Early Western Travels*, I, cited, 36 n., 37 n., 38 n., 40 n., 42 n., 43 n., 65 n., 66 n., 68 n.; "Early Lead-mining in Illinois and Michigan", cited, 120 n. *See also* Bibliography
Tonica Indians. *See* Indians, Tonica

Townshend, Charles, 133
Township system, recommended for proposed Illinois colony, 119
Trade, 8, 11, 87, 130, 132, 134, 135, 142, 153 n.; French monopoly of, threatened, 3; comparison of French and English methods of managing, 28, 78, 84-86; attempts to regulate, 55, 77, 79, 80-81, 89, 93, 98-100, 131; rivalry between France and England for predominance in, 77, 84; conditions of, in Illinois country, 1765-1775, 77-102; rush of English to participate in western, 82; French attempt to monopolize, 88; benefit of, to Great Britain, 94-96; contraband, 86 n., 97 n., 126 n.; management of, transferred to colonies, 102, 138; effect on, through establishment of colony in Illinois, 118, 125
Traders, British, 21 n.; regulations for, 16, 80-81, 93, 96-97; behavior of, 19; character of, 28; methods employed by, 32, 61, 85-86; rush to Illinois country, 82; rivalry among, 83-84; fear to enter Indian country, 87-88; route followed by, 90-95; Spanish, 23, 61, 64 n.; French, necessity of repelling invasion of, 23; methods employed by, 28, 30, 35, 40, 41, 61, 64 n., 85; take oath of allegiance to English crown, 41; route followed by, 82, 87; rivalry of, with British, 83-84; purchase goods from British, 86
Transactions of the Illinois State Historical Society for 1907, cited, 45 n.
Trottier, François, 9

Ulloa, Gov., 93
United States, 95 n.

Vandalia Company, 144
Vandalia grant, 137, 140
Van Schaack, Henry C., "Captain Thomas Morris in the Illinois Country", cited, 36 n. *See also* Bibliography
Villiers, Neyon de, gives up command of Fort de Chartres, 35-36
Vincennes (Post Vincennes, Post Vincent, St. Vincent), 3, 6 n., 35, 40 n., 42, 87 n., 98 n.
Viollet, P., *Histoire du droit français*, 10 n. *See also* Bibliography
Virginia, 98 n., 105, 118, 157 n.; settlers from, in Ohio Valley, 3; party from, attacked by Indians, 63 n.; establishes Augusta County, 103; residents of, in Mississippi Land Company, 105, 109 n.
Visitation, chapel of, 11
Viviat, Louis, 9, 69, 147 n., 160
Volney, C. F., *View of the United States*, cited, 8 n. *See also* Bibliography

Wabash Land Company, 160, 161 n.
Wabash River, 3, 6 n., 22, 35, 36, 42, 44, 60, 61, 63 n., 87, 93, 98 n., 105, 106, 110
Wabash settlements, 47
Wallace, Lieut. Hugh, letters to, from Johnson, 44 n.
Wallace, J., *Illinois and Louisiana under French Rule*, cited, 40 n., 58 n., 66 n., 70 n. *See also* Bibliography
Walpole, Thomas, 140 n.
Walpole Company, 140, 144. *See also* Vandalia Company
Walton, F. P., *The Scope and Interpretation of the Civil Code of Lower Canada*, cited, 25 n. *See also* Bibliography
Washington, George, 105, 144 n.; letter from, to Crawford, 108 n.

Washington, George, Writings of (ed. Ford), cited, 108 n., 127 n., 144 n.
Washington, John, 105
Washington, Samuel, 105
West, the, 58, 77, 79, 84, 86, 87, 94, 108 n., 113, 119 n., 121 n., 123, 127 n., 131, 135. 141, 144 n., 160 n., 161; treatment accorded, 13, 14; Shelburne's plan for, 15; Gage in touch with, 18; inability of government to control, 20; no provision for, in proclamation of 1763, 23; extension of English law to, discussed, 24–25; occupation of posts in, 27; Pontiac determines to rehabilitate French power in, 29; value of, to Great Britain, 93 ff.; Hillsborough's statement regarding, 100; propositions for establishment of colonies in, 129 n.; opposition to establishment of colonies in, 139 n., 144 n.; Haldimand left in charge of, 149 n.; condition of Indian affairs in, 157 n.
West, Company of the, 6
West Florida. *See* Florida
Wharton, Joseph, Jr., 116 n.
Wharton, Joseph, Sr., 116 n.
Wharton, Samuel, 69 n., 116 n.
Wharton, Thomas, letter from, to B. Franklin, 130 n.
Wilkins, Lieut.-Col. John, 68 n., 70 n.; complaints of, against French in Illinois, 63 n., 70; takes command at Fort de Chartres, 64; letters from, to Gage, 64 n., 96 n., 98 n., 155 n., 156 n.; to Barrington, 67 n., 88 n., 97 n., 98 n.; efforts of, to bring about order in Illinois, 65, 69; discussion as to authority of, in establishing court, 66–67; proclamation of, concerning justices, 67 n., 70 n.; heads party faction in Illinois, 71; abolishes court of judicature, 71–72, 145; confronted with Indian problem, 73, 74; relations of, with Roman Catholics, 74; effort of, to regulate trade, 96 n.; letter to, from Gage, 155 n.; dismissed from Illinois post, 155–156; goes to England, 157–158
Williams, David, 69
Willing, Thomas, letter from, to Haldimand, 156 n.
Winsor, Justin, *Narrative and Critical History of America*, cited, 6 n., 7 n., 11 n., 27 n., 31 n., 32 n., 38 n., 42 n.; *Mississippi Basin*, cited, 27 n., 29 n., 31 n., 32 n., 33 n., 35 n., 38 n., 42 n.; *Westward Movement*, cited, 66 n., 70 n., 111 n., 127 n., 134 n., 136 n. *See also* Bibliography
Wisconsin River, 88

York, Chancellor, 160